IIC STUDIES

Studies in Industrial Property and Copyright Law

Volume 24

· HART ·
PUBLISHING

OXFORD AND PORTLAND, OREGON
2005

Published by the Max Planck Institute for Foreign and International Patent, Copyright and Competition Law, Munich

IIC STUDIES

Studies in Industrial Property and Copyright Law

Josef Drexl and Annette Kur (editors)

International Property and Private International Law – Heading for the Future

HART PUBLISHING
OXFORD AND PORTLAND, OREGON
2005

Hart Publishing
Oxford and Portland, Oregon

Published in North America (US and Canada) by
Hart Publishing c/o
International Specialized Book Services
5804 NE Hassalo Street
Portland, Oregon
97213-3644
USA

Hart Publishing is a specialist legal publisher based in Oxford, England.
To order further copies of this book or to request a list of other publications please write to:

Hart Publishing, Salter's Boatyard, Folly Bridge,
Abingdon Road, Oxford OX1 4LB
Telephone: +44 (0)1865 245533 or Fax: +44 (0)1865 794882
e-mail: mail@hartpub.co.uk
WEBSITE: http//www.hartpub.co.uk

British Library Cataloguing in Publication Data
Data Available
ISBN 1–84113–539–9 (paperback)

Typeset by Hope Services (Abingdon) Ltd.
Printed and bound in Great Britain on acid-free paper by
Lightning Source, UK Ltd

Contents

II. European Issues

III. International Issues

Annex

Preface

The relationship between intellectual property and private international law, fascinating and multi-faceted as it may be, is loaded with a peculiar tension. Both fields have similar features; they are markedly different from general civil law and civil procedural law, and each of them has become the domain of specialists cultivating their own terminology and patterns of thinking. Both are also inherently international. While this is obvious in the case of private international law, it also applies to intellectual property, which, on account of its ubiquity and the problems resulting therefrom with regard to protection of rights in foreign countries, has always figured among those legal areas where international protection systems and multilateral harmonisation efforts have been considered as factors of key importance.

Whereas the existence of conflicts ensuing from the unauthorised use of protected subject-matter abroad has always been witness to the fact that an area of common interest exists between private international law and intellectual property, the relationship between the two fields has long been tense, or was even neglected. This is due not least to the high degree of specialisation referred to above; it is not easy for the specialists in each field to communicate with each other in a language that is precise and sophisticated enough to express the relevant nuances, yet at the same time is understandable to both sides. Nevertheless, in view of the exponential increase in conflicts involving trans-border elements that have arisen in a world characterised by global trade and borderless communication structures, it has become essential to enhance one's ability to understand and employ the other discipline's tools and structures, not least with a view to probing their appropriateness for mastering the challenges of the future.

The meeting arranged under the title Jurisdiction and Choice of Law in Intellectual Property Matters—Perspectives for the Future (Europe and World-Wide) in July 2003 by the Max Planck Institute for Intellectual Property, Competition and Tax Law, of which the contributions compiled in this volume are the fruit, represents one of the many steps that have to be taken on the long journey towards a better understanding between private international law and intellectual property, with the ultimate aim to devise a future system of international and regional jurisdiction and applicable law that is better adapted to the increasingly supranational character of exploitation and conflicts of rights than are traditional schemes. Among other things, the meeting marked the culmination of a project concerned with the elaboration of draft provisions on jurisdiction and enforcement of foreign judgements in intellectual property matters that had been conducted at the Max Planck Institute since spring 2001. The solutions endorsed by the Max Planck working group were presented and discussed at the meeting, the topic being complemented by information on the activities by the Hague Conference for Private International Law as well as on the jurisdiction chapter in the project adopted in 2001 by the American Law Institute. As jurisdiction cannot be regulated properly in an international context without addressing choice-of-law issues, the perspectives for development of international rules in the latter field featured as another focal point in the meeting. Framed by these two elements—international jurisdiction on the one hand and perspectives for harmonised choice of law rules in an international context on the other—specific European themes were addressed, namely, jurisdiction, the establishment of a European judiciary in the patent field and its potential relevance for IP in general, the relationship between regional (European) systems and an international jurisdiction convention, and, in the context of choice-of-law issues, the recent proposal for a Regulation on applicable law in non-contractual relationships (Rome II). Furthermore, in order to underline the international perspectives, a special contribution was dedicated to recent developments in Japan.

In the one year that has passed since the meeting, things have developed further, without a breakthrough having been achieved in any of the areas treated in this volume. The authors have to some extent been able to update their written papers, which, however, still reflect the views presented and the thoughts discussed during the lively and most animated sessions that took place in the beautiful surroundings and inspiring atmosphere of the convent of Frauenwörth on the island of Frauenchiemsee in Bavaria.

Josef Drexl
Annette Kur
Munich
August 2004

Abbreviations

(7th, 9th) Cir.	Court of Appeal for the (7th, 9th) Circuit
AJP	Aktuelle Juristische Praxis
ALAI	Association Littéraire et Artistique Internationale
ALI	American Law Institute
All E.R.	All England Law Reports
AMI	Tijdschrift voor Auteurs- Media en Inforamtierecht
Art.	Article
Aw	Auteurswet 1912 (Dutch Copyright Act)
BB	Betriebs-Berater
BC	Berne Convention on the Protection of Literary and Artistic Works
Berk. J. Int'l Law	Berkeley Journal of International Law
BGB	Bürgerliches Gesetzbuch (German Civil Code)
BGH	Bundesgerichtshof
BMM bulletin	Bulletin van de Beneluxvereniging voor Merken- en Modellenrecht
BNA	Bureau of National Affairs
BT-Drs.	Bundestags-Drucksache
BYIL	British Yearbook of International Law
CA	Cour d'Appel/Court of Appeal
Cal.L.Rev.	Californian Law Review
Case W.Res.J.Int'l L	Case Western Reserve Journal of International Law
Cass.	Cour de Cassation
Cass.Civ.	Arrêt de la Chambre civil de la Cour de Cassation
cf.	confer
ch.	chambre
Ch.D.	High Court, Chancery Division
Chicago-Kent L.Rev.	Chicago-Kent Law Review
cl.	clause
Colum. J. L. & Arts	Columbia Journal of Law and the Arts (since 2001)
Colum.-VLA J.L. & Arts	Columbia Journal of Law and the Arts (until 2001)
COM	EU Commission documents
CPC	Community Patent Court
CR	Computer und Recht
CRi	Computer Law Review International

CTMR	Community Trademark Regulation
CRCP	(Proposal for a) Council Regulation on the Community Patent
DGD	Dreyfuss/Ginsburg Draft (Draft Convention on Jurisdiction and Recognition of Judgments in Intellectual Property Matters)
DHCC	Draft Hague Choice of Court Convention
DHJC	Draft Hague Jurisdiction Convention
Doc.	Document
Dw	Databankenwet 1999 (Dutch Database Act 1999)
E.g.	for example
EC	European Community, (Maastricht) Treaty establishing the European Community
ECHR	European Convention on Human Rights
ECJ	European Court of Justice
ECR	Reports of Cases decided by the European Court of Justice
ed., eds.	editor, editors
EEC	European Economic Community
EFTA	European Free Trade Area
EGBGB	Einführungsgesetz zum Bürgerlichen Gesetzbuch (Introductory Act to the German Civil Code)
Einl.MarkenG	Einleitung zum Markengesetz
E.I.P.R.	European Intellectual Property Review
EPA, EPO	Europäisches Patentamt, European Patent Organisation
EPC	European Patent Convention
EPJ	European Patent Judiciary
EPLA	European Patent Litigation Agreement
et al.	and others
et seq.	and following
EuGVÜ	Europäisches Gerichtsstands- und Vollstreckungsübereinkommen in Zivil- und Handelssachen (Brussels Convention)
EuZW	Europäische Zeitschrift für Wirtschaftsrecht
F (2d, 3d)	Federal Reporter (2nd, 3rd series)
F.Supp.	Federal Reporter, Supplement
Fordham Int'l Intell. Prop.L. & Pol'y	Fordham International Intellectual Property Law and Policy
F.S.R.	Fleet Street Reports
GRUR Int.	Gewerblicher Rechtsschutz und Urheberecht, Internationaler Teil
GRUR	Gewerblicher Rechtsschutz und Urheberrecht

ICANN	Internet Corporation for Assigned Names and Numbers
i.e.	that is
IIC	International Review of Industrial Property and Copyright
Int'l IP	International Intellectual Property
IPL	International Public Law
IPQ	Intellectual Property Quarterly
IPR	Internationales Privatrecht (Private International Law)
IPR	Intellectual Property Rights
IPRax	Praxis des internationalen Privat- und Verfahrensrechts
IT	Information Technology
IZPR	Internationales Zivilprozessrecht (International Law of Civil Procedure)
JCP	Juris Classeur Périodique
JDI	Journal du Droit International
J.Int'l.Arb.	Journal of International Arbitration
JWIP	Journal of World Intellectual Property
JZ	Juristenzeitung
Law & Contemp. Probs.	Law and Contemporary Problems
L.Ed.	Lawyer's Edition
lit.	littera
LugÜ	Lugano-Übereinkommen (Lugano Agreement)
Mich.J.Int.L.	Michigan Journal of International Law
Mitt.	Mitteilungen der deutschen Patentanwälte
MMR	Multimedia und Recht
N.D. Ill	United States District Court Northern District of Illinois
NJW	Neue Juristische Wochenschrift
no.	number
note	footnote
OJ EC	Official Journal of the European Communities (L or C series)
op.cit.	pre-cited
Or.L.Rev.	Oregon Law Review
p., pp.	page, pages
para.	paragraph
PCT	Patent Cooperation Treaty
PIL	Private International Law
Prel.Doc.	Preliminary Document
pt.	point

RabelsZ	Rabels Zeitschrift für ausländisches und internationales Privatrecht
Rev.cr.dr.int.pr.	Revue critique du droit international privé
RIDA	Revue internationale du droit d' auteur
R.P.C.	Reports of Patent, Design and Trade Mark Cases
SCT	WIPO Standing Committee on the Law of Trademarks, Industrial Designs and Geographical Indications
S.Ct.	Supreme Court
Sec.	Section
sic!	Zeitschrift für Immaterialgüter-, Informations- und Wettbewerbsrecht
SJ	La Semaine Judiciaire
SJZ	Schweizer Juristen-Zeitung
SZW	Schweizerische Zeitschrift für Wirtschaftsrecht
SZIER	Schweizerische Zeitschrift für Internationales und Europäisches Recht
TDG	Teledienstleistungsgesetz (German Act on telecommunication services)
TRIPS	Trade Related Aspects of Intellectual Property Rights
UFITA	Archiv für Urheber-, Film-, Funk- und Theaterrecht
U.Ill.L.Rev.	University of Illinois Law Review
U.S.C.	United States Code
U.S.P.Q	United States Patent Law Quarterly
UNIDROIT	International Institute for the Unification of Private Law
USPTO	United States Patents and Trademarks Office
v.	versus
Va.J.Int'l.L.	Virginia Journal of International Law
Vol.	Volume
WIPO	World Intellectual Property Organisation
WIPR	World Intellectual Property Review
W.L.R.	Weekly Law Reports
WM	Wertpapier Mitteilungen
WPNR	Weekblad voor Privatrecht, Notariaat en Registratie
WRP	Wettbewerb in Recht und Praxis
ZEuP	Zeitschrift für Europäisches Privatrecht
ZUM	Zeitschrift für Urheber- und Medienrecht
ZVglRWiss	Zeitschrift für Vergleichende Rechtswissenschaft
ZZP	Zeitschrift für Zivilprozess

Part One

Jurisdiction

I.

The Proposed Hague Convention

The Hague Conference Project for a Global Convention on Jurisdiction, Recognition and Enforcement in Civil and Commercial Matters – An Update*

ANDREA SCHULZ**

I. The History of the Hague Judgments Project

Following some preparatory work which had been carried out within the framework of the Hague Conference on Private International Law between 1992 and 1996,[1] the Member States represented at the Diplomatic Conference that concluded the Eighteenth Session of the Conference in 1996 decided "to include in the Agenda of the Nineteenth Session the question of jurisdiction, and recognition and enforcement of foreign judgments in civil and commercial matters".[2]

In accordance with this decision, the Permanent Bureau of the Hague Conference established a Special Commission, which held five meetings of one or more weeks between June 1997 and October 1999. At the meeting in October 1999, which was supposed to be the last meeting of the Special Commission,[3] a "Preliminary Draft Convention[4] on Jurisdiction and

---

* This article is based on the paper given at the workshop organised by the Max Planck Institute for Intellectual Property, Competition and Tax Law at Frauenchiemsee on 20–22 July 2003. It takes into account subsequent developments up to 30 September 2003.

** Dr.iur., LLM, since 1 January 2002 First Secretary at the Hague Conference on Private International Law and responsible for the Judgments Project. Between 1998 and 2001, the author (then working with the German Federal Ministry of Justice in the sections on private international law (PIL) (until June 1999) and copyright (from June 1999 until December 2002)) was a member of the German delegation to the Hague negotiations on the Judgments Project. She can be reached at as@hcch.nl.

[1] For further details, *see Nygh & Pocar*, Report on the Preliminary Draft Convention on Jurisdiction and Foreign Judgments in Civil and Commercial Matters adopted by the Special Commission, Hague Conference (HC) Prel.Doc. No. 11, at 25 *et seq.* (also available at www.hcch.net under "Work in Progress"). Whenever reference is made to the website of the Hague Conference in this paper, only the top-level address will be indicated due to current changes in the Hague Conference website format that may affect the location of individual documents.

[2] Final Act of the Eighteenth Session, Part B, No. 1. Hague Conference on private international law, Proceedings of the Eighteenth Session, Tome I, 1999, p. 47.

[3] According to the working methods of the Hague Conference, each session lasts roughly four years and is concluded by a Diplomatic Conference, which normally adopts (1) the main elements of the work programme for the four years to follow, in particular the next convention project, and (2) the text of a "Draft Convention", which has been elaborated by a Special Commission during the four years preceding the Diplomatic Conference.

Foreign Judgments in Civil and Commercial Matters"[5] was adopted. This was done by vote on the individual provisions, as provided by the Rules of Procedure of the Hague Conference.

Both the structure and the content of the text adopted in 1999 very much resembled the Brussels Convention of 27 September 1968 on Jurisdiction and the Enforcement of Judgments in Civil and Commercial Matters[6] and the Lugarno Convention of 16 September 1988 on Jurisdiction and the Enforcement of Judgments in Civil and Commercial Matters.[7] The text contained rules on jurisdiction as well as on the recognition and enforcement of judgments rendered on the basis of Convention-based jurisdiction in a Contracting State. The chapter on jurisdiction provided for a general defendant's forum (in the defendant's state of habitual residence; Art. 3), where all actions against a particular defendant could be brought, as long as they fell within the scope of the Convention (Art. 1) and were not subject to exclusive jurisdiction under the Convention. Equally open to all actions, independent of the subject matter, were fora based on a choice-of-court agreement (Art. 4), on appearance and submission by the defendant (Art. 5), on a joinder of actions against multiple defendants (Art. 14), counter-claims (Art. 15) and third party claims (Art. 16). In addition, there were rules on specific jurisdiction for certain subject matters – some exclusive (Art. 12), but most of them not (Arts. 6–11).

As far as intellectual property rights are concerned, Art. 12(4)–(6) provided as follows:

---

[4] The Special Commission constituted for each project will normally end its work about one to one-and-a-half years before the envisaged date of the Diplomatic Conference with the adoption of a "Preliminary Draft Convention", thereby leaving time for consultations on the text in the Member States of the Conference and other states participating in the negotiations. The final text then adopted during the Diplomatic Conference, as mentioned above, is called "Draft Convention" as long as it has not been signed by any state entitled to do so. Normally, the Draft Convention is opened for signature on the closing day of the Diplomatic Conference, when the Final Act is signed by all delegations and the text thereby approved as being the result of their negotiations. The first signature by a state entitled to do so then promotes the "Draft Convention" to a "Convention" which will subsequently bear the date of the first signature.

[5] The text of the Preliminary Draft Convention and its Explanatory Report by *Nygh* (Australia) *& Pocar* (Italy) have been published in HC Prel.Doc. No. 11 (*supra* note 1).

[6] OJ EC 1998 No. C 27/1. On 1 March 2002, the Brussels Convention was replaced by Regulation (EC) No. 44/2001 on Jurisdiction and the Recognition and Enforcement of Judgments in Civil and Commercial Matters of 22 December 2000 (OJ EC 2001 L 12/1) (the Brussels I Regulation) for 14 of the 15 EU Member States. The Convention is, however, still in force between the 14 EU Member States, now bound by the Regulation, and Denmark. In this paper, the Conventions of Brussels and Lugano, together with the Brussels I Regulation, will be referred to as "the European instruments".

[7] OJ EC 1988 L 319/9.

(4) In proceedings which have as their object the registration, validity, [or] nullity [, or revocation or infringement,] of patents, trade marks, designs or other similar rights required to be deposited or registered, the courts of the Contracting State in which the deposit or registration has been applied for, has taken place or, under the terms of an international convention, is deemed to have taken place, have exclusive jurisdiction. This shall not apply to copyright or any neighbouring rights, even though registration or deposit of such rights is possible.

[(5) In relation to proceedings which have as their object the infringement of patents, the preceding paragraph does not exclude the jurisdiction of any other court under the Convention or under the national law of a Contracting State.]

[(6) The previous paragraphs shall not apply when the matters referred to therein arise as incidental questions.]

Thus, the validity of intellectual property rights with required registration or deposit was subject to exclusive jurisdiction where it was the principal issue of the action. The delegates present in October 1999, however, did not consider themselves in a position to decide whether exclusive jurisdiction should also extend to proceedings where validity could arise as an incidental question, in particular infringement proceedings. At that time, the IP community largely ignored the negotiations in The Hague and provided very little input there. One can only speculate about the reasons for this lack of interest.[8]

It was not until the late 1990s that this attitude changed on a global scale. International, regional and national developments had contributed to this change. The internet and electronic commerce were becoming ever more important, and legislators were struggling to deal with them. In the United States of America, the Digital Millennium Copyright Act (DMCA) was being discussed, in the European Union there was a debate on the Directives on Electronic Commerce and on Copyright in the Information Society (all three involving, *e.g.*, the problem of liability of internet Service Providers (ISPs) for content posted by their clients, and the questions of jurisdiction and applicable law for such liability); and the Conventions of Brussels and Lugano were revised, thereby stirring up the waters with regard to the

[8] It has to be pointed out, however, that in many countries, different ministries are responsible for PIL (this is often a responsibility of the ministry of justice) and intellectual property (copyright is sometimes a responsibility of ministries of culture or education while patents and trademarks, as well as other industrial property rights, lie with the ministry of economic affairs). This does not facilitate consultation. In addition, in many countries both intellectual property and PIL are specialisations a student can acquire at a rather late stage of his or her studies, and normally this involves a choice between the two (and other subjects). Thus, while many people who specialise in, say, PIL, have some basic (or more comprehensive) knowledge of contract law, tort law or family law, because part of those areas might be compulsory, a choice for PIL as a specialisation often excludes the choice for intellectual property law. During negotiations within, *inter alia*, WIPO and the Hague Conference, the author has experienced that this definitely leads to both a lack of dialogue and even fear and avoidance of the other area.

internet and electronic commerce.[9] In addition, specialised international organisations started to look across the neatly drawn boundaries between IP and PIL. The Hague Conference on Private International Law, for instance, had to examine IP issues during the negotiations on the Judgments Project, and the WIPO started looking at trademarks on the internet (voluntarily) and conflict-of-laws issues in copyright (rather forcibly – during the negotiations on a Treaty on Audiovisual Performances in December 2000 which, up to now, has still not been finalised).[10]

In The Hague it was easy to get the impression that, once the IP community became alerted that there was "something going on" in The Hague that could affect IP rights, they wanted to bring everything to a temporary halt because they had been taken by surprise. This, in return, surprised the Hague Conference (that had published all documents on its website at www.hcch.net and therefore assumed that anyone interested would be sufficiently informed) as well as the delegates from Member States, who had consulted their "usual stakeholders" throughout the negotiations. It turned out, however, that specialised IP bodies were in most cases not among the latter, as international governmental and non-governmental organisations specialised in either PIL or IP had clearly respected the (imagined) boundaries of their respective areas in the past. The same had been true of lobby groups, although it seems that negotiators in both areas could clearly benefit from input coming from outside their "inner circle", no matter whether the latter is an IP or a PIL circle.

During the consultations carried out in the Member States of the Hague Conference on the Preliminary Draft Convention adopted in October 1999, it turned out that the text seemed hardly acceptable for any state other than those that were party to the Conventions of Brussels and Lugano and perhaps a few others with similar or at least compatible legal – and in particular procedural – systems. Moreover, the method applied to adopt the text raised concerns in some more consensus-oriented systems: according to the rules of procedure of the Hague Conference, the text had been adopted by vote, and on many occasions there had been a very narrow majority, thus leaving a large minority of almost half of the delegations dissatisfied. A final text resembling the Preliminary Draft Convention – and therefore being something like a copy of the Conventions of Brussels and Lugano – was therefore likely to be acceptable mainly to those states that were already parties to those Conventions. With only few other states joining the new Convention, it would have been likely to add little to the existing legal situation. The

[9] What had been seen by the delegates revising the Conventions of Brussels and Lugano (to whom the author belonged) as a mere clarification of Art. 13(1) No. 3 of the (previous) Brussels Convention (the issue of targeting of electronic advertisements) was seen by the information technology (IT) community as a major change to their detriment in the jurisdiction rules.

[10] The author was deputy head of the German delegation to these negotiations.

negotiating parties in The Hague therefore decided in April 2000 to suspend formal negotiations and conduct informal discussions on how to reach consensus on specific issues. Informal meetings hosted by individual states were held in Noordwijk (The Netherlands), Washington, D.C. (USA), Ottawa (Canada), Basel and Geneva (Switzerland), and Edinburgh (Scotland/United Kingdom) in 2000 and 2001.[11] The Geneva meeting in January 2001 was the first meeting ever to focus on IP issues. Following a two-day conference organised by the WIPO on "Private International Law of Intellectual Property" which also touched, *inter alia*, on the Hague Judgments Project, the Hague Conference organised a one-day meeting on the Judgments Project only, taking advantage of the presence of numerous IP experts as well as many "habitual" Hague delegates. The major aim was to examine whether different IP rights might require different treatment under the Hague draft. While there was a strong preference to reserve issues of validity of registered industrial property rights exclusively to the state of registration where this was the principal issue of the claim, there was no clear tendency as to whether exclusive jurisdiction should be extended to infringement proceedings, bearing in mind that in many infringement proceedings invalidity is the standard defence.[12]

Discussions on infringement proceedings were continued at another meeting in Ottawa in March 2001, where the tort jurisdiction under Art. 10 was examined, in particular in light of the internet. Discussions focused on cases where an act occurring in one single state produced effects in a number of different states, as can be the case with defamation, environmental damage or IP infringement. It was generally welcomed that Art. 10(4), first part, of the 1999 Hague Draft[13] limited jurisdiction based on the injury arising in that particular state (while the act had been committed abroad) to the (part of the) injury arising there.[14] There were doubts, however, about the appropriateness of Art. 10(4), final part. This provision allows consolidation of all claims for worldwide damages in a state where (part of) the injury arose, if the injured person has his or her habitual residence in that state. All states party to the Convention would subsequently be obliged to recognise the resulting judgment. When it became clear that this consolidation would be possible directly by virtue of the Convention, even in states which today do not extend their jurisdiction to the global damages, and that recognition and

[11] *See*, for a summary description of the informal meetings, the report produced by the Permanent Bureau (Prel.Doc. No. 15) at www.hcch.net under "Work in Progress".

[12] The meeting report (Prel.Doc. No. 13) is available at www.hcch.net under "Work in Progress".

[13] *Supra* note 5.

[14] This provision amounts to a codification of the decision of the European Court of Justice in the *Shevill* case, ECJ, decision of 7 March 1995, Case C-68/93, *Shevill v. Presse Alliance SA.*, [1995] ECR I-415.

enforcement would be possible under the Convention, the working group adopted a paper suggesting the deletion of that final part.[15]

After this series of informal meetings, delegations felt sufficiently confident that they could now come to agreement when they went back to formal negotiations. Moreover, it was agreed that the next step should not be based on voting but be consensus-based. Because it was felt that the latter might require more time, the decision was made to split the Diplomatic Conference (which was the only remaining "formal" step, as the Special Commission had terminated its work in October 1999) into two parts. The first part took place in June 2001 and produced a draft entitled "Interim Text".[16] Wherever it was impossible to reach unanimity – even in cases of a single person or delegation opposing a proposal –, the text was placed in square brackets. The number of square brackets, options, variants and alternatives makes the text very difficult to read, to say the least. For anyone who did not participate in the meeting, it is almost incomprehensible. Moreover, it does not reflect how weak or strong the support or opposition to a particular provision was, because the requirement of unanimity was applied very strictly.

Initially, it had been envisaged to hold a two-day meeting of the Special Commission on General Affairs and Policy of the Hague Conference[17] immediately following the first part of the Diplomatic Conference in June 2001, in order to decide how to proceed. Given the complexity of the text, this was felt to be impossible. Therefore, delegates reconvened in April 2002. That meeting showed that some delegations still had a strong interest in a global instrument covering all kinds of civil and commercial cases, and containing specific bases of jurisdiction for all of them. Others stressed that the meeting in 2001 had demonstrated that it would be impossible to reach unanimity on all these issues within a reasonable time. In light of the time and effort that had already been spent on the project and in an attempt to reconcile both positions, it was therefore decided to change first of all the working method: the Permanent Bureau of the Hague Conference was invited to establish an informal working group, reflecting the legal traditions of the Member States of the Hague Conference, that would try to draft a text that could then serve as a basis for future work. The group was supposed to use a "bottom-up approach", and take the basis of jurisdiction in previous drafts that seemed least controversial, namely, choice-of-court clauses in business-to-business (B2B) cases. The group was further invited to gradually examine

[15] During the turbulences of the Diplomatic Conference (First Part) held in June 2001, which led to the adoption of a revised draft, it was however "forgotten" to present this proposal.

[16] Available at www.hcch.net under "Work in Progress".

[17] This is a plenary meeting of Member State representatives that now meets annually and decides on the work programme of the Conference, within the four-year framework set up by the Diplomatic Session (*supra* note 3).

other bases of jurisdiction on which consensus seemed possible. The Commission on General Affairs listed a general defendant's forum, submission, counter-claims, branches, trusts, and physical torts as possibilities.[18]

The informal working group encompassed participants from Argentina, Brazil, China, Egypt, the European Commission, Germany, Italy, Japan, Mexico, New Zealand, the Russian Federation, South Africa, Spain, Switzerland, the United Kingdom and the United States of America. It was chaired by Professor Allan Philip from Denmark. The Permanent Bureau submitted a paper to facilitate the discussions of the group, which dealt with choice-of-court clauses in B2B cases as well as with submission, counter-claims and the general defendant's forum.[19] During the three meetings held by the group,[20] a text on choice-of-court clauses in B2B cases was drafted.[21] It was however not possible to reach a consensus on the other bases of jurisdiction.

The text produced by the group was submitted to the Commission on General Affairs and Policy of the Conference at its meeting in April 2003. The Commission decided as follows:

> The Special Commission on General Affairs and Policy requests the Secretary General to communicate to the Member States the draft text on choice-of-court agreements elaborated by the informal working group on the Judgments Project. He should at the same time ask them to inform him, before the end of July 2003, whether they would agree that this text should be put as the basis for work before a Special Commission to be convened in December 2003, with a view, in due course, to be forwarded to a Diplomatic Conference. On the basis of the reaction by Governments to such letter, the Secretary General shall determine whether there is sufficient support for the reference of the draft to a Special Commission and, if so, convoke it.
>
> The Special Commission on General Affairs and Policy affirms that any decision to convene a Special Commission in December 2003 concerning the draft text on choice-of-court agreements shall not preclude any subsequent work on the remaining issues with regard to jurisdiction, recognition and enforcement of foreign judgments in civil and commercial matters.

The consultation subsequently carried out by the Secretary General demonstrated that there was sufficient support for a Special Commission to be convened on the basis of the draft produced by the informal working group. Consequently, a Special Commission meeting will be held in The Hague from 1 to 9 December 2003.

---

[18] This last expression was used in order to exclude mere financial damages and damages to intangible rights (intellectual property, reputation). *See*, for the Conclusions of the Commission, www.hcch.net under "General Affairs and Policy".

[19] Prel.Doc. No. 19, available at www.hcch.net under "Work in Progress".

[20] *See* the reports of the three meetings (Prel. Docs. Nos. 20, 21 and 22) at www.hcch.net under "Work in Progress".

[21] Prel.Doc. No. 8 (General Affairs), available at www.hcch.net under "Work in Progress".

II. The Draft Text on Choice-of-Court Agreements in B2B Cases Produced by the Informal Working Group on the Judgments Project

1. The Aims of the 2003 Hague Draft

The Convention suggested by the informal group is limited to choice-of-court clauses in B2B cases. It has three aims, namely to ensure that: the chosen court *must* hear the case when seized by one of the parties, thereby excluding any discretion, *e.g.* under the doctrine of *forum non conveniens* (Art. 4); any other court has to decline jurisdiction (Art. 5); and a judgment rendered by the chosen court has to be recognised and enforced under the Convention (Art. 7).

The limitation, which allowed focus to be placed more clearly on how best to strengthen party autonomy with regard to choice-of-court clauses in B2B cases, led to a complete departure from the structure of the 1999 and 2001 Hague drafts. This concerns in particular the previous division of grounds of jurisdiction into "good grounds" (the so-called white list of conventional bases of jurisdiction, the use of which entitled the judgment rendered to recognition and enforcement under the Convention), "bad grounds" (the so-called black list of jurisdictional bases available under some national laws which would even prevent a court from rendering a judgment on such a basis, and not only exclude transborder recognition and enforcement), and "tolerated grounds" (the remaining "grey area" of bases of jurisdiction available under national law: their use was permitted as long as the jurisdictional basis in question was not black-listed, although the resulting judgment would not be entitled to simplified recognition and enforcement under the Convention regime). The new draft, while focusing on just one basis of jurisdiction, namely choice-of-court agreements, aims for a certain degree of harmonisation[23] in this respect while leaving everything beyond

---

[22] The draft text and a report with comments on the provisions, drawn up by the Permanent Bureau and reflecting the discussions in the informal working group, is available at www.hcch.net under "Work in Progress" (Prel.Doc. No. 22).

[23] Because the informal working group was neither a plenary meeting of all Member States of the Hague Conference nor a body mandated by the former to make such decisions, it preferred to leave some issues to the decision of all Member States. With regard to the formal validity of a choice-of-court agreement, it was left open whether a complete harmonisation should be achieved, or whether it should be possible for a choice-of-court agreement that did not meet the Convention standards to be valid under national law (*i.e.* whether a grey area of formal validity should be permitted). As to substantive validity, the group found it impossible to agree on (exhaustive) Convention standards. It was found equally impossible to agree at least on a choice-of-law rule determining that the substantive validity of the clause should be judged according to the law chosen by the parties (or, if no law had been chosen, according to the law determined by the conflict-of-laws rules of the designated forum; assuming for these purposes that the designation was valid).

choice-of-court clauses in B2B cases to national law. It therefore no longer contains grounds of jurisdiction for specific subject matters such as contracts, torts, or the validity of certain IP rights. However, the jurisdiction based on a choice-of-court clause is "content-neutral", as long as the matter at issue is not excluded from the scope of the Convention (Art. 1(2) and (3)) and "arises in connection with a particular legal relationship", as agreed by the parties (Art. 4).

It is hoped that a Convention along these lines could provide a valuable alternative to arbitration, in particular in cases of low value, where the costs of an arbitration might seem out of proportion as compared to the value of the case, or in cases where, for some reason, *e.g.* effects on third parties or the possibility to join them to the proceedings even against their will, it seems desirable to obtain a court judgment instead of an arbitral award. The Convention thus does not aim at entering into competition with the – most successful – 1958 New York Convention on the Recognition and Enforcement of Foreign Arbitral Awards, but intends to complement it. This complementarity is also reflected to some extent in some wording of the draft, which echoes the New York Convention.

2. Consequences of the 2003 Hague Draft for IP Rights

To sum up, party autonomy is the value most cherished by the draft. What does this mean for IP rights? As stated above, they are not excluded from the (limited) scope of the envisaged new Convention[24] with the exception of "agreements between a natural person acting primarily for personal, family or household purposes (the consumer) and another party acting for the purposes of its trade or profession, or between consumers" (Art. 1(2)(a)); and "proceedings relating to the validity of patents, trademarks and [other intellectual property rights – to be defined]" (Art. 1(3)(k)).

a) Validity as Principal Issue of the Claim

There was consensus in the working group that claims directly aiming at a determination of the validity of a patent or registered trademark with effect *erga omnes* (and therefore also affecting the entry in the register concerned) should be excluded from the scope of the Convention. This consensus seems to extend also to unregistered trademarks and other registered industrial property rights.

Questions remained, however, as to which other intellectual property rights should be covered by this exclusion from the scope of the Convention, and in which words to express this – by listing individual IP rights, by referring to certain *categories* of rights (*e.g.* "registered intellectual property rights"), or by other means. The problem with the latter solution, however, is that some rights may be – or even have to be – registered in some countries, while in other states they are unregistered. In addition, some rights exist

[24] The exclusions from the scope of the Convention are defined in Art. 1(2) and (3).

in a registered and an unregistered form within the same state. This applies, *e.g.*, to designs, copyright and trademarks. Furthermore, new registration duties are sometimes created for some rights. Making the exclusion from scope dependent on registration would therefore lead to somewhat arbitrary results, depending on the choice of a national legislature whether to require registration or not. Moreover, one would have to find a solution for those rights that did not have to be registered but may be. The solution of mentioning specific IP rights, on the other hand, bears the risk of casting in stone solutions which might need to be adapted over time, *e.g.* with the creation of new IP rights.

Therefore, two options seemed to emerge: either a general catch-all phrase excluding proceedings having the validity of *any* intellectual property right as their principal issue,[25] or an exclusion limited to the obvious and undisputed area of proceedings having the validity of patents and (registered or unregistered) trademarks as their principal issue.

While the drafting policy of these two solutions seems to be fundamentally different, the results might not differ very much, assuming that a satisfactory "incidental question rule" can be found. The reasons for this are the following.

The Convention as it is drafted now is limited to choice-of-court agreements in B2B cases. This means that it will cover litigation concerning IP rights only where the parties to the proceedings have entered into some kind of contract beforehand, which contains *inter alia* a choice-of-court clause. Such a contract could be a licensing agreement, an agreement that one party should not make use of a certain IP right, or another, similar agreement. Where a dispute then arises between the parties, it will have to be decided whether it arose "in connection with (this) particular legal relationship" (*see* Art. 2(1)(a)) in order for the Convention to apply. So far, reports from practitioners seem to suggest that validity as a principal issue arises in particular with regard to patents, to a lesser extent with regard to trademarks and other (registered) industrial property rights, and almost never with regard to copyright and (other) – in particular unregistered – rights. Therefore, even if one chose to exclude "proceedings relating to the validity of intellectual property rights" while at the same time making clear that this applied only to claims where this was the principal issue, the exclusion would in practice not cover very many cases beyond patents and trademarks, if any at all. And where it did, those cases would be subject to exclusive jurisdiction in most states concerned anyway, which means that *not* excluding them would involve difficult disconnection issues with regard to other existing and future international instruments.

---

[25] One suggestion in this context was to exclude "proceedings relating to the registration and validity of intellectual property rights, but not to licensing". Others felt that the last part should be better covered by a general "incidental question" rule, which was also required for the other exclusions mentioned in Art. 1(3).

b) Validity as Incidental Question

aa) Examples of Incidental Findings on Validity Article 1(4) provides that "[Proceedings are not excluded from the scope of the Convention if a matter referred to in paragraph 3 arises merely as an incidental question]".

In patent and (to a lesser extent) trademark cases, the defendant often objects to a claim by alleging the invalidity of the IP right. This also applies to the sort of cases that would be covered by a convention along the lines of the 2003 Hague Draft, *i.e.* where there is an agreement between the parties that contains a choice-of-court clause for disputes arising between them in connection with the particular legal relationship. It has to be stressed in this context that the convention would not apply to the so-called sheer piracy cases, *i.e.* infringement cases between two parties not related by any contract. While the latter is probably the biggest group of cases in which the standard defence would be invalidity, this can also arise in cases where the licensor sues for royalties that have not been paid, or for damages arising from an alleged exploitation of the IP right beyond the limits covered by the licence.[26]

In some legal systems, an invalidity defence has to be brought by a counter-claim. These cases would, in many jurisdictions, not be considered as "incidental question cases" because the *principal* issue of the counter-claim is validity, and consequently the exclusion in Art. 1(3)(k) applies to the counter-claim. Jurisdiction for the counter-claim on validity is then governed by national law, and so are the effects of the judgment.

In other countries, invalidity can be raised as a defence in proceedings brought, *e.g.* for the payment of royalties. While the principal finding of the judgment is whether royalties are due or not, on its way to this decision the court has to deal with the invalidity defence. The 2003 Hague Draft reflects that a court seized on the basis of a choice-of-court clause should be enabled to decide the principal issue falling under the Convention even in situations in which an incidental finding on the validity might be required.[27]

---

[26] This last example shows that it would be wise to move away from the opposition of "infringement" versus "contract". In some jurisdictions, this would be considered a contract case, while in others it would be a tort case. Again, it must be recalled that in many countries the plaintiff only has to plead the facts, and it is for the court to find the legal basis. There are countries where the court would apply tort and contract rules cumulatively or alternatively, and the application of this Convention should not depend on such differences of national procedural law. Decisive for the application of this Convention should be the fact that the two parties had entered into a contract beforehand that contains a choice-of-court clause. The court seized would then have to determine whether the case "arose in connection with" the particular legal relationship. This concept has long been applied in arbitration.

[27] Many licence agreements, however, *e.g.* for trademarks, contain a "no challenge clause". The licensee undertakes a contractual obligation not to challenge the validity of the right. However, if (s)he does so in spite of the clause, *e.g.* when being sued for non-payment of the license fee, it depends on national procedural law what influence the clause

bb) Effects of an Incidental Finding on Validity The effect of such an implicit or incidental finding on validity is different in different legal systems. A common feature, however, is that these findings normally have a limited effect only. It therefore seems desirable, in a Hague Convention on Choice of Court Agreements, to also explicitly limit the effect of an incidental finding on validity. Examples to be found in national laws are that (a) sometimes the finding acquires the effect of *res judicata*, but only *inter partes*; (b) in other legal systems there may be broader collateral estoppel effects; and (c) in a third group of states, the implicit finding does not create any binding effect for subsequent proceedings even between the same parties.

Validity judgments creating effect *erga omnes* are normally excluded from party autonomy under national law[28] because the state that grants the protection of the IP right concerned also wants to reserve the decision on the existence of the right to the authorities it deems fit. This does not apply, however, if the principal issue is contractual litigation between private parties. Therefore, the working group chose to state in the Convention that the incidental finding on validity reached in litigation between private parties linked by a contract would create subsequent effects only between the parties to these proceedings. Thereby it is clear that neither third persons nor, in particular, the registering institution will be bound by the finding on the incidental validity issue under this Convention. According to Art. 1(4), second sentence, a judgment resulting from such proceedings shall have effect under this Convention only as between the parties – and thus neither oblige any registration authority to amend the registries accordingly, nor allow any competitor to use the right that might have been found invalid in the proceedings.

Although this approach respects party autonomy while at the same time holding the parties to the consequences of their agreement, some members of the informal working group felt that this did not go far enough. First consultations carried out on Art. 1(4) confirmed that important parts of the IP community as well prefer a rule excluding *any* – even *inter partes* – effect of the incidental validity finding in subsequent proceedings. Therefore, it was suggested to go back to Art. 12(6) of the 2001 Interim Text that was drafted

will have on the proceedings. In many cases, it will not make them inadmissible or ill-founded, but will only give the licensor a right to damages for breach of contract. The fact that such clauses are widely used therefore does not make an "incidental question rule" in the Convention superfluous.

[28] National law, as a coherent and conclusive system, can exclude certain issues from party autonomy by simply establishing a rule of exclusive jurisdiction for it. The same mechanism can be used in a double convention like the Conventions of Brussels and Lugano. There, the provision on choice-of-court clauses is always "subject to" the provisions on exclusive jurisdiction. In a convention limited to choice-of-court clauses only, however, the limits set by any rules on exclusive jurisdiction are not contained in the same instrument, because it does not establish any such rules. Therefore, the respective subject matter as such would have to be excluded from the scope of the convention.

by the IP working group[29] – an approach also taken in paragraph (2) of the MPI Draft.

3. Other Elements of the 2003 Hague Draft

In light of diverging case law under the 1958 New York Convention on Foreign Arbitral Awards, Art. 6 of the Draft makes clear that the Convention does not prevent either party from requesting interim relief elsewhere. It is of course conceivable that the parties may have entered into a choice-of-court agreement expressly covering not only the merits of the case but also interim relief. Such a clause should then be honoured.

The present text is limited to *exclusive* choice-of-court clauses in the jurisdiction chapter. That is, the obligation of the chosen court to take the case and not to exercise any discretion to decline jurisdiction does not exist where the choice-of-court agreement was non-exclusive, thereby allowing one or all parties to seize a court other than the chosen court. If they have another option, there is no need to limit any discretion not to take the case that might exist under the national law of the court chosen and seized. The same is true of the obligation of any court other than the chosen court to decline jurisdiction: where the parties themselves have retained the freedom to seize a court other than the chosen court by making their clause non-exclusive, the Convention does not impose any obligation on the court seized but not chosen to decline jurisdiction.

The approach of the chapter on recognition and enforcement is slightly more generous because, at the enforcement stage, there is no convincing reason not to recognise and enforce a judgment rendered by the chosen court, even if the choice was not exclusive. The fact that the parties nevertheless honoured the clause and took their case before the court previously chosen by them is good reason to treat the resulting judgment the same way as a judgment based on an exclusive choice-of-court clause.

III. Conclusion

Thus, negotiations in The Hague are still going on, the next step being a Special Commission in December 2003 on the Draft Text on Choice of Court Clauses in B2B Cases. The meeting will show whether agreement on such a limited, but nevertheless novel Convention can be achieved. It would

---

[29] Art. 12(6) of the 2001 Interim Text:

[6. Paragraphs 4 and 5 shall not apply where one of the above matters arises as an incidental question in proceedings before a court not having exclusive jurisdiction under those paragraphs. However, the ruling in that matter shall have no binding effect in subsequent proceedings, even if they are between the same parties. A matter arises as an incidental question if the court is not requested to give a judgment on that matter, even if a ruling on it is necessary in arriving at a decision.].

be the first global instrument on jurisdiction, recognition and enforcement in civil and commercial matters. Even with a limited scope, this would be a major achievement.

With regard to intellectual property rights, a lot will depend on the positions taken on (1) which validity issues as a principal issue, concerning which IP rights, to exclude from the scope of the Convention, and (2) the drafting of an "incidental question rule".

II.

The MPI Proposal

Jurisdiction and Enforcement of Foreign Judgments – The General Structure of the MPI Proposal*

ANNETTE KUR**

I. Background

As in other parts of the IP community, notice was first taken in the Max Planck Institute of the endeavours undertaken by the Hague Conference to promulgate an international jurisdiction convention when the 1999 preliminary draft text was published. Having been made aware of the 1999 Draft Hague Judgments Convention (DHJC) in the course of participation in an AIPPI working group, the personal involvement of this author with the topic grew stronger with the realisation that the misunderstandings about the structure and potential practical impact of the DHJC among the IP community were no less widespread and profound than the oft-lamented unfamiliarity of PIL specialists with the specific character of intellectual property. This engagement resulted in several publications[1] and, from 2001, in the formation of a working group consisting of current and former members of the MPI research staff as well as of participants from Finland, Sweden, and Switzerland.[2]

The primary aim of the MPI project was, and still is, to help fill the vacuum created by the Hague Conference's abandonment of IP infringement matters subsequent to the Commission meeting in April 2001.[3] In that

---

* Prof. Dr.jur, Max Planck Institute for Intellectual Property, Competition and Tax Law, Munich; University of Stockholm. The author can be reached at annette.kur@ip.mpg.de.

** See also the text of proposed Art. 21a plus comments printed in the Annex to this volume.

[1] *See e.g. Kur*, International Hague Convention on Jurisdiction and Foreign Judgments: A Way Forward for IP? (2001) E.I.P.R. 175.

[2] The following persons have been/are permanent or temporary members of the working group: *Fritz Blumer*, Switzerland; *Jordan Gimbel*, USA/Sweden; *Lydia Lundstedt*, Sweden; *Wolf Meier-Ewert*, Germany, *Marcus Norrgård*, Finland; *Alexander Peukert*, Germany; *Dieter Stauder*, Germany; *Dorothee Thum*, Germany.

[3] It was pointed out during the Frauenchiemsee meeting that this statement ought to be qualified, as IP infringement matters still form part of the present efforts by the Hague Conference to conclude a core convention in the area of jurisdiction clauses in B2B contracts (*see* the contribution by *Andrea Schulz*, in this volume). While this is true, the fact remains that the Hague Conference deals with IP matters only to the extent that they are covered by a contract, which will not frequently be the case; *see also* the contribution to this volume by *A. Peukert*.

respect, its motives are similar to those underlying the ALI project.[4] The approach taken is however different in so far as it does not propose, like the *Dreyfuss/Ginsburg* draft preceding the ALI principles,[5] an instrument solely dealing with matters of IP litigation, but still departs from the original concept of the 1999 DHJC, *i.e.* to conclude an international convention encompassing jurisdiction and enforcement in civil and commercial matters as a whole. Therefore, unlike the ALI principles, the MPI project – at least for the time being – is restricted to the formulation of rules that are specific for IP,[6] whereas it is submitted that general rules, such as the principle of defendant's forum, etc., can be taken from the 1999 DHJC text (or whatever may replace it in the future).[7] However, the working scheme presently followed by the MPI project does not mean that the idea originally endorsed by *R. Dreyfuss* and *J. Ginsburg* to conclude a separate convention on jurisdiction and enforcement in IP matters is rejected for good; it simply reflects the fact that at this stage, attention in the MPI project is focused on the contents of provisions with specific relevance for IP litigation rather than on rules with a more general character or on the regulatory framework.

In this context, it deserves to be pointed out that another motive for launching the MPI project was the wish to assume a pro-active role in the discussions concerning the substantive rules proposed in the ALI project and its predecessor, the *Dreyfuss/Ginsburg* draft.[8] Departing from a European

---

[4] At the Frauenchiemsee meeting, *A. Kur*'s presentation was preceded by a lecture by *Richard Fentiman* on the jurisdiction chapter of the ALI project (for details *see* the following note). This publication deviates slightly from the program followed at Frauenchiemsee, as *Richard Fentiman*'s two lectures are published together (at 129 in this volume).

[5] The draft convention by *Rochelle Dreyfuss* and *Jane Ginsburg* was first published, under the title "Draft Convention on Jurisdiction and Recognition in Intellectual Property Matters", on the WIPO homepage, at www.wipo.int/pil-forum/en, as a contribution to the Forum on Intellectual Property and Private International Law, held at Geneva in January 2001. A slightly revised version is published in 77 Chicago-Kent L. Rev. 1065 (2002). The project was adapted by the American Law Institute in 2003, now under the title "Intellectual Property: Principles Governing Choice of Law, and Judgments in Transnational Disputes" (in the following: ALI project), and the two original authors have been joined by a third reporter, Prof. *François Dessemontet* from Lausanne, Switzerland. In its present form, the full text of the *Principles* is not publicly available. As regards the chapter on jurisdiction, which will be the main focus of the following article, the present version is however still quite close to the two earlier versions referred to. For more details, *see* the contributions by *Richard Fentiman* and *Andrea Schulz*, in this volume; *see also Dreyfuss/Ginsburg*, Principles Governing Jurisdiction, Choice of law, and judgments in Transnational Disputes, 2003 CRi 33.

[6] The MPI proposal in its present form, with additional remarks completing the outlines contained in this article, is printed in the Annex to the contribution.

[7] In order to prevent misunderstandings, it must be emphasised that relying on the 1999 DHJC text as a general framework for the present draft is merely a matter of working convenience and does not express the view of the MPI working group that the 1999 DHJC still is, will be, or should remain unchanged in the future.

[8] *See supra* note 5.

background, it is no wonder that the MPI project follows more closely the structure of legal rules applying in Europe, and thereby also the structure of the 1999 DHJC, which largely corresponded to the system reflected in the Brussels and Lugano Conventions. Providing for a European-inspired model of reference for regulations governing jurisdiction and enforcement in trans-border IP conflicts as an alternative to the rules promulgated in the framework of the ALI project is hoped to further and enrich the forthcoming debates.[9]

To embark on a major project like this would, however, be pointless under any aspect if those taking part in it were unconvinced of the usefulness and feasibility of efforts to conclude an international Convention on jurisdiction and enforcement covering IP matters. In that respect again, the MPI working group concurs with the view of the ALI project reporters that to elaborate a set of internationally accepted rules in this field is a timely and highly desirable aim. It is submitted that

- establishing a catalogue of commonly accepted jurisdiction rules would considerably enhance legal security in this field, in particular if
- the application of national rules considered inappropriate in an international context are excluded by "blacklisting" them, and
- a link is established between jurisdiction rules and rules governing acknowledgement and enforcement of foreign judgments, meaning that judgments handed down by a competent court are "automatically" enforced (subject only to an *ordre public* clause).

There is also concurrence with the ALI reporters in that the benefits of an agreed-upon catalogue of international jurisdiction rules are particularly valuable in view of the ever-increasing need to solve conflicts with multi-territorial implications in an efficient and satisfactory manner. As we watch the territoriality principle tending to clash with a reality characterised by largely globalised markets and limitless communication structures, we have to be aware that courts will have to tackle the task of adjudicating cases involving multi-state or even global infringements to an extent that was unknown previously. Although they may be available in principle, the instruments for this task are still poorly developed and in need of refinement, thereby taking into account two different, yet related objectives: First, it should be possible to enjoin an infringer, in one lawsuit conducted before one competent court, from continuing his business in all the countries where it takes place, and to claim sanctions for the infringement in its entirety. On the other hand, tendencies of national courts must be controlled and contained to decide claims with a multi-territorial or even global impact, without the assumption of competence being based on generally accepted rules reflecting fairness and

---

[9] The European aspects of the MPI draft were elaborated in more detail in *Kur*, Principles Governing Jurisdiction, Choice of Law and Judgments in Transnational Disputes: A European Perspective, 2003 CRi 65.

equity in international relations, and without fully understanding and evaluating the international nature of the conflict.

II. Main Features of the MPI Proposal

1. Holistic Approach

When the 1999 DHJC was published, the first alarmed reactions came from the patent community, where the possibility to consolidate infringement proceedings outside the country of registration met with nearly unanimous disapproval. The concerns also reached the area of trademark law, although the majority opposing the idea of consolidated proceedings may not have been as dominant as in patent law. Copyright and related rights played a minimal role, if any, in the debates. By contrast, the *Dreyfuss/Ginsburg* draft as well as the ALI project in its present stage are nearly exclusively inspired by specific problems raised by copyright infringement on the internet, where the practical need for consolidation of claims relating to a multiplicity of countries before one competent court is particularly obvious. The authors have even wondered whether patent law should remain entirely excluded from the scope of application of the ALI Principles, considering that the differences between TRIPS member countries are still more profound in substantive patent law than in trademark and copyright law, and that patent claims are more "territorially grounded".[10]

It may indeed appear tempting to avoid having to take a firm position with respect to the contentious issue of exclusive jurisdiction in patent litigation, and to concentrate instead on those legal areas where fast and efficient solutions are needed most, and where an agreement seems to be within easier reach than in the patent field. However, this would mean that trademark as well as industrial design law would also have to be excluded, as the problems first and most prominently voiced with respect to patent law have become topical in those areas, too. As a result, it would hardly be possible to maintain the claim that the principles should pertain to intellectual property disputes in general; they would de facto be confined to copyright and neighbouring rights only. It is submitted that, not least with a view to the increasing overlap between different fields of intellectual property rights, such a selective approach is neither theoretically desirable nor practically feasible.

The MPI proposal has therefore chosen to adopt a holistic approach. This means, first, that equal importance is attributed in the considerations to all areas of intellectual property law. Second, the proposal seeks to avoid as

---

[10] In the Comments on Chapter I – Scope of the *Principles*, (b) – possible exceptions – 2. Patents. In contrast to that, it is sometimes held – and was confirmed by participants in the Frauenchiemsee conference – that harmonisation of patent law is particularly far advanced. Indeed, the differences presently existing in patent law between TRIPS member countries seem to result from the manner in which lawsuits are conducted (discovery, jury trial etc.) rather than from divergences in substantive law itself.

much as possible discriminating between the different categories of IP law. Instead of formulating separate rules, the proposal endorses the principle that, wherever possible, solutions should be devised that at least as a matter of principle can be applied indiscriminately in the fields concerned, although, for practical reasons, their relevance may vary between the different areas.

2. Limited Choice of Fora – The General Rule

In accordance with the Brussels Convention, on which it was originally modelled, the 1999 DHJC aimed at restricting the possibilities for parties to choose the competent court in IP infringement cases (apart from invalidity matters), to a foreseeable minimum. By contrast, the ALI project – in accordance with the *Dreyfuss/Ginsburg* draft preceding it – expressly intends to abandon that rigid scheme and identifies a whole range of competent fora that may have adjudicatory competence in IP litigation. In pursuance of that objective, courts and the parties shall be encouraged to engage in consultations with the aim to consolidate proceedings in related actions pending before courts in different countries.

While certainly interesting and worth discussing, the practicability[11] of that innovative approach would depend to a large extent on the readiness as well as the ability of judges and the parties to enter into fruitful, efficient negotiations on the matter. In an international environment, which typically involves language problems as well as misunderstandings resulting from different legal backgrounds, there is no reason to be overly optimistic in that respect.

Pending further deliberations on the ALI project's novel approach, the MPI proposal endorses the more traditional and cautious concept reflected in the 1999 DHJC and the Brussels system, namely that in principle, the choice of fora in IP infringement and validity cases shall remain restricted, and that the rules determining the competence of a given court shall be as clear and unambiguous as possible.

Based on that principle, proceedings concerning the infringement of intellectual property rights[12] according to the MPI proposal may (only) be conducted in the country

a) where the right is protected (and allegedly infringed),
b) whose courts have been declared competent in a contractual agreement between the parties,[13] and/or
c) where the defendant is habitually resident.

---

[11] The benefits of the proposed solution from the perspective of economic game theory are highlighted in the article by *Moore & Parisi*, Rethinking Forum Shopping in Cyberspace, 77 Chicago-Kent L.Rev. 1325–1347 (2002).

[12] On proceedings concerning (in)validity, *see infra*, 4.

[13] On jurisdiction clauses in contractual agreements, *see* the contribution by *Alexander Peukert* in this volume.

If jurisdiction is solely founded on the fact that the right is protected and infringed in the forum state (a, above), the court's competence is restricted to adjudication of the infringement occurring[14] in that particular country. By contrast, the courts at defendant's forum – *i.e.* the courts in his or her country of habitual residence – as well as the courts chosen by contractual agreement between the parties, are competent to decide all infringement claims raised against that defendant, *i.e.* they may exercise jurisdiction even with respect to infringements occurring in other countries, unless the matter is subject to exclusive jurisdiction.

3. Exceptions to the General Rule

Notwithstanding the general rule, the MPI proposal provides for two exceptions:

- Proceedings conducted against multiple defendants, and
- Proceedings concerning internet-related behaviour.

The first exception concerns a situation which is the object of proposals also in the DHJC and in the *Dreyfuss/Ginsburg* draft as well as the ALI project. In the framework of the MPI project, the issue has been examined more closely by *Marcus Norrgård* and is treated in a separate contribution to this volume.[15]

The second exception is specific to the MPI proposal. It takes account of the fact that a more flexible solution than that outlined sub 2) above is needed for infringements occurring in the digital environment. It would be unrealistic to ignore the fact that in the brave new world of cyberspace, potential infringers are more mobile than the traditional kind of enterprises typically involved *e.g.* in patent conflicts, and are more prone to moving their business establishments into countries where they can easily escape efficient prosecution. Therefore, the MPI proposal contains a rule providing, in infringement cases concerning behaviour related to the internet, additional opportunities to consolidate proceedings before one single court that is competent to adjudicate the infringement as a whole.

---

[14] Art. 12a, paragraph 6 of the MPI proposal contains the following definition of the place where an infringement occurs:

> (1) For the application of paragraph 4, 2nd sentence, an infringement is held to occur in a Contracting State where the right exists, provided that
> a) the activity or omission by which the right is claimed to be infringed has commercial effect or, if commercial effect is lacking, a substantial impact in that Contracting State, or
> b) the activity by which the right is claimed to be infringed is intentionally directed towards that Contracting State.
>
> [(2) Courts shall deny jurisdiction if the defendant has taken reasonable steps to avoid creating a commercial effect in, or directing activity to, that Contracting State.]

[15] At 35.

Admittedly, it may appear difficult or even arbitrary to discriminate between traditional infringements on the one hand and acts committed in e-commerce on the other. However, undertaking this somewhat questionable differentiation allows for a better containment of the number and type of cases where a deviation from the general, clear and simple rules set out above can and must be tolerated. In particular with respect to patent infringement suits, with their often quite traditional structure, it seems advisable and important to keep the choice of competent fora to a clearly defined and foreseeable minimum. This aim can hardly be achieved other than by confining the applicability of a rule permitting multi-territorial jurisdiction of courts outside the defendant's forum to those situations when the need actually arises, *i.e.* when the allegedly infringing act is carried out on the internet or similar media.

In order to determine which courts other than those at defendant's forum can exercise multi-territorial jurisdiction in internet infringement cases, the MPI proposal applies two criteria, one positive and the other negative. First, an essential part of the activities causing the alleged infringement must have occurred in the forum state.[16] The second, negative requirement stipulates that the activities causing the infringement are not aimed at the market in the country of defendant's habitual residence, and do not have substantial commercial effect there. These criteria are intended to capture the aspect that the alleged infringer cannot rely on justified interests in the continuation of the relevant business in his or her own home country, thereby reducing in importance one of the chief motives for the privilege otherwise granted to a defendant, *i.e.* that consolidation should only take place before her or his home courts.

Whereas the first requirement basically appears to comply with other proposals that have been made in this context, the second, negative condition is more unusual, and it is expected that it will meet with certain misgivings. Admittedly, it would entail a considerable reduction in scope for the possibility of consolidating proceedings. Its wording could even invite the argument that the intended effects are easily circumvented if the defendant carries out some token business in its home market. It should be emphasised, therefore, that the proposed wording is not meant to be final. The restrictive approach was, however, deliberately applied in order to highlight the fact that to promulgate a rule instituting an exception from the principle of territorial confinement generally restricting the competence of courts at the

---

[16] It is a disadvantage that this requirement involves an assessment – what is an "essential part" of activities? – that does not live up to the standards of clarity and certainty that, at least according to continental European traditions, are desirable in principle for the determination of jurisdiction. However, when it comes to rules designed to apply in the fuzzy world of cyberspace, it will be necessary to provide for a certain amount of flexibility that can hardly be achieved otherwise. *See also* the comments on Art. 12a in the Annex to this volume.

forum delicti commissi is a very sensitive issue. As understandable as the reasons may be for a plaintiff wanting to consolidate proceedings outside the defendant's home country – protection of the defendant's interests remains an important objective in the context of international jurisdiction rules and should not be discarded too readily.

3. Irrelevance of the Injured Party's Habitual Residence

Pursuant to the ALI project, competence to render decisions with transborder effects shall be vested in (a) the courts in the country where the defendant substantially acted in furtherance of the alleged infringement,[17] and (b) the courts in a country to which the alleged infringement was intentionally directed, "if the injured person has his or her habitual residence or main place of business there".[18] The practical effect of the clause cited in the last half-sentence would regularly amount to permitting a person claiming infringement of his or her rights to lodge world-wide claims with the courts in his or her home country.[19]

A similar rule was found in Art. 10.4 of the 1999 DHJC.[20] As a general principle, it was set out that the competence of courts whose jurisdiction is solely based on the *forum delicti commissi* rule is regularly restricted to adjudication of harmful events occurring in the forum state. However, pursuant to paragraph 4, last sentence, the territorial restriction should not apply with respect to courts situated in the injured party's home country.

It appears plausible that this approach was (*inter alia*) a reaction to the ECJ's frequently criticised judgment in the *Shevill* case,[21] where it was held that the plaintiff, an alleged victim of libel, could not claim damages for the infringement as a whole before her home courts, but had to restrict her claim to the damage inflicted by the (few) copies of the foreign magazine spreading the disparaging message that had been sold in the forum state. The consequence that she would have to revert to the courts in the publisher's home country

---

[17] Art. 5.1 a) of the draft Principles, contending that this includes preparatory acts.

[18] Art. 5.1 b) of the draft Principles in connection with 5.2, last half-sentence. Pursuant to Art. 5.1 b), an infringement is also considered as being "intentionally directed" to the forum state if the defendant did not take reasonable steps to avoid acting in or directing activity to that state.

[19] This result is underpinned and justified by references to cases decided by courts in the USA (*Calder v. Jones*, 465 U.S. 783 (1984); *Keeton v. Hustler Magazine, Inc.* 465 U.S. 770 (1984)) and Australia (*Dow Jones & Co. v. Gutnick* [2002] HCA 56 (High Court Australia, Dec. 10, 2002)) concerning the publication of defamatory content in print media or over the internet.

[20] It was clarified during the Frauenchiemsee meeting that it had been decided at the 2001 Diplomatic Conference to delete the last half-sentence in Art. 10.4 DHJC, but that unfortunately, it has been "forgotten" to change the text accordingly.

[21] *Shevill v. Presse Alliance SA*, C-68/93, 1995 ECR I-415.

in order to claim sanctions for the infringement in its entirety may indeed appear as overly burdensome.[22]

Whereas it may therefore be justified to extend the reach of jurisdiction of courts located in an injured party's home country in cases of defamation or other personal injury torts, the MPI proposal strongly endorses the view that such a rule would be out of place in the context of intellectual property litigation. First, intellectual property cases regularly do not involve an element of moral hazard inflicted upon a natural person, with the exception of only those extremely rare cases where the *droit moral* of an author is at stake. Second, unlike the typical situation in defamation cases with a private party claiming remedies from a media company, the relative strength of the parties involved in an IP conflict is generally equal. On the contrary – it could even be correct to claim that in the majority of cases, the holder of an allegedly infringed right is the stronger party. With the specific aspects motivating a deviation from the general rule in defamation cases lacking with respect to intellectual property litigation, the MPI proposal does not accept any extension of a court's jurisdiction on the ground that it is located in the injured party's – *i.e.* usually: the plaintiff's – home country.

4. Proceedings Concerning (In)validity of IP Rights

Finally, with regard to the contentious question as to the scope of exclusive jurisdiction vested in the courts situated in the state of grant or registration of an IP right,[23] the following rules are suggested in the MPI proposal:[24]

- Proceedings having as their object the registration or validity of an IP right must be conducted exclusively before the courts in the state of grant or registration.[25]
- If the validity issue arises as an incidental question, courts in another state than the state of grant or registration may render a decision on the merits (provided that they are competent on other grounds, as e.g. the courts at the defendant's forum). However, an incidental ruling on validity will only have legal effect between the parties, and will not affect subsequent proceedings, even if they are conducted between the same parties.

---

[22] *See e.g. Schack*, Entscheidungszuständigkeiten in einem weltweiten Gerichtstands- und Vollstreckungsübereinkommen, 1998 ZEuP 931, 948; by the same author, Internationale Urheber-, Marken- und Wettbewerbsverletzungen im Internet, 2000 MMR 135, 139, in note 45; *Stauder/Kur*, Extraterritoriale Jurisdiktion und Streitbeilegung, in: *Schricker/Dreier/Kur* (eds.), Geistiges Eigentum im Dienst der Innovation, 2001, at 151, 155.

[23] The topic is also contentious in the framework of the Regulation 44/2001 on jurisdiction and enforcement of judgments in civil and commercial matters (Brussels-I-Regulation; the previous Brussels Convention), Art. 22.4. The issue was recently brought before the ECJ by a reference for preliminary decision by the Düsseldorf Court of Appeals, 2 U 104/01 (2003 GRUR Int. 1030), ECJ case C-4/03-1.

[24] In that respect, the proposal follows quite closely the structure of the 1999 DHJC plus suggestions made during the first part of the Diplomatic Conference in 2001.

[25] An exception is made from that rule if the judgment becomes effective *inter partes* only. For details, *see* the text of proposed Art. 12a plus comments, in the Annex to this volume.

It is expected that this proposal will raise the same strong misgivings, especially in the patent law community, as did the DHJC text of 1999.[26] As was pointed out above, the view was endorsed by a strong majority among the interested circles that exclusive jurisdiction should not only apply to (in)validity issues in a narrow sense, but that it should also be extended to infringement proceedings in general, the main argument being that validity and infringement are inseparable issues anyway. In the MPI working group, the arguments brought forward in favour of that view have been examined and were found unconvincing. The reasons for adopting instead the approach followed in the 1999 (and 2001) DHJC[27] are briefly summarised in the following lines.

a) Points of Departure

It is uncontested in general that the courts in the country of registration/protection provide for the most appropriate and competent forum for infringement suits. This, however, is not the decisive point. The only relevant question is whether the possibility to choose another forum should be *totally precluded for now and for the future*. It is submitted that it is better to maintain than to discard the option for making a choice, provided that the interests of the parties are safeguarded to the best possible degree, and that misuse can be prevented.

b) The Plaintiff's Interests

It is not easy to understand why a rule granting the plaintiff[28] the opportunity to choose between the courts in the country where the right is protected and allegedly infringed, and the defendant's forum, should have detrimental rather than beneficial effects for him. This applies in particular in view of the fact that taking the case to the defendant's forum would offer the possibility, in cases of multi-territorial infringement, to claim sanctions for the infringement as a whole, which would be impossible in the absence of such a rule. The positive effects would of course only accrue under the condition that the choice of forum made by the plaintiff is based on sound and rational deliberations. No one doubts that litigating abroad, in the defendant's home

---

[26] As a prophylactic reaction to those misgivings, the MPI proposal also provides for compromise solutions to be discussed. *See* the comments on proposed Art. 12a, in the Annex to this volume.

[27] As to the state of discussions in the Hague Conference, *see* the contribution by *Andrea Schulz* to this volume.

[28] It has been argued that it would be wrong to assume that the plaintiff regularly is the holder of an IP right that is allegedly infringed; alleged infringers as well might take the initiative to launch proceedings before courts of their own choice. Whereas that observation is correct in principle, it is important to note that, according to the system underlying the DHJC, which is also endorsed in the MPI proposal, the court seized with proceedings in which substantive remedies are claimed for infringement of IP rights will prevail over a court seized first with proceedings concerning declaration of non-infringement in the same matter; *see also* the text below (*sub* d).

country, can be dangerous, especially if the courts are not familiar with the law in the country of protection, which they have to apply in the assessment, and if the procedural rules tend to disfavour a foreign plaintiff. However, would it be appropriate to exclude any choice for the plaintiff, just because it may turn out to be unwise in a given case? The holders of patents and other intellectual property rights are usually deemed to be grown-up, rationally minded and well-informed people, all the more so as they can rely on the advice given to them by their experienced (patent) attorneys. Why should they be treated in the same way as naive and uneducated consumers who must be protected from their own decisions?[29]

c) The Defendant's Interests

There is more reason to worry about the defendant, who does not have a choice herself, but must abide by the decision made by the plaintiff. In the proposal, the ensuing need to protect the interests of the defendant to the best possible degree is achieved by reserving the power to exercise jurisdiction in (normal) infringement cases to the courts in the state where the defendant is habitually resident (unless the case is brought before the courts in the country of registration/protection, or before the courts that have been indicated as competent in a contractual agreement between the parties). This means that the alternatives a defendant has to face (absent contractual relations involving a jurisdiction clause) are being sued either in the country where the right is protected and allegedly infringed, or in her own jurisdiction.[30] It is submitted that the resulting hardships for the defendant would appear acceptable.

d) Prevention of Misuse

The fear that a jurisdiction rule granting a choice of forum in IP infringement proceedings may lead to misuse primarily concerns the so-called torpedo problem, which has emerged in the context of the Brussels Convention/Regulation. However, the situation in the DHJC is different from the Brussels system on that point. Article 21, the provision in the DHJC incorporating the *lis pendens* rule, stipulates in paragraph 6 that if an alleged infringer has initiated proceedings for a declaration of non-infringement with a court that is competent according to the provisions of the convention, the court second seized prevails if the claim lodged there seeks the grant of

[29] In other words: The position of the plaintiff and the risks to which he might expose himself when trying to enforce a European patent before an American court should not be our primary concern. If litigating in the US is dangerous and expensive, then don't go there as a plaintiff, if you have a choice – and according to the proposal, nobody would ever take away, or interfere with, that freedom of decision.

[30] An exception has to be made for internet infringements, *see supra*, where the interests of the defendant are intended to be safeguarded by the positive/negative requirements set out above, and for the multiple defendants rule, as explained below.

substantive relief in the same case.[31] The same approach is also endorsed in the MPI proposal. Fears of abusive torpedo litigation are therefore unfounded.

e) Inter Partes Effect of Invalidity Rulings

It is true that, in particular in patent cases, validity issues will regularly be brought up in the framework of infringement litigation. As was pointed out above, the MPI proposal, in line with the 2001 DHJC text, proposes that if the validity issue is raised as an incidental question, it can be decided by other (competent) courts than those in the state of registration or grant, with the decision only having *inter partes* effect. Against that solution, it has been argued that the effects of a finding of invalidity between the parties would regularly prove to be fatal for the right-owner, as in spite of the restrictions with respect to the legal effects of the judgment, the right would no longer be respected by anyone in practice. Even if this is true, the argument is not fully convincing. If the right is disrespected by others than the party involved in the first lawsuit, nothing would prevent the right-holder from undertaking a second effort to enforce his right *vis-à-vis* (a) subsequent infringer(s). Of course, he would be ill-advised to launch proceedings in the same country where the first negative judgment was handed down, and where the second attempt would most likely fail as well. Instead of making the same mistake twice, the right-holder can and regularly will initiate proceedings in the country where the right has been registered.[32] If the first court was wrong, there is nothing to stop the second, presumably more competent, court from handing down a more favourable decision, which can be enforced without difficulties under the Convention. If, on the other hand, the right-holder fails even before the court in the country of registration, this implies the confirmation that the first court was right after all. It is not easy to understand why this should be a matter for concern rather than a principally welcome consequence of the fact that foreign courts can be trusted at least in some cases to make a correct assessment of complex issues like the validity of patents or other intellectual property rights.

f) Public Policy Concerns

Finally, account must be taken of the fact that, in spite of being effective only between the parties, a foreign judgment on infringement involving (in)validity matters will have direct consequences on the market in the country of registration. It has been argued that this effect clashes with the sovereign powers of the state having issued the right at stake, as it ought to be

[31] *See* the text of Art. 21.6, 1999 DHJC.

[32] It has been pointed out that the plaintiff would not retain this freedom in a case in which he is obliged by contract to sue in the country where the first and the second etc. infringer(s) are domiciled. In this case, the plaintiff would indeed have to rely on the confinement of the legal effects of the first judgment.

a matter for domestic authorities only to allow or forbid measures having actual or potential effects on, *inter alia,* consumer prices.[33]

To some extent, the issue corresponds to the discussion regarding the possibility to submit patent or trademark conflicts to arbitration. The situations appear parallel or at least comparable, insofar as a decision handed down by an arbiter also entails an impact on the market, regularly without the deciding person qualifying as a judge, an ordinary court or a competent authority in the usual meaning of domestic law.

Indeed, for public policy reasons, intellectual property disputes, in particular disputes involving invalidity of a patent or trademark, were formerly considered inarbitrable in many jurisdictions. Meanwhile, however, the majority opinion seems to have changed, as most countries by now have assumed a positive attitude towards arbitration, as *e.g.* the United States.[34] Even in a country like Germany, where decisions on patent validity are in principle a matter for the patent office only, arbitration awards are considered unproblematic at least when the arbiter, although taking the (in)validity of the right into account, does not address the issue explicitly in his findings.[35] Furthermore, it seems to be a generally accepted practice in international arbitration that decisions involving the (in)validity of a patent are enforced even in countries where the issue, according to domestic law, would have been excluded from arbitration, provided that the law applied in the arbitration proceedings allows for that possibility.[36]

In the same vein, it is contended in this proposal that the public policy aspects concerning the impact on the domestic market of a foreign judgment involving a finding on (in)validity *inter partes* do not weigh so heavily that they command a total prohibition for foreign courts to exercise jurisdiction. This is ultimately a question of party autonomy.[37] If the decision of a right-holder is generally respected not to enforce her right at all in case of infringement, or to settle the case out of court by agreement with the infringer, or to submit the issue to binding arbitration – why should it not be acceptable to grant the option to have the case decided with effect *inter partes* by a foreign

---

[33] It seems that the Düsseldorf Court of Appeals, in its decision to refer the matter of exclusive jurisdiction in infringement proceedings involving validity matters to the ECJ (*supra* note 23), attributes specific relevance to this argument.

[34] For the United States, *see* 35 U.S.C. § 294 (a) (1994). Generally, on public policy and the (in)admissibility of arbitration in IP disputes, *see Grantham,* The Arbitrability of International Intellectual Property Disputes, 14 Berk. J.Int'l Law 173 (1996).

[35] *Pagenberg,* The Arbitrability of Intellectual Property Disputes in Germany, in: Worldwide Forum on the Arbitration of Intellectual Property Disputes (conference paper, 1994).

[36] This means that the legal principle prohibiting arbitration involving an assessment of validity, insofar as it still applies at all in a given country, is generally not considered to form an important part of *ordre public.*

[37] The aspect of autonomy is also emphasised in the article by *Grantham,* 14 Berk. J.Int'l Law 173 *et seq.* (1996) with respect to the admissibility of arbitration in intellectual property disputes.

court having general jurisdiction under the rules set out in an international agreement? From the point of view of public policy, it is hard to see why the latter option should raise more ponderous or essentially different misgivings than the other possibilities mentioned.[38]

III. Concluding Remarks

For the time being, chances to conclude a comprehensive international agreement on jurisdiction and enforcement, of which the MPI proposal could become part, seem to be minimal. Nevertheless, having developed and debated the ideas presented in the previous article may still prove to have some use for the future, be it as a contribution to the somewhat more limited discussions to be conducted with respect to the present efforts by the Hague Conference, or as an alternative model to some of the features proposed in the jurisdiction chapter of the Principles proposed in the ALI project.

[38] If the option to litigate before a foreign court resulting in a decision with *inter partes* effect only should raise concerns under competition law in an individual case, these concerns should be taken into account just as in other situations when the conflict is dealt with in a manner other than by submitting it to the competent authority in the country of registration or grant.

Provisional Measures and Multiple Defendants in the MPI Proposal

MARCUS NORRGÅRD*

I. Provisional and Protective Measures in Intellectual Property

1. Introduction

There are several kinds of provisional and protective measures. In general civil and commercial matters, perhaps the most important type is the attachment order, which is a seizure of property in order to safeguard the payment of a monetary claim (*Mareva injunction*, *Arrest*). Attachment orders are also used in intellectual property matters, but the typical type of provisional and protective measure in intellectual property matters is the interim or preliminary injunction. With such an injunction, the court prohibits the defendant from continuing an infringement on an intellectual property right. Another typical type of provisional and protective measure in intellectual property matters is the order to secure evidence of an infringement (*search order*). The importance of preliminary injunctions and orders to secure evidence is emphasised by Art. 50(1) of the TRIPS Agreement, which reads as follows:

> 1. The judicial authorities shall have the authority to order prompt and effective provisional measures:
>
> (a) to prevent an infringement of any intellectual property right from occurring, and in particular to prevent the entry into the channels of commerce in their jurisdiction of goods, including imported goods immediately after customs clearance;) to preserve relevant evidence in regard to the alleged infringement.

The purpose of part I of this article is to study provisional and protective measures in intellectual property disputes.[1] This means, first and foremost, that the focus is on the two typical types of measures in intellectual property.

The fundamental principles and values brought forward in the draft proposal by the Max Planck working group on international jurisdiction (MPI

---

* Juris doktor, acting professor at the Swedish School of Economics and Business Administration, Helsinki, Finland. The author can be reached at marcus.norrgard@hanken.fi.

[1] Questions of *lis pendens* and enforcement and recognition will not be dealt with expressly in this article. It would, however, seem natural that provisional and protective measures do not give rise to a *lis pendens* effect in relation to instituted proceedings as to the merits of the case in another state and vice versa. Furthermore, provisional and protective measures issued *ex parte* would not be enforceable outside the forum state.

proposal)[2] are taken as starting points. This means, for instance, that the holistic approach of the MPI Proposal is accepted. Equal importance is thus attributed to all areas of intellectual property law and discrimination between different categories of intellectual property rights is avoided as much as possible. This does not, however, mean that the provisions necessarily have an identical impact in all fields of intellectual property law.

2. Similarity between Preliminary Injunctions and Final Injunctions

Preliminary injunctions and attachment orders (and search orders) illustrate the division between two larger groups of measures: measures that have the same effect as a judgment on the merits, and measures whose effect is less than that of a judgment on the merits. Preliminary injunctions in intellectual property disputes typically fall into the former group. If the court enjoins the defendant, the effect of such a preliminary injunction is typically the same as with a final injunction ordered in a judgment on the merits. The latter type is represented, for instance, by attachment orders and search orders. Their effects are somewhat less than that ordered in a judgment on the merits.

The preliminary injunction enjoining the defendant from continuing an infringement requires special attention when it comes to drafting a provision on international jurisdiction in the field of intellectual property. Since, in its effect, a preliminary injunction is so similar to a final injunction, it needs to be considered whether there should also be similarity in the jurisdiction provisions. This would mean that the jurisdictional strictness represented in the MPI Proposal is extended to include preliminary injunctions as well. There must not be an imbalance between the provisions on jurisdiction applying to, on the one hand, cases on the merits and, on the other, preliminary injunctions. Such an imbalance might lead to forum shopping flourishing uncontrollably. Since there is no such similarity for attachment and search orders, the same does not apply to them.

3. Different Approaches

a. The 1999 DHJC

The provision on provisional and protective measures in the 1999 Draft Hague Convention, Art. 13, is worded as follows:

> Article 13 Provisional and protective measures
>
> 1. A court having jurisdiction under Articles 3 to 12 to determine the merits of the case has jurisdiction to order any provisional or protective measures.
>
> 2. The courts of a State in which property is located have jurisdiction to order any provisional or protective measures in respect of that property.

---

[2] The MPI proposal is available at http://www.ip.mpg.de/Enhanced/Deutsch/Arbeitsgruppen/int_zustaen_haag-projekt/dhcalternativedraft5amended.htm.

3. A court of a Contracting State not having jurisdiction under paragraphs 1 or 2 may order provisional or protective measures, provided that –

   a) their enforcement is limited to the territory of that State, and
   b) their purpose is to protect on an interim basis a claim on the merits which is pending or to be brought by the requesting party.

The concept of provisional and protective measures is not defined in the 1999 DHJC except for the limited definition in Paragraph 3. The drafters, however, had in mind the classification of measures made by the International Law Association.[3] Provisional and protective measures thus perform two principal purposes: a) they provide a preliminary means of securing assets from which an ultimate judgment may be satisfied; or b) maintain the status quo pending determination of the issues at trial.[4] This definition does not include measures whose purpose is to obtain evidence for use in the trial on the merits.[5] Measures designed to discover or preserve evidence were discussed, but the Special Commission did not accept an extension of the definition.[6]

The reference to "any" provisional and protective measures means that the court seized decides on the basis of its own national law (including choice-of-law rules) what provisional and protective measures are available and what the requirements for such measures are.[7] The choices seem, nonetheless, to be limited to the two types of measures defined in the *Nygh & Pocar* Report.

The courts having jurisdiction under Arts. 3 to 12 have jurisdiction to order provisional and protective measures. According to Art. 3, the defendant may be sued in the courts of the state where that defendant is habitually resident. A court chosen by the parties on the basis of a choice-of-court agreement also has jurisdiction to order provisional and protective measures (Art. 4), as does any court (except in cases of exclusive jurisdiction) if the defendant proceeds on the merits without contesting jurisdiction (Art. 5). Measures may also be issued by courts having jurisdiction in contract disputes (Arts. 6-8), over branches (Art. 9), and in tort (Art. 10) and trust cases (Art. 11). Finally, courts having exclusive jurisdiction (Art. 12) have jurisdiction to order provisional and protective measures. A court having jurisdiction to adjudicate a dispute on the basis of Art. 14 on multiple defendants does not, however, have jurisdiction to order measures on the basis of Paragraph 1.

---

[3] *Nygh & Pocar,* Report of the Special Commission (Prel.Doc. No. 11), http://www.hcch.net/doc/jdgmpd11.pdf, at 68.

[4] International Law Association, Report of the 67th Conference, Helsinki, 1996, at 202.

[5] *Nygh & Pocar, supra* note 3, at 69.

[6] *Id.*, at 69.

[7] *Id.*, at 69.

The 1999 DHJC does not explicitly deal with extraterritorial injunctions. In the Nygh & Pocar Report it is nevertheless stated that orders made on the basis of Paragraph 1 may have extraterritorial effect (*i.e.*, effects not limited to the territory of the state of the court).[8] The value of such extraterritorial measures is diminished to some degree by the fact that provisional and protective measures ordered *ex parte* are not enforceable outside the forum state, since the recognition or enforcement of a judgment or decision may be refused if the document that instituted the proceedings was not made known to the defendant (Art. 28(1)(d)).

Nevertheless, the wide range of courts having jurisdiction to order provisional and protective measures might invite widespread forum shopping. In an intellectual property context, it must be considered whether there is a real need for such a wide range of competent courts.

The notion of property and the location of such property might turn out to be problematic in intellectual property disputes (Art. 13(2)). First, it has to be laid down whether the concept of property includes intellectual property. Second, even if property were to include intellectual property, it might be difficult to ascertain where intellectual property is located. From an intellectual property viewpoint, it would be better to refer to established concepts such as place of registration.

The wording of Art. 13(3) might also lead to some IPR-related questions. It is uncertain whether a preliminary injunction enjoining the defendant from infringing the plaintiff's right is a measure whose purpose "is to protect on an interim basis a claim on the merits which is pending or to be brought by the requesting party". Due to the similarity between preliminary and final injunctions, it could be argued that a preliminary injunction "enforces" rights. It does not "protect" rights.

It is likewise uncertain whether orders to preserve evidence protect claims. Taking into account that orders to preserve evidence do not fall within the concept of provisional and protective measures as used in the 1999 DHJC, the question has obviously been left unanswered.

b. The 2001 DHJC

In the Summary of the Outcome of the Discussion in Commission II of the First Part of the Diplomatic Conference 6–20 June 2001 (the 2001 DHJC) a new version of the DHJC was presented. Art. 13 had undergone major changes, but no consensus was reached on the final wording. The alternatives presented were as follows:

> [Alternative A
>
> 1. A court seised and having jurisdiction under Articles [in the white list] to determine the merits of the case has jurisdiction to order provisional and protective measures.

---

[8] *Nygh & Pocar, supra* note 3, at 70.

2. A court of a Contracting State [may] [has jurisdiction to], even where it does not have jurisdiction to determine the merits of a claim, order a provisional and protective measure in respect of property in that State or the enforcement of which is limited to the territory of that State, to protect on an interim basis a claim on the merits which is pending or to be brought by the requesting party in a Contracting State which has jurisdiction to determine that claim under Articles [in the white list].
3. Nothing in this Convention shall prevent a court in a Contracting State from ordering a provisional and protective measure for the purpose of protecting on an interim basis a claim on the merits which is pending or to be brought by the requesting party in another State.
5. In paragraph 3 a reference to a provisional and protective measure means

 a) a measure to maintain the status quo pending determination of the issues at trial; or
 b) a measure providing a preliminary means of securing assets out of which an ultimate judgement may be satisfied; or
 c) a measure to restrain conduct by a defendant to prevent current or imminent future harm.]

[Alternative B

A court which is or is about to be seised of a claim and which has jurisdiction under Articles [3 to 15] to determine the merits thereof may order provisional and protective measures, intended to preserve the subject-matter of the claim.]

The 2001 DHJC shows in a sufficiently clear manner that no consensus was reached on provisional and protective measures during the intergovernmental negotiations. In addition to these two alternatives, there was a further alternative that would provide that provisional and protective measures are excluded from the scope of the Convention (with the exceptions stated in Art. 1(2)(k)). It is submitted that provisional and protective measures under no circumstances may be excluded from the scope of the Convention. These measures (especially preliminary injunctions) are too important in intellectual property litigation to be excluded from a convention dealing with jurisdiction in intellectual property disputes.

The major change in Paragraph 1 is that it is not enough that a court has jurisdiction; it must also be seized of the case. As for the 1999 DHJC, it was expressly stated in the Nygh & Pocar Report that it is not necessary for the court exercising jurisdiction under Paragraph 1 to be seized or about to be seized of the substantive dispute.[9]

Paragraph 2 is in essence a combination of Paragraphs 2 and 3 in the 1999 DHJC. In the 2001 DHJC, Paragraph 2 gives a court, even where it does not have jurisdiction to determine the merits of the case, jurisdiction to order a provisional and protective measure (a) in respect of property in that state or (b) the enforcement of which is limited to the territory of that state. In both cases the purpose of the measure must be to protect, on an interim basis, a claim on the merits that is pending or is to be brought by the requesting party in a Contracting State that has jurisdiction to determine that claim.

---

[9] *Nygh & Pocar, supra* note 3, at 69.

Thus, Paragraph 3 of the 1999 DHJC has been deleted. Instead Paragraphs 3 and 4 of the 2001 DHJC deal with the *lis pendens* effect of a claim on the merits in one state on provisional and protective measures in another state. As long as the provisional and protective measure applied for is of the kind defined in Paragraph 4, there is no *lis pendens* effect. If, however, the measure applied for in another state would, for example, be one of interim payment, there might be a *lis pendens* effect.

Alternative B of the 2001 DHJC is substantially shorter than Alternative A. According to Alternative B, a court that is or is about to be seized of a claim and that has jurisdiction under the relevant Articles to determine the merits thereof may order provisional and protective measures to preserve the subject-matter of the claim. In its brevity, it obviously leaves some questions unanswered. It does, however, exclude measures whose purpose is not the preservation of the subject matter of the claim. It is uncertain whether preliminary injunctions fall within the requirement of preservation of the subject matter. Again, it could be argued that preliminary injunctions enjoining infringements "enforce" rights, which is something other than preservation. Although arguments against such an interpretation can be expressed, it is clear that the provision creates some uncertainty for intellectual property.

c. *The Dreyfuss/Ginsburg Draft (DGD)*

In the Draft Convention on Jurisdiction and Recognition of Judgements in Intellectual Property Matters (DGD),[10] Art. 19, a provision on provisional and protective measures has been included.[11] The inclusion of the provision is based on the argument that "the time-value of information and the inability to return (or forget) what has been learned makes the availability of preliminary relief particularly important in intellectual property disputes".[12] Furthermore it stated that "this provision offers courts a great deal of flexibility in insuring the maintenance of the status quo pending adjudication".[13] Article 19 of the DGD reads as follows:

> Article 19 Provisional and Protective Measures
>
> 1. The court where the action is properly pending under the rules of this Convention has jurisdiction to determine the merits of the case has jurisdiction to order any provisional or protective measures, including trans-border injunctions.
> 2. The courts of a State in which intellectual or tangible property is located have jurisdiction to order any provisional or protective measures in respect of that property.
> 3. Courts in other Contracting States not having jurisdiction under paragraphs 1 or 2 may order provisional or protective measures, provided that –

[10] *Dreyfuss & Ginsburg*, Draft Convention on Jurisdiction and Recognition of Judgements in Intellectual Property Matters, http://www.kentlaw.edu/depts/ipp/intl-courts/docs/treaty10_10.pdf.

[11] *See also Dreyfuss & Ginsburg*, Principles Governing Jurisdiction, Choice of Law, and Judgements in Transnational Disputes, 2003 CRi 33.

[12] *Dreyfuss & Ginsburg, supra* note 10, at 51.

[13] *Id.*, at 51.

a. their enforcement is limited to the territory of that State; and
b. their purpose is to protect on an interim basis a claim on the merits which is pending or to be brought by the requesting party.

The provision lays down three different grounds for jurisdiction. First of all, the courts where the case is properly pending, that is, the courts that have jurisdiction to hear the case on the merits and where the case is pending, have global jurisdiction to issue provisional and protective measures. At least the following courts have jurisdiction to issue provisional and protective measures, including trans-border injunctions: a) The defendant's forum (Art. 3); b) a court chosen by the parties (Art. 4); c) a court having jurisdiction where the defendant proceeds without contesting jurisdiction (Art. 5); d) courts of any state where the defendant substantially acted (including preparatory acts) in furtherance of the alleged infringement (Art. 6(1)(a)); e) courts of any state to which the alleged infringement was intentionally directed (Art. 6(1)(b); f) courts of any state in which the alleged infringement foreseeably occurred.

Although the reach of jurisdiction to adjudicate the case on the merits is limited to the forum state when jurisdiction is only based on e) or f) *supra* (Art. 6(2) and 6(3)), no such limitation applies to provisional and protective measures. Thus, there are very many courts having jurisdiction to issue preliminary trans-border injunctions enjoining the defendant. Too many courts to choose from invites forum shopping. Due to the above-mentioned similarity between final and preliminary injunctions, the jurisdiction as to preliminary injunctions must not automatically be wider than the jurisdiction to issue final injunctions.

Second, the courts of a state in which intellectual or tangible property is located have jurisdiction to order any provisional or protective measures in respect of that property. Here the unresolved question of the DHJC as to what the concept of property includes has been explicitly addressed by including "intellectual or tangible property". The problem of location of intellectual property might, however, still lead to uncertainty as to the proper forum. It is not clear whether this is a reference to where the right is in force or where the right is registered, or whether it is something completely different. The notion of location is too problematic to be included.

Furthermore, it should be asked what it means that a court has jurisdiction to order measures in respect of intellectual property located in the forum state. Will such a measure have effects outside the forum state? If it does, is that really what has been strived for? From the point of view of intellectual property, all those unfamiliar and vague expressions should be struck.

Third, courts in other Contracting States not having jurisdiction under Paragraphs 1 or 2 may under certain circumstances order provisional or protective measures. Those circumstances are: a) the enforcement of the measures is limited to the territory of the forum state; and b) the purpose of the measure is to protect, on an interim basis, a claim on the merits that is pending or is to be brought by the requesting party.

In addition to Art. 19, the DGD also includes a provision on injunctions in Art. 31, which reads as follows:

> Article 31 Injunctions
>
> 1. In the ordinary course, injunctive relief is available; nonetheless courts may decline to enjoin activities within their territories if:
>
> a. health and safety are at issue, or
> b. the judgement conflicts with fundamental cultural policies in the State where enforcement is sought, and
> c. damages would afford an effective remedy for that territory.

Article 31 on injunctions is not a provision on jurisdiction, but a provision on the substantive requirements for injunctions. It is not clear whether the provision applies both to preliminary and final injunctions, but since it is in no way limited, it is likely meant to apply to both. In this article, questions of substantive law and the requirements for injunctions will not be dealt with, because it is questionable whether substantive issues should be addressed at all in a convention on jurisdiction.

4. Proposal for a Provision

a. Text

Taking into account the considerations above, it is submitted that a provision on provisional and protective measures should be worded as follows:

> Article 13 Provisional and Protective Measures
>
> 1. A court which has jurisdiction under Articles 2 or 14 may order any provisional or protective measures, including measures having effect outside the state of the court.
> 2. A court of a Contracting State which does not have jurisdiction under Paragraph 1 may order provisional or protective measures the enforcement of which is limited to the territory of that state.

b. Comments

aa) General Applicability of the Provision Although the proposed provision on provisional and protective measures is primarily drafted for intellectual property disputes, it is not specific in the sense that it could not be applied in other types of cases. On the contrary, the proposed provision would most likely also work in other fields of law. The differences of opinion as to the wording of a provision on provisional and protective measures that were aired in the 1999 DHJC and the 2001 DHJC do, however, clearly show that political consensus on the wording seems difficult to reach. The task of the MPI Working Group is, however, limited to presenting a proposal on a provision that reflects the needs of intellectual property law.

bb) The Concept of Provisional and Protective Measures Under a purely literal interpretation it is not obvious what types of measures the concept of provisional and protective measures includes. The measures have to be "provisional" and "protective". Provisional is a reference to the interim nature of the measure, which means that its duration is limited in time. It enters into force (at the earliest) when it is issued, and ceases to be effective after a given period of time or when a judgment is given. The protectiveness of the measures could be construed as referring to the dichotomy between "protection" and "enforcement". A protective measure means that the underlying right or claim is protected not enforced. On the basis of an attachment order a creditor is not, for example, allowed to collect the debt from the debtor. The seized property is only secured so that the debtor cannot dispose of it in a way that harms the interests of the creditor.

This dichotomy does not hold true for preliminary injunctions in intellectual property disputes. Intellectual property involves a right to exclude others from using the right in question. This right is usually only effectively protected through a preliminary injunction, which, on the one hand, protects the claim on the merits and, on the other, enforces it. Instead of the concept of provisional and protective measures, the distinct concepts of provisional or protective measures are used in order to avoid any misunderstandings as to whether preliminary injunctions enjoining the defendant from continuing acts of threatened or actual infringement come under the scope of the provision.

Another way of dealing with preliminary injunctions would be, instead of including them in the scope of the provision, to exclude them from the scope of the provision altogether. Since it would not be acceptable to exclude preliminary injunctions from the scope of the Convention, the jurisdiction for preliminary injunctions would have to follow the jurisdiction of disputes on the merits. That would, however, lead to intricate demarcation problems: when is a measure of the type that is regarded as a provisional and protective measure and when is it not? It is far better to have a broad definition of provisional and protective measures and take the broadness into account when drafting the provision on jurisdiction for provisional and protective measures.

In the Nygh & Pocar Report, measures to secure evidence are not included in the concept of provisional and protective measures.[14] Evidence-preserving measures are, however, important in intellectual property disputes. The TRIPS Agreement requires that Contracting States provide for provisional measures to preserve evidence (TRIPS 50(1)(2)). Thus, it is essential in intellectual property that such measures be included in the concept of provisional and protective measures. It must be noted, however, that parts of the ordinary civil proceedings that are not provisional and protective (such as discovery) would have to fall outside the scope of the definition.

cc) Paragraph 1 In line with the general rule in the MPI proposal of favouring the defendant's habitual residence, Paragraph 1 gives the courts in the

---

[14] *Nygh & Pocar*, *supra* note 3, at 69.

state where the defendant is habitually resident the widest jurisdiction. This rule has, however, been modified in light of the proposed Art. 14 of the MPI proposal on multiple defendants. In order for a multiple defendant provision to have the needed effect, the reach of jurisdiction must also be extra-territorial for the non-residing defendants.

According to Paragraph 1, a court in a state where the defendant has his habitual residence may order any provisional and protective measures, including measures having effect outside the forum state. This essentially means that extra-territorial preliminary injunctions, measures preserving evidence in foreign countries, and attachment orders regarding property outside the forum state may be issued by the courts of the state where the defendant has his habitual residence.

In a multiple-defendant dispute, a court having jurisdiction on the basis of Art. 14 has extra-territorial jurisdiction also regarding the defendants not having their habitual residence in the state of the court. Otherwise, there might be situations where no court has jurisdiction over all defendants, although the actions against the defendants are closely connected.

Paragraph 1 is in balance with the provisions on jurisdiction regarding disputes on the merits. It does not encourage forum shopping and opportunistic behaviour, because it does not confer any wider jurisdiction than does the jurisdictional provisions regarding disputes on the merits.

It suffices that a court has jurisdiction according to Arts. 2 or 14. The said court need not be seized or about to be seized of the claim. Thus, the proceedings as to the merits can be instituted in some other state.

dd) Paragraph 2 The jurisdiction of courts other than those defined in Paragraph 1 is limited to measures whose enforcement is limited to the forum state. In principle Paragraph 2 gives a wide range of court jurisdiction. It first and foremost makes redundant any references to the problematic concept of "location of property".[15] Any court where "property is located" would have jurisdiction to, for instance, issue an attachment order with respect to that property. Courts in states where an infringement has occurred have jurisdiction to issue, for example, preliminary injunctions and search orders that are limited to that state. This is in line with what has been proposed in the MPI proposal Art. 12a(3) and (4): In disputes on the merits, courts in Contracting States where the right has been registered have jurisdiction only with respect to infringements occurring in that state's territory (unless regulated otherwise in 12a(5)).

Paragraphs 1 and 2 together reach a fair balance in intellectual property matters. On the one hand, there is a need for effective enforcement of IPRs. On the other, there is a need to predict where actions are going to be commenced. If there is a need for preliminary injunctions with extraterritorial effects, these can be ordered by the defendant's forum. On the other hand,

[15] *Cf.* the 1999 DHJC, the 2001 DHJC and the DGD.

there may be a need to secure evidence and attach property. Such orders can either be made by the defendant's forum (with extraterritorial effects) or by some other court (for example, where property is located). This solution also shows the importance of the defendant's forum as the main forum.

5. Conclusion

Provisional and protective measures, especially preliminary injunctions and orders to preserve evidence, are important in intellectual property. It is, therefore, vital that a convention on jurisdiction does not exclude provisional and protective measures from its scope. Furthermore, it is of utmost importance that jurisdiction provisions on such measures take into account the special needs of intellectual property. Preliminary injunctions prohibiting the defendant from continuing acts of infringement or threatened infringement are very similar to final injunctions ordered in a judgment on the merits. Therefore, special account needs to be taken so that the jurisdiction provisions on provisional and protective measures do not encourage forum shopping.

Reach of jurisdiction is a question that must be addressed explicitly in a provision on provisional and protective measures. The principal rule is that only the courts of the country of the defendant's habitual residence have global jurisdiction. In addition, a court that has multiple-defendant jurisdiction on the basis of Art. 14 of the ADHC has global jurisdiction. The jurisdiction of all other courts is limited to the country of the court.

In conclusion, the proposed Art. 13 was worded as follows:

Article 13 Provisional and Protective measures

1. A court which has jurisdiction under Articles 2 or 14 may order any provisional or protective measures, including measures having effect outside the State of the court.

2. A court of a Contracting State which does not have jurisdiction under Paragraph 1 may order provisional or protective measures the enforcement of which is limited to the territory of that State.

II. Multiple Defendants in Intellectual Property Disputes

1. Introduction

The purpose of this part of the article is to present a proposal for a provision on international jurisdiction in intellectual property infringement cases with multiple defendants. The proposal is based on the Alternative Draft for Provisions on Proceedings Involving I.P. Rights (MPI proposal) proposed by the Max Planck working group on international jurisdiction.[16]

[16] *See supra* note 2.

The fundamental principles and values brought forward in the MPI proposal are taken as starting points. The holistic approach of the MPI proposal is accepted, which means that equal importance is attributed to all areas of intellectual property law and that discrimination between different categories of intellectual property rights is avoided as much as possible. This does not, however, mean that the provisions necessarily have an identical impact in all fields of intellectual property law.

The grounds for jurisdiction proposed in the MPI proposal constitute a starting point for the discussion on multiple defendants. Thus, only the courts in the state where the defendant is habitually resident have jurisdiction to rule on all infringements of that defendant (Art. 12(4)(1) MPI proposal). The courts of the country of registration (Art. 12(1)(1)) or the country where the judgement shall have legal effect *erga omnes* (Art. 12(1)(3)) have exclusive jurisdiction in cases concerning the validity of intellectual property rights.

2. The Importance of Consolidation

It is clear, in light of the Draft Hague Convention on Jurisdiction and Foreign Judgments in Civil and Commercial Matters (the 1999 DHJC) and the MPI proposal, that they first and foremost deal with situations involving only one defendant. The 1999 DH C originally included a provision on multiple defendants. It was deleted during the intergovernmental negotiations.[17] This, however, cannot imply that there is no need for a multiple-defendants rule. It is well known that the courts in Europe have been confronted with multiple-defendant situations in intellectual property disputes within the framework of the Brussels Convention and Regulation.[18]

Nevertheless, I will make a short detour into the reasons for a provision on multiple defendants.[19] In the Nygh & Pocar Report, which is a commentary to the 1999 DHJC, it is submitted that the purpose of the provision on multiple defendants (Art. 14 of the 1999 DHJC) is to avoid a serious risk of inconsistent judgments that might result if the plaintiff had to sue the defendants separately in different jurisdictions.[20]

As for the Brussels Regulation (and Convention), procedural economy and the avoidance of inconsistent judgements have been stated as reasons for

[17] Summary of the Outcome of the Discussion in Commission II of the First Part of the Diplomatic Conference 6–20 June 2001, www.hcch.net/doc/jdgm2001draft_e.doc.

[18] *See*, for instance, *Pertegás Sender*, Cross-Border Enforcement of Patent Rights, 2002, at 88 *et seq*.

[19] It should be noted that in the Draft International Copyright Code (May 2001) by Professor J.L. Sterling the question of consolidation and jurisdiction has altogether been avoided by proposing the creation of an International Copyright Tribunal (which would only hear copyright cases).

[20] *Nygh & Pocar*, Report of the Special Commission (Prel.Doc. No. 11), www.hcch.net/doc/jdgmpd11.doc, at 72.

Art. 6(1).[21] In intellectual property matters, fragmentation of litigation in the respective countries of each defendant and the resulting "excessive litigational burden", have been stated as reasons for the consolidation[22] of proceedings involving multiple defendants in a single country.[23]

A pro-consolidation stance is taken in the Draft Convention on Jurisdiction and Recognition of Judgements in Intellectual Property Matters (DGD)[24] and the Principles Governing Jurisdiction, Choice of Law, and Judgements in Transnational Disputes.[25] In the commentary to the DGD, it is submitted that consolidation is especially important for intellectual property.[26] Several reasons for consolidation are put forward.[27] First, rights in intangible works can easily be utilised around the globe, which can lead to infringements in multiple jurisdictions.[28] Second, consolidation might temper the impulse to expand the reach of domestic laws to cover foreign infringements.[29] Third, consolidation provides a way to avoid inconsistent judgements.[30] Fourth, consolidation would further the goals of the TRIPS Agreement in that it would be possible to institute proceedings in courts that act quickly.[31] Fifth, consolidation preserves litigation resources and reduces opportunities for harassment.[32] Sixth, consolidation might add to the willingness to settle.[33]

Some negative consequences of consolidation are also presented in the commentary to the DGD. Greater enforcement of intellectual property rights could be viewed as a negative consequence. Accordingly, it would be more desirable to tolerate infringements, particularly for remote jurisdictions.[34] Moreover, some negative consequences in connection with class

---

[21] *See*, for example, *Kropholler*, Europäisches Zivilprozessrecht, 2002, at 174; *Pålsson*, Brysselkonventionen, Luganokonventionen och Bryssel I-förordningen, 2002, at 129 *et seq*.

[22] It should be noted that the concept of consolidation includes more than just multiple-defendant situations. Consolidation also includes consolidation of multiple infringements committed by the *same* infringer. The consolidation scenarios thus fall into two classes: Single-defendant consolidation and multiple-defendant consolidation. *See*, for a similar distinction, *Moore & Parisi*, Rethinking Forum Shopping in Cyberspace, 77 Chicago-Kent L.Rev. 1325 (2002).

[23] *Pertegás Sender*, *supra* note 5, at 88 *et seq*.

[24] *Dreyfuss & Ginsburg*, Draft Convention on Jurisdiction and Recognition of Judgements in Intellectual Property Matters, http://www.kentlaw.edu/depts/ipp/intl-courts/docs/treaty10_10.pdf (downloaded 4.9.2003).

[25] *Dreyfuss & Ginsburg*, Principles Governing Jurisdiction, Choice of Law, and Judgements in Transnational Disputes, 2003 CRi 33.

[26] *Dreyfuss & Ginsburg*, *supra* note 11, at 36.

[27] For a discussion regarding the DGD *see also Moore & Parisi*, *supra* note 9.

[28] *Dreyfuss & Ginsburg*, *supra* note 11, at 36.

[29] *Id.*

[30] *Id.*

[31] *Dreyfuss & Ginsburg*, *supra* note 11, at 37.

[32] *Id.*

[33] *Id.*

[34] *Id.*

action in the United States have been aired against consolidation provisions.[35] Inaccurate results might follow if a single court is forced to apply the law of many states.[36] Consolidation might provide the plaintiffs with undue power, which can lead to settlements of meritless claims.[37] On the other hand, it has been argued that consolidation might also increase the plaintiff's interest in settling knowing it only has one chance to win.[38]

Other arguments against consolidation might include, for instance, the obligation of some of the defendants to defend their cases in remote jurisdictions where the language used is not their mother tongue. The remoteness of the forum would lead to higher litigation costs for those defendants, because of higher travel expenses for the parties' representatives and possible witnesses. Language issues might lead to translation costs (including translation of court documents).

Reasons of predictability might also be used to argue against consolidation. If a provision on consolidation is too vague and does not clearly state where cases may be consolidated, it might become impossible to make any prediction as to the place of litigation. Such uncertainty might have negative consequences for business. For e-commerce, it has been stated that a predictable framework for jurisdiction and the recognition and enforcement of foreign judgements would support the growth of the e-commerce industry by allowing businesses to more accurately manage the risks and costs associated with litigating in foreign courts.[39] The consequence of legal uncertainty may, on the other hand, be that companies limit their product offerings or that consumers become wary of purchasing goods and services over the internet.[40] These arguments are valid also when discussing provisions on multiple defendants: predictability is important.

It is submitted that the *pros* outweigh the *cons*. The reasons against consolidation should be taken into account in the drafting of the provision. They do not, however, amount to insurmountable obstacles. Consolidation is of special importance in intellectual property matters. The question is thus not whether there should be a provision on multiple defendants, but how it should be drafted.

3. Different Approaches

a. Flexibility Versus Rigidity

There are at least two different approaches regarding how to formulate a provision on multiple defendants. One is more flexible and the other more

---

35 *Dreyfuss & Ginsburg, supra* note 11, at 37.

36 *Id.*

37 *Id.*

38 *Id.*

39 *Haines*, The Impact of the Internet on the Judgements Project: Thoughts for the Future (Prel.Doc. No 17 of February 2002), www.hcch.net/doc/gen_pd17e.doc, at 5.

40 *Haines, supra* note 26, at 5.

rigid. The rigid solution is displayed in the 1999 DHJC and the Brussels I Regulation, according to which the plaintiff may choose a suitable forum from among a narrow range of appropriate choices.[41] The flexible solution can be found in the DGD, which identifies a set of courts with adjudicatory authority over the parties. For cases where parallel litigation is ongoing in several territories, the courts seized with parts of a multinational dispute are encouraged to cooperate with one another and with the parties to choose a forum for centralised dispute resolution.[42] The view adopted in the DGD is that forum shopping in intellectual property disputes cannot be controlled without the element of consultations between the courts and the parties.[43] Although consultations are only a part of the pro-consolidation philosophy represented in the DGD, consultations nevertheless represent a completely different strategy compared to the solution adopted in the Brussels I Regulation and the 1999 DHJC, since these make no use of consultations at all.

The solution adopted in the DGD has been considered in a game-theoretic study by Moore & Parisi. In their view a system where neither party has the opportunity to make strategic choices about the forum leads to fewer problems than a system where only one of the parties can choose the forum.[44] In the DGD one party cannot control where the dispute is adjudicated due to the possibility of consultations. Thus opportunistic behaviour by the parties is likely to be minimised.[45]

Consultations do, however, involve an element of uncertainty. If forum shopping in the rigid systems decreases the possibility of predictability, consultations would decrease it even further because then it would be impossible to say, *ex ante*, what court most likely will adjudicate the dispute. It is thus submitted that a rigid system is more predictable than a flexible one, and thus better for business.

In the DGD efficiency of litigation is emphasised. It is, however, doubtful how efficient the consultation system would be. Consultations between several judges and the parties would obviously take time. Since there is no higher authority to resolve conflicts in the consultation process, it is possible that the consultations would lead to unsatisfactory consolidation solutions or to no solutions at all.

To sum up, a rigid system with a limited number of competent courts, with no consultation procedure, is preferable over a flexible system. It is, however, submitted that, as long as there is no supranational intellectual property court deciding all cases, there is no optimal jurisdictional system.

---

[41] *Cf. Dreyfuss & Ginsburg, supra* note 11, at 3, where a distinction is made between the Brussels Convention and the 1999 DHJC.

[42] *Id.*, at 4.

[43] *Id.*, at 3.

[44] *Moore & Parisi, supra* note 9, *at* 1.

[45] *Id.*

b. The 1999 DHJC Does Not Take IPRs into Account

The 1999 DHJC is very similar to the solution adopted in the Brussels Regulation. Art. 14 of the 1999 DHJC lays down the requirements for consolidation of multi-defendant litigation. If the requirements for consolidation are met, the court is, in principle, under an obligation to hear the case. However, it is possible, in exceptional circumstances, for the court to decline jurisdiction on the basis of Art. 22. The 1999 DHJC does not take into account the special needs of intellectual property rights.

Article 14 enables forum shopping in that it does not clearly state which defendant's forum is the most suitable. Although Art. 14 requires a close connection between the actions against the defendants and a substantial connection between each defendant and the forum state, it is likely that there is more than one place of litigation, from which the plaintiff may choose the place best suited to his purposes.

Forum shopping should be minimised. Thus, the number of possible fora should be limited. Preferably only one court in a multiple-defendant dispute should have jurisdiction.

The notion of "inconsistent judgements" in the 1999 DHJC is problematic. In the Nygh & Pocar Report, it is stated that judgments are inconsistent when the findings of fact or conclusions of law, in relation to the same issues on which they are based, are mutually exclusive.[46] In multi-state intellectual property disputes, the infringement claims are based on rights in force in different countries. Thus, a finding of infringement in country A (of a right in force in A) is, in a strict interpretation, not inconsistent with a finding of non-infringement in country B (of a right in force in B), although the protected subject matter might be the same or very similar. In intellectual property matters, there might be a need for a more liberal interpretation in order to promote consolidation.

The 1999 DHJC takes no stand as to the reach of jurisdiction. In intellectual property matters, it is very important to know whether the court seized of the matter has jurisdiction to give a ruling that has effect outside the forum state or whether the effect of the ruling is limited to the forum state. This question needs to be addressed.

4. Provision on Multiple Defendants

a. Proposed Wording

Article 14 Multiple Defendants

1. A plaintiff bringing an action against a defendant in a court of the state in which that defendant is habitually resident may also proceed in that court against other defendants not habitually resident in that state if–

   a) the claims against the defendant habitually resident in that state and the other defendants are closely connected, and

[46] *Nygh & Pocar, supra* note 7, at 72.

b) as to each defendant not habitually resident in that state, there is a substantial connection between that state and the dispute involving that defendant.

c) the defendant habitually resident in that state is the main infringer.

[2. Paragraph 1 shall not apply to a co-defendant invoking an exclusive choice-of-court clause agreed with the plaintiff and conforming with [Article 4].]

3. The Courts having jurisdiction under this Article shall have jurisdiction also with regard to infringements occurring outside the forum state.

b. Comments on Article 14

The purpose of Art. 14 is to enable consolidation of claims against more than one defendant in a situation where the claims are closely connected to each other. It is submitted that a provision on multiple defendants is a vital element of a jurisdiction system in intellectual property cases. Although intellectual property rights can be characterised as territorial, practice shows that they are utilised in a global manner. Global utilisation not only means registration, but also enforcement in more than one country.

If the infringements are committed in several countries by one infringer, the question of jurisdiction can be resolved on the basis of Art. 12a(3)(2) and 12a(4)(1) of the MPI proposal. The court where the defendant is habitually resident has jurisdiction to rule on all infringement claims against that defendant, irrespective of the place of infringement. If several infringers commit infringements only in one country, litigation can be consolidated in the country of registration (Art. 12a(3)(1) and 12a(4)(2) of the MPI proposal). If, however, the infringements are committed in more than one country by more than one infringer, the situation cannot be resolved without a provision on multiple defendants. It is thus important to include such a provision in the MPI proposal.

The provision on multiple defendants would have a structure similar to that of Art. 14 of the 1999 DHJC. There are four basic requirements for the provision's application. First, at least one of the defendants needs to be habitually resident in the country of the court. Second, there has to be a close connection between the actions against the defendants. Third, there has to be a substantial connection between each defendant and the forum state. Fourth, the defendant habitually resident in the country of the court has to be the main infringer.

According to the proposed wording of Art. 14 of the MPI proposal, the claims against the defendant habitually resident in that state and the other defendants not habitually resident can be consolidated to one forum state if the claims are closely connected. This requirement of close connection differs from the stricter alternative proposed in the 1999 DHJC, where the wording is that the actions are so closely connected that they should be adjudicated together to avoid a serious risk of inconsistent judgements.

The notion of inconsistency might be a problem in the field of intellectual property.[47] Since intellectual property rights are registered and valid only in

[47] *Cf. Dreyfuss*, An Alert to the Intellectual Property Bar: The Hague Judgements Convention, 2001 U.Ill.L.Rev. 101, 132.

the registration country, there can, strictly interpreted, never be inconsistency between judgements that concern rights registered in different countries. Such a strict interpretation would render the multiple defendant provision virtually useless. A more liberal approach would better serve the interests of the intellectual property system.[48] It must, however, be observed that procedural economy is not on its own a sufficient condition for consolidation. Basically, this means that consolidation cannot be invoked only because it is cheaper to litigate in one country than in several countries. There need always be a close connection between the actions.

The proposed close connection requirement does not require a risk of inconsistency of judgements. It does, however, require a close connection as to the claims or the facts in the case (legal closeness). If, for instance, the trademark in dispute is (virtually) identical in countries A and B, there is a close connection between disputes regarding the marks in A and B. Also, if the intellectual property rights in question have been infringed in several countries through the use of one product (although the rights may differ), there might be a close connection between the actions.

It is not enough that the actions are closely connected. There must also be a substantial connection between the forum state and the dispute. This requirement is needed in order to safeguard that a defendant is not sued before a clearly inappropriate forum. The wording is taken directly from Art. 14(1)(b) of the 1999 DHJC. This requirement, which in essence tries to ensure that the forum has a strong interest in the dispute, would probably work well for intellectual property.[49]

Forum shopping is a negative consequence of a jurisdictional system with too many options of where to institute proceedings. In the DGD, consultations are proposed as the remedy for forum shopping. Here, however, the number of competent courts is limited by submitting that only the courts of the main infringer's habitual residence have jurisdiction. This approach might be criticised because it favours the "really bad guys" at the expense of smaller infringers because the main infringer (the "really bad guy") can litigate in a court of the country of his habitual residence, whereas smaller infringers have to litigate in a foreign court. This observation is accurate, but at least two arguments in favour of the proposed solution should be taken into account. First, in its most typical form, a multiple-defendant situation arises when a group of companies infringes a number of national intellectual property rights by marketing a certain product in several countries. In such a case the parent company is the main infringer, and the subsidiaries must litigate in the country of the parent company. Such a solution can hardly be characterised as unfair or unbalanced. The alternative in that situation would be to decide the case in a country where one of the subsidiaries is located. Even then only one of the subsidiaries would have the benefit of litigating in

---

[48] *Dreyfuss*, *supra* note 34.

[49] *Dreyfuss*, *supra* note 34.

a court of his habitual residence. All other subsidiaries would have to litigate in a foreign court. Taking account of all parties' interests, choosing the courts of the country of the parent company's habitual residence is the most balanced solution.

A similar situation might arise in a case where an infringing product is manufactured in country A and marketed in countries B, C and D by three different companies, one of which is habitually resident in B, one in C and one in D. Assuming that the same right is not in force in all four countries, one must ask how a balanced solution is to be reached, if the actions against the infringers are consolidated. If the actions are consolidated in B, C or D, two of the "smaller" infringers must litigate in a foreign court, which probably is less appropriate than the forum of the main infringer, which in this case would be A.

It could also be left open which court is the most appropriate. Such a solution would, however, be less satisfactory. Since the question of jurisdiction would, as long as there is no supranational court system for these questions, be decided by national courts, too many jurisdictional options would leave the door open for unwanted forum shopping. Thus, the most balanced and fair option is to consolidate proceedings in the courts of the country of the habitual residence of the main infringer.

In paragraph 2 it is stated that paragraph 1 shall not apply to a co-defendant invoking an exclusive choice-of-court clause agreed upon with the plaintiff and conforming to the provision on choice-of-court agreements. The paragraph is in brackets and awaits further results on provisions regarding the choice-of-court agreements.

In paragraph 3 the reach of jurisdiction is defined. The court seized of the multiple-defendant dispute shall have global jurisdiction, that is, jurisdiction to adjudicate all the infringement claims made against the defendants. This is an important addition to the rule on defendant's forum. It is thus not only the defendant's forum (Art. 12a) that has global jurisdiction, but also the main infringer's forum in a multiple-defendant dispute. Otherwise the multiple-defendant provision would be rendered meaningless.

5. Conclusion

In conclusion, intellectual property requires a multiple-defendant provision. The question is how to draft it. In this article a proposal for a provision has been made that builds upon the MPI Proposal made by the Max Planck working group on international jurisdiction.

The system of streamlining litigation proposed in the Draft Convention on Jurisdiction and Recognition of Judgments in Intellectual Property Matters (DGD) was not accepted, since it requires consultations between the courts seized of parts of multinational litigation and with the parties.

Article 12 of the Draft Hague Convention on Jurisdiction and Foreign Judgments in Civil and Commercial Matters (1999 DHJC) was not accepted as a model for a multiple defendant provision, either. The possibility of forum shopping, the open question of reach of jurisdiction and the strict requirement of close connection between the actions are questions where intellectual property poses special needs.

Finally, a provision on multiple-defendant disputes was presented. It is worded as follows:

> Article 14 Multiple Defendants
>
> 1. A plaintiff bringing an action against a defendant in a court of the state in which that defendant is habitually resident may also proceed in that court against other defendants not habitually resident in that state if—a) the claims against the defendant habitually resident in that state and the other defendants are closely connected, and
>
> b) as to each defendant not habitually resident in that state, there is a substantial connection between that state and the dispute involving that defendant.
>
> c) the defendant habitually resident in that state is the main infringer.
>
> [2. Paragraph 1 shall not apply to a co-defendant invoking an exclusive choice-of-court clause agreed with the plaintiff and conforming with [Article 4].]
>
> 3. The Courts having jurisdiction under this Article shall have jurisdiction also with regard to infringements occurring outside the forum state.

Contractual Jurisdiction Clauses and Intellectual Property

ALEXANDER PEUKERT*

I. Relevance

1. Proceedings Pertaining to Intellectual Property

As a starting point in analyzing the impact of choice-of-forum clauses on international I.P. litigation, a fundamental distinction has to be made: jurisdiction to adjudicate contractual disputes, for example proceedings that relate to contractual payment, obligations to produce, etc.,[1] follows other rules than do proceedings that have as their object the infringement or (in)validation of intellectual property rights. This article does not discuss possible rules of jurisdiction for actions in contracts other than those based on choice-of-court clauses, even if the actions relate to intellectual property.

Rather, the following article centres on aspects of forum-selection clauses in connection with I.P. infringement and (in)validity matters. Accordingly, the proposal made by a working group of the Max Planck Institute for Intellectual Property in Munich (MPI proposal) is limited to proceedings pertaining to the grant, registration, validity, abandonment, or revocation of

---

* Dr.iur., Research Fellow, Max Planck Institute for Intellectual Property, Competition and Tax Law, Munich. The author can be reached at a.peukert@ip.mpg.de.

[1] *See* Art. 6 of the Preliminary Draft Convention on Jurisdiction and Foreign Judgments in Civil and Commercial Matters (DHJC), available at http://www.hcch.net/e/conventions/draft36e.html; Art. 6 Summary of the Outcome of the Discussion in Commission II of the First Part of the Diplomatic Conference 6–20 June 2001 (2001 interim text), available at ftp://ftp.hcch.net/doc/jdgm2001draft_e.doc; Art. 5(1) Brussels I Regulation.

The *Dreyfuss/Ginsburg* approach (Draft Convention on Jurisdiction and Recognition of Judgments in Intellectual Property Matters, WIPO 2001, available at http://www.wipo.int/pil-forum/en/documents/pdf/pil_01_7.pdf; amended version of June 7, 2002 for ALAI Study Days, Neuchatel, September 16, 2002, on file with the author; in the following: DGD) also contains a rule for contractual disputes pertaining to intellectual property. According to Art. 6 DGD, an action to enforce an agreement pertaining to intellectual property may be brought in any country whose rights are covered by the agreement. With regard to cases involving consolidation, the court where a claim regarding contract rights is seized shall consider whether the court has the most significant relationship to the contract, based, in particular, on where the parties reside, where the intellectual property was developed, and where the rights that are the subject of the contract are to be exercised (*see also* Art. 12(4)(c) DGD).

an I.P. right (in the following: (in)validity matter)[2] and to the infringement, including declaration of non-infringement, of I.P. rights (in the following: infringement matter). If the plaintiff alleges that the defendant infringed his or her I.P. right, if he or she asks for a declaratory judgment that an I.P. right is invalid, or that the defendant is not the owner of the right, it is normally not a case where the parties had already established a contractual relationship before the dispute arose. In sheer piracy cases, there is normally no contractual relationship between the right-holder and the alleged infringer. Where there is no contractual agreement between the parties, there is no choice-of-court clause, either.[3] Only in very rare cases do right-holder and infringer agree on a competent court after the dispute comes up.[4] Therefore, forum-selection clauses are of relevance only where the litigating parties have concluded an agreement that governs the use of an I.P. right (in the following: licensing agreement).

These licensing agreements occur in all areas of life and they are becoming more and more important. This holds true for the B2B sector that uses licensing agreements to organise the international transfer of technology and other creative products as well as for cases involving consumers, where licensing agreements are a common feature of today's distribution of digital products, particularly of software.[5] Many I.P. licensing agreements contain forum-selection clauses, not only in B2B cases, but also in B2C cases.[6]

---

[2] According to the Proposed Alternative Draft for Provisions on Proceedings Involving I.P. Rights of the Max-Planck-Institute for Intellectual Property (in this volume annex II; in the following: MPI proposal), an (in)validity matter in this sense is also given if the decision entails a prohibition of further use of the right in the Contracting State of registration, even if the issue of invalidity has not been raised expressly in the proceedings. This provision applies only to registered rights and acknowledges that a prohibition of further use equally deprives the right-holder of an exploitation of a trademark or patent as does the revocation of the right. *See* Art. 12a(1) 2nd sentence MPI proposal; MPI proposal comments, at 2.3; infra III.3.b) (2) (b).

[3] *Schulz*, Report on the First Meeting of the Informal Working Group on the Judgments Project – October 22–25, 2002, Prel.Doc. No. 20, November 2002, at 12, available at ftp://ftp.hcch.net/doc/jdgm_pd20e.doc.

[4] *Schack*, Internationale Urheber-, Marken- und Wettbewerbsrechtsverletzungen im Internet, Internationales Zivilprozessrecht, 2000 MMR 135, 137.

[5] *Dreyfuss/Ginsburg, supra* note 1, at 24, with reference to the Uniform Computer Information Transactions Act (UCITA) in the U.S.; for German law, *see Hilty*, Der Softwarevertrag – ein Blick in die Zukunft – Konsequenzen der trägerlosen Nutzung und des patentrechtlichen Schutzes von Software, 2003 MMR 3 *et seq.*

[6] *See* the International Chamber of Commerce (ICC) Survey regarding business practices on jurisdictional issues, available at http://www.iccwbo.org/law/jurisdiction/. According to this study, 49% of all international contracts in all business sectors specify a court that is granted jurisdiction to deal with disputes; 37% designate a court with exclusive jurisdiction. In the sectors that rely heavily on intellectual property rights (marketing, media and publishing sector/telecommunications and information sector), this share amounts to 50% and 78% (with respect to exclusively chosen courts 33% and 56%), respectively.

A forum-selection clause possibly bears different causes of action. One might be of a purely contractual nature, for example a claim for licensing fees under a patent license agreement. As already indicated, this cause of action adheres to the rules that apply to claims over contracts.[7] However, does a choice-of-court clause as part of a licensing agreement have any relevance for (in)validity and infringement matters as defined above?

2. Infringement Matters

In order to have relevance in such matters, a forum-selection clause has to cover not only purely contractual disputes, but also directly I.P.-related causes of action, *i.e.* (in)validity matters and infringement claims. With regard to the latter, a common situation might be that the licensor alleges that the licensee exceeded his contractual powers, thereby violating not only his contractual obligations but also infringing the I.P. right. Furthermore, it is conceivable that the right-holder will claim infringement – after having terminated the licensing agreement – whereas the licensee bases his ongoing exploitation of the I.P. right on the allegedly terminated agreement. If the contract at stake contains a choice-of-court clause, the plaintiff may file suit in the chosen court not only because of breach of contract but also because of infringement of the I.P. right. On the other hand, the defendant may file a motion to dismiss if the plaintiff institutes legal proceedings in the forum delicti, disregarding the forum-selection clause. Cases like this have regularly been subject to court decisions. In Europe as well as in the U.S., courts decide the question whether a claim for infringement has to be filed in the chosen forum by construing the forum-selection clause according to the applicable substantive law. Since none of the existing proposals on jurisdiction covers substantive law or conflicts of law, its applicability underlies the choice-of-law rules of the forum.[8] German courts have held that a forum-selection clause governs infringement actions if the judgment can be based on breach of contract as well as on tort.[9] Moreover, a choice-of-forum clause that reads that certain courts are competent to decide any disputes in connection with the contract also applies to a claim in tort that relates to the contract.[10]

---

[7] *Supra* note 1.

[8] *See Haines*, Choice of Court Agreements in International Litigation: Their Use and Legal Problems to Which They Give Rise in the Context of the Interim Text, Prel.Doc. No. 18, February 2002, at 7, available at ftp://ftp.hcch.net/doc/gen_pd18e.doc.

[9] German Federal Labour Court, 1970 NJW 2181; *Bork*, in: *Stein-Jonas* (ed.), ZPO, 21. ed. 1993, § 40 German Code of Civil Procedure No. 1; Munich Court of Appeals, 1989 WM 605 (Art. 17 Brussels Convention); Stuttgart Court of Appeals, 1974 BB 1270; *Nygh/Pocar*, Report on the Preliminary Draft Convention on Jurisdiction and Foreign Judgments in Civil and Commercial Matters, adopted by the Special Commission, Prel.Doc. No. 11, at 43, available at ftp://ftp/hcch/net/doc/jdgmpd11.doc.

[10] Stuttgart Court of Appeals, IPRax, 1992 88; *Geimer*, Internationales Zivilprozessrecht, 4. ed., 2001, No. 1719; *Roth*, Gerichtsstandsvereinbarungen nach Art. 17 EuGVÜ und kartellrechtliches Derogationsverbot, 1992 IPRax 67.

According to U.S. courts, whether or not a forum-selection clause applies to infringement claims depends on what the specific clause at issue says.[11] Thus, the particular circumstances of the case are decisive.[12] What is more important for the following discussion is that forum-selection clauses as part of licensing agreements have a particular relevance for infringement actions between the parties of the contract.[13]

3. (In)validity Matters

The interdependence of (in)validity matters – normally raised in the form of declaratory judgments – and choice-of-court clauses, however, has until now been of a more theoretical nature. The reason is twofold: As far as these matters are subject to exclusive jurisdiction according to existing law, forum-selection clauses are ineffective.[14] Even if this is not the case, for example with regard to copyright and neighbouring rights, validity issues usually only come up as incidental matters, not as an isolated claim or counterclaim for declaration of (in)validity of an I.P. right.[15] At least theoretically, a licensee may be sued for license fees and he or she will then challenge the original ownership of the plaintiff or plead that the term of protection has lapsed by filing a respective invalidity counterclaim in the chosen forum,

---

[11] *See* for example *Omron Healthcare v. Maclaren Exports,* 28 F.3d 600, 602 (7th Cir. 1994) (deciding that the clause "The parties hereto agree that all disputes arising out of this Agreement which cannot be resolved amicably between the parties shall be referred to the High Court of Justice in England which will have exclusive jurisdiction to determine such disputes." applied to trademark infringement because the agreement contained an implicit license to use the trade mark); *John Wyeth & Brother Ltd. v. Cigna Int'l Corp.,* 119 F.3d 1070, 1074 (3d Cir. 1997) (applying the forum-selection clause "This Agreement shall be governed by and construed in accordance with English law, and the English Courts shall have exclusive jurisdiction in relation to any dispute arising under or out of or in relation to this Agreement." to product liability claims); *Morgan Trailer Mfg. Co. v. Hydraroll, Ltd.,* 759 A.2d 926, 931 (2000) (holding that the clause "This Agreement and each contract made between the parties hereunder for the sale of the Products will in all respects be interpreted in accordance with the laws of England and the parties hereby submit themselves to the exclusive jurisdiction of the English Courts." does not cover non-contract claims like misappropriation of trade secrets); *Symeonides,* Choice of Law in the American Courts in 2002: Sixteenth Annual Survey, 51 The American Journal of Comparative Law 1, 67–68 (2003).

[12] *Schulz,* Reflection Paper to Assist in the Preparation of a Convention on Jurisdiction and Recognition and Enforcement of Foreign Judgments in Civil and Commercial Matters, Prel.Doc. No. 19, August 2002, at 13, available at ftp://ftp.hcch.net/doc/jdgm_pd19e.doc; Prel.Doc. No. 20, *supra* note 3, at 12.

[13] *See also* Prel.Doc. No. 19, *supra* note 12, at 13.

[14] *See* for example Art. 22(4), 23(5) Brussels I Regulation.

[15] MPI proposal comments, *supra* note 2, at 2.3; *Schulz,* Report on the Work of the Informal Working Group on the Judgments Project, in Particular in the Preliminary Text Achieved at Its Third Meeting – 25–28 March 2003, Prel.Doc. No. 22, June 2003, available at ftp://ftp.hcch.net/doc/jdgm_pd22e.doc, 10–11.

solely relying on the choice-of-forum clause.[16] The answer to the question of whether jurisdiction in deciding the counterclaim may be derived from the contractual clause will also depend on the interpretation of the particular clause at issue.

In sum, forum-selection clauses may well have significant relevance for jurisdiction in infringement matters, and to a more limited degree also in (in)validity matters as defined above. If the parties agree on a clause that reads broadly enough to include infringement or even (in)validity actions that are connected with the contract, the question has to be resolved in how far an envisaged convention should acknowledge this freedom of contract.

II. Survey of Current Approaches

In the following, we give an overview on how the current drafts of the Hague Conference on Private International Law, the *Dreyfuss/Ginsburg* approach and the MPI proposal tackle this problem.[17]

1. Hague Convention

a) The preliminary draft of a Convention on Jurisdiction and Foreign Judgments in Civil and Commercial Matters of October 30, 1999 (DHJC)[18] as well as the interim text that presents the outcome of discussion in Commission II on the first part of a diplomatic conference held on June 6–20, 2001 (2001 interim text) were based directly on the Brussels and Lugano Conventions model in that they too distinguish between general, special, and exclusive jurisdiction, limit the choice of fora, restrict forum shopping, and foster consolidation of similar claims pending before several fora.[19]

---

[16] MPI proposal comments, *supra* note 2, at 2.3. Under German law, a licensee may terminate a patent licensing agreement and is thereafter not obliged to pay royalties if the patent is declared invalid; *see* Supreme Court of the German Reich, 1936 GRUR 1056, 1058; 1943 GRUR 35, 38; German Federal Supreme Court, 1957 GRUR 595, 596; 1961 GRUR 466, 468; *Benkard,* PatG, 9th ed. 1993, § 15 German Patent Act No. 109–110 with further references; for Swiss law *see Hilty,* Lizenzvertragsrecht, 2001, §§ 8, 10.

[17] The American Law Institute also initiated a project dealing with international jurisdiction (see http://www.ali.org/, International Jurisdiction and Judgments Project; *Dreyfuss/Ginsburg,* Principles Governing Jurisdiction, Choice of Law, and Judgments in Transnational Disputes, 2003 CRi 33). As no drafts have yet (August 2003) been made publicly available, we will not specifically address this proposal. The "Preliminary Draft No. 1 of Principles Governing Jurisdiction, Choice of Law and Judgments in Transnational Disputes of the American Law Institute" (January 17, 2003; in the following: 2003 ALI Principles) is on file with the author and will be considered where relevant, infra, at III.

[18] *Supra,* note 1; *see* the explanatory memorandum of *Nygh/Pocar,* Prel.Doc. No. 11, *supra* note 9.

[19] MPI proposal comments, *supra* note 2, at 2.2.; *Dreyfuss,* An Alert to the Intellectual Property Bar: The Hague Judgments Convention, 2001 U.Ill.L.Rev. 421, 427.

(1) With respect to choice-of-court issues in general, the drafts promote from the beginning the principle of autonomy that underlies Art. 4 as the provision that provides for effective choice-of-court clauses to settle any dispute that has arisen or may arise in connection with a particular legal relationship.[20] In the course of discussion about the pros and cons of forum selection in general, it has been pointed out that a choice of court by the parties provides predictability, reliability, and legal certainty for the parties involved, is a very common feature in B2B agreements, and prevents application of the principle of forum non conveniens.[21]

Both the DHJC and the 2001 interim text address basic principles that regulate forum-selection clauses: the jurisdiction chosen by the parties shall be exclusive unless the parties agree otherwise.[22] An exclusive choice of court does not allow lis alibi pendens (Art. 21(1) DHJC/2001 interim text),[23] and hinders the exclusively chosen court from declining jurisdiction in exceptional circumstances (Art. 22(1) DHJC/2001 interim text).[24] All other courts have to decline jurisdiction[25] or dismiss the case for lack of jurisdiction.[26] Whereas some questions were at least in 2001 no longer controversial (limitation of choice to personal, not to subject-matter jurisdiction,[27] formal requirements,[28] acceptance of jurisdiction[29]), others were heavily disputed.[30] Particularly, no consensus could be found with regard to the requirements that apply to substantive validity of choice-of-court clauses, in how far these requirements are subject to an autonomous regulation under the convention, and which court is competent to decide this matter under which applicable law.[31] This assessment also holds true for the lawfulness of

---

[20] Prel.Doc. No. 11, *supra* note 9, at 43.

[21] Prel.Doc. No. 18, *supra* note 8, at 3, 20; Prel.Doc. No. 19, *supra* note 12, at 15.

[22] Art. 4(1) 1st sentence DHJC (*supra* note 1); Art. 4(1) 1st sentence 2001 interim text, *supra* note 1.

[23] Prel.Doc. No. 19, *supra* note 12, at 20.

[24] Id., at 16–17.

[25] Prel.Doc. No. 18, *supra* note 8, at 7 *et seq*. for a comparison of national laws.

[26] Art. 4(1), 2nd sentence, 2001 interim text, *supra* note 1; Prel.Doc. No. 19, *supra* note 12, at 17.

[27] Prel.Doc. No. 19, *supra* note 12, at 14.

[28] Prel.Doc. No. 11, *supra* note 9, at 44, 45; Prel.Doc. No. 18, *supra* note 8, at 10; Prel.Doc. No. 19, *supra* note 12, at 7.

[29] Art. 4(3) 2001 interim text, *supra* note 1; Prel.Doc. No. 19, *supra* note 12, at 23.

[30] These are, for example, the questions of whether a specific connection between the forum chosen and the dispute or the parties is necessary (Prel.Doc. No. 11, *supra* note 9, at 43; Prel.Doc. No. 18, *supra* note 8, at 4), and whether the dispute has to be of an international character (2001 interim text, *supra* note 1, at 3 No. 15; Prel.Doc. No. 11, *supra* note 9, at 41; Prel.Doc. No. 19, *supra* note 12, at 14).

[31] Proposals vary from leaving this decision out of the convention (Prel.Doc. No. 11, *supra* note 9, at 42), referring the decision to the law of the chosen forum with regard to consent and capacity (Art. 4(1) 3rd sentence 2001 interim text, *supra* note 1) or to substantive validity in general (Art. 4(5) 2001 interim text, *supra* note 1, at 4 No. 24, 25 No. 27; Prel.Doc. No. 19, *supra* note 12, at 7 *et seq*.).

the forum-selection clause as such. Proposed Art. 4(5), 1st sentence, of the 2001 interim text declares that the parties cannot be deprived of the right to enter into agreements conferring jurisdiction.[32] This provision aims to clarify that the lawfulness of a forum-selection clause is autonomously regulated by the convention without leaving room for national laws imposing conditions on this aspect. If this question were to be left to ongoing national legislation that imposes differing standards of voiding clauses, the aim of the convention, to provide reliability and predictability for the parties, would be lost.[33] Another very controversial issue was the relationship between choice-of-forum provisions and consumer transactions and employment contracts.[34] These political differences led to the suggestion to limit the whole convention to B2B contracts.[35] Nevertheless, it is important to notice that one case that was named to exemplify the need to protect consumers relates to the purchase of software packages over the internet[36] and thereby directly to intellectual property cases.[37]

Finally, as another basic principle, both the DHJC and the 2001 interim text set out that exclusive jurisdiction under Art. 12 renders choice-of-court clauses ineffective.[38] This relationship is generally acknowledged. Nevertheless, the core problem to be solved is which actions fall under exclusive jurisdiction of certain courts and which actions will be subject to parties' discretion.

(2) This assessment particularly concerns I.P. law as a possible subject of a worldwide convention on jurisdiction. Although both the DHJC and the 2001 interim text take I.P. law into account, no substantive consensus could be reached.

Art. 12(4) DHJC states that "in proceedings which have as their object the registration, validity, [or] nullity [, or revocation or infringement,[39]] of

---

[32] 2001 interim text, *supra* note 1, at 5 No. 28; Prel.Doc. No. 11, *supra* note 9, at 43.

[33] Prel.Doc. No. 11, *supra* note 9, at 42; Prel.Doc. No. 19, *supra* note 12, at 8–11.

[34] *See* 2001 interim text, *supra* note 1, at 7–10.

[35] Prel.Doc. No. 19, *supra* note 12, at 10.

[36] Prel.Doc. No. 18, *supra* note 8, at 15.

[37] Software is subject to copyright protection and possibly to patent protection; *see* Art. 10 TRIPS; for patentability of computer programs in Europe and Germany *see* Art. 52(2)(c) European Patent Convention, § 1(2) No. 3 German Patent Act; German Federal Supreme Court, 2002 GRUR 143–146. *See* further the Proposal for a Directive of the European Parliament and of the Council on the patentability of computer-implemented inventions of February 20, 2002, available at http://europa.eu.int/comm/internal_market/en/indprop/comp/com02-92en.pdf. According to this proposal (at 2), the European Patent Office alone granted more than 20,000 patents for computer-implemented inventions.

[38] Art. 4(3), 12 DHJC (*supra* note 1); Art. 4(5), 12 2001 interim text, *supra* note 1; *see id.*, at 5 No. 29; Prel.Doc. No. 11, *supra* note 9, at 46.

[39] *See* additionally Art. 12(5) DHJC (*supra* note 1): In relation to proceedings which have as their object the infringement of patents, the preceding paragraph does not exclude the jurisdiction of any other court under the convention or under the national law of a Contracting State.

patents, trade marks, designs or other similar rights required to be deposited or registered, the courts of the Contracting State in which the deposit or registration has been applied for, has taken place or, under the terms of an international convention, is deemed to have taken place, have exclusive jurisdiction; however, this shall not apply to copyright or any neighbouring rights, even though registration or deposit of such rights is possible". The wording of this article and the number of square brackets makes it plain that this proposal is nothing more than a first suggestion, leaving many questions to the first diplomatic conference.[40] During the 2001 Diplomatic Conference, three proposals relating to the treatment of I.P. in the convention were made.[41] The proposals differ with respect to exclusive jurisdiction of courts in infringement cases (yes/no), and exclusive jurisdiction in proceedings that have as their object the registration, validity, nullity or revocation of registered and other I.P. rights.[42] As a new feature in comparison with the DHJC, Art. 12(6) of the 2001 interim text explicitly excludes decisions on incidental questions from exclusive jurisdiction, thereby opening the possibility to adjudicate these matters in the chosen court.

b) A major change in the way to pursue the intention to develop a worldwide convention on jurisdiction, recognition and enforcement of judgments has come about after a meeting of Commission I on General Affairs and Policy of the Nineteenth Diplomatic Session of the Hague Convention in April 2002. As an expression of the lack of consensus on many issues, it was decided that the starting point for the future work of the Conference should no longer be a Brussels/Lugano Convention-like scope, but a core area and possible additions that the Contracting States could more likely agree on. This "core area" included, *inter alia*, choice-of-court agreements in B2B cases, but not infringement and (in)validity actions pertaining to intellectual property.[43] Following this approach, preliminary document no. 19 explained the impacts and issues to be resolved if the convention were limited to choice-of-court clauses in B2B cases. Such a "minimum convention" would contain only one "white rule on jurisdiction", *i.e.* choice of court by the parties, possibly a black list of prohibited grounds of jurisdiction, and a large grey area, because rules of jurisdiction under national law would remain in force.[44]

---

[40] Prel.Doc. No. 11, *supra* note 9, at 66, 67.

A report of an experts' meeting on the intellectual property aspects of the future convention of February 2001 shows that no consensus on the various questions of exclusive or non-exclusive jurisdiction for (in)validity or infringement matters, respectively, could be achieved. *See* Permanent Bureau, Report of the experts meeting on the intellectual property aspects of the future Convention on jurisdiction and foreign judgments in civil and commercial matters, Prel.Doc. No. 13, April 2001, available at ftp://ftp.hcch.net/doc/jdgmpd13.doc, at 4, 10.

[41] 2001 interim text, *supra* note 1, at 13 No. 80.

[42] 2001 interim text, *supra* note 1, at 13.

[43] Prel.Doc. No. 19, *supra* note 12, at 6.

[44] Id., at 7 *et seq*.

The discussions of an informal working group resulted in a draft text on choice-of-court agreements of March 2003 (DHCC).[45] In this paper, forum-selection clauses in general and I.P. matters in specific are dealt with according to the following principles.

(1) The preamble of the proposed convention emphasises the principal advantages of choice-of-court clauses by stating that the promotion of international trade and investment through enhanced judicial cooperation requires a secure international legal regime that ensures the effectiveness of choice-of-court agreements by parties to commercial transactions.[46] The convention applies to agreements on the choice of court concluded in civil or commercial matters.[47] In such agreements two or more parties designate, for the purpose of deciding disputes that have arisen or may arise between them in connection with a particular legal relationship, the courts of one or more states or one or more specific courts.[48] However, the convention does not apply to agreements between a consumer and another party acting for the purposes of its trade or profession, between consumers, or to individual or collective contracts of employment.[49] In case of doubt, a forum-selection clause is deemed to be exclusive unless the parties have provided otherwise.[50] Art. 3 DHCC regulates formal requirements for an effective choice-of-court agreement. It envisages only minor changes to the respective provisions in the DHJC and the 2001 interim text and establishes similar requirements as Art. 23(1) and (2) of the EC regulation on jurisdiction. Whereas the members of the informal working group agreed that Art. 3 DHCC should specify maximum requirements, it is an open question whether it should also impose minimum requirements in the sense that courts are obliged to void forum-selection clauses that do not meet the prerequisites listed in Art. 3 DHJCC.[51] As to substantive validity, the proposed draft text does not include a separate Article. However, the rule addressed to the court chosen (and seized, Art. 4 DHCC) and the rule addressed to the court seized but not chosen (Art. 5 DHCC) impose the obligations contained in those Articles only "unless the court finds that the agreement is null

[45] Preliminary Result of the Work of the Informal Working Group on the Judgments Project, Prel.Doc. No. 8, March 2003, available at ftp://ftp.hcch.net/doc/jdgm_pd8.doc (DHCC). *See* Prel.Doc. No. 22, *supra* note 15, passim.

[46] Preamble DHCC, *supra* note 45.

[47] Art. 1(1) DHCC, *supra* note 45.

[48] Art. 2(1)(a) DHCC, *supra* note 45.

[49] Art. 1(2) DHCC, *supra* note 45.

[50] Art. 2(1)(b) DHCC, *supra* note 45.

[51] Prel.Doc. No. 19, *supra* note 12, at 7; Prel.Doc. No. 20, *supra* note 3, at 5; Report on the Second Meeting of the Informal Working Group on the Judgments Project – January 6–9, 2003, Prel.Doc. No. 21, January 2003, at 7 and Art. 3 ("only"); Prel.Doc. No. 22, *supra* note 15, at 14.

and void, inoperative or incapable of being performed".[52] Finally, Arts. 15 and 16 of the DHCC stipulate the possibility for Contracting States to refuse to enforce – upon ratification – choice-of-court agreements either if there is no connection between the chosen court and the parties or the dispute, or if all relevant elements of the dispute are connected with a state other than the chosen one.[53]

(2) Aside from these general principles regarding choice of court by the parties, Art. 1(3)(k) DHCC expressly deals with I.P. matters. The provision reads in its current version (March 2003) that the "Convention shall not apply to proceedings relating to validity of patents, trademarks and (other intellectual property rights – to be defined)".[54]

Additionally, Art. 1(4) DHCC states – albeit in square brackets – that

> proceedings are not excluded from the scope of the convention if a matter referred to in paragraph 3 arises merely as an incidental question. However, a judgment resulting from such proceedings shall have effect under this Convention only as between the parties.

Obviously, there are still open questions with regard to I.P. matters. Systematically, Art. 1(3)(k) is part of an extensive list of proceedings that are exempted from the scope of the convention and that will thereby remain subject to national law (so-called "grey area" jurisdiction). The rationale behind this provision is that probably all national laws contain rules on exclusive jurisdiction for specific subject matters. In those areas, the freedom of parties to choose a court is limited.[55] To handle this fact, the working group preferred to exclude a wide range of subject matters from the scope of the convention as a whole, as the current draft contains only one "white" jurisdiction, *i.e.* a forum-selection clause, instead of introducing the possibility for Contracting States to enter reservations/declarations with regard to specific proceedings that shall be exempted.[56]

The documents of the Hague Conference that preceded the DHCC deal explicitly with I.P. matters. Whereas a general exclusion of all I.P.-related litigation has been rejected due to the enormous reduction of applicability of

---

[52] Prel.Doc. No. 22, *supra* note 15, at 15. *See* for different options to solve questions of lawfulness, consent, and capacity Prel.Doc. No. 19, *supra* note 12, at 7–11; Prel.Doc. No. 21, *supra* note 51, at 12. Prel.Doc. No. 20, *supra* note 3, at 6 *et seq.*, makes it clear that Contracting States will not likely agree on harmonised standards of capacity or consent and that a general escape clause receives approval.

The discussion again touched upon click-wrap agreements and their legal treatment; *see* Prel.Doc. No. 20, *supra* note 3, at 9; Prel.Doc. No. 21, *supra* note 51, at 7, 10, with regard to electronic and other forms of contracts.

[53] Prel.Doc. No. 21, *supra* note 51, at 7–10.

[54] It follows e contrario that infringement proceedings are subject to the agreement insofar as the forum-selection clause covers this kind of action too (*supra* 1).

[55] Supra, note 14.

[56] Prel.Doc. No. 20, *supra* note 3, at 11.

the convention and the fact that choice of forum is particularly common in license agreements as defined above,[57] the problem remains unsolved how to delimitate I.P.-related proceedings that are or are not subject matter of the convention.[58] Since both the DHJC and the 2001 interim text – and in the end the DHCC as well – did not propose a theoretically and practically conclusive framework for how to treat these questions, two alternative academic proposals have been launched that shall be summarised below with regard to choice-of-court clauses and I.P.-related litigation.

2. Dreyfuss/Ginsburg Draft

The Draft Principles on Jurisdiction and Recognition of Judgments in Intellectual Property Matters by Professor *Dreyfuss* and Professor *Ginsburg* (in the following DGD) are meant to help national courts to develop a consistent, and if possible, uniform approach to jurisdiction over multinational intellectual property litigation.[59] Following the notion that claims like this raise unique issues by the intangibility of the rights at stake,[60] the DGD is based only in part on the work of the Hague Conference. Instead, it constitutes a separate and self-contained convention on jurisdiction and recognition of judgments in intellectual property matters.[61]

The freedom of the parties to select a forum is already mentioned in the summary of the main points of the *Dreyfuss/Ginsburg* principles.[62] Art. 3 DGD regulates agreements pertaining to choice of court. Its wording – that the parties basically may confer jurisdiction to a court of their choice (para. 1) and what formal requirements have to be observed (para. 2) – refers to Art. 4 of the Hague Conference drafts.[63] However, Art. 3.3 DGD contains a novel feature in that it attaches the validity of a non-negotiated forum-selection clause to the "reasonableness" of the choice in light of a number of

[57] Supra, I.

[58] Prel.Doc. No. 19, *supra* note 12, at 13; Prel.Doc. No. 22, *supra* note 15, at 9–11.

Prel.Doc. No. 20, *supra* note 3, at 12, distinguishes between copyright and other I.P. rights. It examines that, whereas even in (in)validity matters relating to copyright no exclusive jurisdiction existed under national laws, this was different with regard to other I.P. rights. Therefore, the working group suggests including copyright, but excluding patents, trademarks (both registered and unregistered) and other registered industrial property rights.

Prel.Doc. No. 21, *supra* note 51, at 12, cites a report that was received from one Member State that strongly supports the inclusion of all I.P. rights as long as the convention was limited to choice-of-court clauses.

[59] *Dreyfuss/Ginsburg*, *supra* note 1, at 1.

[60] With regard to choice-of-court clauses infra III. 2.

[61] *Dreyfuss/Ginsburg*, *supra* note 1, at 3.

[62] *Id.*, at 2.

[63] *Id.*, at 22.

criteria.[64] If the rendering court's jurisdiction is based on a non-negotiated contract clause whose forum designation is unreasonable in the sense of Art. 3.3 DGD, recognition and enforcement of that judgment may be refused.[65] *Dreyfuss* and *Ginsburg* justify this handling of unilateral forum designations merely with the uniqueness of I.P.-related contracts, but with a general rejection of the proposals submitted by the Hague Conference with respect to substantial validity.[66]

Based on the notion that basically all intellectual property claims are considered sufficiently transitory to be heard in any state's court,[67] exclusive jurisdiction that deprives the parties of the right to select a forum is only established in proceedings that have as their sole object the obtaining of a declaration of the invalidity or nullity of a patent registration:[68] All other infringement and (in)validity proceedings (even if not raised as an incidental matter) are subject to the parties' discretion to choose a forum.[69]

3. MPI Working Group

Finally, an MPI working group chaired by Professor *Kur* proposed one comprehensive provision that deals with jurisdiction in infringement and (in)validity matters, and that is based on the framework established by the

---

[64] The criteria are:

(a) the location of the non-contract-drafting party;
(b) the availability of online dispute resolution or other forms of virtual representation;
(c) the resources of the parties; in particular, of the non-contract-drafting party;
(d) the sophistication of the parties; in particular, of the non-contract-drafting party;
(e) the substantiality of the connection between the designated forum, and the parties or the substance of the dispute, including whether the designated forum would have had jurisdiction over the non-drafting party in the absence of a forum-selection clause, and
(f) whether the terms of the agreement were sufficiently apparent with respect to accessibility, typographic readability, and national language so as not to cause surprise;
(g) for registered rights, whether the designated forum was established by the state to foster expertise in adjudicating disputes of this type.

[65] Art. 17(2)(d) DGD, *supra* note 1.

[66] *Dreyfuss/Ginsburg*, *supra* note 1, at 24; for a more detailed discussion, *see infra* 3 a.

[67] *Id.*, at 31.

[68] Art. 7.2 DGD, *supra* note 1; *Driessen*, International Jurisdiction and Recognition and Enforcement of Foreign Judgments in Intellectual Property Cases, available at http://www.kentlaw.edu/depts/ipp/intl-courts/drafttreaty-06.doc, 63. This exclusive jurisdiction seems also to apply if the proceeding is initiated as a counterclaim (Art. 8(1) DGD, *supra* note 1); *see Dreyfuss/Ginsburg*, *supra* note 1, at 32: ". . . if the other requirements of these Principles are met . . .".

[69] *Driessen*, *supra* note 68, at 49.

DHJC or the 2001 interim text, as appropriate.[70] It therefore also relies on the fundamental distinction between general, special and exclusive jurisdiction to foster the consolidation of claims and legal certainty for all parties involved. Furthermore, the draft follows a horizontal approach that seeks to avoid as much as possible discriminating between the different categories of I.P. law.

Paragraph 1 establishes exclusive jurisdiction in proceedings in which the relief sought is a judgment on the grant, registration, validity, abandonment or revocation of registered I.P. rights (unless the judgment would only become effective *inter partes*), on the validity or ownership of all other I.P. rights, and – as a novel feature – in the case of relative invalidity based on a prohibition of further use of the rights. With respect to all other categories of proceedings, parties are free to choose a forum. This is made clear by paragraph 2, which excludes proceedings from exclusive jurisdiction where the (in)validity matter arises as an incidental question and by paragraph 3, 1st sentence, which refers to valid agreements under Art. 4 of the Hague drafts (*supra*) in infringement proceedings.

4. Summary

When comparing the three current proposals, one can observe a tendency to give effect to choice-of-court clauses pertaining to intellectual property only insofar as the proceeding relates to infringement matters or (in)validity matters if raised as an incidental question. However, substantive differences emerge in the course of a more detailed analysis. Whereas the *Dreyfuss/Ginsburg* approach contains a very limited scope of exclusive jurisdiction prevailing over party autonomy, the MPI proposal extends exclusive jurisdiction to (in)validity matters with regard to unregistered I.P. rights. The Hague Conference has not yet found a common basis to resolve this issue. Even after the Conference has focused on choice-of-court agreements, the question in how far I.P. law shall be subject to an autonomous worldwide regime is not definitely answered.

The fundamental goal is to draw the line between the area where party autonomy should be decisive to provide for a reliable, predictable framework in international jurisdiction, and the remaining area where specific aspects (particularly sovereignty) demand consideration and thereby prevail over the freedom of the parties to choose a forum and to depart from the statutory bases of jurisdiction. In order to help establish this delimitation, the pros and cons of the various proposals will be discussed in the following section.

---

[70] Supra, note 2; *Kur,* Principles Governing Jurisdiction, Choice of Law and Judgments in Transnational Disputes: A European Perspective, 2003 CRi 65–72.

III. Pros and Cons of Choice-of-Court Clauses in I.P.-Related Proceedings

1. General or Partial Exclusion of Intellectual Property Rights from the Convention

The fundamental option to exclude all proceedings relating to I.P. rights from the scope of a convention is unanimously rejected in all three current proposals. The drafts acknowledge the ever-growing relevance of I.P. in general, and with regard to a worldwide convention on jurisdiction in specific.

This is even truer in light of the approach to limit the convention to choice-of-court agreements in B2B cases, because contractual disputes with regard to I.P. licensing agreements that would doubtless be governed by the convention are hardly distinguishable from I.P. matters.[71] For example, the question of whether the licensee is obliged to pay license fees may depend on a termination of the contract that is effective only if the licensed I.P. right actually is not subject to protection.[72] The problem becomes even more evident if the contract at stake involves not only I.P. rights but also trade secrets, which will certainly also be subject to the convention. In such a case, the problem would arise of whether a contractual dispute that relates to a trade secret as well as to subject matter protected by I.P. law falls under the convention or not. It is obvious that a solution like this would seriously hamper the aim of promoting international trade and investment by way of a predictable and reliable international legal regime on jurisdiction.

A selective approach, excluding certain I.P. rights while letting others come under the rules of a future convention,[73] is also neither theoretically desirable nor practically feasible, not only because of many overlaps between different fields of intellectual property and a limited flexibility of the convention in case of the development of future I.P. rights, but also in light of choice-of-court agreements pertaining to intellectual property. The reason is that many B2B licensing agreements cover various I.P. rights. For example, a publishing contract may contain not only a transfer or grant of copyright, but possibly a transfer of rights in the title of the work that is subject to trademark protection. Moreover, software-related transactions have to take into account that software may be protected by copyright as well as patent law.[74] Again, it would cause severe legal uncertainty if the convention did not cover both categories of I.P. rights as possible subjects of a particular licensing agreement.

---

[71] Prel.Doc. No. 19, *supra* note 12, at 13; Prel.Doc. No. 21, *supra* note 51, at 12; *Dreyfuss/Ginsburg*, *supra* note 1, at 1 *et seq*.

[72] *Supra*, I. 4.

[73] *See* Prel.Doc. No. 20, *supra* note 3, at 12.

[74] *See supra* note 37.

Thus, the horizontal approach taken in the MPI proposal is advisable not only in light of general considerations, but particularly with respect to choice-of-court agreements in I.P. matters.

2. Forum Selection and Intellectual Property in General

Assuming that all categories of intellectual property rights will be part of the convention, the next question is in how far this field of law raises specific problems with regard to choice-of-court agreements. In addressing this issue, we do not refer to the problem of what kind of I.P.-related proceedings shall not be subject to parties' discretion because of exclusive jurisdiction (*infra*, c), but to whether there are peculiarities of I.P. infringement or (in)validity matters that generally demand recognition in the context discussed in this article.

aa) In other words, before going into a more detailed discussion, it must be made clear whether the nature of I.P. rights as the subject of a contract that contains a choice-of-court clause (in contrast to tangible goods as the subject of a relevant agreement) requires special treatment with regard to the regulation of choice-of-court clauses under an autonomous regime of a worldwide convention.

In the context of this question, commentators often mention the "issues uniquely raised by the intangibility of the rights at issue".[75] Admittedly, there are a number of issues that are presented by I.P. rights alone. Among them are the following.

Intangible goods subject to protection under I.P. laws, in contrast to tangible things, can never be used up, and their use by one person does not deprive anyone else of that use. They are potentially ubiquitous.

To achieve protection, it is partly necessary to apply for registration that is granted only after expert examination according to national law. The principle of territoriality of I.P. rights is closely connected with the latter fact. It reflects *inter alia* the fact that every national law balances the conflicting interests of right-holders on the one hand and users on the other differently by tailoring rights and exceptions. These aspects show that sovereignty is an important feature when it comes to intellectual property and its protection.

However, these characteristics of I.P. should result in special legal treatment only where practical reasons are given. In all other situations, the general rules should also apply to I.P.-related matters. In this article, we deal solely with the problem of whether the uniqueness of I.P. touches on the general rationale and acceptance of choice-of-court agreements and their relevance for infringement and (in)validity matters.[76]

bb) In our view, this is not the case. First and most important, the concept that exclusive jurisdiction is not subject to derogation by party autonomy

---

[75] *Dreyfuss/Ginsburg*, *supra* note 1, at 1; MPI proposal, *supra* note 2, Art. 12a(3) 3rd sentence.

[76] Supra, I. 2.

provides a system to recognise certain special aspects of I.P. law, especially the interests that are connected with the territorial scope of I.P. rights.[77] This works just as well as with, for example, rights in rem in immovable property.[78]

Second, the arguments that favour acceptance of choice-of-court agreements in international trade (legal certainty, lower costs through consolidation of claims, respect of party autonomy) apply both to contracts that govern tangible goods and to those that govern intangible goods. On the contrary, the often worldwide scope of I.P.-related license agreements that are deliberately entered into makes it particularly important to provide for a reliable, predictable basis of jurisdiction in this area.[79] Finally, most other issues that are subject to discussion in The Hague do not demand specific consideration in light of I.P.-related matters. The reason for this is that questions of formal and substantial validity and exclusivity pertain to contractual issues of forum selection, but have nothing to do with the subject of the contract at stake.

Even with regard to the regulation of B2C cases, I.P.-related litigation does not give rise to the application of different solutions than in other B2C transactions. At first glance, it seems that the *Dreyfuss/Ginsburg* approach does not follow this view.[80] However, in analyzing the arguments that *Dreyfuss* and *Ginsburg* put forward, it emerges that their proposal is not particularly based on the uniqueness of I.P. as the subject of B2C transactions, but is founded on the fact that the authors drafted a complete convention and that they pursue the protection of the weaker party to a non-negotiated contract in a slightly different way than the 1999 and 2001 Hague drafts.[81] The *Dreyfuss/Ginsburg* proposal addresses issues that are connected with internet transactions that differ from agreements concluded using other means of communication; but it does not rely on unique issues of I.P. as the subject of such a transaction. Admittedly, as *Dreyfuss* and *Ginsburg* point out, choice-of-court clauses are a more and more common feature in B2C contracts

---

[77] *See* infra, III. 3. b).

[78] *See* Art. 1(3)(i) DHCC, *supra* note 45.

[79] *Stauder/Kur,* Exterritoriale Jurisdiktion und Streitbeilegung, in: *Schricker/Dreier/Kur* (ed.), Geistiges Eigentum im Dienst der Innovation, 2001, 151, 165.

[80] *Contra*: *Dreyfuss/Ginsburg, supra* note 1, at 3. *See also* 2003 ALI Principles, *supra* note 17, Art. 3.4.

[81] Their arguments are (*Dreyfuss/Ginsburg, supra* note 1, at 24):

- Generic prohibitions are not desirable because non-negotiated clauses in I.P.-related contracts are an important feature of international trade (shrinkwrap/clickwrap contracts).
- It is not appropriate to rely on states' domestic contract law because this is, due to a wide variety in the scope of protection, not predictable.
- The home law of the consumer is difficult to determine in internet cases.
- The problems posed by non-negotiated contracts that contain choice-of-forum clauses are not confined to consumers, but also concern small enterprises.

relating to software and other products subject to protection by I.P. laws. Moreover, in many cases it will be difficult to decide whether the person purchasing software acts "primarily for personal, family, or household purposes" or "for his/her trade or profession" (for example when the software is partly used for professional purposes). Only in the latter case does the envisaged convention on choice-of-court agreements apply. If a court holds that the natural person acts as a consumer, the case falls under the "grey area" where Contracting States are free to impose limitations to party autonomy with regard to choice-of-court clauses as they see fit (see Art. 1(2)(a) DHCC). Nonetheless, the same delimitation has to be carried out where a natural person enters into a contract that has nothing to do with intellectual property (for example the booking of a flight on the internet). The ever-growing importance of forum-selection clauses in I.P.-related B2C contracts thus stresses the necessity of a thoughtful treatment of B2C cases in general.

To sum up, the rationale and advantages of choice-of-court clauses and the compromise that may be found with regard to purely contractual aspects of forum selection, such as the protection of weaker parties to non-negotiated contracts as well as to formal and substantial validity, can be applied without reservation to I.P.-related transactions.

3. Forum Selection in (In)Validity Matters

However, these considerations do not serve to answer the question of how to delimit the cases that will be subject to parties' discretion on the one hand and the cases that will fall under the exclusive jurisdiction of certain courts on the other hand. In the following, we adhere to the generally acknowledged principles that, insofar as a regulation provides for exclusive jurisdiction, forum-selection clauses are not effective,[82] and that one has to distinguish between (in)validity and infringement matters.

a) As a starting point, we support the intention formulated in the preamble of the DHCC. Especially in B2B cases, choice-of-forum clauses are a good means to consolidate claims and to provide for legal certainty in international trade. Therefore, limitations to party autonomy in the form of exclusive jurisdictions should be kept to a minimum range of cases that have to be conferred to the courts of a state due to specific reasons. The following section summarises the justifications for subjecting certain (in)validity matters to exclusive jurisdiction.

---

[82] *See*, for example, Art. 23(5) Brussels I Regulation. Note that this system only works if the rules on exclusive jurisdiction are within the same instrument, or have at least the same "rank". Where, however, an international convention regulates forum-selection clauses only, rules on exclusive jurisdiction may be found in national or supranational (EC) law. Unless there is a caveat in the convention itself, the convention could – depending on the relationship between the convention and national or supranational law – prevail, thereby enabling choice-of-court clauses to override national rules on exclusive jurisdiction.

b) (1) Basically, we can refer to the general arguments in favour of conferring jurisdiction to the courts of the state where an I.P. right has been registered or is deemed to have been registered under the terms of an international convention if the respective ruling has effect erga omnes. These assertions are, above all, respect for foreign administrative officials, concerns of institutional competence and specialised examination by trained national officials.[83] Besides, exclusive jurisdiction of the courts in the country of registration brings international jurisdiction into line with choice of law, because the forum where the proceeding has to be filed will apply the law of the forum.[84]

However, the MPI proposal does not apply this solution to judgments on the validity of registered rights that become effective inter partes, because only decisions affecting the legal existence of the right in its entirety should be reserved to the courts in the country of registration (act of state doctrine).[85] Given that a choice-of-court clause actually governs a civil action in which the relief sought is a declaration of invalidity of a registered right with effect inter partes (*supra*, 1c), a future convention should acknowledge this mutual consent of the parties. Not only does the registration of the right, and thus the existence of the right in relation to third parties, remain unaffected, but a decision like this does not reach beyond the contractual relationship between the parties involved.

---

[83] *See* MPI proposal comments, *supra* note 2, at 2.1; *Dinwoodie*, Private International Aspects of the Protection of Trademarks, available at http://wipo.int/pil-forum/en/documents/pdf/pil_01_4.pdf, 23 *et seq.*; *Dreyfuss, supra* note 19, at 421, 451 *et seq.*; Prel.Doc. No. 22, *supra* note 15, at 10. The 2003 ALI Principles, *supra* note 17, at 7, refer to the control of individual nations over the local conditions under which cultural products are created, exploited, and accessed.

With regard to Art. 16(4) Brussels Convention (= Art. 22(4) Brussels I Regulation) *see Kieninger,* Internationale Zuständigkeit bei der Verletzung ausländischer Immaterialgüterrechte: Common Law auf dem Prüfstand des EuGVÜ, 1998 GRUR Int. 280 *et seq.*; *Stauder,* Grenzüberschreitende Verletzungsverbote im gewerblichen Rechtsschutz und das EuGVÜ, 1998 IPRax 317 *et seq.*; *Karet,* Suit, Anti-Suit, 1998 E.I.P.R. 76; *Fort Dodge Animal Health v. Akzo Nobel,* 1998 F.S.R. 222 (Ct. App. 1997) (Eng.); *Coin Controls Ltd. v. Suzo International (UK) Ltd.*, 3 All E.R. 45 (Ch. D. 1997) (1997) (Eng.); Prel.Doc. No. 11, *supra* note 9, at 43.

An alternative proposal suggests that a judgment on (in)validity matters would have effect between the parties only. However, in light of the factual consequences of such a judgment, even if it has legal effect inter partes only, this proposal did not receive support. *Dreyfuss/Ginsburg, supra* note 1, at 31; *Dinwoodie, supra* note 83, at 24; *Dreyfuss, supra* note 19, at 421, 445. Another approach is to vacate the judgment on (in)validity, should a court in the jurisdiction where the right is registered subsequently hold the I.P. right valid in litigation involving third parties; *see Dreyfuss, supra* note 19, at 421, 446.

[84] *See* for immovable, tangible goods *Stoll,* in: *Staudinger* (ed.), Internationales Sachenrecht, No. 125.

[85] *See* MPI proposal, *supra* note 2, Art. 12a(1) 1st sentence; MPI proposal comments, *supra* note 2, at 2.1.

(2) More important with regard to the limitation of the freedom of the parties to choose a court is the fact that exclusive jurisdiction in (in)validity matters with effect erga omnes does not significantly harm the intention to consolidate claims.

(a) It is critical to note, though, that this notion heavily relies on the suggestion not to subject incidental matters to exclusive jurisdiction.

All above-mentioned proposals state that if an (in)validity matter arises merely as an incidental question, the respective provision on exclusive jurisdiction does not apply.[86] However, this judgment shall have no binding effect in subsequent proceedings, so that an (in)validity proceeding may be brought in the state of registration thereafter.[87] Again, we can refer to the general rationale of this acceptance of party autonomy.[88]

With regard to forum selection, a limited competence in incidental (in)validity matters can be justified by the impossibility of deciding contractual disputes (for example on the effectiveness of the termination of a license agreement) without considering the validity of the underlying I.P. right.[89] Since proceedings solely relating to actions of a contractual nature doubtlessly fall under choice-of-court clauses, a regulation establishing exclusive jurisdiction for incidentally raised (in)validity matters as well would seriously hamper the intention to provide for an effective and reliable basis in international I.P. litigation. In many cases, it is not even foreseeable whether the validity of the I.P. right will be of relevance for a contractual cause of action. Besides, the defendant would only need to invoke aspects of validity to successfully request the dismissal of the case in the chosen court. Therefore, the eminent feature of forum-selection clauses in international license agreements, predictability, would be lost. It is, moreover, important to note that the right-holder is able to promote his interest to have an experienced and reliable court decide on (in)validity matters. Finally, the fact that the decision has effects only inter partes leaves open the possibility of litigating the matter again, and it reflects the merely contractual basis of the jurisdiction of the deciding court.

In drafting this limitation of the scope of exclusive jurisdiction, it should be clarified whether a counterclaim is an incidental matter in the sense of the provision. If it is to be the case that the chosen court is not competent to

[86] Whether exclusive jurisdiction according to Art. 22(4) Brussels I Regulation also applies to incidentally raised validity matters is an open question that is currently (April 2003) pending before the ECJ. *See Fähndrich/Ibbeken*, Gerichtszuständigkeit und anwendbares Recht im Falle grenzüberschreitender Verletzungen (Verletzungshandlungen der Rechte des geistigen Eigentums (Q174) – Bericht für die deutsche Landesgruppe, 2003 GRUR Int. 616, 617.

[87] MPI proposal, *supra* note 2, Art. 12a(2); Art. 1(4) DHCC, *supra* note 45; Prel.Doc. No. 22, *supra* note 15, at 12; with regard to the *Dreyfuss/Ginsburg* approach, *see supra* 2 b.

[88] MPI proposal comments, *supra* note 2, at 3.1; critical: *Dinwoodie, supra* note 83, at 23, No. 121.

[89] *Supra*, I. 4.

adjudicate counterclaims on (in)validity,[90] the convention should moreover make clear that the filing of such a counterclaim does not end the otherwise given jurisdiction of the seized court over the first claim.[91] Otherwise, the defendant would be able to undermine the described system of jurisdiction. Furthermore, it seems advisable that the convention should clarify whether the chosen court must or may stay the proceedings if the defendant proves that he or she filed a suit for the declaration of invalidity in the competent court. The obligation of the chosen court to stay the proceedings, at least in the case of patent law, might be a compromise that reflects the reservations of the patent community.

(b) Provided that the convention gives the chosen court the power to decide (in)validity matters if these arise as incidental matters or if they have effect inter partes only, the interests of the parties to have their freedom reflected in international jurisdiction matters are so limited that they do not prevail over the public interest to inalienably confer jurisdiction to the courts in the state of registration in cases where validity erga omnes is the principle issue.

It must be reiterated that (in)validity matters are litigated in connection with forum-selection clauses only if a contractual relationship between the parties existed before the dispute arose.[92] However, it is hard to imagine a case in which a licensee files an isolated claim for revocation of the licensed I.P. right against the licenser and, moreover, in which the forum-selection clause at issue actually applies to this claim.[93] Thus, the practical relevance of this situation already seems to be minimal. More important, due to the regulation of incidental (in)validity matters (*supra*), the defendant is in a position to contest the validity of the I.P. right in order to avert a negative judgment not only with regard to contractual causes of action, but also in infringement proceedings (*infra* d). The interests of the licensee that go beyond this possibility to defend himself, *i.e.* to (counter)attack the validity of the I.P. right with effect erga omnes, are also beyond his contractual interests and are therefore subject to the public policy limitations of party autonomy in international jurisdiction matters.

---

[90] MPI proposal, *supra* note 2, Art. 12a(2) 2nd sentence; *id.*, at 3.2; Prel.Doc. No. 22, *supra* note 15, at 11–12.

If Art. 1(k) DHCC, *supra* note 45, were interpreted as excluding counterclaims to void the I.P. right from the scope of the convention, the national law of the forum seized would be decisive. In German and European law, counterclaims in matters that fall under exclusive jurisdiction may only be decided by a court actually having this exclusive jurisdiction; *see* § 40(2) German Code of Civil Procedure; Art. 6(3) Brussels I Regulation; *see also Dreyfuss/Ginsburg*, *supra* note 1, at 31.

[91] Prel.Doc. No. 21, *supra* note 51, at 12;*see Coin Controls Ltd. v. Suzo International (UK) Ltd.*, [1997] 3 All E.R. 45, 60g–61d (Ch.D. 1997) (Eng.) on Art. 16(4) Brussels Convention; contra: *Kieninger*, *supra* note 83, at 280, 288.

[92] *Supra* I. 2.

[93] The reason is that such a claim does not seem to be connected closely enough with the contract at stake; *see supra* I. 2. This author has no knowledge of a court decision that ruled that a forum-selection clause applies to an isolated claim on revocation or invalidity.

(c) This consideration has to be qualified in part in light of a novel feature submitted for discussion in the MPI proposal. Paragraph 1, 2nd sentence, declares that the courts in the Contracting State where the right has been registered or is deemed to have been registered have exclusive jurisdiction if the decision would entail a prohibition of further use of the (registered) right in the state of registration, even though the issue of invalidity has not been raised expressly in the proceedings. This provision also limits party autonomy in the case that the requested decision would hinder the right-holder in using his I.P. right in the state of registration, for example in the case of an injunction on the basis that the plaintiff has an older trademark in that country.[94] However, this rule may turn out to be relevant in connection with forum-selection clauses only in specific situations, for example trademark differentiation agreements, where the defendant not only allegedly violates the contract and the I.P. right of the plaintiff, but moreover acts relying on his own registered I.P. right. In such a case, it might well be that the judgment on the infringement also embodies a prohibition of the use of the defendant's I.P. right that can only be brought in the courts of the state of registration. The therefore limited effects of this clause appear to make this additional limitation of choice-of-court agreements acceptable.[95]

c) The MPI proposal also establishes exclusive jurisdiction with regard to (in)validity proceedings pertaining to unregistered I.P. rights if the respective decision would become effective erga omnes.[96]

The rationale behind this provision is to avoid discrimination between different fields of intellectual property law to the best possible degree, and to let the competence to exercise jurisdiction with effect erga omnes rest with the courts in the state with respect to which this effect will accrue. As analysed above, this aim applies equally to the topic discussed in this article. However, the relevance of isolated (in)validity proceedings that fall under a

---

[94] For a general justification *see* MPI proposal comments, *supra* note 2, at 2.3.

[95] Against this basis of exclusive jurisdiction it could be put forward that an injunction to use a younger trademark is regularly connected with a claim for damages and that infringement actions between trademark owners would thus practically fall under the exclusive jurisdiction of the courts in the state of registration. Besides, the rationale of exclusive jurisdiction in (in)validity matters does not apply to relative invalidity of trademarks to the same degree as to absolute invalidity, because relative invalidity of trade marks is at least in some national legislations not subject to official examination. Rather, the holder of the older mark has to oppose registration. This system elucidates that the right-holder has the discretion to decide whether he wants to initiate a proceeding to invalidate a younger trademark or not. Aspects of public policy are obviously not so important as to require an examination ex officio. *See* for example Art. 8 EC Regulation on Trademarks, § 9 German Trademark Act (Markengesetz), Art. 2, 3 Swiss Trademark Act (Markenschutzgesetz); but *see* for U.S. trademark law 15 U.S.C. § 1052(d).

[96] MPI proposal, *supra* note 2, Art. 12a(1) 3rd sentence; MPI proposal comments, *supra* note 2, at 2.3; critical to this approach *Dreyfuss, supra* note 19, at 421, 443; Art. 7.2 DGD, *supra* note 1; *Dinwoodie, supra* note 83, at 22 et seq.; *see* Prel.Doc. No. 22, *supra* note 15, at 10.

choice-of-court clause is minimal.[97] This is even truer when it comes to unregistered rights, where the defendant is not likely to contest the validity of the I.P. right as such instead of invoking invalidity as part of his defence. Moreover, as explained in the MPI proposal, it is questionable whether a declaration of (in)validity of an unregistered IP right can possibly become effective erga omnes.[98] In light of these minimal practical consequences for the principle of party autonomy, and for the sake of clarity and consistency,[99] forum selection by the parties should also not be effective in (in)validity proceedings over unregistered I.P. rights if the judgment handed down has effect erga omnes.

d) In a previous version of the MPI proposal, the exclusivity rule of Art. 12a(3) with respect to unregistered rights was extended to proceedings that have as their principal object the *ownership* of rights. This provision was also intended to form a parallel to rules applying to registered rights. However, in light of the positive features of forum selection in B2B matters in general, we do not retain this solution for the following reasons.

(1) Ownership of *registered* rights is derived either from registration or from an assignment of an I.P. right that is registered for someone else. A claim seeking a declaratory judgment that a registered person or entity is not holding the right is futile and practically irrelevant, since ownership depends exclusively on the registration. If the claim relates to an assignment of rights, the registration of the right as such is not affected. This is why the MPI proposal does not mention ownership-related proceedings in the rule on exclusive jurisdiction for registered rights. Instead, with regard to patent law, one has to distinguish between inventorship and ownership. Whereas proceedings aiming at the ownership as registered will – as shown – not occur, disputes about who the inventor was according to the applicable law are a common situation in patent litigation. In those national patent laws that adhere to the first-to-file principle, these disputes are resolved by giving the true inventor a claim to replace the previous proprietor without invalidating the patent.[100] Only in very few cases will proceedings of this kind possibly be covered by a choice-of-court clause in an agreement between the parties involved. Still, the convention should cover and acknowledge this choice since the decision of the chosen court does not affect the validity of the patent and the question of inventorship is not subject to in-depth examination in the registration process, giving less weight to sovereignty considerations.[101] Contrary to this approach, under

---

[97] Supra I. 4.

[98] MPI proposal comments, *supra* note 2, at 2.3.

[99] *Dinwoodie*, *supra* note 83, at 25.

[100] *See* for example Art. 99(5) European Patent Convention; 35 U.S.C. § 256 (inventorship disputes over issued patents).

[101] *See* Art. 81, 91(1) European Patent Convention; § 37(1)(3) German Patent Act. Accordingly, Art. 22(4) of the Brussels I Regulation does not apply to disputes between an employee and an employer on the question of who is entitled to the patent; ECJ, decision of 15 November 1983, Case C-288/82, *Schroefboutenfabriek B.V. v. Goderbauer*, 1984 GRUR Int. 693, 696.

U.S. patent law, a party who is second to file may establish priority by showing an earlier date of invention (first-to-invent principle).[102] The question of priority of invention when more than one applicant seeks a patent on substantially the same invention is resolved in an interference proceeding that directly affects the pending patent applications involved.[103] Proceedings of this kind should not be subject to the convention on choice-of-court clauses, because it is necessary to compare the inventions,[104] and the primary object of the proceeding is the registration of patents.[105]

(2) With regard to *unregistered* rights, proceedings aiming at a declaratory judgment on the ownership of a right are of practical relevance.[106] They might even be covered by a choice-of-court clause, for example, when a licensee terminates a copyright licensing agreement – that contains a broad choice-of-court clause[107] – due to the fact that the licensor was not the (sole) author of the work. Contrary to the initial version of the MPI proposal, we now suggest giving effect to a choice of court by the parties that may govern proceedings in which the challenge of the ownership of a copyright or other unregistered right is the primary object. First, questions of ownership are, even in cases involving registered rights, only partially subject to exclusive jurisdiction (*supra*). Second, exclusive jurisdiction is unfounded anyway if the respective claim is based on the allegation that the ostensible right-holder was not assigned the right at issue. The aspects that call for exclusive jurisdiction in (in)validity matters do not bear on proceedings seeking a declaratory judgment on initial ownership since states do not execute sovereignty by requiring registration etc. in that respect,[108] and hardly ever will third parties be affected by this decision. The mere fact that rules on initial copyright ownership and the respective choice-of-law rules differ in national laws[109] does not constitute a reason to exclude this matter from the convention.[110]

---

[102] *Chisum*, Chisum on Patents, § 10.01.

[103] 35 U.S.C. § 135; *Chisum, supra* note 102, at § 10.09, § 22.02; *Consolidated World Housewares, Inc. v. Finkle,* 831 F.2d 261, 265 (Fed. Cir. 1987) (exclusive jurisdiction of the USPTO); *Airport Surface Techs., L.L.C. v. FieldTurf, Inc.*, 2003 U.S. Dist. LEXIS 10679 (differentiation between pending applications and issued patents with regard to jurisdiction).

[104] *See* 35 U.S.C. § 135(b).

[105] *See* the proposal at the end of this document.

[106] MPI proposal comments, *supra* note 2, at 2.3.

[107] *Supra* I. 2, 3.

[108] *Supra* III. 3. b) (1).

[109] *See* MPI proposal comments para. 7, *supra* note 2: Some national laws partially apply the work-made-for-hire doctrine, whereas others regard exclusively the author as the owner of copyright. In choice of law, some states subject questions of initial ownership the lex loci protectionis rule, others, the country-of-origin rule; *see Thum* and *van Eechoud*, in this volume.

[110] Note that the recognition of the declaratory judgment on initial ownership of the chosen court might be refused, if this would be manifestly incompatible with the public policy of the state addressed (Art. 7(1)(e) DHCC, *supra* note 45).

e) Instead of providing a list of exclusive jurisdictions, the DHCC excludes these matters from the envisaged convention, leaving them as a large grey area for national law in order to respect existing rules on exclusive jurisdiction, which already exist in other sets of rules outside the convention, like national or supranational law.[111] Again, this approach does not raise specific problems with respect to I.P. and contractual jurisdiction clauses that differ from the difficulties generally produced by this solution. In all cases listed in Art. 1(3) DHCC, the parties of respective contracts relating to these matters have to check in advance to see how the applicable law in the chosen forum deals with the case at issue. This loss of reliability, however, is acceptable because of the limited relevance of proceedings that have as their object the validity of an I.P. right and that are possibly governed by a choice-of-court clause regulated by the autonomous regime of the convention.[112]

Applying the principle of exclusive jurisdiction to (in)validity matters does not necessarily mean that infringement proceedings follow the same rules. Rather, one has to distinguish between (in)validity and infringement matters.[113]

4. Forum Selection in Infringement Cases

a) As already shown,[114] forum-selection clauses as contained in I.P. license agreements may – depending on the exact wording of the clause – apply to alleged infringements of the right underlying the contract, for example where the licensee exceeds his contractual powers. The plaintiff often submits contract causes as well as tort causes of action because the conditions under which the claims have to be recognised differ substantially under national law, for example with regard to the limitation of one or the other action. In other cases, the alleged infringement forms the basis of a claim of contractual nature, such as the declaration of effective exceptional dismissal of the contract. In light of this factual relevance of choice-of-court clauses in connection with infringement claims, it is rightly pointed out that in situations like these the competence of the chosen court to adjudicate contractual and tortious claims is necessary to make sure that the court actually considers all significant facts. Besides, this consolidation reduces costs for the parties and the states involved, and it furthermore prevents repeated proceedings.[115] The plaintiff is put in a position to concentrate all causes of action in one

---

[111] *See* Art. 1(3) DHCC, *supra* note 45.

[112] *Supra* I. 4. To clearly delimit the scope of application of Art. 1(3) DHCC, *supra* note 45, in contrast to Art. 1(4) DHCC, *supra* note 45, the wording of Art. 1(3) should read "have as their object" instead of "relating to". Moreover, Art. 1(4) DHCC should contain a definition of incidental matters as proposed in the 2001 interim text, *supra* note 1, at 13, and the MPI proposal, *supra* note 2, Art. 12a(2) 2nd sentence.

[113] *See* for the Brussels Convention *Jenard* Report, OJ EC 1979 C 59, at 1, 36.

[114] Supra I. 3.

[115] *Dreyfuss/Ginsburg, supra* note 1, at 31.

proceeding, while the defendant profits from the reduction of opportunities for harassment.[116]

Moreover, there is practically no risk that an envisaged convention regulating that a chosen court may also hand down a ruling on infringements may serve as a legal basis for totally inappropriate or unreasonable jurisdiction. This is because in the typical case of relevance, an I.P. license agreement, the right-holder is able to affect the choice of forum.[117] At the same time, it is not likely that the parties would choose a forum that has no connection with the contract or the parties, because that would interfere with the interest of both parties to efficiently enforce the contractual obligations of the other party.[118] Moreover, Art. 6 DHCC sets out that the envisaged convention shall not prevent a party from requesting provisional and protective measures on an interim basis from any court or prevent any court from granting such measures. The right-holder remains free to seize other courts than the chosen court for interim relief, which any court may grant, provided that it has jurisdiction under its national law.[119] There is thus no considerable risk of reducing the effectiveness of the international enforcement of I.P. rights.

b) To acknowledge the competence of the chosen court to decide infringement actions that are covered by the choice-of-forum clause therefore is not only in the interest of all parties concerned.[120] It moreover

---

[116] *Dreyfuss/Ginsburg, supra* note 17, at 33, 35.

[117] However, it should be considered that in the case of exploitation contracts involving individual authors (not authors on the basis of works made for hire) and performing artists, exploiters, as their contracting partner, are often able to dictate the content of the agreement in general and of the forum-selection clause in specific. Therefore, national copyright laws often contain provisions that limit party autonomy in order to grant authors and performers protection in their contractual relationship with exploiters; *see*, for European copyright laws, *Guibault/Hugenholtz,* Study on the Conditions Applicable to Contracts Relating to Intellectual Property in the European Union, available at http//www.ivir.nl/publications/guibault/contracts.html, at 28 *et seq.*; for the right to terminate a contract under U.S. copyright law, *see* 17 U.S.C. §§ 203, 304(c). Freelance authors and performers act for the purposes of their trade or profession and not as consumers. These contracts would therefore be covered by the DHCC, *supra* note 45. To address the issue that authors and performers regularly are the weaker party to an exploitation contract, the convention had to contain a rule that limits the lawfulness of choice-of-court clauses involving freelance authors and performers. A possible solution could be to draft a provision similar to Art. 16, 21 Brussels I Regulation that serves the intention to afford consumers and employees the protection granted by their respective "home" law; *see Peukert,* Protection of Authors and Performing Artists in International Law – Considering as Example Claims for Equitable Remuneration in German and Italian Copyright Law, forthcoming in IIC 2004.

[118] Articles 15 and 16 DHCC, *supra* note 45, contain additional protective measures in that respect.

[119] Prel.Doc. No. 22, *supra* note 15, at 18–19.

[120] *See Schack, supra* note 4, at 135, 137; Prel.Doc. No. 11, *supra* note 9, at 43: "While the provision is most likely to be used in relation to disputes arising out of a contractual relationship, there is no reason why issues such as liability for a tort cannot be referred by agreement to a particular court".

demonstrates the autonomy of the plaintiff in I.P. infringement proceedings to choose between the defendant's forum and the forum delicti according to many national laws and current proposals for an international convention.[121]

c) One must further take into account that the decision in favour of party autonomy in that field in no way determines issues of choice of law.[122] Even given the possibility to choose a court that is competent to settle infringement proceedings relating to a license agreement, the generally accepted rule that the law applying to I.P. infringement cases is the lex loci protectionis, *i.e.* the law of the country where protection is claimed, will remain unaffected.[123] Thus, the interaction of the rules of international jurisdiction and choice of law serves both the above discussed interests of the parties involved and the public interest to apply the law of the country of protection to reflect the specific balance of interests of right-holders and users that is established in the respective national law.[124] Finally, in exceptional cases, a state may refuse to entertain judgments of the chosen court

---

[121] Under the current (April 2003) Hague proposal, the DHCC, *supra* note 45, defendant's forum and forum delicti fall under the large grey area that is not governed by the convention and is thus subject to national law. Whether I.P. infringements are subject to exclusive jurisdiction according to Art. 22(4) of the Brussels I Regulation, and therefore may not be filed in the courts having general jurisdiction (Art. 2 Brussels I Regulation) or the courts having special jurisdiction under Art. 5(3) Brussels I Regulation, is a question currently (April 2003) pending before the ECJ; *see Fähndrich/Ibbeken, supra* note 86, at 616, 617. The same basic principle holds true for the MPI proposal comments, *supra* note 2, at 4, the *Dreyfuss/Ginsburg* approach (Art. 3/5 DGD, *supra* note 1), and the Art. 2/5 2003 ALI Principles, *supra* note 17.

[122] *See also* Art. 16 2003 ALI Principles, *supra* note 17:

> Art. 16.1: When the applicable law is not the supranational law, characterisation of connecting factors is necessary because the applicable law is not necessarily the law of the forum.
> Art. 16.2: As a rule, the choice of forum does not imply a choice of law.

[123] MPI proposal comments, *supra* note 2, at 4.2.

[124] The German Federal Supreme Court held that the lex loci protectionis rule may not be derogated by a party choice of law. *See* 136 Entscheidungen des Bundesgerichtshofs in Zivilsachen (BGHZ), 380 – Spielbankaffaire; *Zweigert/Puttfarken,* Zum Kollisionsrecht der Leistungsschutzrechte, 1973 GRUR Int. 573, 577; *Fezer,* Markenrecht, 3d ed. 2001, Einl. MarkenG No.199; but see *Schack,* Urheberrechtsverletzung im internationalen Privatrecht aus der Sicht des Kollisionsrechts, 1985 GRUR Int. 523, 525; Cologne Court of Appeals, 2000 GRUR 66 – Michael Jackson; *von Welser,* in: *Wandtke/Bullinger* (ed.), UrhR, 2002, before §§ 120 No. 14 (choice of law effective after the dispute has arisen).

In spite of the fact that both the choice-of-law rules that apply to tangible and to intangible goods (the lex rei sitae and the lex loci protectionis) serve the intention to reflect the interests of users in a particular state who have to be sure of the scope of the property right at stake (*see v. Hoffmann,* Internationales Privatrecht, 7th ed. 2002, § 12 No. 9), it is not contested that choice-of-court clauses as contained in agreements pertaining to tangible, movable goods may possibly govern claims for infringement of the property in these goods.

because of a manifest incompatibility of the decision with the public policy of the state addressed.[125]

d) Another way to exclude the possibility of inappropriate or unreasonable jurisdictions on the basis of forum selection by the parties would be to limit their choices to the general and special jurisdiction provided for by the convention.[126] However, such a limitation of party autonomy is neither feasible nor advisable. First, the DHCC contains only one white rule of jurisdiction, *i.e.* jurisdiction founded on a party choice of court, so that reference to other autonomously regulated jurisdictions is out of reach. Second, parties would be deprived of the flexibility that follows from effective choice-of-court clauses and moreover would be obliged to examine whether their choice is compatible with the jurisdictions as incorporated in the convention. Thereby, practically all advantages connected with choice-of-court clauses in international trade would be lost.

e) It can be summarised that there is every reason to believe that an acknowledgement of parties' freedom to choose a court with respect to infringement matters is in line with the general aim to ensure the effectiveness of choice-of-court agreements in international trade and investment and that it does not raise concerns about public interests that outweigh the advantages of forum selection.

5. Reach of Jurisdiction

Finally, if the above-proposed general application of choice-of-forum clauses to infringement matters were accepted, it would raise the question whether the designated court would be competent to adjudicate all conduct that allegedly constitutes infringement of the I.P. right or whether the reach of jurisdiction would be limited in some respect. Two basic options exist to resolve this issue. Either the chosen court may adjudicate all claims raised against the defendant (irrelevant of where the acts that caused the alleged infringement occurred), or this court may be granted competence only for infringements occurring in the territory of the state where the deciding court is situated.

The MPI proposal consolidates infringement matters basically only in the defendant's forum.[127] However, the general pros and cons of consolidation

---

[125] Art. 7(1)(e) DHCC, *supra* note 45.

[126] *See* Art. 3(3)(e) DGD, *supra* note 1: The question of whether the designated forum would have had jurisdiction over the non-drafting party in the absence of a forum-selection clause is one criterion to be considered in the course of deciding about the reasonableness of the choice.

[127] MPI proposal, *supra* note 2, Art. 12a(4). Art. 12a(5) sets out special rules to consolidate infringement matters in internet-related proceedings.

With regard to jurisdiction and the reach of that jurisdiction in infringement matters, Art. 5 of the DGD, *supra* note 1, distinguishes between substantial acts in furtherance of the alleged infringement, intentional direction of the infringement and places where the infringement foreseeably occurred. Art. 5 of the 2003 ALI principles, *supra* note 17, contains an identical provision.

of infringement claims through unlimited reach of jurisdiction of certain courts merely provide guidance when it comes to jurisdiction that is founded not on statutory jurisdiction (for example: defendant's forum), but solely on the fact that the parties conferred jurisdiction to a particular court.

Rather, the decisive point is to what extent the designation of particular courts bars other courts from exercising their power to adjudicate the dispute. In this regard, one has to determine whether the parties concluded an exclusive or a non-exclusive choice-of-court agreement. If the chosen court has exclusive jurisdiction, a court in a state other than the state of the chosen court must basically either decline jurisdiction or suspend proceedings. All claims that are covered by the clause have to be filed in the selected forum. If the forum-selection clause establishes only non-exclusive jurisdiction of the designated court, any other court that is seized but not chosen is not obliged to dismiss the case.[128]

Insofar as an exclusive choice of court deprives all other courts from hearing the case,[129] the chosen court has to adjudicate all respective causes of action, because otherwise, the plaintiff risks suffering a denial of justice due to a negative conflict of competence. Furthermore, it is beyond doubt that the exclusively chosen court is competent to decide all contractual issues, even if they relate to actions that occurred outside the forum state. If the competence of the court were nevertheless limited with regard to tort causes of action, the parallel treatment of contract and infringement matters would be lost. Finally, should a worldwide convention really be restricted to only one "white" rule on jurisdiction, this sole possibility to consolidate multi-state claims should not be disregarded. Therefore, if the exclusively chosen court finds that the clause at issue covers infringement matters as well, the court's jurisdiction is not confined to infringements occurring in the forum state. If the exclusively chosen court declines jurisdiction, courts in other states having jurisdiction according to the applicable law may hear the case.[130]

However, where the parties confer jurisdiction on a non-exclusive basis only, meaning that other courts are not deprived of general or special

---

[128] Art. 2(1)(b) 2nd sentence DHCC, *supra* note 45, raises the presumption that a choice-of-court clause is exclusive. Art. 5 DHCC sets out the priority of the exclusively chosen court. The exceptions of the obligation to decline jurisdiction or suspend proceedings are enumerated in Art. 5(a–c) DHCC. Since the DHCC does not regulate the effects of non-exclusive choice-of-court clauses, this issue is left to national law (grey area). *See* additionally Prel.Doc. No. 19, *supra* note 12, at 17; Prel.Doc. No. 20, *supra* note 3, at 14; Prel.Doc. No. 21, *supra* note 51, at 5.

[129] As shown above (*supra* I. 3.), the court has to construe whether the clause covers the infringement action or not. This will generally not be the case if the infringement is in no way related to the contract at stake. If the chosen court refuses to hear an infringement claim, other courts naturally are free to adjudicate the case according to the otherwise applicable law.

[130] Art. 5(c) DHCC, *supra* note 45.

jurisdiction, the plaintiff is not threatened by a denial of justice. Instead, he or she still has the option to file the infringement claim either in the defendant's forum or in the country where the infringement occurred.[131] Such situations arise when parties expressly[132] intend to establish merely an additional basis of jurisdiction, not to settle all possible disputes in one single forum. Considering this limited effect of a non-exclusive forum selection, it seems reasonable to assume that the reach of jurisdiction is also restricted in the sense that the non-exclusively chosen court is only competent for infringements that occur in the forum state.

IV. Conclusions and a Proposal

Based on the foregoing analysis, the elements a convention on jurisdiction should ideally contain can be succinctly formulated as follows:

(1) Choice-of-court clauses as part of licensing agreements pertaining to I.P. may cover jurisdiction for infringement claims related to the contractual relationship, depending on the exact wording of the forum-selection clause at issue. However, (in)validity proceedings are not likely to be subject to choice-of-court clauses.

(2) It is not advisable to exclude I.P. law in general or in part from an international convention on jurisdiction, recognition and enforcement of judgments.

(3) As far as contractual aspects of choice-of-court agreements are concerned (for example formal or substantial validity), I.P.-related proceedings do not deserve special treatment.

(4) Proceedings in which the relief sought is a judgment on the validity of registered and unregistered rights with effect erga omnes should be subject to exclusive jurisdiction of certain courts and therefore exempted from the possibility to designate a competent court. However, the chosen court should be competent to adjudicate claims where the (in)validity matter arises as an incidental question or where the judgment would become effective inter partes only.

(5) Infringement actions that relate to the contract containing a forum selection may, depending on the interpretation of the clause under the law applicable in the chosen forum, be decided by the chosen court.

(6) An exclusively chosen court has jurisdiction for all infringement claims raised against the defendant, provided that these actions are covered by the clause. If the parties confer jurisdiction on a non-exclusive basis, the chosen court is competent only with regard to infringements that occur in the forum state.

---

131 *See* for a discussion of jurisdiction in infringement claims MPI proposal comments, *supra* note 2, at 4.

132 *See* Art. 2(1)(b) 2nd sentence DHCC, *supra* note 45 (presumption of exclusivity).

The relevant provisions in the current Hague proposal for a convention on choice-of-court agreements in B2B cases that reflect these conclusions could read as follows:

Article 1: Scope

3. This convention does not apply to proceedings that have as their object[133]

. . .

k) –a judgment on the grant, registration, validity, abandonment, or revocation of a patent, a mark, an industrial design or any other industrial property right required to be registered or protected on the basis of registration, unless that judgment would only become effective inter partes,

[– a prohibition of further use of the right in the Contracting State of registration, even if the issue of invalidity has not been raised expressly in the proceedings, or][134]

– a judgment on the validity of any other intellectual property right if the judgment would become effective erga omnes.[135]

4. Proceedings are not excluded from the scope of the Convention if a matter referred to in paragraph 3 arises merely as an incidental question. However, the ruling in that matter shall have no binding effect in subsequent proceedings, even if they are between the same parties.[136] A matter arises as an incidental question if the court is not requested to give a judgment on that matter, even if a ruling on it is necessary in arriving at a decision.[137]

---

133 *See supra* note 112.

134 For the rationale of this provision, *see supra* III. 3. b) (2) (b).

135 *See supra* III. 3. c); MPI proposal comments, *supra* note 2, at 2.3.

136 *See* Prel.Doc. No. 22, *supra* note 15, at 12; MPI proposal comments, *supra* note 2, at 3.2.

137 *See supra* note 112.

III.

Current Developments in Patent Law

The EPLA Project and the Forthcoming Community Patent System – A Model for IP in General? ★

JAN WILLEMS★★

In order to speculate on an answer to this question it seems necessary first to have a closer look at both the European Patent Litigation Agreement (EPLA)[1] project and at the Community patent system, as far as litigation is concerned, and then to have a look at the differences between them and the advantages and disadvantages of both systems. Finally a conclusion will be drawn.

I. The European Patent Judiciary

1. History

The EPLA was born out of the long-felt need for uniform decisions about the different parts of the European bundle patent. This need, already present before, was felt more and more strongly as the internal market of the European Union became a reality.

It goes without saying that it is an anomaly in an undivided internal market to have different scopes of protection of totally uniformly worded claims. And yet, this is the unavoidable result of having different courts looking at that patent and at its alleged infringements on the basis of different sets of rules of procedure and especially different rules on evidence.

An intergovernmental conference, organised on the initiative of the French government, was held in Paris in 1999. This conference created a working party in which all Contracting States to the European Patent Convention (EPC) were represented. The mandate given to this group was "to (among other things) present a draft optional protocol to the EPC which would commit its signatory states to an integral judicial system, including uniform rules of procedure and a common court of appeal".

The working party met a number of times. At first the main issue of the discussion was whether only a common court of appeal should be created,

---

★ This article is a modified version of a presentation given at a conference at Frauenchiemsee on 21 July 2003, organised by the Max Planck Institute for Intellectual Property, Competition and Tax Law.

★★ The author is a legally qualified member of the Boards of Appeal of the EPO but expresses of course only his purely personal opinions.

[1] European Patent Litigation Agreement.

thereby leaving first-instance proceedings to the national courts, or whether it would be preferable to create a totally new *supra*national court with a first and a second instance. Ultimately the solution chosen was that of a totally new central *supra*national court structure with two instances. Nevertheless, the working party realised that it would not be acceptable for the users of the system to have all their proceedings in only one place in Europe, and that this would also not be very efficient. Therefore the local presence of the court in first instance was guaranteed by the creation of regional divisions of the court, with seats in the Member States for which they were created and not at the central seat of the court.

The EPLA as it is finally devised will create a new legal entity called the European Patent Judiciary (EPJ). It will include (and be administered by) an Administrative Committee (*cf.* the Administrative Council of the EPO). Furthermore it will contain a European Patent Court, consisting of a Court of First Instance, a Court of Second Instance and a Registry. The Court of First Instance will consist of a Central Division and a number of Regional Divisions: every Member State or group of Member States that can claim at least two judges experienced in patent law can request the creation of a Regional Division.

Not to be confused are the ideas of the central and regional divisions, being only organisational units, and the panels, sitting on individual cases. These panels will consist of two legal judges: a judge-rapporteur (in principle coming from the division before which the case is pending) and a chairman (in principle coming from another division and having in any case a different nationality). Furthermore the panel will include a technical judge.

The registry will have sub-registries in all Member States, all having access to the same electronic registers. The problem of finding the necessary number of experienced judges is solved by also using – part time – judges from national courts, who will go on acting as national judges for that part of their time they do not need for the "European" work.

On the one hand, that solves the problem of the scarcity in Europe of experienced patent judges, and on the other hand – possibly not less important – this construction promotes the harmonisation of European patent law and national patent law, as the same judges will be dealing with both.

2. Competence of the Court

The EPJ will be competent for all proceedings regarding the infringement, threatening infringement (including actions for a declaration of non-infringement) and/or validity of European bundle patents in the Member States that have acceded to the EPLA. Moreover, it will deal with actions for damages or compensation in respect of the protection conferred by a published European patent application.[2]

[2] Therefore, actions concerning *e.g.* the ownership of a patent would remain under the national jurisdiction, as will be the case with the Community patent.

This competence shall, after a transitional period of seven years, be exclusive and therefore no longer belong to the national courts.

3. Powers of the Court

The EPJ court shall have the necessary powers to fulfil its function. It will be able to:

- give injunctions regarding infringing actions;
- declare forfeited infringing goods and goods used for manufacturing them;
- order a party to pay damages, be it in money or in other forms;
- order a party to give information about other persons in the chain of supply of the infringing goods;
- order that its decision will take the place of any declaration or other act by a party;
- sanction any order by an astreinte, a huge sum of money to be paid by the non–obeying party to its opponent;
- revoke wholly or in part a European patent, if necessary by reformulating the claims of the patent;
- give provisional and protective measures:

  preliminary injunctions,
  orders for inspection ("Saisie contrefaçon"),
  freezing orders ("Mareva injunctions"),
  orders for sequestration and
  protective measures regarding a person's trade secrets or other confidential information.

4. Harmonisation of Substantive Law

As most of the existing Member States of the EPC have harmonised their substantive patent law in accordance with the Strasbourg Convention[3] and the Luxembourg Community Patent Convention,[4] their substantive law is to a great extent harmonised. More recently acceded Member States of the EPC, however, have not necessarily attained this degree of harmonisation. Therefore it was felt to be a good idea to harmonise substantive patent law in the EPLA in order to ensure that at least the Member States to the EPLA would have as harmonised a substantive law as possible. A number of articles in the EPLA thus define such concepts as infringing actions and indirect infringement, what limitations there are to the effect of a European patent, prior use and reversal of the burden of proof in the case of new products.

---

[3] Convention on the Unification of Certain Points of Substantive Law on Patents for Invention, Strasbourg 1963

[4] Luxembourg 1975, 1985.

5. Language of Proceedings

The language of proceedings in appeal will be that used in the proceedings in the first instance. As regards the first instance, one has to distinguish between the Central Division and the Regional Divisions. The language of the proceedings before the Central Division will be the language in which the European patent is granted. The language of the proceedings before the Regional Divisions will be determined according to the principles of the London protocol on languages. That is to say that if proceedings take place before a Regional Division in a Member State that has as (one of) its official language(s) one of the official languages of the European Patent Organisation, the language of the proceedings will be that language. All Member States that do not have one of the languages of the European Patent Organisation as an official language (or that have more than one of the languages of the EPO as an official language) will have to designate any one official language of the EPO as the language of the proceedings before a Regional Division in that Member State.

6. Effect of Decisions

If the European Patent Court revokes a patent (totally or in part), that decision will be valid for all Member States for which it is given.[5]

7. Sanctions

As has already been said, the European Patent Court will be able to sanction infringements by ordering the infringer to pay damages and/or to forfeit the infringing goods or the devices used to manufacture these goods.

Apart from the sanction on an infringement that has taken place there is, however, a need for a sanction on non-compliance with an order of the Court (be it an injunction or any other order). This sanction will be an astreinte. The astreinte stems from the Benelux countries, which have had experience with it for many years now. The astreinte is not a fine. A fine is a payment to be made to the authorities as a punishment for a violation of a rule. An astreinte has to be paid not to the authorities but to the opposing party, and is meant not so much as a punishment but rather as an incentive not to violate the order. That difference is visible in the sometimes quite clear disproportionality between the potential damage done by a violation and the much larger amount of the astreinte.

[5] There has been some dispute about the question of whether a revocation decision should automatically be valid for all designated Member States of the EPLA, but that approach seems difficult to align with the bundle character of the European patent that means that the patent can be slightly different in different Member States and can also have different proprietors in different Member States.

Furthermore, an astreinte received by a party from its opponent does not reduce the claim for damages: the astreinte is not a kind of advance on the damages.

II. The European Community Patent Court

As regards history it may be briefly remembered here that after much time and energy had been invested in the Community Patent Convention it turned out not to be a viable project because industry announced it would not be using the system created by the politicians. This was because its language regime would be too expensive and its proposed litigation system too uncertain.

When the jurisprudence of the Court of Justice cleared the way for this, attention turned to creating a community patent by way of a Council Regulation instead of dealing with such a Community title in a separate treaty.

The Commission had learned its lesson from the history of the Community Patent Convention and started its new Community patent project by listening to the users. The result of these consultations was a fine proposal: the Proposal for a Council Regulation on the Community Patent (COM (2000) 412 final, 1 August 2000). It envisaged the creation of a Community intellectual property court, having a chamber for first instance and a chamber of appeal. The proposal expressly did not propose giving jurisdiction to the Court of First Instance, because of the lack of experience of this court in patent matters and because of the unacceptably long duration of the proceedings before that court.[6]

This proposal took into account the clear wishes of the users of the system[7] and would have been easily compatible with the ideas developed in the working party on the litigation protocol, where the same wishes of the users had been listened to. Things seemed to be going in the right direction at last.

The politicians in the Council, however, did not turn out to have drawn the same wisdom from history as the Commission had, and the whole project got bogged down in a squabble about languages and translations. After a long standstill, a common political[8] approach was reached by Member States of the EU in March 2003 and from there the work was taken further.

---

[6] Of course this new court should be subjected to the jurisdiction of the Court of Justice.

[7] Also regarding the language regime; Community patents would be granted in one of the official languages of the EPO and only the claims would have to be translated, and only into the two other official languages of the EPO.

[8] The adjective "political" is not necessarily a good omen, as it was the politicians who created the Community Patent Convention that suited them but not the users of the system. History will teach us whether the same error is being repeated now.

As regards the creation of a Community patent, work is at this moment being done regarding the necessary modifications of the European Patent Convention, allowing the Union to become a member of that convention and enabling the European Patent Office to grant Community patents if the Union is designated in the application.

As regards the litigation aspects, the creation of a specialised patent court is envisaged inside the Court of Justice (ECJ) and, more particularly, inside the Court of First Instance. According to the draft European Constitution, the role and the structure of the ECJ will be clarified. According to Art. 28 of the Constitution, the court will be named "The Court of Justice". It will comprise the "European Court of Justice", the "High Court" (nowadays still called the Court of First Instance[9]) and "specialised courts".

One of these "specialised courts" will be the "Community Patent Court" (CPC) proposed in Art. 30 of the draft Council Regulation on the Community patent of 16 April 2003 (8539/03). The CPC will have exclusive jurisdiction for litigation concerning infringement and/or threatening infringement and the validity of community patents (Art. 30 of the revised text of the Proposal for a Council Regulation on the Community Patent (CRCP)).[10] It will also be competent to deal with claims for a declaration of non-infringement (Art. 34 CRCP). Moreover, it will deal with claims for compensation for the use of the invention after the publication of the application (Art. 35 CRCP). Finally, it will deal with claims concerning the prior use of the invention (Art. 36 CRCP).

The CRCP is silent about the structure of this Community Patent Court. All we had until recently was the common approach of 3 March 2003 (7159/03), saying that the CPC will have its seat in Luxembourg, that it will sit in panels of three judges and that the judges will be assisted by technical experts. Furthermore it was stipulated that the language of the proceedings will be the official language of the Member State where the defendant is domiciled.

Since 23 December 2003, however, we know somewhat more about the ideas of the Union regarding its future Community Patent Court: the Commission has presented a proposal for a Council decision conferring jurisdiction on the Court of Justice in disputes relating to the Community patent (COM (2003) 827 final) and a proposal for a Council decision establishing the Community Patent Court and concerning appeals before the Court of First Instance (COM (2003) 828 final).

From these proposals it appears that the EU now envisages a Community Patent Court, consisting of seven judges (Art. 2 COM (2003) 828), assisted

[9] Thereby preventing the anomaly of calling the second instance the "Court of First Instance".

[10] Interinstitutional file 2000/0177 (CNS) 10404/03.

by a number of technical experts not disclosed in the text of the proposal,[11] appointed to the CPC as assistant rapporteurs in the sense of Art. 13 of the Statute of the Court of Justice. These experts will take part in the proceedings and in the deliberations but will have no vote.

The CPC will sit in panels of three judges but envisages the possibility of an enlarged configuration and of a single judge. Details will have to be found in the rules of procedure, still to be set up (Art. 8 COM (2003) 828).

Parties will have to be represented by a lawyer authorised to appear before a court in a Member State, who can be assisted by a European patent attorney, having the right to address the Court (Art. 11 COM (2003) 828 juncto Art. 19 of the Statute of the Court of Justice).

1. Powers of the Court

The powers of the CPC do seem sufficiently broad. Article 43 of the CRCP gives the court the power to give injunctions, to seize infringing goods and to order "other penalties adapted to the circumstances or suitable for guaranteeing compliance with the orders" mentioned in this article.

Also, it is clear that the CPC will have the power to order damages to be paid (Art. 44 CRCP juncto Art. 1 COM (2003) 827). Will the Court feel that this allows damages or compensation to be effected by other means than the payment of cash? Such means might include calling back infringing products from customers, publishing rectification texts in letters and/or advertisements, providing names of customers and/or suppliers of infringing goods. It remains to be seen. The CPC will further be able to "prescribe any necessary interim measures" (Art. 42 CRCP and Art. 14 COM (2003) 828 juncto Art. 39 Statute of the Court of Justice and Art.243 EC Treaty).

It remains to be seen how broadly this will be interpreted by the CPC. The seizure of evidence is expressly mentioned in Art. 42 of the CRCP, but will the CPC decide that it comprises, *e.g.*, orders for freezing assets (Mareva injunctions) and/or sequestration of infringing products?

Appeals of the decisions of the CPC will be open to the Court of First Instance (in the draft Constitution: the High Court) that will be enlarged by three judges, forming a specialised patent chamber (Arts. 5 and 6 COM (2003) 828).

The time limit for filing an appeal will be two months after the notification of the decision (Art. 26 COM (2003) 828), and it may be based on points of law or on points of fact. Nevertheless, new facts and new evidence may only be brought in if their submission by the party concerned could not reasonably have been expected in the first instance. Therefore the

---

[11] According to the Legislative Financial statement accompanying COM (2003) 828, seven of these assistant rapporteurs are envisaged in the first instance (for inorganic chemistry, organic and polymer chemistry, biochemistry and biotechnology, general physics, mechanics, information technology and electrical engineering, respectively). For the second instance three experts are thought to be sufficient.

appeal will not be a totally fresh retrial of the whole case, with parties being able to correct any mistake they made in first instance.

2. Selection of Judges

There is still some uncertainty about how the procedure for selecting and appointing judges will turn out in practice.

According to the now published proposals, the Council will appoint an advisory committee, composed of seven members chosen from among former members of the Court of Justice (including the Court of First Instance and the CPC) or "lawyers of recognised competence."[12] This advisory committee will give an opinion on the adequacy of the profile of candidates and it may attach to its opinion a list of candidates possessing the most appropriate level of experience, provided that the list comprises at least two candidates for each vacancy to be filled (Art. 3 COM (2003) 828). The candidates themselves will have to be presented by the Member States. The judges will be appointed by the Council from the candidates presented by the Member States after consultation of the advisory committee.

Although this system seems fine on paper, it far from guarantees that indeed judges with the necessary experience will be appointed, as the Council is not bound by the opinion of the advisory committee nor by their list of appropriate candidates. The ever-present risk of political deals and politically motivated appointments would in my view only be sufficiently suppressed if either the Council were bound by the list of candidates the advisory committee attached to their opinion, or if the candidates were not presented by the Member States but were selected after open application proceedings, allowing everyone to file an application. Personally I do not understand why, as long as the final appointment is up to the Council, such a narrow approach is taken to the question of who could be a candidate.

Moreover it seems questionable to fix the number of judges in the CPC in the Statute of the Court of Justice itself. It is foreseeable that, if the Community patent is a success, the number of cases would by far exceed the capacity of seven judges. Why not fix a much larger maximum number in the Statute and leave it to the CPC and the Council to adapt the factually appointed number of judges to the needs of the moment?

III. Differences Between the EPJ and the CPC Systems

The first clear difference is that, although both courts will be dealing with the same classes of proceedings, the EPJ deals with a multiplicity of titles: all national parts of the European patent. These will in most cases be the same, but not necessarily so. Moreover, the different parts of the European patent can be subject to different legal provisions in different Member States;

[12] Recognised by whom?

although European patent law is harmonised to a large extent there still are differences. The CPC, in contrast, will be dealing with a unitary title that will be subject to one uniform legal regime.

A further difference is that the EPJ will have a technician aboard as one of the judges, while the judges of the CPC will be "assisted" by technical experts in the capacity of assistant rapporteurs. It is too early to say much about this issue as long as a more detailed set of rules has not been published, but it is clear that there is a danger here of technical expertise being provided to the court without the control of the parties. That danger is already present in the case of a technically qualified judge, but it seems still greater in the case of technical experts: while the role of the technical judge is not that of an expert but of a technical interpreter, the role of a technical expert clearly goes beyond that.[13]

Another, most important, difference is the language regime. A lawsuit before the EPJ will always have one single language of proceedings. As regards the proceedings before the CPC this is not clear, especially not for cases in which there are multiple defendants, a quite common event in patent litigation. It seems that in such cases each defendant will be allowed to use their own official language as long as that is an official EU language.

Next to the matter of languages, the second-most important difference is that in the degree of centralisation. The EPC sits not only in a central division, but also in a number of regional divisions. In principle every Member State can assure that its subjects will be summoned before a division of the EPC in his or her own country.

As regards the CPC there is only one seat. Although in principle the possibility is open that the CPC can also have sessions in other states, there is no regional registry where a case can be filed, there are no "local" judges, and so forth.

Of course it could be argued that under the provision that allows the CPC to sit in other places than its own seat could, if taken very literally, be subsumed a factual set-up in which a number of judges of the CPC had their permanent seats elsewhere. That, however, seems to me to be in such a clear contradiction to what the authors of the Council decision have in mind that such an interpretation seems hardly likely. Moreover, it does not seem feasible with a total number of only seven judges.

IV. Advantages and Disadvantages

The main advantage of the Community patent system seems to be that it necessarily covers the whole market, while the EPJ courts only cover a number of Member States, thereby only reducing the problem and not really solving it.

---

[13] This is not to say that having a technical judge on the panel is an ideal solution.

The main advantages of the EPJ system seem to be its regional accessibility, its relatively simple language regime and resulting inexpensive functioning and its links with the national courts.

A disadvantage of the Community patent project seems to be that it will not be possible to make use of experienced national judges. Therefore it will be difficult to find sufficient experienced judges (which will initially not enhance the trust of the users in the system), and it will be more difficult to harmonise national and *supra*national patent jurisprudence.

The main disadvantage of both systems is that they seem hardly compatible with each other in the sense that they do not seem to make an integration of both systems easy.

Having said that, it should not be forgotten that there are similarities between the two systems: both have a single, *supra*national, centralised court for patent cases, both deal with infringement and validity, and both take care that in some way technical expertise is available to the court.

The Community patent system, however, seems to have two crucial disadvantages that should be corrected before it is too late: the language regime and the excessive centralisation. The language issue is not only a problem when it comes to the question of translation of (the claims of) the patent but certainly also in regard to litigation.

The possibility of more than twenty possible languages makes it illusory to think that the parties and the judges would be able to understand the language of a proceeding without both a translation of the documents of the case and simultaneous interpretation of the oral proceedings. That seems to pose some problems not only of a financial nature (which are so evident that they do not need further discussion here), but also of a Babylonian nature. Anybody who has dealt in practice with proceedings comprising simultaneous translations knows how much of what is said is lost in translation.

Moreover, problems can easily arise in the written submissions. If the language of the proceedings is *e.g.* Greek or Portuguese, most judges will not be able to understand the documents as presented to the court, so they will have to be translated into a language the judges do understand. Which language? It is hardly imaginable that every judge will be able to determine into which language his or her documents are to be translated.[14] That would lead to differences of opinion among the judges based on different translations of he original submissions. Therefore the CPC will probably have to adopt a single language as the "working language" of the court. Nowadays it is difficult to imagine that that would be French (originally the working language of the Court of Justice and the Court of First Instance), especially in patent matters, where the large majority of the prior art will be in English. Most experienced patent judges, because of this, will be able to deal with

[14] Although that is now the case according to Art. 36 of the Rules of Procedure of the Court of First Instance. It seems hardly practicable to maintain such a system in view of the rather different proceedings the CPC will be dealing with.

English, but hardly any of them with French, as a language to discuss and deliberate in. If the working language among the judges will thus probably be English anyway, why not save a lot of costs and possible translation errors in opting for a system with "English only"?

The other possibly lethal error in the CPC proposal is that of the centralisation at one seat, Luxembourg. The absence of local judges and regional registries is not only of eminent psychological importance for the acceptance of the court, but it will also have consequences for the ease with which speedy decisions can be delivered. In patent cases, provisional measures, especially provisional injunctions, play a crucial role.

The possibility – or impossibility – of achieving quick provisional measures may very well be one of the decisive factors in the acceptance of the community patent by the users. Users, already wary about the translation costs of the community patent, should not be frightened away by making it de facto impossible to uphold the patent.

It also seems questionable whether a single court, sitting in a place that is notoriously difficult to reach by plane, would be in compliance with Art. 6 of the European Human Rights Convention.[15] According to, *e.g.*, the *Airey* case,[16] the access to a court should not only be formally possible but should also be effective. In my view that means that when it is not possible to get quick interlocutory measures in a field of law in which that is essential, it is very questionable whether creating such a court, and giving it exclusive competence, would not be a violation of Art. 6 of the ECHR. The very least that should be done to deal with this aspect is to maintain the national jurisdiction for interlocutory measures.

However, all these problems are really problems of patent people (only). The question in the title of this article, however, does not deal with patent law, but asks whether these (patent) systems could function as a model for other IP disciplines.[17]

V. The Answer Is No

This brings us back to the question in the title. In my opinion, the answer to the question is: "No, these systems should not be used as a model for IP in general". There are several reasons for this negative answer.

---

[15] Although the Union as such is not a party to this convention, it is bound to it indirectly, as all its Member States *are* parties to the convention and will have to act in accordance with it, also when voting in the Council.

[16] *Airey v. Ireland*, decision of 9-10-1979, A.32. In this case it was held necessary for a Member State to provide for legal aid in such cases where a litigant could not be expected to present his case effectively. If the absence of legal aid could be held a violation of Art. 6, why not then the placement of a court in a place very difficult to reach?

[17] Seen from that angle, an important further disadvantage of both systems, however, is that they both are too specialised and only deal with one very particular field of law: patent law.

As the systems are very different, it seems probable that for at least one of them the answer should be negative. This "no" could and should only be changed if in the near future a way is found to harmonise them and to integrate them into one coherent system.

A more important argument for the "no" answer is that these systems certainly should not be seen as exemplary in terms of the way they were developed. What we see here is that urgently necessary developments in European patent litigation are handled by two different authorities without any co-ordination.[18] The result is two systems that are not compatible enough to merge in the future because of their totally different structural set-up. This could make the confusion in Europe even worse than it already is. Certainly sooner or later the two systems should be harmonised with each other. Again: this "no" could only be changed if a way were found to integrate them into one system.

It seems nearly superfluous to point out that such a co-ordination between the judicial systems governing the Community patent on the one hand and the European bundle patents on the other hand is necessary: both patent systems will be existing in parallel and will contain patents that are verbally identical.[19] It is hardly possible to imagine a system where these identical patents would be interpreted by two[20] wholly different courts using two wholly different sets of procedural rules (which as such already should lead to diverging decisions, as different rules of evidence will lead to another set of facts to be taken into account by the court).

The question therefore is hardly whether the two systems should be co-ordinated but how this should be done. That discussion would take us far outside the scope of the present article, though. But is the negative answer to the title question of this article a problem as such? I do not think so: why should patent courts have to function as a model for other kinds of IP?

There is no reason at all why a system of litigation that is suitable for patents should also have to be recommendable for copyright and/or trademark disputes. The law on all three subjects is totally different. Moreover, it is in a totally different state of harmonisation. Finally, the different disciplines of intellectual property make totally different specialisations necessary: while patent cases can hardly be tried by judges without any technical background, that requirement does not exist for trademarks or for copyright (although nowadays a certain knowledge of information technology seems indispens-

[18] For reasons of fairness, however, it should be pointed out that the working party on the EPLA has invited the EU as an observer to all of its meetings from the very start but that the Union has hardly made use of this invitation and even has expressly stated that it had no interest in taking part in this project.

[19] Applications will designate the European Union and will probably also designate Member States of the EPC that are not (already) Member States of the Union.

[20] Disregarding for the moment the fact that there will in reality be a third "supreme" instance interpreting European patent law: the Enlarged Board of Appeal of the European Patent Office.

able). The grounds for grouping these subjects in one basket called "intellectual property" are mainly historical and bear hardly critical scrutiny. So there is no reason why they should be subject to the same system of litigation.

If we accept that, the only way the EPLA/CPC initiatives could act as a "model" were if they pointed to the possibility of creating specialised courts for these fields of law as well. The desirability of further specialised *supra*-national courts has to be weighed very carefully, however, as this could lead to the existence in a number of years of lots of specialised *supra*national courts. That would not only be very disorderly and obscure but it would also be a waste of human resources. It would also hinder proceedings in which more than one issue was at stake, *e.g.* combinations of passing off and copyright.

VI. "No" But . . .

However, I would like to take you one step beyond IP. We all know that IP people are very special and that IP law is even more special. Nevertheless, there are also other fields of law that share one of the peculiarities of IP law, namely, the cross border effect. I mean the problems caused by the divergence between the legal situation – having different states with their own separate legal systems and jurisdictions – and the economic situation in a common market – where people and businesses are operating in a number of territories as if it were one territory.

This is not only a problem with patents, trademarks, copyrights, etc., but certainly also for unlawful competition, transport, insurance, environmental issues, banking, and insolvency, to name a few.

What we really need in Europe, therefore, is a European court for all civil litigation that has interstate aspects and in which it is undesirable that the same issue could be decided upon differently.

Such a court could be realised in the framework of the Court of Justice of the EU, *e.g.* by creating[21] a "court for international civil proceedings" as a "specialised court" in the sense of Art. 28 of the European Constitution.[22] Such a court could deal with all civil litigation (probably with the exception of family law) having cross-border aspects.

If Member States are prepared to sacrifice a certain amount of their judicial autonomy by creating a community court for Community patents, there is no reason to think they would not be prepared to do the same with certain well-defined other types of litigation, if that is what is needed in practice in a real internal market. That this is not necessarily unrealistic daydreaming may become clear from the example of the EPLA project, where a number

---

[21] Next to the CPC, whose separate identity is justified by the necessary technical knowledge (whether that is introduced by way of technical judges or by way of technical assistant rapporteurs).

[22] And, as long that is not there, in the sense of Art. 225a of the Nice Treaty.

of states turned out to be willing to sacrifice their own jurisdiction on bundle patents. Their number would certainly increase if such a project were to be realised inside the European Union instead of in the framework of the European Patent Organisation.

An essential requirement for a viable system, however, would be that the Commission and the Council relinquish their centralised conception of the court system and allow this court to have regional divisions in Member States, *e.g.* along the pattern developed by the EPLA working party.[23]

Furthermore, a realistic solution should be sought for the language problem. On this issue the Union could be inspired by the EFTA, today consisting of Iceland, Liechtenstein and Norway. Although none of them have English as an official language, nevertheless the official language of the EFTA Court is English. Perhaps the EU could at some future time muster the political courage to comply with requirements of reality and follow the example of its smaller sister, thereby doing away with the problems pointed to earlier in this article.

So, on reconsideration, although the initiatives of the EPLA and the CPC in my view neither could nor should function as a model for further *supra*national courts, they could certainly function as an example of how it is possible to develop a *supra*national court for civil litigation with cross-border aspects, especially if both initiatives are allowed to cross-fertilise.

If the political will is there, this would be one small step for the Commission and the Council, but it would be one giant leap forwards for all Europeans.

VII. Conclusion

Both projects have their advantages and disadvantages, but it seems that generally the working party on the EPLA has had a better ear for the wishes of the system's users.

Nevertheless, a co-ordination of both projects is necessary and the most sensible way to do this should be to somehow subsume the EPLA system under the Community system. To that end, however, it would be necessary to redesign that system in such a way that is acceptable for the users.

Europeans should moreover start thinking about a (Community) court for all civil litigation that involves cross-border aspects and influences the functioning of the internal market.

---

[23] As a transitional solution one could imagine national courts sitting as Community courts of first instance, *cf.* the Community trademark courts, but a truly international jurisdiction would require the participation of lawyers from different Member States.

The Relationship Between Regional (Patent) Judiciary Systems in Europe and International Conventions – Smooth Coexistence or Confusion?

STEFAN LUGINBUEHL*

I. Introduction

When it became clear that the first concluded Convention on the recognition and enforcement of foreign judgments in civil and commercial matters by the Hague Conference on Private International Law[1] would probably not take effect, the United States took the initiative, in 1992, to encourage new work in that field,[2] including intellectual property. The reason for the failure of the first Convention was mainly the complexity of the texts[3] and the faltering interest of the members of the European Community (EC) to conclude the necessary bilateral agreements[4] with signatory states of the Hague Convention after the Brussels Convention[5] entered into force among them in 1973. The lack of interest has two main reasons. First, it seems that the need for a convention on recognition and enforcement with regard to European judgments is not that great,[6] probably not least because the world-wide

* Jurist, European Patent Office; member of the Swiss Delegation to the First Part of the Diplomatic Conference of the Commission II of the Hague Conference on Private International Law; former Deputy Head of the Swiss Delegation to the Working Party on Litigation of the European Patent Organisation. The author gratefully thanks Dr. Lukas Buehler and Dr. Romina Mossi for their very valuable contributions to this article. He expresses his personal views and may be contacted at sluginbuehl@epo.org.

[1] The Hague Convention of 1 February 1971 on the Recognition and Enforcement of Foreign Judgements in Civil and Commercial Matters; for on overview, *cf. Coester-Waltjen*, Die Anerkennung gerichtlicher Entscheidungen in den Haager Übereinkommen, 1993 RabelsZ 263, at 284 *et seq.*

[2] *Cf. Jametti Greiner & Bucher*, La dix-septième session de la Conférence de La Haye de droit international privé, 1994 SZIER 55, at 58.

[3] *Cf. Kessedjian*, Preliminary report on International Jurisdiction and Foreign Judgments in Civil and Commercial Matters, March 1997, No.7, available at www.acca.com/gcadvocate/hague/juris/; *McClean*, The Hague Conference's Judgments Project, in: *Fawcett* (ed.), Reform and development of private international law, essays in honor of Sir Peter North, 2002, 255, at 257 and Preliminary Document No. 17 of May 1992.

[4] *Cf. von Mehren*, Recognition and Enforcement of Foreign Judgments: A New Approach For The Hague Conference?, 57 Law & Contemp.Probs. 271 at 275 (1994).

[5] EEC – Convention on Jurisdiction and the Enforcement of Judgements in Civil and Commercial Matters of 27 September 1968, consolidated text at OJ EC C 027, at 1 (26 January 1998).

[6] *Cf. Coester-Waltjen, supra* note 1, at 289.

acceptance seems less problematic than, *e.g.*, judgments of US courts in Europe.[7] Second, the Brussels Convention, which was concluded between the states of the EC, is more extensive. It also includes rules on *jurisdiction* in civil and commercial matters[8] and consequently it is ascertained which court has international jurisdiction to adjudicate initially on the merits of the case.[9] The interest of businesses in legal certainty in that regard could thus be ensured.[10] The states of the EC were, therefore, not too interested in the applicability of the Hague Jurisdiction Convention between themselves anymore.[11] With the accession of Denmark, Greece, Ireland, Portugal, Spain and the UK to the EC, the territorial scope and significance of the Brussels Convention further increased[12] and the interest in the Hague Convention continued to falter. This effect increased with the conclusion of the Lugano Convention[13] between the EC and EFTA[14] states in 1989, a project that was mainly initiated by Switzerland.[15] The result was the creation of a judicial area on jurisdiction and the recognition and enforcement of judgments in civil and commercial matters covering the entire territory of Western

---

[7] *Cf. von Mehren*, Recognition and Enforcement of Foreign Judgments: Would an International Convention be useful? 1993 RabelsZ 449, at 452 *et seq.*

[8] For a definition of the term "civil and commercial matters", *see* Preliminary Draft Convention on Jurisdiction and Foreign Judgments in Civil and Commercial matters and Report by *Nygh* & *Pocar*, Hague Conference on Private International Law, Preliminary Document 11 of August 2000, at 29 *et seq.*, available at www.hcch.net/e/workprog/jdgm.html; for the Brussels and Lugano-Conventions, *cf. Kropholler*, Europäisches Zivilprozessrecht, Kommentar zur EuGVO und Lugano-Übereinkommen, 2002, Art. 1 No.1 *et seq.*; *Walter*, Internationales Zivilprozessrecht der Schweiz, 2002, at 164 *et seq.*; *but also Kropholler*, Die Auslegung von EG-Verordnungen zum Internationalen Privat- und Verfahrensrecht – eine Skizze –, in: *Basedow et al.* (eds.), Aufbruch nach Europa: 75 Jahre Max-Planck-Institut für Privatrecht, 2001, 583 *et seq.*

[9] *Cf. Kessedjian*, *supra* note 3, No.8.

[10] *Cf. Nygh*, The preliminary draft Hague Convention on jurisdiction and foreign judgments in civil and commercial matters, in: *Borchers & Zekoll* (eds.), International Conflict of Laws for the Third Millenium, essays in honour of Friedrich K. Juenger, 2001, 261 at 266.

[11] *Cf. Wagner*, Die Bemühungen der Haager Konferenz für Internationales Privatrecht um ein Übereinkommen über die gerichtliche Zuständigkeit und ausländische Entscheidungen in Zivil- und Handelssachen, Ein Sachstandsbericht nach dem 1. Teil der Diplomatischen Konferenz, 2001 IPrax 533, at 534.

[12] *Cf. von Mehren*, *supra* note 7, at 449 *et seq.*

[13] EC-EFTA Convention on Jurisdiction and the Enforcements of Judgments in Civil and Commercial Matters of 16 September 1988, OJ EC No. L 319/9 (25 November 1988).

[14] European Free Trade Association; www.secretariat.efta.int/; the EFTA state Liechtenstein does not participate in the Lugano Convention.

[15] *Cf. Volken*, Das Lugano-Übereinkommen, Entstehungsgeschichte und Regelungsbereich, in: *Schwander* (ed.), Das Lugano-Übereinkommen, Europäisches Übereinkommen über die gerichtliche Zuständigkeit und die Vollstreckung gerichtlicher Entscheidungen in Zivil- und Handelssachen, St. Galler Studien zum internationalen Recht, 1990, 37, at 43.

Europe.[16] Meanwhile, the Brussels Convention had been transformed into an EC Council Regulation[17] (EC Regulation 44/2001). There were, however, no major changes in regard to the relevant rules that apply to intellectual property litigation. Since Denmark did not participate in the adoption, three instruments exist in Europe side by side yet all different to some extent. The accession of new states to the EC on 1 May 2004 further enlarged the territorial scope of this judicial area to include central and Eastern Europe, a development that had already begun with the accession of Poland to the Lugano Convention[18] in 2000. The disadvantage of the EC Regulation 44/2001, as well as the Brussels and Lugano Conventions (European instruments) is that countries outside of Europe are basically excluded from this circulation of judgments.[19]

The United States' initiative of 1992 was based on the desire to facilitate the recognition and enforcement of judgments of US courts abroad[20] and to improve predictability in the enforcement. Recognition and enforcement practice were to be to clarified and simplified.[21] At the same time, the use of exorbitant jurisdictional grounds against persons not domiciled in one of the Contracting States of the Lugano and Brussels Convention was seen as problematic from a constitutional point of view.[22]

The United States proposed to the Hague Conference to create a so-called *mixed convention*;[23] that is, a mixture of a "single" and a "double convention". In a "single convention" the question of jurisdiction of Contracting States is only dealt with indirectly,[24] *i.e.*, as a condition for the recognition of

---

[16] *Cf. von Mehren, supra* note 4, at 275.

[17] EC; No. 44/2001 of 22 December 2000, OJ EC No. L 012/1 (16 January 2001). It entered into force March 1, 2002. *Cf. Beaumont*, The Brussels Convention becomes a regulation: Implications for legal basis, external competence, and contract jurisdiction, in: *Fawcett* (ed.), *supra* note 3, at 9 *et seq.*; *Rodriguez*, Die Revision des Brüsseler und Lugano-Übereinkommens im Kontext der Europäisierung von IPR und IZPR, Jusletter 4. Februar 2002, www.jusletter.ch.

[18] *Cf. Jametti Greiner*, Zur Erweiterung des Geltungsbereichs des Lugano-Übereinkommens in den mittel- und osteuropäischen Raum, insbesondere zur Situation Polens, 1998 AJP 707 *et seq.*

[19] *Cf. Walter & Walther*, International Litigation: Past Experiences and Future Perspectives, in: *Cottier & Caplazi* (eds.), 25 Swiss Papers on European Integration 41 (2000); *Jametti Greiner & Bucher, supra* note 2, at 58; but also *cf. von Mehren, supra* note 4, at 280.

[20] *Cf. Barbosa*, From Brussels to The Hague – The Ongoing Process Towards Effective Multinational Patent Enforcement, 32 IIC 729, 730 *et seq.* (2001); Hague Conference on Private International Law, U.S. State Department Collects Views To Evaluate Hague Treaty Draft, 17 WIPR (07/03) 21, at 21 (2003).

[21] *Cf. von Mehren, supra* note 7, at 454.

[22] *Cf. Jametti Greiner & Bucher, supra* note 2, at 58; *von Mehren, supra* note 7, at 454.

[23] *Cf. Baumgartner*, The Proposed Hague Convention on Jurisdiction and Foreign Judgments, Veröffentlichungen zum Verfahrensrecht, Band 32, *Stürner & Walter* (eds.), 2003, at 3.

[24] The Hague Convention of 1 February 1971 on the Recognition and Enforcement of Foreign Judgments in Civil and Commercial Matters is essentially a single convention.

judgments. In a "double convention", both jurisdictions, the direct (which the courts of the Contracting States are permitted to exercise) as well as the indirect, are regulated.[25] The mixed convention basically follows the approach of a direct jurisdiction but it is not "closed" and limited as such, and therefore allows a restricted use of jurisdiction based on national law.[26]

The Hague Conference responded positively to the initiative of the United States and it was decided at the 17th session to place the matter on the agenda for future work by the Conference.[27] A special commission elaborated a Preliminary Draft for a Hague Jurisdiction Convention (DHJC) during five meetings, which was then presented to a Diplomatic Conference to be held in two parts. The first one was held in June 2001. This draft included different proposals on the relationship of the Hague Convention with other conventions, which were submitted by delegations to the special commission. Because of disagreement in many different fields, including intellectual property, the proposals could not be discussed in depth before the conference.[28] This did not change at the conference itself. The various interests and views, mainly between the European states and the United States,[29] made it impossible to reach the necessary consensus in due time. Among these issues were patents, trademarks, copyrights and other intellectual property rights, as well as the relationship with other instruments on jurisdiction and enforcement of judgments.[30] It was decided to postpone the second part of the Diplomatic Conference until a way could be found to approach critical issues and examine whether the conditions for a successful conclusion of the negotiations could be met.[31]

One still ongoing discussion concentrates on the question of whether intellectual property should be excluded from the scope of the convention[32]

---

[25] The Lugano and Brussels Conventions are double conventions.

[26] *Cf.* Preliminary Draft Convention on Jurisdiction and Foreign Judgments in Civil and Commercial Matters and Report by *Nygh & Pocar, supra* note 8, at 26 *et seq*.

[27] *Cf. Jametti Greiner & Bucher, supra* note 2, at 61.

[28] *Cf.* Preliminary Draft Convention on Jurisdiction and Foreign Judgments in Civil and Commercial Matters and Report by *Nygh & Pocar, supra* note 8, at 117.

[29] *Cf. Hess*, Steht das geplante weltweite Zuständigkeits- und Vollstreckungsübereinkommen vor dem Aus?, 2000 IPRax 342, at 343; *von Mehren*, The Hague Jurisdiction and Enforcement Convention Project Faces an Impasse – A Diagnosis and Guidelines for a Cure, 2000 IPRax 465 *et seq.*; *Baumgartner, supra* note 23, at 6 *et seq*.

[30] At least four more major areas were numerated: The internet and e-commerce; activity based jurisdiction (jurisdiction based on "doing business"), as well as consumer and employment contracts, Preliminary Document No. 16 of February 2002, at 5, available at www.hcch.net/e/workprog/jdgm.html.

[31] *Cf.* Preliminary Document, No. 16 of February 2002, *supra* note 30, at 4; *McClean, supra* note 3, at 266.

[32] *Cf. Lucas*, The Hague Convention on Jurisdiction and Foreign Judgments in Civil and Commercial Matters, IIPI, Judicial Capacity Regarding Intellectual Property Enforcement and Dispute settlement, 12–13 September 2002, presentation available at www.iipi.org/activities/IPCourts_agenda.htm.

and regulated in a separate protocol or another kind of instrument of international law. A separation could help to find a way out of the current deadlock. This would make it possible for experts in intellectual property and the respective litigation to further explore compromises. But it would seem necessary that a clear deadline for an agreement be set to avoid a discussion on these important issues without a clear end. The question just rises whether the Hague Conference on Private International Law would be willing to follow a project that concentrates on highly controversial IP issues.

The discussions concerning the entire project showed that for the time being a "mini-convention" on exclusive choice-of-court clauses[33] seems to have the highest chances of realisation.[34] A proposal prepared by an informal working group was submitted to the special commission in December 2003.[35] Further meetings of the commission on this subject-matter had been held and it was decided to convene for a Diplomatic Conference probably in 2005 to further negotiate and conclude the convention. Any subsequent work on the remaining issues shall, however, not be precluded.[36] The period for further reflections should therefore also be used to examine the impact of various proposals concerning the relationship of the future Hague convention on jurisdiction and foreign judgments in civil and commercial matters (Hague Jurisdiction Convention, HJC) as proposed in the DHJC, as well as the impact of the latest proposal for an HCC on the regional European (patent) judiciary systems. This can also be done independently of the issue of regulating intellectual property in a separate instrument, since the question of this relationship will also have to be answered there.

II. Possible Impact of the Preliminary Draft Convention as it Stands After the First Part of the Diplomatic Conference, 6–20 June 2001

The DHJC includes an annex with three proposals for an Art. 37, which would regulate the relationship of the Convention with other such

---

[33] *Cf. Markus*, Neue Entwicklungen im internationalen Zuständigkeitsrecht (insb. LugÜ), in: *Gauch & Thürer* (eds.), Zum Gerichtsstand in Zivilsachen, Probleme der nationalen und internationalen Zuständigkeit, Symposien zum schweizerischen Recht, 2002, 127, at 139.

[34] *Cf.* Preliminary, Doc. No. 8 (corrected) of March 2003, at 3; *Schulz*, Report on the second meeting of the informal working group on the judgment project – January 6–9, 2003, Preliminary Document No. 21 of January 2003, at 4, both available at www.hcch.net/e/workprog/jdgm.html.

[35] *Cf.* Work.Doc. No 49 E, Revised, available at www.hcch.net/e/workprog/jdgm.html.

[36] *Cf. Schulz*, Report on the Work of the informal working group on the Judgment Project, in particular on the preliminary text achieved at its third meeting – 25–28 March 2003, Preliminary Document No. 22 of June 2003, at 5, available at www.hcch.net/e/workprog/jdgm.html

instruments.[37] At the first part of the Diplomatic Conference a fourth proposal was added and two alternatives discussed[38] to regulate the relationships with conventions in relation to *particular* matters (Article 37A DHJC).[39] It seems obvious that the negotiations showed the desire to differentiate between the questions of the HJC's relationship with other general instruments including provisions of jurisdiction, recognition and enforcement of judgments in relation to civil and commercial matters, and its relationship with instruments that only regulate a limited part of the scope of the HJC. The European instruments would clearly fall under the first category. So far, no decision was made on any of these proposals.

1. Relationships with Other "General" Conventions Containing Provisions on Jurisdiction, Recognition and Enforcement with Regard to Patents

a) *First proposal for Article 37 DHJC*

> 1. The Convention does not affect any international instrument to which Contracting States are or become Parties and which contains provisions on matters governed by the Convention, unless a contrary declaration is made by the States Parties to such instrument.
> 2. However, the Convention prevails over such instruments to the extent that they provide for fora not authorised under the provisions of Article 18 of the Convention.
> 3. The preceding paragraphs also apply to uniform laws based on special ties of a regional or other nature between the States concerned and to instruments adopted by a community of States.

From this suggestion of a provision it seems clear that the European instruments would basically prevail. The HJC would apply whenever the European instruments do not provide for a ground of jurisdiction or cannot be invoked for the enforcement of a foreign judgment. However, a "contracting out" clause gives Contracting States of the European instruments the possibility to decline their precedence. Such a waiver only seems realistic if the compromises reached with the HJC do provide for a better

---

[37] With regard to a possible conflict of the HJC and other instruments in general, especially in the absence of a disconnection clause, and which kind of clause is permissible in the new treaty, *cf. Schulz*, The relationship between the judgments project and other international instruments, Preliminary Document No. 24 of December 2003, available at www.hcch.net/e/workprog/jdgm.html.

[38] *Cf.* Summary of the Outcome of the Discussion in Commission II of the First Part of the Diplomatic Conference 6–20 June 2001, Annex I, available at www.hcch.net/e/workprog/jdgm.html.

[39] *Cf. also*, however, the impact on particular matters and especially the European Patent Litigation Agreement if one of the alternatives concerning the relationship with general conventions were applicable, in: *Luginbuehl*, A Stone's Throw Away from a European Patent Court: The European Patent Litigation Agreement, 25 E.I.P.R. 256, at 266 *et seq*. (2003).

all-round package, including intellectual property, than the current European instruments, so that all states bound by the European instruments would disconnect. Paragraph two of that proposal would make it clear that a disconnection of the HJC would not include Art. 18 DHJC. This provision deals with the grounds for jurisdiction that are prohibited by the HJC, the so-called black list. It sets forth the principle that grounds for jurisdiction provided for by the national law of a Contracting State are admissible only if they are based on a substantial connection between either the dispute or the defendant and the state concerned. The court that has to apply it in each specific case has to decide whether or not there is a substantial connection underlying each rule of jurisdiction.[40] A judgment based on such a prohibited ground shall not be recognised or enforced.[41] The list of examples in the provision includes the highly controversial justification in lit. e) regarding the carrying on of commercial or other activities by the defendant, or simply, "doing business", in the United States. The general nature of this connection would make it possible to bring a suit against the defendant even when the claim has no specific relationship with the activity by the defendant in the state of the court seized.[42] There was no consensus on whether this justification should be excluded from the list of prohibited grounds or not. An agreement not to include it would certainly have an impact on the jurisdiction in patent disputes in Europe. It would thus be quite easy to argue for jurisdiction of US courts[43] in patent infringement cases and, consequently, to "neutralise" the jurisdiction rules of the European instruments.[44] A certain imbalance and a stronger influence of US jurisdiction, not least with regard to the interpretation of European patent law, would be the consequence. This would, however, imply that the court asked to enforce the judgment based on that justification would have no possibility to refuse the recognition or enforcement of it, or that it would interpret Art. 18 DHJC in the same way as the court rendering the decision did.

The chances that a jurisdiction based on "doing business" will be accepted by European states are, however, rather low, since they judge this justification from a fundamental point of view as exorbitant. Thus, it is not

---

[40] *Cf.* Preliminary Draft Convention on Jurisdiction and Foreign Judgments in Civil and Commercial matters and Report by *Nygh & Pocar, supra* note 8, at 75.

[41] Article 26 DHJC.

[42] *Cf.* Preliminary Draft Convention on Jurisdiction and Foreign Judgments in Civil and Commercial Matters and Report by *Nygh & Pocar, supra* note 8, at 77.

[43] There are, however, "continuous and substantial" business contacts necessary to provide jurisdiction, *cf. Wagner, supra* note 11, at 534.

[44] This becomes even more evident in view of the general rule of Art. 2 DHJC, which provides that the HJC jurisdiction rules should already be applicable if the parties are habitually *resident* in the same Contracting States. In contrast, the European instruments request for the *domicile* in a Contracting State of the party sued.

to be expected that they will introduce it into their national law to possibly correct the emerging imbalance.

b) *Second Proposal for Article 37 DHJC*

1. a) In this Article, the Brussels Convention [as amended], Regulation [...] of the European Union, and the Lugano Convention [as amended] shall be collectively referred to as "the European instruments".
   b) A State Party to either of the above Conventions or a Member State of the European Union to which the above Regulation applies shall be collectively referred to as "European instrument States.
2. Subject to the following provisions [of this Article], a European instrument State shall apply the European instruments, and not the Convention, whenever the European instruments are applicable according to their terms.
3. Except where the provisions of the European instruments on –
   a) exclusive jurisdiction;
   b) prorogation of jurisdiction;
   c) lis pendens and related actions;
   d) protective jurisdiction for consumers or employees

are applicable, a European instrument State shall apply Articles 3, 5 to 11, 14 to 16 and 18 of the Convention whenever the defendant is not domiciled in a European instrument State.

4. Even if the defendant is domiciled in a European instrument State, a court of such a State shall apply –
   a) Article 4 of the Convention whenever the court chosen is not in a European instrument State;
   b) Article 12 of the Convention whenever the court with exclusive jurisdiction under that provision is not a European instrument State; and
   c) Articles 21 and 22 of this Convention whenever the court in whose favour the proceedings are stayed or jurisdiction declined is not a court of a European instrument State.

Note: Another provision will be needed for other conventions and instruments.

The brackets in the definition of the European instruments of paragraph one have meanwhile been partly filled, now that EC Regulation 44/2001 has become reality and received a number. However, it remains unclear when the Brussels Convention will be revised and when the already revised Lugano Convention[45] will enter into force. The reasons for this lack of clarity are, first, the delays in regard to the transfer of the Brussels Convention into EC Regulation 44/2001, which consequently also delayed the negotiations concerning the revision of the Lugano Convention. Second, since Denmark is not taking part in the adoption of that regulation,

[45] *Cf. Jametti Greiner*, Die Revision des Brüsseler und des Lugano-Übereinkommens, 1999 AJP 1135 *et seq.*; *Markus*, Revidierte Übereinkommen von Brüssel und Lugano: Zu den Hauptpunkten, 1999 SZW 205 *et seq.*, *Rodriguez*, *supra* note 17.

the Brussels Convention has to be revised. Negotiations with Denmark were not able to be concluded until now. And last but not least, the European Court of Justice (ECJ) was asked by the Council for an opinion on the situation regarding the competence to negotiate and conclude a revision of the Lugano Convention since the adoption of EC Regulation 44/2001.[46] The answer is still pending but an opinion of at least a split competence between the EC and its Member States should be expected. Re-negotiation of the revised Lugano Convention will therefore follow.

aa) Paragraphs Two and Three of the Second Proposal for Article 37 DHJC

It was made clear in paragraph two that the European instruments should in general prevail over the HJC. In comparison to the first proposal for an Art. 37, several exceptions were included in paragraphs three and four. Deserving special mention is the proposal regarding the defendant's forum in Art. 3 of the DHJC, which follows the habitual residence of the defendant. In contrast, the European instruments request the *domicile* in a Contracting State of the party sued. With a view to intellectual property, the reservations in paragraph three regarding jurisdiction in questions of prohibited grounds (Article 18 DHJC), which has already been explicated above, *torts* (Article 10 DHJC) and multiple defendants (Article 14 DHJC) are of particular interest. Upon closer examination, and possibly with the exception of Article 18 of the DHJC, this paragraph is less problematic than it seems in terms of a coexistence with the European instruments and a special eye on patent litigation. First, the regulation with regard to multiple defendants, which became famous in Europe[47] in cross-border injunctions concerning European patents,[48] seems to be of no importance anymore, as it was agreed at the First Diplomatic Conference to delete this article.[49] Second, the exceptions in that paragraph only apply if the defendant is not domiciled in a European instrument State. In view of Article 10, there would be no interference of the HJC with the relevant Article 5(3) of the European instruments, since the *tort* jurisdiction of the latter is only applicable if the defendant is domiciled *in* a European instrument State. The coexistence would therefore be smooth in that respect.

[46] *Cf. Markus, supra* note 3, at 130; *Furrer*, Internationales Zivilprozessrecht im Wandel – Quo vadis?, 2002 SJZ 141 at 149.

[47] Article 6(1) of the European instruments

[48] *Cf. Brinkhof*, Geht das grenzüberschreitende Verletzungsverbot im niederländischen einstweiligen Verfügungsverfahren zu weit?, 1997 GRUR. Int. 489 at 491 *et seq*.; *Stauder & von Rospatt & von Rospatt*, Cross-Border Protection of European Patents, 29 IIC 497, 504 *et seq*. (1998); *von Meibom & Pitz*, The Reach and Limitations of European Transborder Jurisdiction, 2 JWIP 593 at 599 *et seq*. (1999); *Guidicelli*, Cross-Border Injunctions für Europäische Patente, 2001.

[49] *Cf.* critical remarks in this book by *Norrgård*, Provisional Measures and Multiple Defendants in the MPI Proposal.

bb) Paragraph Four of the Second Proposal for Article 37 DHJC

Paragraph four is more problematic in terms of a coexistence with the European instruments. It is suggested that, even if the defendant is domiciled in a European instrument State, the courts of that state would have to apply the provisions in regard to: a) choice of law whenever the court chosen is not in a European instrument State; b) exclusive jurisdiction whenever the courts with exclusive jurisdiction under the HJC provision are those of a country that is not an European instrument State; and c) *lis pendens* and exceptional circumstances for declining jurisdiction if the court in whose favour the proceedings are stayed or jurisdiction is declined is situated in a state outside of the area of the European instruments.

The impact of lit. a on the European instruments and their regulation with regard to patent litigation will not be explored, since it was agreed upon by the working group on the judgment project that the conclusion of a special convention on agreements on the choice of court in civil and commercial matters should be further explored and a respective proposal elaborated and possibly submitted to a special commission.

Paragraph 4, lit. b, pleads for a priority of the rules of the HJC with regard to exclusive jurisdiction based on Article 12 of the DHJC even if the defendant is domiciled in a European instrument State and whenever the courts of a country that is not an European instrument State have exclusive jurisdiction under this provision. The question is, therefore, first, what impact this regulation has on the respective provisions of the European instruments. Article 22(4) of the EC Regulation 44/2001 and Article 16(4) of the Lugano and Brussels Conventions stipulate that in proceedings concerned with the registration or validity of patents, the courts of the European instrument State in which the deposit or registration has been applied for, has taken place, or is, under the terms of an European instrument convention, deemed to have taken place should have exclusive jurisdiction regardless of the domicile of the parties to the respective proceedings. The exclusive jurisdiction in proceedings concerned with the registration or validity of *European patents* is underscored by Article 22(4) of EC Regulation 44/2001 and Article Vd, Protocol one, of the Lugano and Brussels Conventions. The registration and validity proceedings include proceedings relating to validity, existence or lapse of a patent or an alleged right of priority by reason of an earlier deposit.[50] In contradiction of Swiss legal views,[51] the ECJ[52] seems not to

[50] ECJ, decision of 15 November 1983, Case 288/82, *Duijnstee v. Goderbauer.*

[51] *Cf. Mäder,* Die Anwendung des Lugano-Übereinkommens im gewerblichen Rechtsschutz, 1999, at 71 *et seq.*; *von Büren & Marbach,* Immaterialgüter- und Wettbewerbsrecht, 2002, No.798 in combination with No.812.

[52] Decision of the ECJ, *supra* note 50. It should be noted that this decision basically concerns a dispute between an employee and an employer.

qualify actions for vindication of a patent as registration or validity proceedings and consequently also excludes them from the exclusive scope.[53] Article 12 of the DHJC includes three somewhat controversial alternatives concerning the question of when the courts should have exclusive jurisdiction with regard to intellectual property. It is undisputed, however, that the courts of an HJC Contracting State should have exclusive jurisdiction in proceedings regarding the grant, registration, validity, abandonment, or revocation of a patent, among other things. The two regulations would therefore be congruent, although the HJC will again be interpreted autonomously.

Less congruent is the proposal that HJC Contracting States should also have exclusive jurisdiction in patent infringement proceedings.[54] The issue of whether there should be exclusive jurisdiction has been discussed extensively and is highly controversial.[55] The arguments shall not be repeated here. It seems clear, however, that validity and infringement are closely related in patent proceedings, since in most infringement cases the validity of the patent is immediately questioned. In the majority of countries infringement and validity are treated by the same court at the same time. It is argued that a provision with a non-exclusive jurisdiction of the HJC Contracting State in patent infringement proceedings would accept an approach that has been rejected in the patent laws of most countries.[56] It is a fact, however, that the Lugano and Brussels Conventions also do not provide for exclusive jurisdiction in infringement cases.[57] This raises the question of why this split between infringement and validity proceedings was not corrected when the Brussels Convention was transferred into EC Regulation 44/2001 and why this fact was not criticised[58] as much. Besides the view of UK courts that they

---

[53] *Cf. Stauder*, Kommentierung des Europäischen Patentübereinkommens, Protokoll über die gerichtliche Zuständigkeit und die Anerkennung von Entscheidungen über den Anspruch auf Erteilung eines europäischen Patents (Anerkennungsprotokoll), in: *Beier & Haertel & Schricker* (eds.), Münchner Gemeinschaftskommentar, 6. Lieferung, 1984, Art. 1 No.11; *Kropholler*, Europäisches Zivilprozessrecht, Kommentar zur EuGVO und Lugano-Übereinkommen, *supra* note 8, Art. 22 No.48.

[54] Art. 12(4) and (5), as well as alternative B Art. 12(5A) DHJC, Summary of the Outcome of the Discussion in Commission II of the First Part of the Diplomatic Conference 6–20 June 2001, *supra* note 38.

[55] *Cf. Sir Laddie*, Commentary: Hague *v.* Brussels Convention, in: *Hansen* (ed.), 6 Fordham Int'l. Intell. Prop. L. & Pol'y, Fordham University School of Law, Chapter 34 (2001); *Kur*, International Hague Convention on Jurisdiction an Foreign Judgments: A Way Forward for I.P.?, 24 E.I.P.R. 175 *et seq.* (2002); *Sir Laddie*, The interaction between the Hague Convention and patent rights, in: *Hansen* (ed.), 7 Fordham Int'l Intell.Prop.L. & Pol'y, Fordham University School of Law , Chapter 93 at 93–5 (2002); *Fawcett*, Special rules of private international law for special cases: What should we do about intellectual property?, in *Fawcett* (ed.), *supra* note 3, 137 at 151 *et seq.*

[56] *Cf. Sir Laddie*, in: *Hansen* (ed.), 7 Fordham Int'l Intell.Prop.L. & Pol'y, *supra* note 55.

[57] *Cf. Kropholler*, Europäisches Zivilprozessrecht, Kommentar zur EuGVO und Lugano-Übereinkommen, *supra* note 8, Art. 22 No.50 *et seq.*

[58] *Cf.* however, *Fawcett*, *supra* note 55, *at* 165 *et seq.*

cannot treat an infringement action where the validity of a foreign patent is at stake,[59] it seems that there is still distrust existing among the countries on a world-wide level.[60] A judgment may have vast consequences, such as the payment of high damages or even the closing down of local factories. On the one hand, there is consequently a certain lack of trust in the application of foreign patent law not least by courts with a profoundly different court system in infringement cases.[61] On the other hand, some states obviously seem to fear that foreign courts would influence the interpretation of their substantive law in an undesirable way and possibly influence their policy.[62] This is even more evident since it is and should be the aim of the HJC that the judgments will have to be recognised and enforced among the Contracting States of the HJC without great blocking possibilities. It seems that even the EC is starting to fear intervention in its possible future Community IP rights. During the latest negotiations for an HCC the European Commission suggested excluding such rights from the scope of the convention, because it desires exclusive jurisdiction for its future Community courts with regard to any Community IP dispute. This standpoint is clearly in line with the approach of the UK courts. Not least with a view to the future HJC it is to be expected that other states will insist on the same right. One may therefore wonder whether the time is indeed ripe for such a broad world-wide agreement on jurisdictional cooperation.

A union of infringement and validity proceedings would have as a consequence the revision of the current proposed paragraph 6 of Article 12 of the DHJC. This paragraph tries to tackle among other things the well-known problem of whether the patent infringement court should have jurisdiction to decide on the question of validity if this problem is brought up as an incidental question. While courts in the United Kingdom[63] took the view that, as mentioned earlier, the courts of a Member State are precluded by a combination of Articles 16 and 19 of the Brussels and Lugano Conventions[64] from

---

[59] The higher instance, Düsseldorf District Court, has meanwhile filed a request with the ECJ for a preliminary ruling with regard to this problem. The matter is still pending (*cf. GAT Gesellschaft für Antriebstechnik v. LuK Lamellen und Kupplungsbau Beteiligungs GmbH & Co.KG*, registered as 4/03 before the ECJ).

[60] *Cf. also* Stauder & Kur, Extraterritoriale Jurisdiktion und Streitbeilegung, in: *Schricker/Dreier/Kur* (eds.), Geistiges Eigentum im Dienst der Innovation, 2001, 151 at 165.

[61] *Cf. Sir Laddie*, in: *Hansen* (ed.), 7 Fordham Int'l Intell.Prop.L. & Pol'y, *supra* note 56, Chapter 93 at 93–3; *Kur, supra* note 55, at 177.

[62] *Cf. also Chisum*, Normative and Empirical Territoriality in Intellectual Property: Lessons from Patent Law, 37 Va.J.Int'l.L 603 at 610 *et seq.* (1997) as well as *Ortman v. Stanray Corp.*, 371 F.2d 154, 152 U.S.P.Q. (BNA) 163 (7th Cir. 1967) and *Packard Instrument Co. v. Beckman Instruments, Inc.*, 346 F. Supp. 408, 175 U.S.P.Q. (BNA) 282 (N.D. Ill. 1972).

[63] *Coin Controls Ltd. v. Suzo International (UK) Ltd. and others* All E.R. 45 (Ch.D.) (1997), *Fort Dodge Animal Health Ltd. v. Akzo Nobel NV*, 29 IIC 804 (1998).

[64] Articles 22 and 25 EC Regulation 44/2001.

trying an infringement action where validity of a foreign patent is an issue, the Court of Appeal in the Netherlands took a slightly different view and declared that the jurisdiction must be decided on the basis of the claim stated in the summons.[65] In principle, it has to stay the infringement proceedings until the foreign court has pronounced judgment in the nullity issue except the court takes the view that the challenge to validity clearly has no chance of succeeding.[66] The suggested provision pleads for a solution of giving the infringement court the right to decide on the validity if it is in question incidentally. The ruling should, however, have no binding effect in subsequent proceedings, even if they are between the same parties. The reason lies in the fact that the effect of an incidental finding on validity differs in a variety of legal systems.[67] The result of the current proposal would be a split of validity and infringement proceedings[68] if a counterclaim for revocation is brought up in an infringement case.

Paragraph 4, lit. c, provides that the provisions of *lis pendens* (Article 21 DHJC) and exceptional circumstances for declining jurisdiction (Article 22 DHJC) are applicable whenever the court in whose favour the proceedings are stayed or jurisdiction is declined is not a court of a European instruments state. Both proposals are a compromise between the Anglo-Saxon doctrine of *forum non conveniens* and the principle of priority.[69] Their application is of a general nature and will impact all proceedings, including patent proceedings, whenever the HJC is applicable. The question of *lis pendens* is regulated only to a certain extent in the European instruments. While the question was basically left to national law in the Brussels and Lugano Conventions,[70] it is now included in EC Regulation 44/2001 with its Article 27 in combination

---

65 For an overview *cf. Bragiel,* "A Funny Thing Happened on the Way to the Forum" – Actionability in the United Kingdom of Infringements of Intellectual Property Rights Committed Abroad, IPQ, 135 *et seq.* (1999); *Wadlow,* Enforcement of Intellectual Property in European International Law, 1998, 1–51 *et seq.*

66 *Expandable Grafts Partnership v. Boston Scientific BV,* F.S.R. 352 (1997)*; cf. Brinkhof,* The Enforcement of Patent Rights in the Netherlands, in: Festschrift für Dieter Stauder, 31 IIC 706, at 715 (2000); *Fawcett, supra* note 55, at 144; *Barbosa, supra* note 20, at 737 *et seq.*

67 *Cf. Schulz,* Report of the work of the informal working group on the judgments project, in particular on the preliminary text achieved at its third meeting – 25-28 March 2003, *supra* note 36, at 12, *Dogauchi/Hartley,* Preliminary Draft Convention on Exclusive Choice of Court Agreements, Draft Report, Prel.Doc. No. 25, at 12, available at www.hcch.net/e/workprog/jdgm.html.

68 *Cf. Fawcett, supra* note 55, at 162.

69 *Cf. Bucher,* Vers une convention mondiale sur la compétence et les jugements étrangers, 2000 SJ 77 at 105 *et seq.; Nygh, supra* note 10, at 281 *et seq.*; *Wagner, supra* note 11, at 543 *et seq.*

70 The ECJ declared in *Zelger* v. *Salinitri,* 7 June 1984, Case 129/83, that Art. 21 of the Brussels Convention must be interpreted as meaning that the court first seized is the one before which the requirements for proceedings to become definitely pending are first fulfilled, such requirements to be determined in accordance with the national law of each of the courts concerned.

with Article 30. The precise point in time when a claim is deemed to be pending before a court consequently varies in Europe. Some states decided that it is the date of filing the claim at the court, while others decided that a valid pending claim is given as soon as the defendant is properly informed. Yet other states regard a court as seized of a matter in which notification is required before filing as soon as the documents are delivered to the person or authority responsible for service.[71] In the territory where EC Regulation 44/2001 applies, the precise point of *lis pendens* is now fixed at the date of the filing with the responsible authority.[72] It is, however, on the condition that the plaintiff has subsequently not failed to take the steps required to have service effected on the defendant.

It is suggested that this *lis pendens* rule also be incorporated into the revised Lugano Convention.[73] The provision differs slightly from that of the DHJC. On the one hand, Article 21 of the DHJC requires, for a stay of proceedings of the second court seized, that between "the same parties" (*inter easdem partes*) the "same cause of action, irrespective of the relief sought" (*eadem res*) is *lis pendens* abroad. In regards to the requirement of *eadem res*, the DHJC is more precise than the European instruments.[74] With a view to the exact point of *lis pendens*, paragraph 5 of Article 21 of the DHJC, on the other hand, provides that a court shall be deemed to be seized when the document instituting the proceedings or an equivalent document is lodged with the court; or, if such document has to be served before being lodged with the court, when it is received by the authority responsible for service or served on the defendant. This solution obviously leaves more room for a particular national regulation.[75] Unlike the solution in EC Regulation 44/2001, it could still be the time of serving the document on the defendant that is the relevant point of *lis pendens*.

The proposal in paragraph six of Article 21 of the DHJC is of particular interest with regard to patent proceedings; it suggests that, if in the action before the court first seized the plaintiff seeks a determination that it has no obligation to the defendant, and if an action seeking substantive relief is

[71] *Cf.* Preliminary Draft Convention on Jurisdiction and Foreign Judgments in Civil and Commercial matters and Report by *Nygh & Pocar, supra* note 8, at 87.

[72] In the Principles and Rules of Transnational Civil Procedure of ALI/UNIDROIT it was also suggested that the exact time of *lis pendens* is "the time a claim is first asserted", which provides for the same approach; *cf.* Principle 28.2., Discussion Draft No. 4, April 18, 2003, http://www.ali.org/TransCivilDD4.pdf.

[73] *Cf.* Art. 23a Proposal for a revised Lugano Convention and *Markus, supra* note 45, at 214 *et seq.*; *Rodriguez, supra* note 17, No.70 *et seq.*

[74] *Cf. also Walter,* Ausländische Rechtshängigkeit und Konnexität nach altem und neuem Lugano-Übereinkommen, in: *Spühler* (ed.), Internationales Zivilprozess- und Verfahrensrecht, 2003, 127 at 141 *et seq.*

[75] The same suggestion is also made in Intellectual Property: Principles Governing Jurisdiction, Choice of Law, and Judgements in Transnational Disputes of ALI/UNIDROIT, Preliminary Draft No. 1, January 17, 2003, Article 11.6.

brought in the court second seized, then the court first seized shall suspend the proceedings at the request of a party if the court second seized is expected to render a decision capable of being recognised under the HJC. This principle would stop the effects of so-called "torpedo actions".[76] It would no longer be possible to block a faster jurisdiction from dealing with proceedings concerning a patent and/or an alleged infringement by an action for declaration of non-infringement of the same patent before another court where the judicial system is not particularly quick. This regulation would certainly be a step forward as regards the abuse partly exercised in Europe.[77]

The court seized may also decline jurisdiction in favour of the court second seized under the principles of Article 22. The *forum non conveniens* doctrine, which is not incorporated into the European instruments and which in continental Europe is not greeted with much enthusiasm, can however only be implemented in a very limited way. The court first seized may only suspend its proceedings if in the particular case it is clearly inappropriate for that court to exercise jurisdiction and if a court of another state has jurisdiction and is clearly more appropriate to resolve the dispute. The concept is rather that of a transfer of jurisdiction than of declining jurisdiction.[78] Thus, if a European court were of the opinion that a case of infringement of an Argentinean patent should be dealt with before a court in Argentina, *e.g.* because there is a closer relation to the matter in dispute, although the defendant has its domicile in Europe, it could decline jurisdiction based on these principles. This providing the court with such a possible discretion has been criticised.[79]

c) *Third Proposal for Article 37 DHJC*

Judgments of courts of a Contracting State to this Convention based on jurisdiction granted under the terms of a different international convention ("other Convention") shall be recognised and enforced in courts of Contracting States to this Convention which are also Contracting States to the other Convention. This provision shall not apply if, by reservation under Article . . ., a Contracting State chooses –

a) not to be governed by this provision, or
b) not to be governed by this provision as to certain designated other conventions.

This proposal concentrates on the recognition and enforcement of decisions rendered on the grounds of jurisdiction of other conventions. Judgments

---

[76] *Cf. Franzosi*, Worldwide Patent Litigation and the Italian Torpedo, 19 E.I.P.R. 382 *et seq.* (1997).

[77] *Cf. also Kur, supra* note 55, at 180; but *also Franzosi*, Torpedoes Are Here to Stay, 33 IIC 154 *et seq.* (2002). In that regard, *cf. also* the interesting ECJ decision of 9 December 2003, Case C-116/02, *Gasser v. MISAT.*

[78] *Cf. Nygh, supra* note 10, at 284.

[79] *Cf. e.g. Walter, supra* note 8, at 104.

based on the jurisdiction of a European instrument concerning patents could therefore be recognised and enforced in a European instrument State, although party to the HJC, if it does not express a reservation under this article. This provision would therefore be in smooth coexistence with the European instruments with regard to its recognition and enforcement provisions as long as no European instrument State expressed a reservation concerning jurisdiction under the terms of one of these instruments. A reservation by one or several Contracting States of the European instruments seems again not very realistic, not least because these states are bound among each other by the European instruments. A possible disconnection would therefore be realised by all Contracting States. Nevertheless, the limitation of this proposal to the recognition and enforcement of judgments based on jurisdiction granted under the terms of a different international convention does not mean that the jurisdiction and enforcement provisions of the HJC would be excluded. They are applicable without any restriction. If no reservation were given, a holder of a European patent would therefore basically be able to choose whether to enforce a judgment rendered by a court in a European instrument State based on the regulations of the HJC or the European instrument. This proposal could therefore lead to misuse and legal uncertainty.

d) *Fourth Proposal for Article 37 DHJC*

> Article 2 .Territorial scope
> Insert the words in brackets in the chapeau of paragraph 1, as follows:
> 1. The provisions of Chapter II shall apply in the courts of a Contracting State unless all the parties are habitually resident in that state [or in the territory of a regional economic integration organisation that is a Contracting Party under Article [. . .]. However, even if all the parties are habitually resident in that [Contracting] State [or Party] –
> [. . .]

Whereas the first three proposals took the approach of a disconnection of the general rules in a more or less extensive way by a special regulation, this proposal suggests limiting the territorial scope of the HJC. The application of the general territorial scope of the HJC would be excluded if both parties have their habitual residence in the same Contracting State or in the territory of a regional economic organisation that is a Contracting Party, that is to say, in the EC. The entire Chapter II, which includes the jurisdiction part of the HJC would therefore be excluded as soon as both parties are habitually resident in the territory of the EC. This would clearly appear to be the most extended disconnection of the HJC jurisdiction regulations with a view to the European instruments. However, Article 2 of the DHJC[80] again lists the exceptions of paragraph four of the second proposal.[81] Furthermore, the proposal would not include the Contracting States of the Lugano

80 *See* Annex.
81 *Cf.* 2.1.2.b

Convention that are not members of the EC since the EFTA would not be able to become a party to the HJC. The limitation of scope with regard to the territory of the EC would consequently reduce the Hague Jurisdiction Convention to a "single" convention in that area that only deals with recognition and enforcement. Judgments rendered in a Contracting State of the HJC would in any case be enforceable in another Contracting State based on the applicable provision of the HJC. The proposal that looked more extensive than the second proposal for an Article 37 of the DHJC at the beginning actually leads to a more limited solution. If therefore a holder of a European patent who habitually resides in Switzerland would like to sue an infringer in the United Kingdom, the HJC jurisdiction rules would apply. However, if the holder resides in Germany, it would be EC Regulation 44/2001 that is applicable.

2. Relationship with other Conventions Containing Provisions on Jurisdiction, Recognition and Enforcement, in Particular of Patents

First Proposal for Article 37A

This Convention shall not affect any conventions to which the Contracting States are or will be parties and which, in relation to particular matters, govern jurisdiction or the recognition or enforcement of judgments.

Second Proposal for Article 37A

This Convention shall not affect any conventions to which the Contracting States are or will be parties and which, in relation to particular matters, govern jurisdiction or the recognition or enforcement of judgments, provided that the application of such other convention shall not affect the rights and obligations under this Convention of any State Party that is not a Party to such other convention.

Basically, there is a common understanding that the HJC should not affect conventions to which the Contracting States are or will be parties and which, in relation to particular matters, govern jurisdiction or the recognition or enforcement of judgments. In Europe there are several agreements or projects for such agreements that regulate particular matters with regard to jurisdiction and recognition and enforcement of patents, which would consequently be treated primarily based on the basic principle of lex specialis derogat legi generali.[82] To be mentioned are e.g. the EPO protocol on recognition[83] and the possible European Patent Litigation Agreement

---

[82] With regard to the problem of the differentiation of specificity and generality, *cf. Schulz*, *supra* note 37, at 18.

[83] Protocol on Jurisdiction and the recognition of decisions in respect of the right to the grant of a European patent of 5 October 1973. *Cf. Stauder*, in: *Beier & Haertel & Schricker* (eds.), *supra* note 53.

(EPLA).[84] The future[85] Community Patent Regulation[86] with its Community Patent Court[87] would not be included in the current proposals. This is derivable indirectly from the terminology of the proposals for an Article 37, which always use the term "instruments" whenever more than only conventions should be considered. The wording would therefore have to be changed if this regulation should fall under the applicability of this provision. Since it is the idea of the EC that Community IP rights should exclusively be dealt before Community courts, it would seem the easier solution to let the possible Community Patent Regulation and directly related instruments[88] prevail over the HCJ rather than foreseeing all kind of exceptions with regard to the jurisdiction, recognition and enforcement in the HJC. This would, however, provoke the question whether patent rights should not be excluded completely from the scope of the jurisdiction convention.

In dispute is the question whether these "special" conventions should affect the rights and obligations of the HJC Contracting States that are not parties to these conventions. The above-mentioned special conventions were introduced mainly to specialise the current general proceedings, to make them more efficient and to improve legal certainty. It could therefore be a disadvantage for certain holders of European patents if these special agreements were not binding for all HJC Contracting States. Such a regulation could again lead to legal uncertainty, since the courts would have to decide on the applicable jurisdiction and enforcement provisions. Without a common court of the HJC states[89] ensuring a harmonised interpretation of these rules, there is a great risk that the different courts will also apply the provisions differently.[90]

---

[84] *Cf.* in this book: *Willems,* The EPLA Project and the Forthcoming Community Patent System – A Model for IP in Gerneral?, and *Luginbuehl, supra* note 39.

[85] *Cf. Luginbuehl,* Europäische Patentorganisation: Gemeinschaftspatent seiner Realisierung ein Schritt näher, 2003 sic! 378 *et seq.*

[86] *Cf.* Proposal for a Council Regulation on the Community Patent – Revised Text, Presidency, Doc. No. 15086/03 (PI 122), Brussels, 21 November 2003.

[87] *Cf.* the critical words regarding the court regulations in: *Pagenberg,* Community Patent – Main Features and Comments, 34 IIC 281, 283 *et seq.* (2003); *Tilmann,* Gemeinschaftspatent mit einem zentralen Gericht, 2003 GRUR Int. 381 *et seq.*

[88] *Cf.* Proposal for a Council decision establishing the Community Patent Court and concerning appeals before the Court of First instance, COM (2003) 828 final, 2003/0324 (CNS), Brussels, 23 December 2003, and Proposal for a Council decision conferring jurisdiction on the Court of Justice in disputes relating to the Community patent, COM (2003) 827 final, 2003/0326 (CNS), Brussels, 23 December 2003.

[89] *Cf. Sir Laddie,* in: *Hansen* (ed.), 6 Fordham Int'l Intell.Prop.L. & Pol'y, *supra* note 55.

[90] *Cf. von Mehren, supra* note 29, *at* 466; *also cf. H.P. Walter,* Die Auslegung staatsvertraglichen und harmonisierten Rechts: Gewicht und Bedeutung von Entscheidungen ausländischer Gerichte und der Beschwerdekammern des EPA, 1998 GRUR 866 *et seq.*

III. Possible Impact of the Draft Text on Choice of Court Agreements on the Regional (Patent) Judiciary Systems in Europe

A draft provision dealing with the relationship of the Convention on exclusive agreements on choice of court (Draft Hague Choice-of-Courts Convention; DHCC) with other international instruments has been introduced only in the latest proposal.[91] This draft provision reads as follows:

> Art. 23 Relationship with other international instruments
>
> 1. For the purpose of this Article, "international instrument" means an international treaty or rules made by an international organisation under an international treaty.
>
> 2. Subject to paragraphs 4 and 5, this Convention does not affect any international instrument to which Contracting States are parties and which contains provisions on matters governed by this Convention, unless a contrary declaration is made by the Contracting States by such instrument.
>
> 3. This Convention does not affect the ability of one or more Contracting States to enter into international instruments which contain provisions on matters governed by this Convention, provided that these instruments do not affect, in the relationship of such Contracting States with other Contracting States, the application of the provisions of this Convention.
>
> 4. Where a Contracting State is also a party to an international instrument which contains provisions on matters governed by this Convention, this Convention shall prevail in matters relating to jurisdiction except where—
>
> a) the chosen court is situated in a State in which the instrument is applicable; and
>
> b) all the parties are resident [only] either in a State in which the instrument is applicable or in a non-Contracting State.
>
> 5. This Convention shall not restrict the application of an international instrument in force between the State for the purposes of obtaining recognition or enforcement of a judgment. [However the judgment shall not be recognised or enforced to a lesser extent than under this Convention.]
>
> 6. [Notwithstanding] [Subject to] paragraphs 4 and 5, this Convention does not affect the ability of one or more Contracting States to continue to apply or to enter into international instruments which, in relation to specific subject matters, govern jurisdiction or the recognition or enforcement of judgments, even if all States concerned are parties to this Convention.

The European instruments would obviously prevail over the HCC, where the chosen court is situated in a state in which one of the instruments and the HCC is applicable and all the parties are resident either in a state in which the same instrument and the HCC is applicable or in a non-HCC Contracting State.

---

[91] *Cf.* Work. Doc. No 110 E, Revised, available at www.hcch.net/e/workprog/jdgm.html.

The subject has until now only been discussed in the responsible informal working group. It became clear that there can be only one case of an overlap between the HCC and the European instruments in regard to jurisdiction; that is to say, where a court in a state in which the European instruments apply was chosen and one of the parties is resident in a state where the European instruments apply, but the other is resident in a state that is party to the Hague Convention.

It seemed to be the general feeling in the working group that the HCC should take precedence in such a case. These feelings were consequently implemented into Art. 23 DHCC. It was, however, also proposed that the HCC should not seek to prevail over other instruments binding a HCC Contracting State in its relations with non-Contracting States. This would again be an approach questioning the idea of a multilateral agreement. An alternative proposal which was also discussed would be to replace paragraph 4 b) with the following: "b) a party is resident in a non-HCC Contracting State in which the instrument is applicable, or there is some other relevant connection between the parties or the dispute and such a State". The question rising here would be whether "doing business" in that state would constitute a relevant connection in the sense of the aforementioned paragraph.

The general applicability of the HCC would certainly have an impact on the European instruments and the regional European (patent) judiciary system. The question therefore is what the scope of the HCC should be in regard to patent litigation. As discussed in the context of the drafts for an HJC[92] also for this convention it is suggested that it should not apply to patent rights, except in proceedings pursuant to a contract which licenses or assigns such patent rights, possibly including proceedings for infringement of the right to which the contract relates. The court chosen based on the HCC could therefore not deal with patent infringements. Furthermore, validity issues in general would be out of the scope of the convention as long as the question of validity is a principle matter of the issue and does not arise merely as an incidental question (Art. 2(2)(k) in combination with Art. 2(3) DHCC). It is, however, proposed that recognition or enforcement of the judgment may be refused to the extent that it is inconsistent with a judgment on the validity of the patent right rendered in the state under the law of which the patent right arose.[93] A judgment where the question of validity is decided incidentally to contractual questions would consequently not even have an *inter partes* effect beyond the judgment on the contractual dispute.[94] In addition, it is still under discussion whether the recognition or enforcement of such a judgment could be postponed or refused at the request of one of the parties if proceedings on validity are pending in the state under the law of which *inter alia* the patent right arose. Such a refusal would not prevent a

---

[92] *Cf.* II 1 b) bb).

[93] *Cf.* Art. 10 (2) DHCC.

[94] *Cf.* also II 1 b) bb).

subsequent application for recognition or enforcement of the judgment.[95] A regulation of this kind would only make sense if there is a contradiction of the decisions on the question of the validity of the patent to be expected.

It that regard it has furthermore to be decided whether the chosen court could stay its proceedings in which the question of validity was raised incidentally until this question is decided by the responsible court in the state where the patent right arose.[96]

The proposal makes clear that there would again be a split of proceedings if a counterclaim on validity was tried. It is no surprise that this proposal has already been criticised because it would result in the "toggling" of a dispute between the chosen court and the courts of the country that created the intellectual property rights for the purpose of deciding a single issue.[97] The main reason for that proposal was that the grant of registered industrial property rights is an act of state,[98] and that the invalidation of such an act should not be subject to party autonomy but limited to the authorities of the state whose authorities had granted the right.[99] It was argued that an exclusion from the scope of the HCC would preserve the status quo in this respect, since in many national laws as well as international instruments this is subject to exclusive jurisdiction.

As mentioned above, the proposal includes litigations concerning licenses and assignments with regard to intellectual property rights, including patent rights, into the scope of the convention. Such an approach seems more than questionable: The realisation of this proposal would pick out only a small piece of the versatility and mutuality of intellectual property litigation and especially patent litigation. Additionally, license agreements are often directly related to the validity and infringement of a patent, which would be entirely out of the jurisdiction of the chosen court, unless the Diplomatic Conference decides that the chosen court can decide about the infringement of the patent to which the license contract relates. But in any case, such a cascade regulation seems not very desirable and could provoke delays and abuse. Furthermore, it could also provide for legal uncertainty and it would have to be clarified what the exact impact on the possible future European Patent Court would be.

With regard to the conventions on particular matters it seems still open whether they should prevail on the HCC. The best solution would seem, with a view to the principle of *lex specialis derogat legi generali*, that the HCC

---

[95] *Cf.* Art. 10 (3) DHCC.

[96] *Cf.* Art. 6 DHCC.

[97] *Cf.* Hague Conference on Private International Law, U.S. State Department Collects Views To Evaluate Hague Treaty Draft, *supra* note 20, at 22.

[98] *Cf. Dogauchi/Hartley, supra note* 67, at 11; *cf.*, however, already *Ulmer*, Die Immaterialgüterrechte im internationalen Privatrecht, Max-Planck-Institut für ausländisches und internationales Patent-, Urheber- und Wettbewerbsrecht, Schriftenreihe zum gewerblichen Rechtschutz, Band 38, 1975, at 9.

[99] *Cf. Schulz, supra* note 36, at 10.

would only prevail with regard to any choice-of-court agreement within the scope of the "special" convention. This would certainly presume that the case falls within the scope of the HCC and that a choice-of-court agreement is not excluded by the "special" convention. As regards the applicability of the HCC to the EPLA Contracting States, it would be the easiest solution if the European Patent Judiciary,[100] the international organisation to be created by the EPLA,[101] became a party to the HCC. This would, however, provoke very difficult (political) problems.

IV. Conclusion

The different proposals here basically seek to highlight in detail the aspects for which co-ordination is needed between the HJC and the European instruments, and to strike a balance between their respective requirements.[102] Depending on the proposal, this balance goes more in the direction of the applicability of the HJC or of the regional instruments. The relationship to the regional (patent) judiciary systems in Europe is consequently more or less problematic. Some of the proposals of coexistence are, however, very complicated and difficult to understand.[103] But if one bears in mind that the basic aim of the Hague Conference is to create a world-wide applicable convention on jurisdiction, recognition and enforcement of judgments in civil and commercial matters, there should be no room anymore for regional conventions on the same general aspects. This would be different regarding conventions in relation to particular matters which provide for highly special solutions. An agreement on that point, however, only seems possible if in the end a compromise is reached that ensures not only legal certainty but also a common interpretation of the conventions. Legal certainty seems currently only within reach if a balance between the court jurisdictions can be achieved. But even this overview of the proposals for a disconnecting clause has brought to light the obvious risk that the US jurisdiction could prevail over the other jurisdictions. Some of the proposals would make it easy for US courts to declare jurisdiction, which would have a certain imbalance effect of jurisdiction between the continents. It would consequently give the US courts a greater opportunity to keep their citizens and companies away from foreign jurisdiction but as a consequence also to introduce their views on the interpretation of foreign substantive law[104] and

---

[100] *Cf. Luginbuehl*, A New Court Would Help Resolve the European Patents Mess, 4 European Affairs, No. 1, 109 at 111 (2003).

[101] *Cf. Luginbuehl, supra* note 39, *at* 260.

[102] *Cf.* Preliminary Draft Convention on Jurisdiction and Foreign Judgments in Civil and Commercial matters and Report by *Nygh & Pocar, supra* note 8, at 118.

[103] *Cf. also Bucher, supra* note 69, at 118.

[104] *Cf. Geller,* International Intellectual Property, Conflicts of Laws and Internet Remedies, 22 E.I.P.R. 125 at 127 (2000); but also *Jansen/Michaels*, Die Auslegung und Fortbildung ausländischen Rechts, 2003 ZZP 3 *et seq.*

not least also in the patent field, which is a very important economic policy instrument. This would not be a desirable thought for Europe as long as the substantive (patent) law has not yet been harmonised between these two continents and its common interpretation ensured.

Another point that makes the Europeans and maybe others hesitant is the typical US preference for unilateral solutions and for exercising international leadership in transnational litigation on US terms only.[105] But there are also the well-known differences existing between their judicial systems and that of the United States. With regard to patent proceedings it seems just not imaginable to some and, as the judgments show, sometimes actually without plausible reasons that a jury of non-technicians and legal experts may decide correctly in a highly technical patent case.[106] Furthermore, a common court should be established that ensures a harmonised interpretation of the conventions.

As long as there is no convergence on these points and the parties involved do not give up their conviction of the superiority of their own system,[107] it will be difficult to create the necessary trust in each other's jurisdiction[108] and to conclude an agreement that will suit the actual needs of the users. As long as this approach is not reality, the Europeans will understandably continue to insist on a partly exclusive jurisdiction of their courts and that the regional judiciary systems, including such on particular matters as intellectual property, prevail to some extent.[109] The HJC and the European instruments would exist in parallel in a more or less complicated relationship. One may only hope that the confusion can somehow be kept under control for the sake of the users of the system and the judges who would have to apply the resulting complicated conflict regulations.

---

[105] *Cf. Baumgartner, supra* note 23, at 46.

[106] For a US point of view, *cf. Adamo*, International Panel: Compare and Contrast the Crucial Issues in Determining Choice of Jurisdiction, IBC's Ninth Annual Conference on International Patent Disputes, London 2–3 June 2003.

[107] *Cf. von Mehren, supra* note 29, at 466.

[108] *Cf. Hess, supra* note 29, at 343.

[109] *Cf. Sir Jacob*, International Intellectual Property Litigation in the Next Millennium, The Deioma Lecture, October 1999, 32 Case W.Res.J Int'l L. 507 at 514 *et seq.* (2000); *Kur, supra* note 55, at 183.

Part Two

Choice of Law

I.

General Principles

Choice of Law and Intellectual Property

RICHARD FENTIMAN*

We may begin with an imaginary case, though one grounded in reality.[1] C (the claimant) and D (the defendant) are both resident in Dystopia. C claims in proceedings in Dystopia that D has infringed its copyright by conduct in Utopia, a neighbouring state. D is liable under Utopian law, but not that of Dystopia. Both states subscribe to the principle of territoriality. Utopian law protects against infringements in Utopia; Dystopian private international law treats foreign copyright claims as justiciable, and C argues that Utopian law governs as the law of the place of infringement. There are no special choice-of-law rules in Dystopian law governing such cases, but the general rule is that issues in tort are governed by the law of the place of the wrong. This rule is, however, qualified. A court may apply a law other than the *lex loci delicti* if it has a more significant relationship with the wrong.[2] Dystopian law provides that such a relationship shall be determined by reference to factors such as the policies of the forum and of any other relevant state; the expectations of the parties; and the requirements of justice.[3]

Which law governs? D's counsel will no doubt argue that the common residence of the parties is decisive because it suggests that Dystopia has an interest in regulating the parties' relationship. He may urge that the connection with Dystopia is reinforced if it transpires that the infringing act was orchestrated in Dystopia, following decisions made there. If, as a result, Dystopian law governs D will have won not merely the choice-of-law contest, but outright. This is because Dystopian copyright law – the *internal* law of Dystopia – protects only against infringements in Dystopia, offering no protection against infringements elsewhere.

But C's counsel may reply that the fact that Dystopian copyright law does not apply in such cases has a different implication. It suggests not merely that C has no rights under Dystopian law (as D's counsel contends), but that it was never intended that Dystopian law should apply in such cases at all. She might suggest that Dystopian law therefore has no interest in the matter – for what could be better evidence of a state's interests than the fact that its legislation does not apply in a given case? Conversely, Utopian law plainly was intended to apply in such cases, and irrefutably has an interest in governing.

* Reader in Private International Law, University of Cambridge, e-mail: rgf1000@cam.uc.uk.

[1] *Pearce v. Ove Arup Ltd* [1999] 1 All ER 769 (CA).

[2] A test resembling that under Sections 11 and 12 of the UK Private International Law (Miscellaneous Provisions) Act 1995.

[3] Rather in the manner of the *American Restatement Second, Conflict of Laws*, §6.

Which argument prevails? Posit the following outcome. The court finds for the claimant and applies Utopian law. The judge holds that inevitably Utopian law should govern. As the words of the relevant Dystopian and Utopian statutes made clear it was the policy of the latter to govern such cases and the policy of the latter not to do so. Differently expressed Utopian law has a legitimate and overarching claim to protect copyright owners from infringements within Utopia, while Dystopian law has none. Moreover, let us speculate that the judge identifies a conceptual flaw in the defendant's argument. The defendant's counsel had assumed that the fact that Dystopian law did not apply to infringements elsewhere meant only that, if Dystopian law were the governing law, C would have no claim. But in truth (the judge said), it indicated that Dystopian law could never be the applicable law, because it showed that it had no conceivable relationship with the wrong.

But we may elaborate further. Suppose that the Dystopian Law Reform Commission, troubled by this decision, considers legislation in this area. What should be the choice-of-law rule? Those considering the matter are mindful of the advantages of flexibility, reflected in the existing rule, described above. But they quickly conclude that a special rule is required for intellectual property infringements. They decide that the law of the country whose protection is sought by the claimant should apply without qualification; by doing so they favour invariable resort to the *lex protectionis* – in effect, the law of the country where the infringement occurs. In a case such as that previously considered the law of Utopia would thus apply without argument. The Law Reform Commission comes to this conclusion for several reasons. First, the law of the place of infringement has an overriding – indeed, unique – interest in governing, which should be respected. Secondly, it would be pointless to provide a flexible exception to that rule because no other law could have a more significant relationship with the wrong. Thirdly, it might lead to inefficiency to provide for such an exception because it would encourage litigation to identify the most significantly related law when the answer is clear at the outset. Fourthly, any other conclusion might lead to absurdity because it implies that the most significantly related law might be one that has no interest in regulating the issue.

As this suggests, it is perhaps obvious which law should govern the infringement of intellectual property rights. The arguments for the *lex protectionis* seem compelling, even unassailable. But the reasons are not always easy to state. And the conceptual dilemmas at the heart of the problem are not always exposed. The purpose of the following remarks is to explain the conceptual background to this troubling area, and to articulate the theoretical problems at its core. In doing so, the discussion is more limited than it might have been. For ease of exposition, it takes as its central case the infringement of copyright, rather than the infringement of other rights, or issues concerning the transfer or ownership of intellectual property. And its purpose is not to supply solutions, but to expose the logic of the problem.

I. A Special Case?

Which law should govern rights in intellectual property?[4] The question conceals several distinct issues, each at first sight comfortably familiar. The creation of such rights on the one hand, and their subsequent enjoyment on the other, pose problems belonging respectively to the law of property, and the law of tort. And voluntary dealings in such property, by way of transfer or licence belong, no doubt obviously, to the law of contract.[5] But discerning the law applicable to issues in intellectual property is less straightforward than this implies. True the issues arising may be classified in familiar ways. And it is easy enough in principle to approach the problem using techniques familiar to the conflicts lawyer. The task as ever is to identify the law having the most significant relationship with the issue in question, even if in the end we favour some canonical rule not an open-textured test – such as the rule that the *lex protectionis* governs the infringement of intellectual property rights. This in turns involves a familiar litany of questions: which state is most interested; what are the parties' expectations; which solution best captures the law's economic and social context? But this belies some profound difficulties, and the proper choice-of-law regime for intellectual property is a matter of much debate.

The following remarks are not intended to suggest how the necessary choice-of-law rules might be formulated, with particular solutions to specific problems.[6] Their purpose instead is to consider the relationship between intellectual property and choice of law at a strategic and conceptual level. It is at best a prolegomenon to considering the question – though one that largely supplies the answer. Our concern in particular is with the ways in which (rightly or wrongly), the character of intellectual property apparently cabins and controls the role of the choice-of-law process. The distinctiveness (if not uniqueness) of intellectual property might be thought to arise in three ways:

> First, intellectual property protection has a public character – though whether it truly belongs to private or public law is a keenly contested issue. Respect for national interests, both economic and cultural, becomes especially important in this context. Rights in

---

[4] The literature is large, and growing. The present article draws in particular on the following sources: *Ulmer*, Intellectual Property Rights and the Conflict of Laws, 1978; *Fawcett and Torremans*, Intellectual Property and Private International Law, 1998; *Ginsburg*, Recueil des cours, 1998; *Goldstein*, International Copyright: Principles, Law and Practice, 2001; *Lucas and Lucas*, Propriété Littéraire et Artistique, 2nd ed., 2002; *Cornish*, Intellectual Property, 5th ed., 2003; *van Eechoud*, Choice of Law in Copyright and Related Rights, 2003.

[5] Although which issues are contractual, and which proprietary, may be debated.

[6] Such as those canvassed by the American Law Institute; *see* Intellectual Property: Principles Governing Jurisdiction, Choice of Law, and Judgments in Transnational Disputes, Preliminary Draft No.2 (2004).

intellectual property are exclusive rights, granted or protected by a state, to engage in some economic activity (in the form of production or exploitation) within (or connected with) that state.[7] To what extent such rights exist is deeply a matter of economic concern to that state. Equally they may reflect a state's cultural policies, its interest in fostering particular creative endeavours. This has a double effect. On the one hand, it makes the application of foreign law unusually problematic. It may seem to infringe the sovereignty of the state whose rights are in question. And if not that state may still have a stronger interest in establishing and enforcing such rights. On the other hand the public character of intellectual property protection often means that application of the *lex fori* is mandated where the enforcement of local rights is involved.

Second, the protection of intellectual property under national law flows to an unusual degree from international conventions that represent the subject's founding precepts, its basic law. The question which law governs issues in intellectual property is not therefore at large; whatever the ideal solution conformity with those cardinal principles is required.[8]

Third, intellectual property protection is characteristically territorial in scope. What this means is less clear than might be thought. The "territorial" connections that attract the protection of a given country's laws may be variously defined. And it is debatable whether the concept is any longer apt, as globalisation renders borders increasingly porous. But to varying degrees, and with varying success, national intellectual property protection is limited by national boundaries.

As we shall see, which law governs issues in intellectual property depends inevitably upon how we understand the impact of these considerations. Each of these special considerations warrants scrutiny, although as we shall see, only the third has a controlling influence on choice of law in intellectual property.

1. State Interests and Choice of Law

The character of rights in intellectual property as state-protected rights, which are both exclusive and economically sensitive, gives the law in this area a regulatory character, and ensures that every state has a legitimate interest in the protection of intellectual property rights according to its laws. But in the end this matters less in the choice-of-law process than might be thought. Consider how the public character of intellectual property protection manifests itself. It gives rise to two particular problems in this context: the problem of *application;* and the problem of *mandatoriness*.

The application of one country's laws by the courts of another is a familiarly difficult task. It arises in all but the simplest of cases, and is far from unique to intellectual property disputes. But the state interests involved in the protection of intellectual property rights might seem to give the problem a special dimension. It means that some courts are reluctant to determine questions involving foreign intellectual property law. This is not – or is not merely – because the application of foreign law may be difficult, or even because there is a risk that foreign law may be applied wrongly. Such

[7] *Cornish, op.cit.*, at 17–18.

[8] *Ulmer, op.cit.*, at 6–14.

problems are endemic in the choice-of-law process. Rather the problem here is that *any* risk that foreign law may be misapplied – even if no greater than in connection with other matters – is unacceptable in an area of such interest to the state whose law is in question.

The problem of mandatoriness concerns the application of the law of the forum, not of foreign law. It arises because the regulatory character of intellectual property protection means that a court is likely to be obliged to apply its own law in any case to which it applies. Suppose (say) a copyright infringement occurs in Utopia. Utopian copyright protection will likely extend to the owner. But equally no other law could be applied if proceedings occur in Utopia. Even if claimant and defendant are both resident in Dystopia, such that Dystopia might be regarded as the law with the most significant relationship with the wrong, Dystopian law could not apply. Any such argument would at once encounter the obstacle that the general rules for choice of law are redundant where the application of the *lex fori* is mandatory.

But these difficulties must be viewed in context, and need not distract us. Reluctance to apply the laws of foreign countries is strictly a matter concerning jurisdiction, not choice of law. It does not affect which law should govern but whether foreign intellectual property rights are justiciable at all. This reluctance may be expressed either in a straightforward rule that foreign intellectual property claims are not justiciable, or in a readiness to decline jurisdiction on *forum conveniens* grounds. Nor is the mandatory character of local intellectual property protection significant. The mandatoriness of the law of the forum in certain cases is a common element in the choice-of-law process. It is not a peculiarity of the law of intellectual property.

2. The International Dimension[9]

The law of intellectual property is, of course, not unique in being subject to regulation by international instruments. But the existence of international conventions, the bedrock of the law in this area, has particular importance in this context. Such conventions have a distinctive role in establishing the essential principles of intellectual property protection. Because of the elemental, foundational nature of these *supra*-national norms any rules for choice of law in this area must comply with their requirements. Where copyright and related rights are concerned, it must cohere with the principle of national treatment, embodied in Article 5 of the Berne Convention, and its successors. This ordains that all right-holders shall be given the same protection as nationals of the country under whose law protection is claimed. In particular, some see a choice-of-law rule immanent in Article 5(2), whereby "the extent of protection, as well as the means of redress afforded to the author to protect his rights, shall be governed exclusively by the laws of the country where protection is claimed".

---

[9] *Dessemontet*, Conflict of Laws for Intellectual Property in Cyberspace, 18 J.Int'l.Arb. 489 (2001); *Ulmer, op.cit.*, at 9 *et seq.*; *van Eechoud*, *op.cit.*, at 67 *et seq.*

Whether, and to what extent, the principle of national treatment ordains or implies any particular rules for choice of law is a question that yields no ready answer. Some might say that it argues for application of the *lex fori*,[10] others that it implies that the *lex loci delicti* should govern. For many it justifies application of the *lex protectionis*.[11] But, on inspection, it is more likely that national treatment has no impact at all on the choice-of-law question. Arguably, so far from itself representing a choice-of-law rule, the principle of national treatment has a quite different function, a function that, strictly speaking, lies outside the scope of private international law or, at least, that part of it concerned with choice-of-law rules. This function is to determine the scope of the domestic law of copyright and related rights of the protecting country, however that country may be located in choice-of-law terms. The principle of national treatment does so by ensuring that the law of the protecting country applies as much to foreign right-holders as to nationals, implicitly excluding a role for the *lex originis*.

Two examples illustrate the effect of the principle of national treatment, thus defined as a rule that speaks only to the scope of domestic law, not to the question of choice of law. Suppose, to take a familiar case, that a right-holder commences proceedings in state X for an alleged infringement in that country. Assuming the matter otherwise falls within the scope of its domestic law the courts of state X would have to apply it. They could not apply instead the law governing the origin of the work. That this occurs is the effect of the principle of national treatment, which operates so as to extend state X's domestic law to such cases. Suppose, again, that proceedings are brought in state X for the infringement in state Y of the copyright law of state Y. Assuming that the law of state X permits such actions, it is likely that it will apply the law of state Y to determine the extent of the claimant's rights. It would probably do so on the basis that a copyright infringement is a tort or delict, and that foreign torts and delicts are governed by the *lex loci delicti,* namely the law of state Y. In such a case the application of the law of state Y comes about because the conflicts rules of state X require application of the *lex loci delicti,* not because of the principle of national treatment. National treatment, however, defines the scope of the law of state Y, which the law of state X will apply. It does so by ensuring that its domestic copyright law will apply as much to a right-holder from, say, state Z as it would to a national of state Y itself.

This is not to say, however, that the principle of national treatment is entirely ambivalent as to matters of choice of law. It may indeed be neutral as to how the law of the protecting country is to be identified where an infringement has occurred other than in the forum seised of any dispute. It says nothing explicitly as to whether a *lex loci delicti* test is appropriate, as assumed in the above example, or whether an alternative, whereby the *lex*

[10] For criticism, *see* Ulmer, *op.cit.*, at 11.

[11] *Goldstein, op.cit.* , at 103–104.

fori always governs, is more suitable. In an important, negative sense, however, the principle of national treatment does speak to the issue of choice of law. It does so, as we have seen, by excluding the possibility that the law of the country of origin of the work in question, the *lex originis,* shall be applied in a Contracting State.[12] Indeed, the primary effect of the principle in private international law terms is that it effectively excludes the only alternative to the *lex protectionis* as a choice-of-law rule in matters of intellectual property.

How may we be sure that the effect of the Berne Convention (and cognate instruments) sounds only in domestic law? One response is straightforward. None of the international conventions on copyright and related rights explicitly refers to rules of choice of law. Moreover, it is entirely appropriate to leave the design of the relevant choice-of-law rules to the national law of any state that is seised of a matter. The principle that foreign and local right-holders should be assimilated in terms of the protection they enjoy implies such subsidiarity. Indeed, it is hard to see how matters could be otherwise, given that the relevant conventions impose no obligation on signatory states to adopt any particular choice-of-law rule.

A further justification for thus limiting the principle of national treatment is that it is usually formulated so as to confine its effect to the domestic context. Article 2 of the Rome Convention defines national treatment as the treatment accorded "by the domestic law of the Contracting State in which protection is claimed". So too, Article II of the Universal Copyright Convention speaks of foreigners having the protection that a state gives to its nationals in connection with works "first published in its own territory". It is hard to escape the conclusion that national treatment is simply concerned with treatment under the domestic law of a protecting country, being silent as to choice-of-law matters.

Nor is it surprising that national treatment should have no implications for private international law. It is entirely explicable, for example, that it should be negative in nature, concentrating on eliminating any role for the *lex originis*. The effect of applying a *lex originis* rule to copyright and related rights is that the courts of one country must apply the law of the country in which the work originated in disputes concerning the right-holder's rights. Effectively, this is that of the right-holder's nationality and of the work's creation. Such a procedure has two principal disadvantages. It is impractical, requiring the courts of one country to apply different laws in cases concerning the exploitation and infringements of a given right depending on the country where each originated. It is also discriminatory, potentially affording a foreign right-holder a lesser (or greater) degree of protection in the exploitation of intellectual property rights than that accorded to the nationals of the country of exploitation.

The rationale that underlies and explains the principle of national treatment is that such disadvantages must be avoided. The principle ensures that

---

[12] *Ulmer, op.cit.*, at 9.

if a right-holder from state X exploits its intellectual property rights in state Y it is the law of state Y, not that of state X, which shall determine the extent of those rights and whether they have been infringed. The principle does not, as we have seen, explain on what basis the courts of state Y apply their own law. Do they do so because that law is the *lex fori* or the *lex loci delicti* or simply the *lex protectionis?* It does, however, exclude the possibility that the *lex originis* might be applied.

Again, it is also entirely natural to regard the principle of national treatment as speaking only to the scope of the domestic law of the protecting country, rather than addressing the question (of choice of law) of identifying the *lex protectionis*. It should occasion no surprise that the international intellectual property regime is effectively silent on choice-of-law matters, beyond denying a role to the *lex originis,* the principle of national treatment being Delphic in its implications. By far the most common case in which intellectual property disputes arise is one in which litigation occurs in the country where a given right has been infringed. In such cases, the *lex originis* having been ousted by the principle of national treatment, there are only two ways to analyse the situation. Either we assume that the *lex protectionis* automatically applies, the case being within the scope of its domestic law of copyright and related rights. If so the domestic law of the forum inevitably applies. Or we might see the matter as one of choice of law. If the latter, the only two rules that might be applied are the *lex fori* rule and the *lex loci delicti* rule. Yet in such a case both rules lead to the application of the domestic law of the forum state. However described, therefore, only one law can ever apply in such a case, forum, place of wrong and country of protection being one.

This negative role for national treatment excludes any role for the *lex originis,* and ensures application of the law of protection, but leaves the true choice-of-law questions unanswered. It is arguably what *Ulmer* had in view when he described the principle of the protecting country in the Berne Convention as expressing "not a complete rule of conflict".[13] The reason is that, although it adequately describes which law is to be applied in the event that an infringement occurs in the country whose courts are seised of a matter, it says nothing regarding infringements elsewhere. National treatment is committed to the application of the law of the protecting country where that is congruent with the forum, but silent as to a case where it is not.

Although little may turn on it in practice, it is as well to notice that *Ulmer*'s terminology must be treated with caution. Thus, although, in a generous sense, a rule of conflict, the principle that the law of the protecting country applies is, as we have seen, strictly a rule that determines the scope of the domestic law of the country concerned (by ensuring that it shall extend to non-nationals). As such it is not a choice-of-law rule so much as a rule ensuring that no choice-of-law question ever arises concerning an infringement in

[13] *Ulmer, op.cit.*, at 9

the country whose courts are seised of the matter. As Ulmer implies,[14] the principle of protection is neutral as to the nature of the choice-of-law rule that should be employed in cases to which the domestic law of the forum does not, by virtue of the principle of national treatment, invariably apply.

It is clear, therefore, because it is enshrined in numerous international treaties, that the starting place in understanding choice of law in intellectual property matters must be the principle of national treatment. It is equally clear that the principle ensures that the law of the country of protection shall be applied and not the *lex originis*. Despite appearances, however, national treatment does not supply a choice-of-law rule for such cases. It operates to define the scope of the law of the protecting country by giving it, in effect, extraterritorial scope, extending it to nationals of foreign countries. It also contributes, in a negative way, to determining the nature of the choice-of-law rule for copyright and related rights by excluding the *lex originis* as a potential choice-of-law rule. What it does not do, however, is to ordain or even imply what that choice-of-law rule should be. Our discussion may thus continue unencumbered. Whatever the right solution to the problem of choice of law in intellectual property, it does not depend upon the bedrock of international conventions upon which the law of intellectual property rests.[15]

3. Territoriality and Choice of Law

It is a truism that national intellectual property protection is distinctively territorial, regulating only the enjoyment of rights within the borders of the country concerned. And it is equally true that the concept has become problematic in an era of rapid communications.[16] This is not to deny that the concept is elastic. What constitutes an act "within", or sufficiently connected with, a country is merely a matter of definition. A country can always by legislation extend the range of connecting factors that attract the protection of its laws. In principle, what constitutes an infringement may extend not merely to damage occurring in a given state, but more broadly to acts originating there, or having indirect effects there. For, conceptually, territoriality means only that a territorial connection must exist between particular conduct and a given law. But traditionally the scope of rights in intellectual property is restrictively defined. Copyright, for instance, is invariably conceived as an exclusive right to use or exploit material within the borders of the country concerned. The infringement of those rights involves improperly using or exploiting such material in that country. This is important. For what matters here is not merely that intellectual property protection

---

[14] *Id.*

[15] *See also*, *van Eechoud*, *op.cit.*, at 107, taking the same view.

[16] *Austin*, Social Policy Choices and Choice of Law for Copyright Infringement in Cyberspace, 79 Or.L.Rev. 575 (2000); *Reindl*, Choosing Law in Cyberspace: Copyright Conflicts on Global Networks, 19 Mich.J.Int.L. 799 (1998).

is territorial. It is that territoriality in this context is narrowly defined. To the extent that such rights are not merely territorially limited, but restrictively so limited, the effect on the choice-of-law process is profound.

But this discussion of territoriality may mislead. For what matters to the conflicts lawyer is not that intellectual property rights are territorial; what matters is that territoriality imposes limits upon the applicability of national intellectual property protection. Certainly, the conflicts lawyer is indifferent to whether such protection should be territorial. That is a matter for intellectual property lawyers. What matters is that it is in fact so limited, and that this limitation may affect the normal operation of the choice-of-law process.

a) *Self-limitation and territoriality*

The phenomenon of self-limiting national laws is commonplace in private international law.[17] It is not unique to the protection of intellectual property, nor is the territorial location of acts or events the only means of limiting a law's operation. Any law may prescribe the conditions under which it should apply. Statutes are often restricted in their operation to events or persons within, or otherwise connected with, the country concerned. But not all laws are self-limiting. Many national laws, not being expressly limited in their operation are treated for conflicts purposes as being universal in scope. The self-limiting nature of intellectual property protection may be contrasted with, for example, most internal rules governing issues in contract and tort. These are universal in scope for conflicts purposes, rendered applicable in a given case because the law of which they are part is regarded as applicable for conflicts purposes.

Two contrasting examples make the point. Consider first a case (not involving intellectual property), where the relevant rules of the applicable law are not self-limited – where they are universal in scope. Suppose that the Utopian law of contract provides that a particular form of exemption clause is invalid, and that this rule is not limited to contracts made in Utopia. If Utopian law is held by (say) an English court to govern a given contract the applicability of Utopian law is in effect controlled by English private international law. *Any* exemption clause contrary to the terms of the Utopian statute will be invalid. But this cannot be true where the relevant foreign law is self-limited. Suppose that Utopian law in the previous example provides that certain exemption clauses are invalid only if the contract was made in Utopia. Even if (say), an English court regards Utopian law as the applicable law, it could not coherently apply the Utopian rules concerning exemption clauses to a contract made elsewhere. Suppose, again, that Utopian law is the law applicable to a given copyright infringement. No court could apply Utopian law unless the conditions prescribed by Utopian law for its own

[17] An early influential exploration of the phenomenon is that by *De Nova*, Diritto internazionale, 1959, at 13; the treatment most familiar to English lawyers is *Mann*, Statutes and the Conflict of Laws, 46 BYIL 117, especially 129 *et seq*. (1972–73).

application are satisfied. If the copyright law of Utopia applies only to infringements within Utopia, and if the acts in dispute do not amount to such an infringement, it is self-evident that they cannot be subject to Utopian law. Here the self-limiting character of Utopian law naturally means that the courts of Utopia could not themselves apply their own to such acts. They could not apply their law extraterritorially. But it also affects the extent to which a foreign court could apply Utopian law. Such a court, applying its rules for choice of law, might consider that the law governing the alleged infringement is that of Utopia – perhaps because both parties are resident there. But this inevitably leads to the result that no infringement has occurred, for the copyright protection afforded by Utopian law cannot extend to such cases.

b) Two theories of territoriality

So much may seem obvious, even elementary. But the implications of territorial self-limitation are significant – and which implications we accept will affect our view of the subject. There are two ways to respond to territoriality. We may take a *weak* view of territoriality. We may understand it as defining the *scope* of the applicable law. Or we may take a *strong* view of territoriality. We may see it as defining the *identity* of the applicable law. That is, we may see it as concerning the content of the applicable law, or as concerning the choice-of-law process.

The distinction between these two theories of territoriality is perhaps the crux of the problem of choice of law in intellectual property. It explains why some commentators insist that special choice-of-law rules are required, while others might simply subject such cases to general principles for choice of law. The distinction may be illustrated by reference to the hypothetical with which we began. C claims in proceedings in Dystopia that D has infringed its copyright by conduct in Utopia. C argues that Utopian law governs as the law of the place of infringement, an application of the general rule that issues in tort are governed by the law of the place of the wrong. D replies that the law of Dystopia applies instead because it has a more significant relationship with the issue. If we take the *weak* view of territoriality, we may accept that Dystopian law may be the applicable law. And we would conclude that it confers no rights on C if (as will be the case) it applies only to infringements in Utopia. We would accept that C simply loses on the facts.

On the other hand, if we adopt the *strong* view of territoriality, we would deny that the law of Dystopia could ever be the applicable law. Territoriality means not merely that C has no rights under Dystopian law; it means that Dystopian law is inapplicable – that it cannot apply. There are different ways to express this, although the difference is merely one of idiom. We might say that the territoriality of Dystopian copyright protection indicates that Dystopian law has no interest in governing infringements in Utopia – and so is disqualified from being the applicable law. By contrast, Utopian law has an interest in governing infringements within its territory. So it is the applicable law. But the language of interests sometimes causes unease, because in conjures images of controversial US approaches to interest analysis. So we might prefer the idiom of legislative intent. We might say instead that the Dystopian law of copyright was never intended to address the problem of infringements elsewhere.

If we accept the *weak* view of territoriality, the outcome may at first sight seem unobjectionable, and commonplace. It is inevitable in the conflicts process that the applicable law may not always impose duties or confer rights; that it sometimes provides no remedy. If X sues Y but the applicable law is one whereby X has no right against Y, X simply loses. And, importantly, the fact that it does not do so does not make that law any less the applicable law. But the point has a special resonance in the present context. The territoriality of national intellectual property protection is not a peculiarity of some legal systems, but an inherent and universal feature of such protection. It is systemic. It means that whenever the applicable law is said to be other than the *lex protectionis,* the claimant will lose, for the claimant will have no protection under a law that does not apply. Indeed, those who favour a more flexible approach, avoiding application of the *lex protectionis*, may be seen as taking the part of users rather than right-holders.

Against this, it is of course true that persistent resort to the *lex protectionis* may appear biased towards right-holders. And it might fairly be said that the choice-of-law process should be neutral between particular interest groups – which arguably is best achieved by employing general choice-of-law principles, and perhaps using some flexible "significant relationship" test, whoever might be favoured. But this may not be the point. As traditionally understood the international protection of intellectual property does favour right-holders, for better or worse. To move away from this position is a step with consequences that must be clearly understood. Indeed, to apply general choice-of-law principles is not after all a neutral position. It is one that diminishes the protection currently enjoyed by owners.

Again, the *weak* view may distort the real objectives of the applicable law – the objectives of the internal law of the legal system in question. It may have the effect of conferring on the applicable law a scope it was never intended to have. We cannot by the operation of the conflicts process attempt to confer upon national law a scope it lacks in its own terms. This does not mean, of course, that the weak view confers rights where none exist under the applicable law. But it makes the applicable law relevant in a case where it may have no interest – in which it was (presumably) never intended to apply.

By contrast the *strong* view is immune from these objections. And, unlike the weak view, it may be said to respect the interests of the laws in question. It asserts the interest of the law of the place where infringement occurs, and respects the fact that no other law has an interest. And it gives effect to the legitimate rights of a claimant under the most interested law.

Each of these approaches has particular consequences for the operation of the choice-of-law process in intellectual property cases. Strictly applied, the *weak* view means ignoring the distinctive territoriality of intellectual property protection. And it means that dedicated rules for choice of law in intellectual property are not required – or at least they need not be tailored to accommodate territoriality. By contrast, the *strong* view has two clear consequences, which respect the territoriality of intellectual property rights. On the one hand, it always gives an answer to the question: which law has the most significant relationship (or best connection?) with, say, a copyright infringement? It will always be the law of the country where the claimant's rights are allegedly infringed. On the other hand, it argues for the existence of a specific choice-of-law rule – a rule whereby the law from which protection is sought always applies. As this implies, advocates of the weak view of territoriality will not, or will not automatically, favour application of the *lex protectionis*.[18] But for partisans of the strong view no other law is relevant – and no other choice-of-law rule is possible.

It might be said that, even if we accept the gravitational pull of the *lex protectionis*, we might nonetheless adopt some generalised test of significant connection, or substantial connection. This is because in the end the *lex protectionis* would apply, irresistibly. But it would be wasteful and pointless to apply such an open-textured rule if, in the end, only one law would ever be applied. At the least, efficiency calls for a dedicated rule.

II. Against Territoriality

It is a matter of legitimate debate whether to understand territoriality in its weak or strong sense. But some may deny territoriality even a weak role in the conflicts process. They may insist that any law might govern rights in intellectual property, provided it has a connection recognised by the prevailing choice of law rule. They may insist that the rights conferred by that law should be enforced regardless of any territorial limits to which they are subject. They would treat national laws concerning intellectual property as if they are universal, not territorial, in scope. For some, even a weak theory of territoriality exhibits a narrow, antiquated view of intellectual property protection. For others, it misunderstands the concept of legislative sovereignty. For others still, it reflects a cabined view of the possibilities of the conflicts process.

The first concern is easily met. To report that intellectual property rights *are* territorial, and describe the consequence, is not to approve the fact. Indeed, as we have seen, the conflicts lawyer is not concerned with the territoriality of such rights *per se*, but with the limitation on the scope of intellectual property protection that territoriality provides.

---

[18] *van Eechoud, op.cit.*, at 98.

The issue of legislative sovereignty requires more detailed attention.[19] Some would say that the concept prohibits a state from extending intellectual property protection other than to rights created or exploited within its frontiers. Others would say that it equally prevents a state from deploying choice-of-law rules that purport to alter or extend the scope of foreign intellectual property rights. Certainly the foregoing account accepts that national intellectual property rights are generally territorial. And it accepts that the rules for choice of law cannot purport to extend the scope of foreign (or indeed local) intellectual property rights. But this does not depend upon any particular concept of sovereignty. Most importantly, as we have seen, the inability to use the choice-of-law process to make applicable a law that cannot in its own terms be applied is not a matter of sovereignty. The reason lies in the logic and function of the choice-of-law process.

But there is a different sense in which theories of sovereignty matter in this context. It might be said that a state may purport to give such scope to intellectual property rights as it chooses, through the choice-of-law process. A state might thus declare that, say, the law most closely connected with a copyright infringement shall be applicable *as if* it governs infringements occurring elsewhere. Some may see this as an expression of legislative sovereignty. By this account the problem of self-limitation described above falls away. But the argument from sovereignty supplies no answer to the problem of self-limitation. Clearly a state may legislate as it wishes and purport to ordain the scope of foreign intellectual property rights. Sovereignty is not the issue here. The problem is that it denatures the choice-of-law process to allow it to alter the scope of domestic law.

But conflicts lawyers in particular may respond that the foregoing account depends upon too narrow a view of the choice-of-law process. Some may detect a long-rejected theory of the conflicts process. They may discern a certain recidivism in the focus on the territoriality of local statutes. They may perceive the now superseded thinking of the early statutists, who insisted that the enforcement of rights under foreign law depended upon whether those rights were acquired within the territory of the foreign state concerned.[20] But such disquiet is misplaced. The early writers were not concerned with the choice-of-law process as we now know it. They advocated a theory of recognition, not of choice of law. They supposed that all rights validly acquired in another state should be recognised without attempting to determine whether it is appropriate to apply that law – and that territoriality was the touchstone for such recognition. But this has nothing to do with the difficulties identified above. Few commentators since *Savigny*[21] would doubt that the task is to identify the applicable law according to criteria of

---

[19] *Id.*, at 97 *et seq*.

[20] The statutist position is usually associated with the work of *Huber*; its rejection was most famously advocated by *Savigny*.

[21] *Savigny*, System of Modern Roman Law (trans. Guthrie, 1869), 102–103.

appropriateness. But it is not inconsistent with giving primacy to the choice-of-law process to require that the relevant rules of the applicable law must be applied in the fashion required by that law. This is not to undermine the choice-of-law process but to implement it.

Alternatively, conflicts specialists may advance another answer to the difficulty of self-limiting foreign laws. In choice of law, the law of the forum is always paramount.[22] Arguably, since the private international law of the forum ultimately controls the conflicts process, the connecting factors embodied in the relevant choice-of-law rule also control the scope of the applicable law. The conclusion to be drawn from either argument is that the scope of any given rule of law for conflicts purposes may differ from its scope for internal purposes. The assumption is that the scope of local law depends upon the choice-of-law rules of the forum, not on the local law itself. Differently expressed, it is for the forum to decide whether a foreign legal system has an interest in having its laws applied; it is for the forum to decide whose laws will regulate rights in intellectual property. So the forum can decide to ignore or downplay the territoriality of foreign intellectual property rights in operating its choice-of-law rules. Even if the foreign legal system should consider that it has no interest in being applied (by reference to territoriality), the forum may decide otherwise. This conclusion is in one sense attractive. It ensures that self-limitation in general ceases to be a problem. And in particular it avoids the difficulties occasioned by the principle of territoriality in intellectual property disputes. But more is lost than is gained by this approach, for it undermines, and indeed ignores, the ultimate purpose of the conflicts process, which is the application of the national law most significantly related with a given issue. And it ignores the cardinal principle that a court cannot through its choice-of-law rules bestow on a foreign law an effect it was never intended to have.

To ignore the territoriality of national intellectual property rights altogether is a bold and deeply subversive strategy. It is a means to outflank what some may regard as the outmoded concept of territoriality in domestic law by deploying the choice of law process. But to do so is to misunderstand that process, by attempting to make applicable rules which cannot in truth be applied. To prefer a weak view of territoriality to a strong one is at least defensible, even if it is debatable. But to ignore the territorial nature of intellectual property rights altogether is to render the choice of law process incoherent.

III. Applying the *lex protectionis*

The *lex protectionis*, the law under which an alleged infringement occurs, has perhaps an almost irresistible claim to govern damage to intellectual property

---

[22] *See, e.g., Francescakis*, 1966 Rev.cr.dr.int.pr. 1, 11.

rights. As Ulmer long ago recognised it is uniquely apt as the applicable law.[23] One reason is positive. What law has a greater interest in governing the protection of intellectual property in a given country than that country's law? Another reason is negative. In the majority of cases, given the territorial character of intellectual property protection, what other law could govern? Indeed, what purpose is served by requiring or permitting any other law to apply when no other law has an interest in the matter? It is one thing that the conflicts process sometimes leads to the application of a law which has no claim to govern; it is something else to encourage this result systematically.

Application of the *lex protectionis* has been adopted in the draft Rome II Regulation,[24] which provides that the "law applicable to a non-contractual obligation arising from an infringement of an intellectual property right shall be the law of the country for which protection is sought". Moreover, the realisation that it is fruitless to seek to apply any other law is recognised in the current draft. Article 3 provides that the *lex loci delicti* may in principle give way to another law having a closer connection with the wrong. But no such exception qualifies the rule that subjects intellectual property infringements to the law from which protection is sought.

But this is not the end of the matter. Even if the *lex protectionis* is the general rule special problems arise in two cases – those where a court considers that the content of the applicable law has not been satisfactorily established; and those involving multiple, replica infringements in different countries (involving either one defendant or many).

1. Failure to Establish Foreign Law

A familiar problem in private international law arises when a court considers itself unable to apply foreign law, perhaps because novel or controversial questions of foreign law are involved. A variety of solutions have been adopted.[25] Some systems apply their own law by default. In others a judge may attempt to construct the answer by reference to legal systems contiguous with that in dispute. But no default strategy can avoid the special difficulties that arise in intellectual property disputes. More precisely the principle of territoriality is likely to ensure that a claimant will always lose when it is necessary to apply the law of the forum by default. Because the law of the forum is unlikely to govern an infringement elsewhere the outcome is likely to be that no infringement has occurred.

2. Multiple Claims

Another problem concerns multiple infringements in different countries (a particular problem with online infringements in multiple locations).

[23] *Op.cit.*, at 11 *et seq.*; *see* further, *van Eechoud*, *op.cit.*, at 105 *et seq.*

[24] Proposal for a Regulation of the European Parliament and the Council on the law applicable to non-contractual obligations, C (2003) 427 final.

[25] *Fentiman*, Foreign Law in English Courts, 1995, 281 *et seq.*

Suppose that a claimant has brought proceedings in the country of the infringer's domicile.[26] In principle each infringement is a separate wrong, each subject to the law of the country where each infringement occurs – a conclusion required by the *lex protectionis* rule. Conceptually this is unproblematic. But it has serious practical consequences. It may be both unfair and unrealistic to expect a claimant to sue upon each and every infringement, not least because of the cost and delay involved in seeking to apply the laws of several different countries. The burden and dis-utility involved in applying numerous different laws falls also upon the court. There is also some element of absurdity in applying numerous different laws to what is essentially (if not technically) a single wrong perpetrated by a single wrong-doer. Fairness and efficiency and to some degree common sense suggest that one law should govern in such a case.

Two difficulties might be thought to arise here. One is a matter of design. If one law is to govern, which is it to be – the law of the forum, the law of the parties' common domicile, the law of the first infringement? The third possibility has little to commend it save convenience. But the first and second have some claim to serious attention. Both might be thought to have a connection with each and every infringement insofar as both the location of the forum and the place of the common domicile are factors common to every such claim – they are the only laws having a connection with each such claim. But the problem of design is in the end irrelevant, at least within a traditional model of the conflicts process, for any attempt to identify a single applicable law encounters two more fundamental (and now familiar) problems of principle, involving respectively the territoriality and the mandatory character of intellectual property protection.

Because such protection is territorially bounded, and because no country's law will govern infringements elsewhere, no single law could in practice govern a bundle of claims involving infringements in different states. In such cases there would appear to be no alternative to applying to each infringement each *lex protectionis*. But there may be indirect strategies for easing the difficulty. To the extent that intellectual property protection is harmonised the practical difficulty involved in applying several different laws disappears. Even if harmonisation takes the form of establishing minimum standards this may occur, if only because it becomes easier to apply different laws if they have a family resemblance.

Alternatively, harmonisation may take the form of common agreement that a series of infringements constitutes an infringement under the laws of a single state. An example comes from the EC Cable and Satellite Directive, which ensures that in all Member States the place of uplink, not the place (or places) of receipt of a broadcast is treated as the *locus* of infringement.[27] But nothing would be served merely by stipulating a conflicts solution to a

---

[26] Under, say, the Brussels I Regulation, Art. 2.

[27] Directive 93/83/EEC, OJ 1993 L 248.

problem that ignores the underlying character of intellectual property protection. Certainly one could say that the law of the forum governs in cases of multiplicity, or that of the first infringement, or simply the best-connected law. But this achieves nothing if those legal systems extend protection only to local infringements.

3. Resort to the *Lex Fori – A Solution*?

As this suggests, within the traditional conflicts model, it is perhaps inevitable that the infringement of intellectual property rights can only be governed by the *lex protectionis,* and that the problems of failure in proof and the multiplicity of claims are insoluble, and as such must be tolerated, or absorbed. But in such cases a solution may be offered that does not distort the logic of the choice-of-law process, or denature the content of the applicable law. The problems of failure in the proof of foreign law and multiple proceedings might be solved by adapting the law of the forum so that it applies in such cases. In the former case the *lex fori* might be applied *as if* it governed the facts of the case. And in the latter it might be held that multiple claims involving the same acts and the same parties are governed *as if* the law of the forum applies to each claim.

Such a solution is conceptually coherent and consistent with principle. There is no reason why a legal system cannot regulate the scope of its own law – although, as we have seen, it should not distort the proper application of foreign law. It is open to the *lex fori* to extend the protection of its intellectual property law extraterritorially, to respond to the difficulties of local litigation, although the scope of foreign law cannot be so manipulated. This solution does no violence to the principle that the applicable law must be applied strictly in its own terms. It involves merely amending the terms on which the intellectual property law of the forum applies. Indeed, such a solution is in a sense outside the conflict of laws, because all that is in question is the scope and application of the internal law of the forum.

IV. Re-Imagining the Problem

We have so far considered the problem of choice of law and intellectual property within a traditional conflict-of-laws framework. But in all but the simplest cases, where the *lex protectionis* applies unopposed, the free play of the conflicts process is constrained by the territorial character of intellectual property. Another approach is to contemplate a more radical solution.

The problems here described originate in the difficulty of applying in one state the intellectual property law of another state. This assumes, as the conflicts process always assumes, that the objective is to identify and apply in a given case the laws of a national legal system. The outcome (self-evidently) is a choice of *law*. But what if the process of choosing the relevant standards for decision is "de-legalised", or perhaps (more aptly) "de-localised"? What if the objective is no longer the application of national law, but simply the identification of the norms to be employed to resolve a given case? An analogy might be drawn with the practice of identifying general principles of decision that is common in "delocalised" arbitration. Where such principles are employed the parties' rights and duties are not determined according to the laws of any one national legal system, and the choice-of-law process is redundant. Instead the tribunal applies norms that might variously be described as "denationalised", or *supra*-national. If such a methodology were transposed to the intellectual property area the effect is to substitute for national law something akin to a *lex mercatoria* for intellectual property. Immediately the problems associated with choice of law in intellectual property disappear.

But how is such a delocalised regime to be achieved? Perhaps the parties to a particular dispute might be enabled to ask a court to apply such generally applicable norms. Alternatively a court might be empowered or required to determine multi-state intellectual property disputes in this fashion, either in every case, or in those where a straightforward application of the *lex protectionis* is not possible.

Once again such a radical strategy is attractive, and conceptually satisfying. But it encounters practical obstacles. If left to themselves would litigants opt for such delocalised adjudication? Perhaps the benefits of increased certainty and convenience might be some incentive. But it is perhaps unlikely that either would relinquish whatever tactical or legal advantage they might consider they have under the regular conflicts process. Moreover (and perhaps decisively), how is a court to identify the relevant principles of decision?

V. Conclusion

Our purpose has not been to suggest what choice-of-law rules might govern issues in intellectual property; it has been to identify the logical constraints on the design of such rules. We have seen that three considerations at first sight make this area special: the public character of intellectual property rights; the control of intellectual property protection by *supra*-national norms; and the characteristically territorial scope of such protection. Upon inspection, however, the first and second have no special bearing on choice of law in intellectual property – despite the common assumption that the principle of national treatment, embodied in international conventions, implies a choice-of-law rule. But the third consideration is of decisive importance – at least where the infringement of intellectual property rights is in question. This is not because territoriality is an end in itself. Conflicts lawyers are indifferent as to whether or to what extent intellectual property rights should be spatially limited. But such rights are in fact so limited, and they are universally so limited.

As we have seen, none would dispute this obvious fact. But there may be disagreement about its implications. Some would conclude that only the law of the place of infringement has an interest in being applied, and that no other law, whatever degree of connection it has with a case, can have such an interest. Others would disregard territoriality in the choice-of-law process, and would allow that some law other than the *lex protectionis* might apply (if only exceptionally). But of these two positions, the latter is unattractive, in so far as it ignores the very fact that is most characteristic of rights in intellectual property – their territoriality. Logic dictates that the only law that can realistically apply (as least to infringement claims), is the *lex protectionis* – the law of the country for which protection is sought.

This is not to deny that this conclusion is problematic. In particular, it allows no easy solution to the problem of multiple, cross-border infringements in a digital world. It is inflexible, and contrary to the increasingly popular (if legally awkward) vision of a world with porous borders. But it is a conclusion dictated by the logic of the choice-of-law process, and the phenomenon of territoriality. As we have seen, however, logic permits resort to the internal law of the forum in such cases. Since a legal system can determine the scope of its own law any state might stipulate that each of several parallel claims might be governed as if the law of the forum applies to them all. Involving no more than defining the scope of internal law, the logic of the choice-of-law process is intact.

This means that our discussion must end inevitably (and perhaps disappointingly) in anticlimax. But this itself is not without importance. It is important to grasp why, as *Ulmer* always maintained, the only law that can *meaningfully* govern the infringement of an intellectual property right is the law of the country for which protection is sought. Thus, a claimant suing for infringement somewhere will (obviously) rely upon the law of that country. And it will be no answer for the defendant to suggest that any other law could govern – because better connected, or more closely related, or whatever – for no other law is relevant. As this suggests, the issue in such cases is not truly one of choice of law in the usual sense. It is about the recognition of rights under the only law that could apply. This is not because of any attachment to the territoriality of intellectual property protection. Nor does it disregard the difficulties associated with territoriality in a world of enhanced global communications. It is because the logic of the choice-of-law process requires it.

II.

European Issues

The Proposed Rome II Regulation: European Choice of Law in the Field of Intellectual Property

JOSEF DREXL*

I. Introduction

On July 22, 2003, the European Commission submitted its Proposal concerning a Rome II Regulation on the law applicable to non-contractual obligations.[1] The Proposal is the result of a consultation process starting approximately a year earlier with the publication of the so-called "Preliminary Draft Proposal" for a Rome II Regulation.[2] Earlier steps towards a Rome II Regulation date back to the so-called Vienna Action Plan of 1998 on the implementation of the Amsterdam Treaty in the areas of freedom, security and justice.[3]

Far from expressing a clear position of the Commission on what the law should be, the 2002 Preliminary Draft was designed to launch a public debate on a future Community instrument on choice-of-law rules relating to torts in particular. In this regard, the Draft became a real success. By October 31, 2002, about 80 contributions by governments, the industry and academics had been submitted.[4] The Draft triggered an overall critical debate on several issues. One of those issues was the proposed application of the general choice-of-law rule to infringements of intellectual property rights. No comment supported the general and very broad scope of application of the general rule of Art. 3 of the Preliminary Draft. Comments either argued in favour of an exclusion of intellectual property matters from the scope of

---

* Prof. Dr.jur.LL.M. (Berkeley), Professor at the Institute for International Law of the University of Munich, Director at the Max Planck Institute for Intellectual Property, Competition and Tax Law, Munich.

[1] Commission Proposal of 22 July 2003 for a Regulation of the European Parliament and the Council on the law applicable to non-contractual obligations ("Rome II"), COM (2003) 427 final = http://europa.eu.int/eur-lex/en/com/pdf/2003/com2003_0427en01.pdf (last visited 10 January 2004). For a first comment *see Leible & Engel*, Der Vorschlag der EG-Kommission für eine Rom II-Verordnung, 2004 EuZW 7.

[2] http://europa.eu.int/comm/justice_home/unit/civil/consultation/index_en.htm (last visited 10 January 2004).

[3] Action Plan of the Council and the Commission on how best to implement the provisions of the Treaty of Amsterdam on an area of freedom, security and justice – Text adopted by the Justice and Home Affairs Council on 3 December 1998, OJ EC 1999 No. C 19, at 1.

[4] *See*: Summary and contributions of the consultation "Rome II"; http://europa.eu.int/comm/justice_home/news/consulting_public/rome_ii/news_summary_rome2_en.htm (last visited 10 January 2004).

application of the Regulation or that a specific rule should be formulated confirming the principle of territoriality as an exception to the general choice-of-law rule.

In 2003, the Commission reacted to this criticism by adopting the second approach. Accordingly, the Commission proposes a special choice-of-law rule in Art. 8(1) for IPR infringements, relying on the country-of-protection principle. The second paragraph of the proposed article relates to unitary Community rights. Article 8 of the Proposal reads as follows:

> 1. The law applicable to a non-contractual obligation arising from an infringement of an intellectual property right shall be the law of the country for which protection is sought.
> 2. In the case of a non-contractual obligation arising from an infringement of a unitary Community industrial property right, the relevant Community instrument shall apply. For any question that is not governed by that instrument, the applicable law shall be the law of the Member State in which the act of infringement is committed.

At first glance, this proposal appears anything but revolutionary. The country-of-protection approach builds on the traditional territoriality principle. Everybody in the European Union seems to agree on such a choice-of-law rule, at least as to the issue of infringement. The second paragraph of Art. 8 seems to fill a troublesome gap under existing Community law. It would be most relevant for the application of the Community Trademark Regulation (CMR),[5] whose Art. 98(2), in a most intricate way, still leaves it to the choice-of-law rules of the Member States to decide on the applicable law for issues not covered by the Regulation itself.[6]

However, this preliminary analysis might be treacherous. Things are no longer as they were some years ago. New technology, especially the internet, has changed the landscape of international IPR protection dramatically. In situations in which IPRs are exploited through a single act in the territory of several states (multistate infringement cases), the principle of territoriality reaches its limits. In addition, the principle of territoriality is not as widely accepted as the Commission pretends. Therefore, the Commission Proposal calls us to look closer at the need for a uniform European solution concerning choice of law in the field of intellectual property and at what rules are most appropriate in the European context.

In the following, we will first concentrate on the Rome II process relating to IPRs (*infra* II.), then analyse the objectives of choice-of-law legislation in the European Union under the Amsterdam Treaty (*infra* III.), investigate the need for implementing uniform choice-of-law rules in the EU, in particular, by identifying conflicting domestic choice-of-law rules (*infra* IV.) and finally propose a possible approach to a future Rome II Regulation (*infra* V.).

---

[5] Council Regulation (EC) No 40/94 of 20 December 1993 on the Community trade mark; O.J. EC 1994 No. L, at 11 (initial version).

[6] *See*, in more detail, *infra* IV. 4.

II. The Rome II Debate

As was mentioned above, the 2002 Preliminary Draft earned general opposition to its proposed application of the general choice-of-law rule on torts to IPR infringements. The following analysis will look at the adequacy or rather inadequacy of the now proposed general rule and the two options supported during the debate preceding the Commission Proposal, namely the exclusion of intellectual property issues and the proposed application of the country-of-protection principle.

1. The Proposed General Choice-of-Law Rule on Non-Contractual Obligations

Article 3 of the Commission Proposal provides as follows:

> 1. The law applicable to a non-contractual obligation shall be the law of the country in which the damage arises or is likely to arise, irrespective of the country in which the event giving rise to the damage occurred and irrespective of the country or countries in which the indirect consequences of that event arise.
> 2. However, where the person claimed to be liable and the person sustaining damage both have their habitual residence in the same country when the damage occurs, the non-contractual obligation shall be governed by the law of that country.
> 3. Notwithstanding paragraphs 1 and 2, where it is clear from all the circumstances of the case that the non-contractual obligation is manifestly more closely connected with another country, the law of that other country shall apply. A manifestly closer connection with another country may be based in particular on a pre-existing relationship between the parties, such as a contract that is closely connected with the non-contractual obligation in question.

The formulation of Art. 3(1) and (3) of the Proposal follows by and large the earlier text of the 2002 Preliminary Draft, whereas Art. 3(2) is identical in both versions.[7] This is why earlier criticism on the Preliminary Draft remains valid for this later version of the Commission Proposal.

---

[7] Article 3 of the Preliminary Draft Regulation reads as follows:

> 1. The law applicable to a non-contractual obligation arising out of a tort or delict shall be the law of the country in which the loss is sustained, irrespective of the country or countries in which the harmful event occurred and irrespective of the country in which the indirect consequences of the harmful event are sustained, subject to paragraph 2.
> 2. Where the author of the tort or a delict and the injured party have their habitual residence in the same country when the tort or delict is committed, the applicable law shall be the law of that country.
> 3. However, if it appears from the circumstances as a whole that there is a substantially closer connection with another country and there is no significant connection between the non-contractual obligation and the country whose law would be the applicable law under paragraphs 1 and 2, the law of that other country shall be applicable.

A substantially closer connection with another country may be based in particular on a pre-existing relationship between the parties, such as a contract that is linked to the tort or delict in question.

Article 3(1) provides for the *lex loci delicti commissi* rule. As to the Commission, adoption of this rule has the objective of guaranteeing certainty in the law and of striking a balance between the interests of the person claimed to be liable and those of the injured party.[8] In order to do so, the Proposal has to define the place of the tort, and it opts for the place of the *direct damage.*[9] Neither the law of the country where the relevant act was committed nor the law of the country of indirect damage is relevant. In the case of a traffic accident, for instance, the place of the direct damage is the place of the collision. Direct damage consists in the physical harm and damage caused to the property in the car of the injured party. It is immaterial whether the injured party sustains "indirect" financial or immaterial harm in another country as a consequence of the immediate injury, like costs for medical treatment, loss of income, later pain and suffering.[10]

Whereas the Commentary on Art. 3(1) holds that, in most cases, the country of direct damage would correspond to the law of the victim's habitual residence, this does not seem to be the case in IPR cases. In fact, in IPR cases, this general rule would raise a number of problems. First, the decision not to apply the law of the country in which the infringing act occurred would reject the country-of-protection approach. According to the latter approach, the competent court, in a first step, has to apply the law of the country invoked by the plaintiff, and in a second step, has to answer the question of whether an infringing act was committed in this particular country according to domestic law. This approach is fundamentally different from the one under the *lex loci delicti commissi* rule. Secondly, direct damage in IP cases can only consist in the successful infringement of the invoked intellectual property right. In IPR cases, however, it is not possible to distinguish between the country of the infringing act and the country of successful infringement. Therefore, one might argue, the infringement would have to be located in the country for which the right has been granted and where the infringing act occurred.[11]

Whereas proposed Art. 3(1) might still be applied as a possible, though not a very clear, choice-of-law rule for IPR infringements, paragraph 2 of the said article leads to more inappropriate results. The provision certainly meets

---

[8] Comments on Art. 3 of the Proposal, *supra* note 1, at 11.

[9] *Id.*

[10] Example taken from the comments on the Proposal. The comments also refer to the interpretation of the Brussels Convention for which the ECJ held that the "place where the harmful event occurred" does not include the place where the injured party suffered financial damage following initial damage in another Contracting State; ECJ, decision of 19 September 1995, Case C-364/93, *Marinari v. Lloyds Bank*, [1995] ECR I-2719.

[11] Actually, this is one possible interpretation of the German choice-of-law rule on torts in Art. 40(1) Einführungsgesetz zum Bürgerlichen Gesetzbuch (EGBGB), enacted in 1999, not making an explicit exception for IPRs. *See Sack*, Das internationale Wettbewerbs- und Immaterialgüterrecht nach der EGBGB-Novelle, 2000 WRP 269, at

the needs of persons with the same country of habitual residence who are involved in a car accident abroad.[12] In the field of IPR protection the application of the common national law would contradict the very rationale of the principle of territoriality, namely the respect of the decision of a given national legislature to balance all interests involved – of inventors, creators, exploiters and the public – with regard to acts affecting the national market.

In the field of intellectual property, still, one would be able to take recourse to Paragraph 3 of proposed Art. 3, a provision increasing the power of the judge to decide with more flexibility on the applicable law. Such a flexibility clause might work as a basis for IPR cases in national law.[13] However, too much flexibility is highly problematic in the European context because of the risk that domestic courts may decide differently. The Commission is very well aware of the problem. Therefore, Art. 3(3) may only be applied in exceptional cases in which the obligation is "manifestly more closely connected with another territory."[14] Hence, Art. 3(3) could hardly be used as the legal basis for a general exception for IPR cases. Only in situations in which infringement is argued in the framework of a licensing agreement might the second sentence of Art. 3(3), extending the application of the law of the contract to non-contractual obligations, be considered a workable proposal.

As can be concluded from these ideas, adoption of general choice-of-law rules as proposed in Art. 3 would not serve the needs of intellectual property law adequately. Such rules create at least confusion as to the applicable law and, therefore, should better be avoided. Rules on the law applicable to IPR infringements should either be excluded from the Regulation or the European legislature should provide for a clear-cut IPR-specific rule.

2. Exclusion of Intellectual Property

Given the obvious deficiencies of the Preliminary Draft, many commentators, especially governments and industry, suggested that intellectual property law should be excluded as such from the scope of application of the Rome II Regulation.[15] This view was adopted, for instance, by both the

270 *et seq*. According to the Federal Supreme Court, however, the general choice-of-law rule does not apply to IPRs, since IPRs are only granted for national territories as a matter of substantive law; *see* Bundesgerichtshof (BGH, Federal Supreme Court) of 7 November 2002, 2003 GRUR Int. 470, at 471 – *Sender Felsberg*.

[12] As to the advantages of this clause, *see Leible & Engel*, *supra* note 1, at 11.

[13] According to one possible view under German law, the similar flexibility clause of Art. 41 EGBGB may be construed in the sense of safeguarding continued application of the country-of-protection rule; *cf. Sack*, *supra* note 11, at 272.

[14] *See also* the comments on the provision, *supra* note 1, at 12.

[15] *See* note 2.

German Federal Ministry of Justice and the Max Planck Institute for Intellectual Property, Competition and Tax Law.

The reasons for supporting this exclusion, however, differ. Whereas some commentators, like the German Federal Ministry of Justice, hint at the conflict with the generally accepted principle of territoriality, others argue that the 2002 Preliminary Draft did not really consider the complexity of the IP issue and, therefore, additional studies are needed which however should not delay the Rome II process.[16]

From a legal perspective, the existence of the WIPO Conventions and the WTO/TRIPS Agreement argues in favour of the exclusion. According to Art. 25 of the 2003 Commission Proposal, the Regulation shall not prejudice the application of international conventions to which the Member States are party at the time of the adoption of the Regulation and which lay down choice-of-law rules relating to non-contractual obligations. This brings us to questions of whether the national treatment clause of the WIPO Conventions and of TRIPS include a choice-of-law rule in favour of the law of the country for which protection is claimed (*lex loci protectionis*), and to which issues such a rule would apply. These questions are very much in dispute for the Berne Convention on copyright law in particular.[17] This is not the place to discuss the issue in depth. Nonetheless, it is apparent from the dispute that no choice-of-law rule should be adopted that might contradict the rules of these Conventions and Agreements. Already the uncertainty over the choice-of-law implications of international law argues in favour of the exclusion of intellectual property as such from the scope of the Regulation.

3. Safeguarding the Territoriality Principle

In the consultation process, academics[18] in particular advocated the inclusion of an IPR-specific choice-of-law rule, based on the principle of territoriality, that would provide for the application of the law of the country for which protection is claimed (*lex loci protectionis*). Later, the Commission supported this view in Art. 8(1) of the 2003 Proposal.

---

[16] Position of the Max Planck Institute for Intellectual Property, Competition and Tax Law.

[17] *See*, for instance, *Drexl*, Europarecht und Urheberkollisionsrecht, in *Ganea, Heath & Schricker* (eds.), Urheberrecht Gestern – Heute – Morgen, Festschrift für Adolf Dietz, 2001, at 461, at 467–471 (also with reference to TRIPS). The German Federal Supreme Court supports a choice-of-law interpretation of the Berne Convention; Federal Supreme Court of 17 June 1992, BGHZ 118, 394, at 397 – *Alf* = 24 IIC 539, at 541 (1993). The U.S. Court of Appeals for the 2nd Circuit, however, rejected this view in an obiter dictum: *Itar-Tass Russian News Agency v. Russian Kurier, Inc.*, 153 F.3d 82, 90 (2nd Cir. 1998). In the U.S., the rejection of the choice-of-law meaning of the national treatment clause is not really relevant since the Berne Convention is not directly applicable in the first place.

[18] *See supra* note 4.

Probably most influential was the proposal by the Hamburg Group for Private and International Law.[19] In its comments, the Hamburg Group formulated an Art. 6a that reads as follows:[20]

> 1. The law applicable to a non-contractual obligation arising from an infringement of a copyright or a registered industrial property right shall be the law of the country for which protection is claimed.
> 2. A non-contractual obligation arising from an infringement of a Community industrial property right with a unitary character shall be governed by the law of the Member State where the infringement affects the right.

In its 2003 Proposal, the Commission accepts paragraph 1 of the Hamburg proposal, providing for the country-of-protection principle. As to paragraph 2 on unitary Community rights, the Commission only acknowledged the need for a specific rule in the Regulation. However, whereas the Hamburg Group relied on an IPR-specific effects doctrine, the Commission, adopting the connecting factor already known from Art. 98(2) of the Community Trademark Regulation, prefers application of the law of the country where the infringing act has been committed.[21]

The Hamburg Group rejects the application of Art. 3 of the Preliminary Draft Regulation for the reasons mentioned above.[22] However, the positive justification for integrating the country-of-protection rule is in effect rather dim. The Hamburg Group first refers to the international conventions and agreements in the field of registered rights, patents in particular, arguing that these agreements are governed by the *lex loci protectionis*. Later, a similar argument is made about the Berne Convention[23] despite considerable dispute among academics and national courts on this issue.[24] The Commission adopts the Hamburg view in this regard. As to the comments on the 2003 Proposal, Art. 8(1) and the country-of-protection rule are deemed to preserve current international conventions.[25]

The argument about preserving the application of the Conventions remains problematic at least in the field of copyright law. If the Hamburg Group and the Commission were right about the Berne Convention

---

[19] Members of the Group belong to the Hamburg Max Planck Institute for Foreign Private and Private International Law and the Law Faculty of Hamburg University.

[20] Hamburg Group for Private International Law, Comments of 23 September 2002 on the European Commission's Draft Proposal for a Council Regulation on the Law Applicable to Non-Contractual Obligations, 67 RabelsZ 1 (2003) = http://europa.eu.int/comm/justice_home/news/consulting_public/rome_ii/max_planck_en.pdf (last visited 10 January 2004).

[21] Proposed Art. 8(2) raises a number of concerns which will be discussed *infra* IV. 4.

[22] *Supra* 1.

[23] Hamburg Proposals, http://europa.eu.int/comm/justice_home/news/consulting_public/rome_ii/max_planck_en.pdf, at 24 *et seq*.

[24] *See supra* 2.

[25] *Supra* note 1, at 20.

providing for the application of the *lex loci protectionis*, Art. 8(1) of the Proposed Regulation would not be needed. If the Conventions did not provide for such a rule, proposed Art. 8(2) would implement a rule which would either violate international law or be superseded by the supremacy of international conventions as provided for by Art. 25 of the proposed Rome II Regulation. In the latter case, the proposed rule of Art. 8(1) would create considerable confusion as to the applicable law.

Nevertheless, the Hamburg Max Planck Proposal and the Commission quite rightly deal with the issue of unitary Community industrial property rights. Community Regulations in this field – on Community trademarks, Community designs, Community plant variety rights – do not create uniform Community law in all respects. In particular with regard to sanctions available to the right holder, Community Regulations have to rely on choice-of-law principles.[26] This is where uniform choice-of-law rules are most needed.

In general, the preceding analysis of the debate on the Rome II Proposal argues for a more in-depth investigation of the problems of choice-of-law legislation relating to IPRs in the European Union.

III. Choice-of-Law Legislation in Europe under the Amsterdam Treaty

Until the coming into force of the Amsterdam Treaty,[27] choice-of-law legislation in the European Union mainly existed as a part of secondary legislation adopted with the objective of harmonisation of the law of the Member States. In the field of intellectual property, Art. 1(2)(b) of the Satellite Broadcasting and Cable Retransmission Directive[28] came closest to a choice-of-law rule, but still has to be considered a rule of substantive law.[29] Instead of determining the applicable law, the Directive locates the act of exploitation in respect of satellite broadcasting in the country where the uplink takes place.

1. General Concept of Art. 65(b) EC

The situation has drastically changed with the introduction of Art. 65(b) EC by the Amsterdam Treaty. The provision confers specific power to the

---

[26] The situation will be different in the case of the proposed Community Patent Regulation; *see* in particular Art. 44 of the Revised Proposal of 11 June 2003 for a Council Regulation on the Community patent; http://register.consilium.eu.int/pdf/en/03/st10/st10404en03.pdf (last visited 10 January 2004).

[27] Treaty of 2 October 1997. The Treaty entered into force on 1 May 1999.

[28] Council Directive 93/83/EEC of 27 September 1993 on the coordination of certain rules concerning copyright and rights related to copyright applicable to satellite broadcasting and cable retransmission, OJ EC No. L 248, at 15.

[29] This is the general understanding; *see*, for example, *Schack*, Europäisches Urheberrecht im Werden, 2000 ZEuP 799, 814.

Community for adoption of choice-of-law legislation. This competence is characterised by two elements: (1.) Beyond mere harmonisation, the provision allows creation of uniform choice-of-law rules in the European Union. In order to do this, the Community legislature may even adopt directly applicable regulations that would promote optimal compatibility of choice-of-law rules in the Member States.[30] (2.) The Community may also adopt uniform rules which in individual cases would provide for the application of the law of a non-Member State (principle of universal application).[31]

Of course, the European legislature is only authorised to act, according to Art. 65 EC, "insofar as necessary for the proper functioning of the internal market." However, this requirement needs to be construed in a broad sense.[32] Choice-of-law rules, even when they provide for the application of the law of a non-Member State, promote the free movement of persons within the Union[33] by guaranteeing that all courts in the European Union will apply the same national law to cross-border cases. Uniform choice-of-law rules thereby ensure that no forum shopping takes place within the European Union[34] and that individuals will not have to face sudden and unexpected changes in their legal relationships as a consequence of moving to another Member State when they are sued in their new state of domicile.[35]

In contrast to Art. 95 EC, the objective of Art. 65 EC does not consist in the establishment of the internal market, but rather in creating uniform Community law as such.

This view is supported by the approach of EU institutions to Art. 65(b) EC. Already the European Council in its Tampere Conclusions of October 1999 expressed its will to create an area of freedom, security and justice, so that "the right to move freely throughout the Union, can be enjoyed in

---

[30] As to the advantages of regulations as compared to directives, *see Kreuzer & Wagner*, Europäisches Internationales Privatrecht, in *Dauses* (ed.), Handbuch des EU-Wirtschaftsrechts, Part R, Ergänzungslieferung 10, 2001, note 22.

[31] *See* Art. 2 of the Proposed Rome II Regulation.

[32] *Röben*, in *Grabitz & Hilf* (eds.), Das Recht der Europäischen Union, 13. Ergänzungslieferung, 1999, Art. 65 EGV note 2, arguing in the sense of broad discretion of the legislature. According to *Röben*, after the integration of the third pillar of EU law, including judicial cooperation, Member States are no longer allowed to conclude conventions on choice-of-law rules outside the EC Treaty. Therefore, broad Community power would be needed.

[33] Note that Art. 65 EC belongs to Part 2 Title IV of the Treaty, dealing with the free movement of persons.

[34] In this regard, the Rome II Regulation is the consequence of the Brussels I Regulation, which allows a choice of courts in the EU to some extent and makes judgements executable in all other Member States; as to the argument of forum shopping *see Leible & Engel, supra* note 1, at 8.

[35] This argument is often overlooked even by those commentators who support Community competence for universally applicable choice-of-law rules; *cf. Leible & Engel, supra* note 1, at 9.

conditions of security and justice accessible to all."[36] Accordingly, the European Council invited the Council and the Commission to fully and immediately implement Art. 65(b) EC as laid out in the Vienna Action Plan of 1998.[37] According to this plan, the European legislature would aim at making life simpler for European citizens *inter alia* by promoting the compatibility of conflict-of-law rules and rules on jurisdiction.[38] In more detail, the action plan envisaged adoption of a legal instrument on the law applicable to non-contractual obligations (Rome II) and a revision of the Convention on the law applicable to contractual obligations (Rome I).[39]

In its Green Paper on the Rome I project,[40] the Commission expanded on the objectives of uniform choice-of-law rules in the Union. According to the Commission, national rules on international private law – covering both conflict of jurisdictions and conflict of laws – entails a lack of uniformity and legal certainty as well as the risk that one or more of the parties might take advantage of their case's links to various legal systems to escape the law normally applicable to them.[41] From this reasoning, it follows that the Community should adopt uniform choice-of-law rules even if such rules result in the application of the laws of non-Member States.

2. Art. 65(b) EC and Intellectual Property

However, the question remains whether the rationale of Art. 65(b) EC also applies in the field of intellectual property.

A first argument in favour of uniform choice-of-law rules can be derived from the existence of diverging national rules. In contrast, in a European context in which all Member States have adopted uniform choice-of-law rules, be it based on a silent recognition of the principle of territoriality or the national treatment provisions of international law, there would be no room for forum shopping in respect of diverging choice-of-law rules of the Member States.[42] Therefore, if the argument that IP Conventions provide for the country-of-protection principle were correct, there would be no case to provide for exactly the same uniform European choice-of-law rule under Art. 65(b) EC.

In addition, mere differences between national choice-of-law rules may not suffice to justify uniform choice-of-law rules. The risk of forum shop-

---

[36] Para. 2 of the Tampere Conclusions of 15 and 16 October 1999, http://www.europarl.eu.int/summits/tam_en.htm#top (last visited 10 January 2004).

[37] *Supra* note 2.

[38] Action Plan, *supra* note 2, para. 39.

[39] Para. 40(b) and (c) of the Action Plan (note 2).

[40] Green Paper of 14 January 2003 on the conversion of the Rome Convention of 1980 on the law applicable to contractual obligations into a Community instrument and its modernisation, COM (2002) 654 final, http://europa.eu.int/eur-lex/en/com/gpr/2002/com2002_0654en01.pdf (last visited 10 January 2004).

[41] Part 1.2. of the Green Paper, *supra* note 40, at 9.

[42] *Cf.* similar arguments in the Green Paper, *supra* note 40, Part 1.3 (at. 9).

ping must be real in light of the rules on jurisdiction. As long as the rules on jurisdiction do not give any flexibility to plaintiffs as to the choice of different national courts which then might apply different substantive law, diverging choice-of-law rules alone do not create a danger of forum shopping.

Consequently, the issue of applicable law cannot be dealt with in isolation, but should be considered in the context of the preliminary question regarding jurisdiction. With the exception of Denmark, conflict of jurisdictions in civil cases, including IP disputes, are dealt with in the European Union under the so-called Brussels I Regulation.[43] The Regulation came into force on 1 March 2002. It supersedes the so-called Brussels Convention.[44]

According to the general rule of Art. 2(1) of the Brussels I Regulation, persons domiciled in a Member State shall be sued in the courts of that Member State. Since this Member State of the defendant's domicile is not necessarily the country for which protection is claimed, the competent court may well have to apply foreign law.[45] Article 2(1) of the Brussels I Regulation even enables the plaintiff to litigate multistate infringements of intellectual property rights before a single national court.[46] Obviously, the principle of territoriality in intellectual property law cannot guarantee application of the *lex fori* as the substantive law of the competent court in IP cases. As a result, courts in the European Union have often applied foreign law to intellectual property cases.[47]

---

[43] Council Regulation (EC) No 44/2001 of 22 December 2000 on jurisdiction and the recognition and enforcement of judgments in civil and commercial matters, OJ EC 2001 No. L 12, at 1.

[44] *See* Brussels Convention on Jurisdiction and the Enforcement of Judgments in Civil and Commercial Matters, OJ EC 1972 No. L 299, at 32.

[45] The ECJ has indicated its willingness to deal with infringement cases under Art. 2(1) Brussels I Convention; *see* ECJ, decision of 15 November 1983, Case 288/82, *Duijnstee*, 1983 ECR 3663, para. 23.

[46] However, courts are hesitant to extend their jurisdiction to infringement of rights abroad. In *Fort Dodge v. Akzo Nobel* and *Boston Scientific Ltd. v. Cordis Corp.*, an English court requested a preliminary ruling from the ECJ on whether the territoriality principle in the European Patent Convention excludes the court from deciding on an infringement of a foreign patent; *see Bragiel*, A Funny Thing Happened on the Way to the Forum – Actionability in the United Kingdom of Infringements of Intellectual Property Rights Committed Abroad, 2 I.P.Q. 135, at 152 (1999); *Lundstedt*, Jurisdiction and the Principle of Territoriality in Intellectual Property Law: Has the Pendulum Swung Too Far in the Other Direction?, 32 IIC 124, at 128 (2001). Based on Art. 2(1) Brussels Convention, in *Pearce v. Ove Arup Partnership Limited and others*, 30 IIC 825 (1999), however, the English Court of Appeal (Civil Division) affirmed its jurisdiction for an action against a defendant domiciled in England for an infringement of a Dutch copyright in the Netherlands.

[47] For German case-law *see* Federal Supreme Court (Bundesgerichtshof) of 16 June 1994, BGHZ 126, 252, 255 – *Folgerecht mit Auslandsbezug* (rejecting the application of the German *droit de suite* to auctions held in London); Federal Supreme Court (Bundesgerichtshof) of 2 October 1997, BGHZ 136, 380 – *Spielbankaffaire* (applying the copyright law of Luxembourg). For British law, *see*: *Pearce v. Ove Arup Partnership Limited and others*, Court of Appeal (Civil Division) of 21 January 1999, 30 IIC 825 (1995).

However, the general rule of Art. 2(1) is derogated by exclusive jurisdiction as provided for by Art. 22 No. 4 of the Brussels I Regulation. According to this provision, only the courts of the Member State in which the deposit or registration has been applied for or has taken place have jurisdiction to decide in proceedings concerning the registration or validity of patents, trademarks, designs and other registered rights. This provision on exclusive jurisdiction is interpreted by the ECJ in a narrow sense. An action for declaration of non-infringement does not fall within the scope of this provision.[48]

In particular, exclusive jurisdiction in the sense of Art. 22 No. 4 does not exist for infringement proceedings, leaving a large scope of application to the general defendant's domicile rule in IP cases. However, the plaintiff may also sue in courts of so-called "special jurisdiction." In matters relating to tort, delict or quasi-delict, Art. 5 No. 3 of the Brussels I Regulation[49] confers the right to the plaintiff to sue in the courts of the place where the harmful event occurred or may occur. As an exception to the general defendant's domicile rule, Art. 5 No. 3 needs to be construed in a narrow sense.[50] In general, this rule is interpreted by the ECJ in the sense that it refers either to the place of the event giving rise to the injury or the place where the damage occurred.[51] The provision, which was taken over from the Brussels Convention, was the object of several preliminary rulings of the ECJ.[52] So far, the ECJ has not had the opportunity to decide on the place of the harmful event in IPR infringement cases yet.[53] Nevertheless, there is no doubt about the possibility of applying this provision to IPR infringement cases. Based on the principle of territoriality, some legal commentators interpret this rule in the sense of the country for which protection is claimed.[54] Accordingly, courts in the sense

---

[48] ECJ, decision of 15 November 1983, Case 288/82, *Duijnstee*, [1983] ECR 3663 (on the predecessor provision of the Brussels Convention).

[49] Identical with the same provision of the Brussels Convention and the Lugano Convention.

[50] *See* ECJ, decision of 27 September 1998, Case 189/87, *Kalfelis v. Schroeder*, [1988] ECR 5565.

[51] ECJ, decision of 30 November 1976, Case 21/76, *Handelswekerij G.J. Bier BV v. Mines de Potasse d'Alsace SA*, [1976] ECR 1735, para. 11.

[52] *See also* ECJ, decision of 7 March 1995, Case C-68/93, *Shevill v. Presse Alliance SA*, [1995] ECR I-415 (on whether damage needs to be proven for the application of Art. 5 No. 3); ECJ, decision of 17 September 2002, Case C-334/00, *Fonderie Officine Meccaniche Tacconi*, [2002] ECR I-7357 (application to pre-contractual liability); ECJ, decision of 1 October 2002, Case C-176/00, *Henkel*, [2002] ECR I-2063 (injunctive action by consumer associations against acts of unfair competition).

[53] *See*, however, the decision of the Swedish Supreme Court (Högsta Domstolen) of 14 June 2000, 32 IIC 231 (2001) – *Flootek*, on Art. 5 No. 3 Lugano Convention. On this case, *see Lundstedt*, *supra* note 46.

[54] *Stauder*, Die Anwendung des EWG-Gerichtsstands- und Vollstreckungsübereinkommens auf Klagen im gewerblichen Rechtsschutz und Urheberrecht, 1976 GRUR Int. 465, at 475; *Kreuzer & Wagner*, *supra* note 30, Part Q, Ergänzungslieferung 6, München 1997, note 177.

of Art. 5 No. 3 Brussels I Regulation would apply their own law, provided that the country-of-protection approach is also recognised as a choice-of-law principle.

The preceding analysis shows that a need for uniform choice-of-law rules exists in particular in infringement proceedings. Whereas in proceedings concerning the registration and validity of registered rights, the exclusive jurisdiction solution of the Brussels I Regulation excludes any possibility for forum shopping, in infringement proceedings the plaintiff has the possibility to choose the competent court according to the most favourable applicable law by suing either in the courts of the defendant's domicile or in the courts of the country for which protection is claimed.

According to this analysis, diverging choice-of-law rules in the Member States create a legal imbalance between plaintiffs and defendants to the disadvantage of the latter. A defendant – or infringer of IPR rights – might be tempted to reduce the economic risk of being held responsible for the infringement by establishing his or her domicile or principle place of settlement in a Member State in which the conflict-of-law rules lead to a more favourable applicable law. However, changing one's domicile with the intent of forum shopping may well be too burdensome and, therefore, only hypothetical. Such behaviour may only occur in situations of intentional infringements, namely clear-cut cases of piracy and counterfeiting. Both problems – choice of most favourable jurisdiction by the plaintiff and intentional settlement in specific countries by infringers – can be addressed effectively by uniform European choice-of-law rules in the field of intellectual property.[55]

In light of Art. 65(b) EC, a need for European choice-of-law rules in the field of intellectual property can only be accepted on the basis that national choice-of-law rules differ.

IV. Conflicting Choice-of-Law Rules in the European Union

Several situations may be identified in which conflicting choice-of-law rules exist within the European Union.

[55] In its Proposal of 30 January 2003 on a Directive on measures and procedures to ensure the enforcement of intellectual property rights, COM (2003) 46 final, http://europa.eu.int/eur-lex/en/com/pdf/2003/com2003_0046en01.pdf (last visited 10 January 2004), the Commission misconstrues the international private law situation of IPRs. The Proposal argues that pirates might choose to settle in individual states where sanctions are particularly weak. However, moving to an individual country only creates jurisdiction of the courts of this Member State, whereas, under the principle of territoriality, these courts would apply the law of the country for which protection is sought. To the extent that pirated goods are sold to other Member States, illegal distribution will be governed by the foreign law of the country of distribution.

1. Different National Choice-of-Law Rules in Copyright Law

Whereas in the field of registered rights all Member States follow the principle of territoriality and apply the law of the country for which protection is claimed, the situation is much more complex in the field of copyright law.

The analysis of the existing legal situation has to start with the consideration of the law of the conventions, namely the Berne Convention and the TRIPS Agreement. As a WTO member, the European Community is directly bound by the TRIPS Agreement and indirectly, as a consequence of the "Berne-plus" provision of Art. 9(1) TRIPS, by the Berne Convention. As to the scope of this international law obligation, however, considerable confusion was caused by the ECJ's opinion on the power of the Community to conclude TRIPS.[56] The Court rejected exclusive competence of the Community for TRIPS, nevertheless invoked by the Commission, in favour of a concept of joint competence.[57] According to this concept, exclusive external competence does not arise from the mere existence of internal power of harmonisation (Art. 95 EC). The Court only affirmed exclusive competence to the extent that participation of the Member States in international agreements would impair already *existing* legislation.[58] Beyond this area, the Court held that there only exists joint competence of the Community and the Member States. The notion of joint competence remains ambiguous, in particular with regard to different intellectual property rights. Nevertheless, it is clear that the Court does not want to deprive Member States of their external competence entirely. At the same time, the Court tried to make sure that the Community has some, though not exclusive competence for the whole body of TRIPS. A more thorough analysis leads to the conclusion that, to the extent that there is or will be Community legislation, TRIPS is or will have to be considered part of Community law.[59]

This conclusion has an important impact on the legal status of the national-treatment clause in copyright conventions. In the field of copyright law, only partial harmonisation exists in the European Union. The principle of national treatment, however, covers copyright law in general, including those parts which are harmonised in the Union. Therefore, the national-treatment clause of TRIPS and the Berne Convention has to be considered part of Community law.[60] From its legal nature as Community law, it must follow that the ECJ is competent to decide on the interpretation of the national-treatment clause. This is so even beyond the reach of already existing European harmonisation of copyright law. In the *Assco* case, decided

---

[56] ECJ, opinion 1/94 of 15 November 1994, [1994] ECR I-5267.

[57] *See Drexl*, The TRIPS Agreement and the EC: What Comes Next After Joint Competence?, in *Beier & Schricker* (eds.), From GATT to TRIPS, 1996, at 18.

[58] ECJ, *supra* note 56, para. 99.

[59] *Drexl, supra* note 57, at 31–37.

[60] In this sense *Drexl, supra* note 17, at 476 *et seq.*

together with the *Dior* case, the ECJ affirmed its competence of interpretation of Art. 50(6) TRIPS, relating to procedures on provisional measures in the field of IPR infringements, even for intellectual property rights that have not been harmonised by Community law so far.[61] Thereby, the Court tries to prevent diverging interpretations of TRIPS provisions relating to rights covered by Community law in one case and only by national law in another case. With regard to the national-treatment clause, which has to be applied equally within the scope of Community legislation and outside of it, the situation is no different. Hence, the ECJ is competent to interpret the national-treatment clause of TRIPS and the Berne Convention with binding effect on all courts in the Union and within the full scope of application of the national-treatment clause of the Conventions.[62]

What are the options for the Rome II Regulation in light of this analysis? From the outset it is clear that the Regulation should not adopt a solution that might conflict with a future interpretation of the national-treatment clause by the Court of Justice. Therefore, the analysis has to turn to possible options for interpretation.

There is dispute about whether national treatment has a choice-of-law meaning in the first place. Those who reject such a meaning[63] have to explain how the choice-of-law question will be answered instead. Some argue that the national-treatment clause has to be applied by the competent court as a first step of the legal analysis even before investigating the applicable law.[64] Accordingly, one has to look at national treatment through the lense of choice-of-law rules, namely in the sense of an obligation of non-discrimination in applying choice-of-law rules; application of another law to foreigners would be fully consistent with national treatment. Another interpretation reduces the application of national treatment to substantive law. National treatment only comes into play after the applicable law has been defined in application of national choice-of-law rules.[65] Both interpretations have considerable disadvantages,[66] which do not need to be discussed here.

---

[61] ECJ, decision of 14 December 2000, Joint Cases C-300 and 392/98, *Parfums Christian Dior and others*, [2000] ECR I-11307, para. 50–63.

[62] With this result *Drexl*, *supra* note 17, at 478.

[63] *See* especially the rejection of this meaning by the 2nd Circuit in the U.S., *supra* note 17. This view is shared in Germany by some authors, *see Schack*, Urheber- und Verlagsrecht, 2nd ed., 2001, note 891–893 (at 400 *et seq.*); *Neuhaus*, Freiheit und Gleichheit im internationalen Immaterialgüterrecht, 40 RabelsZ 191, at 193 (1976); *Siehr*, Das urheberrechtliche Folgerecht inländischer Künstler nach Versteigerung ihrer Werke im Ausland, 1992 IPRax 29, at 31. *See also Koumantos*, Private International Law and the Berne Convention, 1988 Copyright 415, at 426 *et seq.*

[64] *Koumantos*, Sur le droit international privé du droit d'auteur, 1979 Diritto di autore 616, at 636; *id.*, *supra* note 63, at 426 *et seq.*

[65] This was the approach of the 2nd Circuit in *Itar-Tass*, *supra* note 17, at 89.

[66] *See Drexl*, *supra* note 17, at 467 *et seq.*; *Fawcett & Torremans*, Intellectual Property and Private International Law, 1998, at 469.

Obviously, the choice-of-law option is more convincing: National treatment requires application of the same substantive law to foreigners and to the nationals of the country whose laws will be applied. In this sense, the national-treatment clause is built on the principle of territoriality. The competent court has to apply the law of the country for which protection is claimed.[67]

It follows that the European legislator should not adopt a choice-of-law rule in conflict with the application of the law of the country of protection. However, there is also a risk that the ECJ would reject a choice-of-law understanding of the national-treatment clause. In this situation, courts in the Union would have to rely on national choice-of-law rules, which diverge to a considerable extent. Greek law, for example, applies the law of the country where the work was made accessible to the public for the first time with regard to all copyright issues, even as to the rights conferred to the author.[68] Portuguese law refers to the law of the country of origin for the acquisition of the right, but applies the *lex loci delicti commissi* rule to infringements.[69] The law of the country of origin is also applied in France, but only as to the definition of the author.[70] In such a scenario, the Community risks continuing with diverging choice-of-law rules. In order to avoid such a situation, the only option consists in the adoption of a European choice-of-law rule based on the application of the law of the country for which protection is claimed.

In addition, there is disagreement among commentators who agree on a choice-of-law understanding of the national-treatment clause as to the scope of application of the Berne choice-of-law rule. This dispute relates to the question of whether national treatment as a choice-of-law rule applies to the scope of protection – rights and limitations – only, or to the acquisition of the copyright as well.[71] This question is most relevant for the definition of the author and first ownership of the copyright, which, according to some national rules and to the U.S. Court of Appeals for the 2d Circuit in *Itar-Tass*

---

[67] *See*, however, *Koumantos*, *supra* note 64, 1979 Diritto di autore 616, at 637; *id.*, *supra* note 63, at 424 *et seq.*, arguing that the Berne Convention would provide generally for the application of the law of the country of origin. *Koumantos* refers to the first sentence of Art. 5(3) Berne Convention, which provides for the protection of works according to the law of the country of origin within this country.

[68] Art. 63 Greek Copyright Act. *See Lucas*, Private International Law Aspects of the Protection of Works and of the Subject Matter of Related Rights Transmitted over Digital Networks, WIPO/PIL/01/1 of 17 December 2000 (http://wipo.int/pil-forum/en/documents/doc/pil_01_1p.doc; last visited 10 January 2004), at 10 (para. 42).

[69] *Siehr*, Das Urheberrecht in neueren IPR-Kodifikationen, 108 UFITA 9, at 17 *et seq.* (1988).

[70] Cass.civ. of 22 December 1959, Recueil Dallow 1960 Jur. 93 – *Rideau de fer*. *See also Kérever*, La règle du "traitment national" ou le principe de l'assimilation, 158 RIDA 75, 113 *et seq.* (1993).

[71] The dominant view supports the last and broad understanding; *see* authors *supra* note 66.

in particular,[72] has to be defined according to the law of the country of origin.[73]

How should the European legislature react to these problems in drafting the Rome II Regulation? Three possible options can be distinguished:

(1.) As a first option, the European legislature could adopt a rule on the application of the law of the country of protection for all issues arising in infringement cases, including initial acquisition and first ownership. By adopting such a rule, the European legislature would change the approach in some Member States that have opted for the country of origin so far. Existing disagreement among Member States on the appropriate approach argues against such a rule.
(2.) As a second option, the European legislature could limit the European rule on the application of the law of the country of protection to the scope of copyright protection, i.e., the author's rights and their limitations. However, such a rule would not add much to the current situation, in which almost all laws in the Member States, with the exception of Greece,[74] already apply this rule. In addition, such a rule might trigger even more diverging national solutions concerning the initial acquisition of the right in comparison to the existing legal situation.
(3.) The last option actually consists in leaving the situation as it is right now. In the future, the pros and cons of the application of the lex loci protectionis and the lex originis could be studied and discussed on a European level in more detail so as to prepare a uniform European rule. This approach, however, would maintain, at least for the time being, the current situation of diverging national choice-of-law rules and legal insecurity about the proper understanding of the national-treatment clause.

Looking at the 2003 Proposal, Art. 8(1) itself does not unveil the Commission's choice of solution. The scope of application of the Regulation's choice-of-law rules is defined in a general way in Art. 11, which, therefore, would also apply to infringements of intellectual property rights. Article 11 only gives an indicative, non-exhaustive list of issues that, for its general character, is all but helpful in solving the problems arising in the copyright field in particular. At best, the Regulation confers power to the ECJ to define the clear scope of the *lex loci protectionis* rule in interpreting Art. 8(1) and Art. 11 of the Regulation. It would be much more advisable for the Commission to deal more sincerely and openly with the issues at stake, which are handled differently under the laws of the Member States, within the framework of the Regulation itself.

2. Multistate Infringements

Another issue lying outside the regulation of the WIPO Conventions and TRIPS relates to the precise understanding of the country-of-protection principle. In drafting the Berne and Paris Conventions more than 100 years ago, diplomacy reacted to the experience that intellectual property rights are

---

[72] *Supra* note 17.

[73] For different interpretations of the Berne Convention, *see Drexl*, *supra* note 17, at 469 *et seq.*

[74] *See Lucas*, *supra* note 68.

ubiquitous and can be infringed universally. Nevertheless, the very concept of national treatment relies on the understanding that infringing acts are limited in scope to national territories.[75]

However, more recent technological developments underline the existence of multistate infringements, characterised by a single exploiting act and simultaneously affecting a number of national territories. Today, of course, the internet is the most prominent example of a medium producing multistate infringements rather as a rule than an exception.[76] In the past, courts both in Europe and the United States had to deal more often with another type of cases, namely cross-border broadcasting.[77] Actually, multistate infringements are not even a development of new technology. Earlier cases related to infringing print publications – book or newspaper – distributed simultaneously in several countries following a single decision made by the infringer.[78]

In multistate infringement cases there is a clear risk that national courts will apply the same choice-of-law rule, namely that of the country of protection, with considerably diverging results. Such divergence may be explained by a number of reasons.

a) Extraterritorial Application

National courts may be tempted to apply the rule of *lex loci protectionis* with extraterritorial effect.[79] As a consequence, different national courts may interpret intellectual property laws very differently when it comes to the question of whether there is an infringement within their own national borders. Two recent cases demonstrate the problem: In 2000, the U.S. Court of Appeals for the 2nd Circuit held in *National Football League v. PrimeTime*[80] that the defendant had infringed the plaintiff's copyright by broadcasting protected works to Canadian subscribers of the defendant's pay-tv services over a satellite – with the uplink taking place from U.S. territory – although there was no infringement in respect of subscribers in the U.S. Actually, the U.S. Copyright Act provides for a limited exception in favour of persons living in remote areas of the U.S. – but not in such areas of Canada (!) – who

[75] *Cf. Geller*, Internationales Immaterialgüterrecht, Kollisionsrecht und gerichtliche Sanktionen im Internet, 2000 GRUR Int. 659 *et seq*.

[76] *See*, on the discussion of the internet, *infra* b).

[77] *See* the comparative analysis of this case-law by *Drexl*, Lex americana ante portas – Zur extraterritorialen Anwendung nationalen Urheberrechts, in Festschrift für Wilhelm Nordemann, 2004, 429 *et seq*.

[78] *Cf. National Enquirer, Inc. v. News Group News, Ltd.*, 670 F.Supp. 962, 970 (S.D.Fla. 1987). In this decision, the U.S. court applied U.S. law to a situation in which only 85 of more then 5 million copies of the infringing newspapers were sold in the U.S.

[79] The term extraterritoriality in the context of IP protection is used predominantly in the U.S.; *see, e.g., Goldstein*, Copyright, 2nd ed. 1998, § 16.2.

[80] *National Football League v. PrimeTime 24 Joint Venture*, 211 F.3d 10 (2nd Cir. 2000). *See also Drexl, supra* note 77.

may not be reached by regular television stations. In a more recent decision,[81] the German Federal Supreme Court applied German copyright law to French-language radio broadcasts transmitted from German territory close to the French border, although practically no German audience existed. The transmission was made possible by the German subsidiary of a French company. The French parent company produced the transmissions in France and sent them to the subsidiary for retransmission to France.

These cases demonstrate the underlying problem. Courts tend to apply their own national law in a biased way, in some instances because they know their law best; in other instances, they want to protect a plaintiff who is a national of their own country. As a consequence, the defendant will be tempted to sue, according to Art. 5 No. 3 of the Brussels I Regulation, in the courts of the country where the harmful event occurred, simultaneously arguing in the sense of an infringement under the IP law of this country, in order to achieve the broadest application of that law.

This tendency to apply national IP law with "extraterritorial" effect was very pronounced in the above-mentioned decision *National Football League*.[82] Whereas in cases in which the plaintiff sues for damages,[83] national courts are able to distinguish between the damage incurred in different territories – and may even refrain from compensating for countries in which there is no infringement according to the law in those countries –, the court in *National Football League* granted an injunction which forced the defendant to stop transmission to Canadian viewers, although the transmission had been legal from the perspective of Canadian law. Accordingly, extraterritorial application of national law in IP cases can produce real clashes of national laws on the basis of a particular choice of jurisdiction by the plaintiff and a tendency of national courts to extend the application of their own law beyond national borders behind the veil of the principle of territoriality.[84]

b) High Number of Possibly Diverging Laws

In cases of multistate infringement, diverging choice-of-law rules are responsible for even more serious contradictions. This is so, for example, with regard to the issue of first ownership in copyright cases. Courts of

---

[81] *See* the decision of the Federal Supreme Court (Bundesgerichtshof) in *Sender Felsberg*, *supra* note 11.

[82] *Supra* note 80.

[83] This was the case in *Sender Felsberg*, decided by the German Federal Supreme Court, *supra* note 11.

[84] In fact, the situation in the U.S. is very peculiar since U.S. courts affirm subject matter jurisdiction based on the judgement that there is an infringement committed within the national territory. Therefore, the argument made about extraterritorial application also holds true for the application of rules on jurisdiction in the U.S. By this extension of U.S. jurisdiction, U.S. courts manage to export U.S. intellectual property law to other countries and protect specific interests, those of the investors in particular, even abroad. *See* the critique expressed by *Drexl*, *supra* note 77.

countries that follow the *lex originis* rule (France, Portugal, Greece, the U.S.) will attribute the right to a different person than will countries following the *lex loci protectionis* approach. Consequently, rules on jurisdiction and on choice of law affect the attribution of rights and the practical outcome of court decisions.

For the application of IP laws on the internet, in particular, discussion has evolved as to whether the *lex loci protectionis* approach should be given up in favour of another, specifically, a *lex originis* approach.[85] The application of the *lex originis* may seem tempting to the European legislature for its closeness to the principle of the country of origin, which applies in other fields of regulation on the internet.[86] However, the *lex originis* has its own drawbacks as a universally applicable choice-of-law rule. In some cases, protection within the European Union would depend on the quality of protection and on policy decisions of legislatures in non-Member States for which the law may not be harmonised under Art. 95 EC.[87]

This very concern supports the view that the principle of territoriality should continue to be applied in internet cases. However, the principle of territoriality would lead to the application of such a multitude of different laws that practice would not be able to handle the problem. It seems that legal territoriality can no longer be applied where territoriality has vanished in reality.

Choice-of-law rules, nevertheless, may be helpful in bringing more precision and uniformity to decisions of domestic courts on the question of whether a given national territory is affected, and may thereby reduce the number of legal orders involved even in internet-related cases. In January 2004, a second version of the Draft IP Principles elaborated in the framework currently conducted under the aegis of the American Law Institute (in the following: ALI Draft Principles) was distributed for consideration by the advisory group.[88] The draft distinguishes between registered and other rights. For registered rights, the Draft Principles propose application of the law of the country of registration. Regarding other rights, the law of the

[85] *See Thum*, Internationalprivatrechtliche Aspekte der Verwertung urheberrechtlich geschützter Werke im Internet, 2001 GRUR Int. 9 (on the discussion within WIPO).

[86] *See* Art. 3(1)(2) Directive on Electronic Commerce, O.J. EC 2000 No. L 178, at 1. Intellectual property rights are excluded from the scope of application of the principle of the country of origin according to a list in the annex to the Directive. *See also* Art. 3(3) of the Directive referring to this list.

[87] Other arguments against the universality principle relate to the difficulties to define the country of origin as the country of first publication and the lack of importance of place of first publication in the internet environment; *see Thum, supra* note 85, at 17–22.

[88] *The American Law Institute*, Intellectual Property: Principles Governing Jurisdiction, Choice of Law, and Judgments in Transnational Disputes, Preliminary Draft No. 2 (January 20, 2004). The Draft Principles, so far, have not been adopted by the ALI Council, and, therefore, have not been made available to the public. Reporters of the corresponding ALI Project are *Jane Ginsburg, Rochelle Dreyfus and François Dessemontet.*

country where the alleged infringing act has a significant impact on the market is preferred.[89] In fact, this second rule may help to control the number of countries whose law has to be applied in cases of multistate infringements. In this regard, the proposal seems to follow a market-oriented effects doctrine known from competition law. This approach would work in the above-mentioned cases of cross-border broadcasting. But, without further explanation, the Draft Principles do not offer any solution for multistate infringements of registered rights.

Still, it is quite doubtful whether the market-impact approach of the ALI Draft Principles would work appropriately for internet cases. The Draft Principles of January 2004 state that the above-mentioned rules do not apply in exceptional cases, for instance, if it is unduly burdensome to decide on the basis of all the laws of the territories where an impact on the market is produced.[90] In such a situation, typical for internet cases, courts should apply the law of the country with the closest connection with the dispute. This is further defined by additional criteria, *i.e.*, the centre of gravity of the alleged infringer's business undertaking and the extent of the activities and the investment of the right holder.[91] The last criterion is not unproblematic since it promotes the application of the law of larger markets in general and the investor-friendly IP law of the U.S. in particular, excluding any other law in internet cases. According to an additional criterion, courts may also prefer the law that conforms best to international standards of the TRIPS Agreement and successive international laws.[92]

Discussion on the internet problem so far has demonstrated that a clear-cut solution in the conflict between universality and territoriality can hardly be found. Nevertheless, the internet discussion demonstrates that the rise of multistate infringements could well trigger a series of perhaps diverging national legislation on choice-of-law rules in the field of IPRs. This may be reason enough for the European legislature to take counteraction.

c) How To Deal with the Problem

Regarding multistate infringements, the national-treatment clause needs to be respected in its private international law dimension by the Community legislature, who must not and should not adopt a principle of universality. However, the national-treatment clause is much too imprecise to be taken as

---

[89] Sec. 301(1) and (2). On the earlier Preliminary Draft No. 1 of 17 January 2003 *see Dreyfuss & Ginsburg*, Principles Governing Jurisdiction, Choice of Law, and Judgments in Transnational Disputes, 2003 CRi 33. This earlier Draft relied on the market impact rule as the sole general choice-of-law rule. *See also Kur*, Principles Governing Jurisdiction, Choice of Law and Judgments in Transnational Disputes: A European Perspective, 2003 CRi 65, comparing the Draft ALI Principles with the jurisdiction rules in the MPI proposal, and also commenting on the choice-of-law principles proposed in the Draft.

[90] Sec. 302(1)(b) Draft Principles No. 2.

[91] Sec. 302(2)(a) Draft Principles No. 2.

[92] Sec. 302(2)(b) Draft Principles No. 2.

the legal basis for answering the question whether an individual intellectual property right was infringed in a given country. By referring to the principle of non-discrimination, national treatment only gives a right to equal protection in comparison to nationals. Therefore, it is the substantive law of the country of protection which has to decide whether an infringement took place in this specific country. Accordingly, national legislating bodies, including the Community legislature, are free to define their own choice-of-law rules in order to bring more precision and legal security to private international law in multistate infringement cases.

From the point of view of European law, the principle of universality could well be implemented between the Member States of the EU based on the supremacy of Community law over national law. Within the scope of application of Art. 307 EC, the Community has to guarantee only that the rights of third states are respected. Although the Community itself is bound by the principle of national treatment,[93] it should not be considered to have an obligation vis-à-vis third members of TRIPS and WIPO to guarantee national treatment between EU Member States. Nevertheless, an intra-European universality rule or rule of origin should be rejected. Depending on whether the country of origin is a Member State of the EU or not, such a rule would create different standards of private international law contrary to the very philosophy of Art. 65(b) EC. In addition, for infringements on the "global" net, it would only reduce the number of national laws that come into play without solving the underlying problem as such.

If the Community legislature adopted a territoriality approach, such a rule could be integrated within a formula applicable to all sorts of infringements. Such a rule could have the advantage of bringing more precision to the general rule of *lex loci protectionis*.

In any event, in the regulation of the internet, international agreement should be preferred to a mere European regulation. For the time being, however, the Community would be free to adopt its specific rule, based on the principle of territoriality, which may well be regarded as a model for future international regulation. The remaining problem consists in finding a generally acceptable formula that would satisfy the needs of the internet.

3. Drawing the Line in Respect of Licensing

Other discrepancies between national choice-of-law rules may arise from the interface of contract law relating to licensing agreements and tort law in cases of infringements.

It is generally accepted that, in the international context, the principle of free choice of law applies in the field of licensing law. The application of different choice-of-law rules to licensing contracts on the one hand and infringement issues on the other hand gives rise to a risk of diverging choice-

[93] On the status of IP Conventions as Community law, *see supra* IV. 1.

of-law results in national courts if domestic laws draw the line between contract law and law on infringement differently. Such a risk arises in particular with respect to German law, which divides the contractual transaction into two parts, namely the part regulating the rights and obligations of the parties (*schuldrechtlicher Vertrag*) and the transfer of the right as such as a second and distinct contract (*dinglicher Vertrag*), producing effects in respect of third parties as well. Accordingly, a dispute exists in Germany as to whether the rule of free choice of law also applies to the assignment of the right.[94] Also under the law of other states, however, a distinction is made between a mere license, allowing the licensee to commit certain acts which would otherwise be considered an infringement on the one hand, and an assignment of proprietary rights on the other hand.[95]

In the field of contracts, the Member States of the European Union apply the Rome Convention.[96] The Convention itself, which is currently being considered for adoption as a Rome I Regulation under Art. 65(b) EC,[97] does not include any specific provision on intellectual property rights. Nevertheless, the Rome Convention is applicable to contractual issues of intellectual property, since licensing agreements are not excluded either.[98] If the Community legislature adopted a rule on IPRs in the Rome II Regulation, European private international law would cover the whole field of intellectual property law. Hence, in such a situation, the ECJ would have full authority to interpret those uniform choice-of-law rules with effect for all Member States' courts. Given the complexity of the interface between licensing law and other issues of intellectual property law, introduction of a uniform rule dealing with this interface of infringement and licensing does not seem to be very recommendable. On the contrary, it would be much wiser to leave it to the ECJ to develop the law progressively in reaction to upcoming referral cases.

Whereas the 2002 Preliminary Draft would have extended application of the *lex causae* of the licensing agreement to issues of infringement committed within a licensing relationship, the 2003 Commission Proposal does not deal with the interface problem. In its Art. 10(1), the 2003 Proposal even explicitly excludes the possibility of the parties in an infringement litigation to choose a law different from the one referred to under Art. 8 after their

---

[94] *Cf. Katzenberger*, in *Schricker* (ed.), Urheberrecht, Kommentar, 2nd ed., 1999, vor §§ 120 ff. note 148.

[95] *See Fawcett/Torremans, supra* note 66, at 545–549. *See also* the decision of the English High Court: *Campbell, Connelly & Co. Ltd. v. Noble*, 1963 All ER 237, distinguishing between the issue of whether the right to renewal of a U.S. copyright could be assigned on the one hand and the interpretation of the contract as to whether the renewal right was assigned together with the copyright on the other hand.

[96] European Convention on the Law applicable to contractual obligations, O.J. EC 1980 No. L 266, at 1.

[97] *See* the Green Paper, *supra* note 40.

[98] *Cf. Fawcett & Torremans, supra* note 66, at 543–593.

dispute arises. The 2002 Preliminary Draft contained a transparent and clear-cut choice-of-law solution, but would have risked conflicting with the national treatment clause of IP Conventions. The 2003 Commission Proposal avoids such fallacies.

4. Unitary Community Rights

The last question relates to unitary Community rights. As we were able to see,[99] the Hamburg Group proposed a specific rule on the applicable national law for such Community rights. According to Art. 6a(2) of the Proposal, infringements of such a right should be governed by the law of the Member State where the infringement *affects the right*. The 2003 Commission Proposal adopts the idea of addressing such rights in Art. 8(2), but sticks to the rule of applying the law of the country where the infringing act was committed (*lex loci delicti commissi*).

Despite the fact that the legal instruments on Community rights establish a proper European IPR regime with the European Union as the country of protection, special choice-of-law rules are needed to fill the gaps left by Community legislation. European law has to refer to the law of the Member States in respect of sanctions in particular. Accordingly, Art. 98(1) of the Community Trademark Regulation[100] provides for injunctive relief in infringement cases, but, according to Paragraph 2 of this Article, "in all other respects," the competent court will apply the law of the Member State where the acts of the infringement or threatened infringement were committed, "including the private international law." Regulations on other unitary Community rights, with the exception of the upcoming Community Patent Regulation,[101] provide for similar rules.

The Hamburg Group justifies the need for a special rule on Community rights basically by two reasons: (1.) In the case of Community rights, the European Union itself has to be considered the country of protection. (2.) As to the connecting factor, the Hamburg Group refers to the situation of multistate infringements. The Group is aware of the fact that the infringement of a Community right may affect several Member States. Accordingly, the application of a number of different national laws is seen as the mere consequence of a multistate infringement to be accepted by the perpetrator.

The 2003 Commission Proposal opts for the different *lex loci delicti commissi* rule without giving a justification for this choice. Nevertheless, the Hamburg Proposal in favour of the *lex loci protectionis* should be preferred. The Commission Proposal only works in situations in which the infringing act was actually committed within the EU. However, a Community right may also be infringed by a behaviour committed outside the Union, for

[99] *Supra* II. 3.

[100] Council Regulation (EC) No. 40/94 of 20 December 1993 on the Community trademark, O.J. EC 1994 No. L 11, at 1.

[101] *See supra* note 26.

instance in the case of advertising put on the internet outside the EU, nevertheless targeting commerce within the EU and thereby infringing a Community trademark. In contrast to the Commission Proposal, application of the *lex loci protectionis* can easily capture such situations. The Hamburg effects rule comes closest to this country-of-protection principle. The latter cannot be applied directly, since the EU at large would have to be considered as the country of origin.

The 2003 Commission Proposal was obviously influenced by the model of unitary Community rights legislation which, for instance under Art. 98(2) of the Community Trademark Regulation, refers to the country where the act of the infringement was committed. In contrast to such rules, proposed Art. 8(2) does not include the formula according to which referral is made to national law including its rules on private international law. In practice, this formula creates considerable problems since Member States may deal differently with the choice-of-law problem, leading to the application of different laws depending on which country is the *locus delicti commissi*. The 2003 Commission Proposal departs from this model, since Art. 20 of the Proposed Regulation makes clear that all choice-of-law rules refer to substantive law only, excluding the rules of private international law. However, Art. 8(2) is not very clear about whether it would replace choice-of-law rules of the type of Art. 98(2) Community Trademark Regulation. The first sentence of Art. 8(2) rather safeguards full application of Community instruments on unitary rights without making an exception for choice-of-law rules contained in such instruments. In addition, the comments on the Proposed Regulation make clear that the second sentence of Art. 8(2), with the choice-of-law rule in favour of the *lex loci delicti commissi*, has only subsidiary application to the extent that the Community instrument neither contains a provision of substantive law "nor a special conflict of laws' rule," apparently giving precedent to Art. 98(2) Community Trademark Regulation.[102] Such regulation would not contribute anything to the current state of the law. It would be much better to replace choice-of-law rules in specific Community instruments on unitary rights with a uniform choice-of-law rule in Art. 8(2) of the Rome II Regulation.

It may be added that the Community legislature would do even better by providing for uniform substantive law as regards all unitary Community rights, including uniform rules on sanctions.[103]

---

[102] In this sense *also Leible & Engel, supra* note 1, at 13.

[103] This approach should also be preferred to the harmonisation of sanctions under national law currently pursued by the Commission in the framework of the adoption of a Directive on measures and procedures to ensure the enforcement of intellectual property rights; Commission Proposal of 30 January 2003, COM (2003) 46 final = http://europe.eu.int/eur-lex/en/com/pdf/2003/com2003_0046en01.pdf (last visited 10 January 2004). *See also* criticism on this Commission Proposal expressed by legal commentators: *Drexl, Hilty & Kur*, Vorschlag für eine Richtlinie über die Maßnahmen und Verfahren zum Schutz der Rechte am geistigen Eigentum – eine erste Würdigung, 2003 GRUR Int. 605, at 607 *et seq*.

V. A Possible Approach of Rome II to Intellectual Property

According to the preceding analysis, a possible approach of the Rome II Regulation to intellectual property could integrate the following elements:

(1.) The Rome II Regulation could implement a choice-of-law rule that brings further precision to the understanding of the current territoriality approach and the current application of the country of protection. Such a rule would be in conformity with the national-treatment clause of the Conventions and would, at the same time, bring more uniformity to the handling of multistate infringements.[104]

(2.) The Rome II Regulation could clarify the scope of application of this more precise choice-of-law rule. In the framework of the Conventions, the lex loci protectionis rule should at least be applied to the scope of protection of intellectual property rights. The European choice-of-law rule may also extend this rule to other aspects of intellectual property law, in particular to the issues of first ownership, the requirements for protection and the subject matter of protection. Such a rule would contradict the choice-of-law rule in some Member States, in particular in the field of copyright law. As an option, the European legislature may also decide to leave the issue open, which would then have to be decided on the basis of the law of the Conventions and TRIPS or national choice-of-law rules.

(3.) Because of the peculiarities of national laws, the interface between contract law and intellectual property law as such should not be addressed by specific rules. Rome I and Rome II would cover the whole field of intellectual property law. In this situation, the ECJ is much better suited to distinguish between the two areas of choice of law by taking into account the specific nature of the problems often arising from national law.

(4.) In the field of unitary Community rights, complete uniform regulation of the substantive rules should be preferred to any choice-of-law approach; uniform choice-of-law rules, excluding the application of the rules of private international law of the country referred to, should be preferred to a piecemeal approach of possibly diverging rules in different Community instruments on such unitary rights that, today, also include referral to the private international law rules of the Member States. Such proposed choice-of-law rules should rely on the country-of-protection approach and should not refer to the country where the infringing act was committed.

(5.) European choice-of-law rules should have universal application as proposed under Art. 2 of the 2003 Commission Proposal.

[104] It was not the purpose of this analysis to formulate such choice-of-law rules. A point of reference for the drafting of such rules could be the discussion taking place within the project of the American Law Institute (ALI); *see supra* note 88.

Comments: The Rome II Regulation Proposal and its Relation to the European Country-of-Origin Principle

MATTHIAS LEISTNER*

I. Introduction

When the following comments were conceived the Rome II Regulation was still subject to a pre-legislative interest group battle in Brussels. A preliminary draft proposal had been published by the Commission for consultation and many comments (mostly of critical nature) had been received. The Commission has now taken a step forward and adopted the official Proposal for a Regulation of the European Parliament and the Council on the law applicable to non-contractual obligations ("Rome II Proposal").[1] Thus, the battle can now be continued on a new and higher stage. The latest developments have been included in the following comments, paying special attention to the favourable fact that the Commission has not, as had been proposed in the consultation process, adopted a country-of-origin principle in the style of private international law for non-contractual obligations arising out of acts of unfair competition. Instead, the traditional continental "market-effects principle" has been retained for unfair competition law, although in a somewhat more sophisticated form (including a proviso dealing with acts of unfair competition aimed directly at a specific competitor). Of course it may be argued that the traditional market-effects principle in unfair competition law is no longer adequate in times of multi-state internet marketing and advertising, and a country-of-origin conflict-of-laws rule may seemingly provide a clear-cut solution for the single market. However, things are not that simple. The following considerations attempt to show that in the field of unfair competition law (and especially in the related field of the far-reaching continental European supplementary unfair competition protection against certain acts of misappropriation) the traditional market-effects principle and its complex interplay with the material country-of-origin provisions in certain areas of European secondary law provides a better solution to the private international law problems that are brought up

---

* Dr.jur.; LL.M. (Cambridge). Former Head of Department at the Max Planck Institute for Intellectual Property, Competition and Tax Law, Munich; at present post-doctoral research scholar of the Bavarian State (based at the Max Planck Institute and the Ludwig Maximilians University, Munich). The lecture form has been maintained, adding only some indispensable references.

[1] COM (2003) 427 final, of July 22, 2003.

by the internet, at least with respect to the proper functioning of the Internal Market.[2]

II. Relevance of Art. 5 Rome II Proposal for IP Protection and the Relationship of the Proposal with the Country-of-Origin Provisions of European Secondary Law

Article 5 of the Rome II Proposal deals with the law applicable to non-contractual obligations arising from unfair competition or other unfair practices. In this respect, Art. 5(1) adopts the traditional continental European market-effects principle.[3] It states that the law of that country shall be applied where the unfair competition or other practices affect competitive relations or the collective interests of consumers.

Obviously, this provision mainly governs advertising. It is, however, also significant for IP protection in several respects. First, in Germany, as in many other European countries, supplementary protection against imitation of certain products is granted on the basis of unfair competition law.[4] However, according to traditional doctrine, supplementary protection under unfair competition law is restricted to protection against particularly unfair imitations. Therefore, such supplementary protection is (in theory) only granted if additional circumstances (beyond the mere fact of imitation itself) exist that qualify the behaviour of the offender as particularly unfair.[5] However, despite this qualification, unfair competition law has in fact been developed in the case law of some fields into a proper supplementary protection instrument for subject matter that does not qualify for exclusive IP protection. The most important example from German case law is the protection of fashion novelties and other general design novelties.[6] Thus, in the future, Art. 5 of

---

[2] It should not be forgotten that the (however questionable, *cf.* the Response of the Government of the United Kingdom in the Consultation process, available at http://www.lcd.gov.uk/consult/general/eurocom.htm) competence of the European Community to draft the Proposal follows from Arts. 61(c), 65 EC Treaty, which require that the instrument be "necessary for the proper functioning of the Internal Market". Therefore in drafting and interpreting the instrument the purpose of at least improving the proper functioning of the Internal Market should play the main role.

[3] For the *proviso* in Art. 5 (2) *cf.* further *infra* III.

[4] *Cf.* for example *Kur*, Protection of Graphical User Interfaces Under European Design Legislation, 34 IIC 50 *et seq.* (2003). On the contrary, British law has never allowed any general principle of unfair competition that clearly extends to the misappropriation of the fruits of another's labour; *cf. Cornish*, Intellectual Property, 4th ed. 1999, 9–38, who points out the resulting trend to press the existing concepts of copyright into service in cutting-edge cases (with reference to Lord *Devlin* in *Ladbroke v. Hill* [1964] 1 W.L.R. 273, 291).

[5] *Cf.* for example *Schricker*, Urheberrecht-Kommentar, 2nd ed. 1999, Einführung, pt. 36 *et seq.*

[6] *Cf.* decisions of the Federal Supreme Court, 1973 GRUR 478 – *Modeneuheit*, 1992 GRUR 448 – *Pullovermuster*.

the Rome II Proposal will be of some relevance for "IP protection" in a broader sense.

Therefore, the more general question of how the market-effects principle in Art. 5(1) of the Rome II Proposal is related to the country-of-origin principle provided for in some acts of Community secondary law is also significant in the field of IP protection in a broader sense.[7] Like Art. 5 of the Rome II Proposal, the country-of-origin principle is relevant mainly with respect to intra-community advertising. Article 3 of the E-Commerce Directive provides a country-of-origin rule regarding electronic commercial communications. Commercial communications in the internet are therefore privileged, at least in comparison to "traditional" intra-community communications. While Art. 3(3), with Annex (pt. 1), of the E-Commerce Directive explicitly excludes, *inter alia,* the area of intellectual and industrial property, unfair competition law is the core field for the application of this rule. As discussed above, this includes supplementary unfair competition law protection against misappropriation, for example, protection for designs. Additionally, in cross-border television Arts. 2, 2a of the "Television without Frontiers" Directive[8] likewise establish a country-of-origin principle. However, the country-of-origin rule in the "Television without Frontiers" Directive is restricted to the "fields coordinated by this Directive", which applies – in this case – only to rules of law *specifically* concerning the fields of broadcasting and distribution of TV programmes, *i.e.* the fields of law that the Directive itself substantively harmonises.[9] Contrast this with the so-called "coordinated area" of Art. 3 of the E-Commerce Directive, which is defined much more broadly,[10] covering virtually all rules directly or indirectly *relevant* to an internet service, having particular regard neither to the specific character of these rules nor to the level of harmonisation in respective fields of substantive law (notwithstanding the far-reaching exceptions from the principle).

The proposed country-of-origin ("Internal Market") provisions in two more recent instruments of European law, *i.e.* the Proposal for a Regulation

[7] The classical IP rights, however, are exempted explicitly from the most powerful and controversial country-of-origin rule, which is provided for in Art. 3 E-Commerce Directive (Directive 200/31/EC of the European Parliament and of the Council of 8 June 2000 on certain legal aspects of information society services, in particular electronic commerce, in the Internal Market, 2000 OJ EC No. L 178/1–16). *Cf.* the following text.

[8] Council Directive 89/552/EEC of 3 October 1989 on the coordination of certain provisions laid down by law, regulation or administrative action in Member States concerning the pursuit of television broadcasting activities (1989 OJ EC No. L 298/23), as amended by Directive 97/36/EC of the European Parliament and of the Council of 30 June 1997 (1997 OJ EC No. L 202/60).

[9] *Cf.* the clear ruling of the ECJ in the *De Agostini*, ECJ, joined Cases C-34/95, C-35/95, C-36/95, *Konsumentenombudsmannen (KO) v. De Agostini (Svenska) and others,* [1997] ECR I-3843, para. 24 *et seq.* (32–34).

[10] *Cf.* Art. 2 lit. h) E-Commerce Directive.

on sales promotion in the Internal Market (Sales Promotion Regulation Proposal)[11] and the Proposal for a Directive concerning unfair business-to-consumer commercial practices in the Internal Market (Unfair Commercial Practices Directive),[12] follow the narrower approach of the "Television without Frontiers" Directive, applying the principle of mutual recognition only to restrictions concerning the unified or harmonised subject-matter as such ("Such restrictions which do not relate to sales promotions as such, continue to apply in so far as they are compatible with Community law . . .",[13] ". . . falling within the field approximated by this Directive . . ."[14]). Outside the scope of the afore-mentioned provisions (*i.e. de lege lata* for most of the non-electronic intra-community trades and services), primary European law, subject to the basic freedoms and the respective jurisdiction of the ECJ along the lines of the *Dassonville/Cassis* doctrine may also prohibit, in intra-community cases, the application of some provisions of national law,[15] chosen according to Art. 5 of the Rome II Proposal, if the national law at least potentially restricts inter-community trade and cannot be justified under Art. 30 EC.

Hence, a certain factual overlap between the choice-of-law rule in Art. 5 of the Rome II Proposal, the country-of-origin principle in European secondary law, and the basic freedoms of primary [European] law cannot be denied. With respect to the Rome II Proposal, the problem, of course, is a general one. However, it has its main impact with respect to intra-community advertising and unfair competition law and, in the way discussed

---

[11] Communication from the Commission on sales promotions in the Internal Market, Doc. COM (2001) 546 final, of 2 October 2001.

[12] Doc. COM (2003) 356 final, of 18 June 2003. Meanwhile, political agreement regarding the Commission's proposal has been reached in the Council. The proposal in its recent form (along the lines of the political agreement in the Council) would no longer contain a (private international law-style) principle of mutual recognition, but instead would only provide for a substantive law provision prohibiting the Member States to impose restrictions on intra-community trade for reasons falling within the field harmonised through the Directive. *Cf.* Council Doc. 9667/04 of May 25 2004). *Cf.* further on the Unfair Commercial Practices Proposal (in its original form) *Leistner,* in: Cambridge Yearbook of European Law Studies 2004; *cf.* further on the new formulation of the country-of-origin principle *infra* note .

[13] *Cf.* Sales Promotion Regulation proposal, Art. 3 (2), and at 24 *et seq.* of the Explanatory Memorandum.

[14] Art. 4 (2) Unfair Commercial Practices Directive proposal.

[15] However as far as the *"Keck"*-doctrine of the ECJ applies (*i.e.* at present for the area of free movement of products, since the *"Keck"*-formula has never been clearly extended by the ECJ into the field of free movement of services) provisions which apply indistinctly and which are not, in law or in fact, discriminatory, do not have to pass the *Dassonville/Cassis* test, if they only prohibit "certain selling arrangements". For the ongoing discussions if this formula really fits the needs of the multistate-marketing-campaigns in the "internet-age" *cf.* further *Craig/de Búrca,* EU Law, 3rd edition 2003, at 647 *et seq.*; *Drexl,* Verbraucherschutz und Electronic Commerce in Europa, in *Lehmann* (ed.), Electronic Business in Europa, 2001, pt. 3 *et seq.*, 19 *et seq.*

above, supplementary IP protection. With respect to supplementary protection of designs against imitations, even a third instrument comes into play: since March 6, 2002, the European Regulation on Community designs, apart from introducing protection for registered designs, provides for broad unitary Community-wide three year protection for unregistered designs based on the mere substantive conditions of sufficient novelty and individual character. This Community right is additional to the potential supplementary unfair competition protection in some national laws. The remedy provided in the Regulation is cease-and-desist orders and the usual accessory means. With respect to further ongoing national sanctions (*i.e.* damage claims), the choice-of-law question is left to the law of the Member States by Art. 89(1) lit. d) of the Regulation, which states that the sanctions shall be provided "by the law of the Member State in which the acts of infringement or threatened infringement are committed, *including its private international law*" (a provision similar to the respective solution in the Community Trademark Directive). The resulting choice-of-law problem in this field will be addressed in the articles of *Schaper* (*infra* Part 2.II) and *Metzger* (*infra* Part 2.II).

For our topic, it is enough to establish that in the field of design protection against misappropriation, apart from national rights, Art. 5 of the Rome II Proposal and the country-of-origin principle have to be considered in the context of the new unitary Community design protection, which itself – as an IP right – is explicitly excluded from the country-of-origin provision of the E-Commerce Directive. This is justified, because in this harmonised area of substantive law, a multi-state advertisement is no longer faced with potentially prohibitive costs of legal analysis. Therefore, in the light of the basic freedoms, a mosaic approach in private international law is less problematic.

To put it more generally: the complex interplay of choice-of-law rules, the country-of-origin principle and the basic freedoms with respect to inter-community cases has to be seen in the light of the existing level and further harmonisation of European secondary law. Choice-of-law rules and the country-of-origin principle have to be modelled and interpreted in a manner that promotes the further accomplishment of the Internal Market.[16] The relation between Art. 5 of the Rome II Proposal and the country-of-origin principle will be analysed from this perspective in the following parts of this article.

First, we will briefly examine and evaluate Art. 5 of the Rome II Proposal in light of the reactions in the consultation process and in comparison to the established rules of private international law in the field of unfair competition law. Then we will move on to consider the relation between the country-of-origin principle and Art. 5 of the Rome II Proposal. This issue can not be considered without further analysis of the character of the country-of-origin

---

[16] *Cf. Drexl,* Internationales Privatrecht als Baustein des Binnenmarkts, manuscript (forthcoming).

principle itself, and the inner connection of this principle with the level of harmonisation in secondary Community law. Finally, we will see the result of the considerations with respect to the appropriate construction of Art. 5 of the Rome II Proposal, and will consider a further perspective with respect to the interaction of possible new Community IP rights and non-harmonised national law.

III. Article 5 Rome II Proposal in Light of the Reactions in the Consultation Process

The principle laid down in Art. 5(1) of the Rome II Proposal is in accordance with the choice-of-law rules in most of the continental Member States. The principle requires the application of the law of the country where the competitive interests collide, *i.e.* where a market is affected (*market-law principle*).[17] The formulation "where competitive relations or the collective interests of consumers are or are likely to be directly and substantially affected" distinguishes between the conflict of interests of competitors on the same market stage and the interests of the corresponding consumers' side of the market and the public in general. This is consistent with the approach of the European Union directives in the field of unfair competition law, which follow the triple objective to protect the interests of competitors, consumers and the public in general.[18] The choice-of-law rule hence reflects the main objective of unfair competition protection, which is to safeguard fair competition as a "level playing field" for competitors, mainly in the sense of *par conditio concurrentium*, which – as an institution – also serves the collective interests of the consumers and the public in general.[19]

Contrary to the opinion of some critics, the explicit rule of Art. 5(1) of the Rome II Proposal is not superfluous in light of the general rule for torts or

[17] *Cf.* for example *Deutscher Rat für Internationales Privatrecht*, Stellungnahme der 2. Kommission des Deutschen Rates für Internationales Privatrecht zum Vorentwurf eines Vorschlags der Europäischen Kommission für eine Verordnung des Rates über das auf außervertragliche Schuldverhältnisse anzuwendende Recht, available at http://europa.eu.int/comm/justice_home/news/consulting_public/rome_ii/deutscher_rat_internat_privatrecht_de.pdf, at 25 *et seq*. with further references.

[18] *Cf.* Sales Promotion Regulation proposal, Explanatory Memorandum, at 15.

[19] Therefore the critique of the *Zentralverband der deutschen Werbewirtschaft*, Position der deutschen Werbewirtschaft, available at http://europa.eu.int/comm/justice_home/news/consulting_public/rome_ii/zaw_de.pdf, at 12, regarding the identical reference to collective interests of consumers in Art. 6 Draft Proposal, was unjustified. The wording of Art. 5(1) Rome II proposal with respect to collective consumer interests correctly reflects the objectives of European unfair competition law and, moreover, clarifies that apart from injunctions brought by the competitors or other individuals, Art. 5(1) Rome II proposal also applies to actions for injunctions brought by consumer associations. *Cf. also* the Explanatory Memorandum, at 15.

delicts under Art. 3 of the Rome II Proposal.[20] Although the market-law principle could also be based upon the flexible opening clause of Art. 3(3) of the Rome II Proposal,[21] this would, however, not guarantee the mandatory and conclusive character of the special rule, which (consistent with the objective of unfair competition law) ensures that preparatory acts in third countries do not trigger the application of the respective countries' law if the acts have no connection with the relevant market. For example, acts that do not yet (potentially) affect a market, or mere successive damages in the enterprise of the competitor that "no longer" harm the market, must not trigger the application of the respective countries' law that would be in no connection with the unfair act at all. Thus, in general the explicit provision of Art. 5(1) of the Rome II Proposal should be met with approval.

In the original Draft of the Rome II Proposal (Art. 6 Draft Proposal), the market-law rule was the only provision concerning non-contractual obligations arising out of acts of unfair competition; an opening clause of any kind was not envisaged. However, it was correctly proposed during the consultation process on the Draft Proposal that a distinction should be made with respect to unfair practices that do not harm a competitor as a reflex of a market distortion but are aimed directly at the competitor and make themselves felt exclusively in relation to that specific competitor without reflexively distorting the market, such as when a commercial secret is violated by a competitor or a competitor inducing a breach of contract of another competitor's customers or enticing another competitor's employees to work for him.[22] In these cases, although a market effect may not always be entirely ruled out, the object of the offence is no longer the market, or fair competition as such (*par conditio concurrentium*), but the offended competitor. The mandatory application of the market-law principle therefore is no longer justified. In these cases, a mandatory conflict rule in favour of the law of the affected market would be erroneous. Rather, the competitor should have the benefit of the general rules of Art. 3 of Rome II with its additional country of residence (seat) rule (Art. 3(2) Rome II Proposal), and the flexible opening clause (Art. 3(3) Rome II Proposal), which, for example in the case of an induced breach of contract, allows the *lex causae* to apply to the act of unfair competition, *i.e.* the law applicable to the contract. The Commission has now adopted this modern view in its official Rome II Proposal, and has formulated a new paragraph 2 of Art. 5 of the Rome II Proposal to provide for the applicability of

---

[20] *Cf. Deutscher Rat für Internationales Privatrecht*, *supra* n. 17, at 26. *Cf. also* the example in the Explanatory Memorandum to the Regulation Proposal, at 16.

[21] This is the solution of the German private international law, *cf.* Art. 41 EGBGB and the Explanatory Memorandum to the law (BT-Drs. 14/343), at 10.

[22] The modern private international law of Switzerland also makes this differentiation in Art. 136 Swiss Private International Law. *Cf.* Sales Promotion Regulation proposal, Explanatory Memorandum, at 16; *cf. also Deutscher Rat für Internationales Privatrecht*, *supra* note 17, at 26.

Art. 3(2) and (3), where an act of unfair competition exclusively affects the interests of a specific competitor.

It may be asked, in the case of our topic (*i.e.* supplementary unfair competition protection against imitations), whether Art. 5(1) or the proviso of Art. 5(2) of the Rome II Proposal should apply, considering that acts of misappropriation are typically targeted against a specific competitor.[23] However, in continental European case law, situations of misappropriation are deeply rooted in the concept of protection against misleading practices (which applies even more so to the much more limited *passing-off* doctrine under British common law) and, therefore, the distortion of the market is central to considerations. This reflects the fact that in the imitation cases the offence is realised via the market only, and that establishment of unfair competition protection in these cases often requires a thorough analysis of the market position of the imitated product. Hence, Art. 5(2) of the Rome II Proposal is not applicable because such acts do not affect *exclusively* the interests of a specific competitor, but often also directly affect the interests of consumers in being protected against misleading practices. Consequently, Art. 5(1) of the Rome II Proposal has to be applied to cases of supplementary unfair competition protection against misappropriating imitations.[24]

In comparison to the Draft Proposal, the formulation of the market-law principle in Art. 5(1) of the Rome II Proposal is both narrower and broader than the original formulation. In reaction to respective propositions in the consultation process,[25] the Commission broadened the formulation by including not only acts that affect competitive relations or the collective interests of consumers, but also acts *likely* to affect those relations and interests. This formulation now clearly includes ex-ante injunctive relief, which aligns Art. 5 of the Rome II Proposal with the jurisdiction rule in Art. 5 No. 3 of Council Regulation 44/2001 of 22 December 2000. A respective amendment has been made in Art. 3(1). Therefore, this gap, which also existed with respect to the general rule of Art. 3 of the original Draft Proposal, has now been closed in both provisions.

Last but not least, the formulation of Art. 5(1) of the Rome II Proposal has been narrowed, as compared to the Draft Proposal, by limiting the provision to acts that *directly* and *substantially* affect the market. This clearly reflects the reactions in the consultation process, where various commentators remarked

---

[23] *Cf.* further on that issue *Leistner*, Unfair competition law protection against imitations – A hybrid under the future Art. 5 "Rome II"-Regulation, in: *Basedow/Drexl/Kur/Metzger* (ed.), Intellectual Property in the Conflict of Laws, Mohr Siebeck 2004, forthcoming.

[24] German private international case law acknowledges that approach. Remarkably, the market effects doctrine in German law even was originally developed by the Federal Supreme Court in a case concerning the imitation of a commercial product (*i.e.* baby-bottles), *cf.* Federal Supreme Court – *Kindersaugflasche*, 1962 GRUR 316, at 318.

[25] *Cf.* for example the Comments of the *Hamburg Group for Private International Law*, 2003 RabelsZ 2, at 19.

that the choice-of-law criteria developed in different national laws to deal with multi-state or spill-over situations[26] (especially relevant with respect to internet marketing campaigns), which all try to exclude, on the basis of a more or less objective (or subjective) standard, the application of the laws of countries where competition is not *substantially* affected,[27] could hardly be based on the original wording of the draft proposal, which included no such limitation at all.[28] The present formulation now at least makes it possible to exclude insignificant influences on third countries in "traditional" media spill-over situations, where an act of unfair competition is neither (subjectively) directed nor (objectively) apt to influence a third market substantially. The "Art.-5(1)-test", whether an act "directly and substantially" influences a third market, will have to be interpreted objectively rather than focussing on the subjective intentions of the offender.[29]

However, it must be admitted that excluding insubstantial effects on competition in foreign markets does not help to solve the problem of "hard-core" multistate-campaign situations, which are particularly relevant for euromarketing campaigns in the Internal Market. In these cases, particularly significant in the internet, the marketing campaign is intended to, and typically does, directly and substantially influence a number of national markets. From the perspective of an advertising company, this leads to a mosaic of applicable laws resulting in potentially prohibitive transaction costs (information costs), such as the cost of legal research to analyse all the applicable laws, undoubtedly hampering the development of Internal Market multistate advertising in Europe. The limitation in Art. 5(1) of the Rome II Proposal does not and cannot help in these cases. This, therefore, brings us to the question of how Art. 5 of the Rome II Proposal co-operates in these cases with the secondary-law country-of-origin principle in electronic communication and cross-border television, and with the basic freedoms of European primary law.

---

[26] As for example the different criteria (language, relevance of disclaimers, currency and so forth) German jurisprudence and doctrine have considered to make the question of *substantial* market effect more operable. *Cf.*, for a short overview with further references, *Leistner,* Werberecht im Internet, in: *Bettinger/Leistner* (ed.), Werbung und Vertrieb im Internet, at 5, at 48 *et seq*.

[27] *Cf.* from German case law, Federal Supreme Court – *Tampax*, 1971 GRUR 153, 154.

[28] *Cf.* as one example *Deutscher Rat für Internationales Privatrecht, supra* n. 17, at 17 *et seq*.

[29] *Cf.* further with special respect to the two relevant strands of thought in German legal doctrine which either focus (subjectively) on the intentions of the offender or (objectively) on the substantiality of the market effect, and the substantially objective core of both approaches, *Leistner, supra* note 26, at 48 *et seq*.

IV. The Relation Between the Country-of-Origin Principle and Art. 5 Rome II Proposal

1. Article 23 Rome II Proposal

First, Art. 23 of the Rome II Proposal must be examined. With respect to the secondary-law country-of-origin principle, Art. 23(2) of the Proposal states that the regulation

> shall not prejudice the application of Community instruments which, in relation to particular matters and in areas coordinated by such instruments, subject the supply of services or goods to the laws of the Member State where the service-provider is established and, in the area coordinated, allow restrictions on freedom to provide services or goods originating in another Member State only in limited circumstances.

Thus, the country-of-origin provisions of the E-Commerce Directive and the "Television without Frontiers" Directive remain untouched. Further, possible future comparable provisions, such as the Sales Promotion Regulation and the Unfair Practices Directive, which may also introduce the country-of-origin principle, will also be covered by Art. 23(2) of the Rome II Proposal.

The new formulation of Art. 23(2) of the Rome II Proposal, as compared to the Draft Proposal, does away with a small flaw in the wording of the original proposal – again reflecting respective propositions raised in the consultation process.[30] The original formulation in the Draft Proposal made reference to restrictions on freedom *to provide services* only; while this seemed sufficient to cover the existing provisions in the field of television broadcasting and e-commerce (which both apply to services), the wording nevertheless disregarded the fact that quite often (and, in the case of commercial communication under the E-Commerce Directive, possibly typically) the *free movement of goods* will also be affected, for example when an electronic advertisement for a certain product is concerned. This is in line with the general observation that, with respect to electronic commerce, the dividing line between free movement of goods and freedom to provide services in the Internal Market becomes thinner and thinner.[31] Thus, to provide an open and – with respect to the basic freedoms – complete framework, Art. 23(2) of the Draft Proposal had to be changed to its present wording, which now rightfully comprises both the freedom to provide services and the free movement of goods. However, the result and starting point for our survey remains the same, namely: the choice-of-law provisions of the Rome II Proposal appear, at first glance, to overlap with the country-of-origin principles in certain areas of secondary Community law and Art. 23(2) provides that the

---

[30] *Cf. Deutscher Rat für Internationales Privatrecht, supra* note 17, at 17.

[31] As the example of music-on-demand services in the internet which allow the user to press his own personal CDs proves manifestly. *Cf. also Drexl, supra* note 15.

latter should prevail while systematically distinguishing the country-of-origin principles clearly from other prevailing choice-of-law rules of Community law, which are dealt with separately in Art. 23(1).

2. The Interplay of Art. 5 Rome II Proposal With Country-of-Origin Rules: Evaluation of the Arguments in Legal Doctrine

This overlap has already been widely addressed. Two extreme positions with respect to that issue can be identified when screening the reactions in the consultation process. These positions are inextricably linked with their respective understanding of the country-of-origin principle itself.[32] Those who tried to interpret the "odious" new rule of the E-Commerce Directive as narrowly as possible, by understanding it as a choice of law including the country of origin's private international law, which typically again results in the application of the wide-spread and more or less similar market-law principles found in national laws, now demand the re-establishment of the predominance of private international law, since the basic freedoms were sufficient to safeguard the completion of the Internal Market.[33] In contrast, those who understood the country-of-origin principle (and in part even the functioning of the basic freedoms[34]), in spite of the explicit statement to the contrary of the E-Commerce Directive,[35] as conflict-of-law rules choosing the substantive law of the origin country, now favour the general introduction of this principle as a clear-cut conflicts rule for non-contractual obligations arising from inner-European unfair advertising in Art. 5 of the Rome II Proposal.[36]

The first solution, that is, to rely upon the basic freedoms of European primary law, seems to be politically unrealistic and, moreover, of little positive effect with respect to the completion of the Internal Market. This is because the current reserve of the ECJ in inner-community advertising cases, resulting from the *Keck* judgment, raises doubts with respect to the efficient application

---

[32] *Cf.* for the discussion in Germany (instead of numerous references, including several doctoral dissertations), the two recent articles, by *Spindler,* Herkunftslandprinzip und Kollisionsrecht – Binnenmarktintegration ohne Harmonisierung?, 2002 RabelsZ 633, and *Grundmann,* Das Internationale Privatrecht der E-Commerce-Richtlinie – was ist kategorial anders im Kollisionsrecht des Binnenmarkts und warum?, 2003 RabelsZ 246, both with comprehensive further references.

[33] *Cf.* for example *Jayme/Pfeiffer,* for the *Institut für ausländisches und internationales Privat- und Wirtschaftsrecht,* Kurze Stellungnahme zu einigen zentralen Aspekten [des Rom-II Vorentwurfs], available at http://europa.eu.int/comm/justice_home/news/consulting_public/rome_ii/ universitat_heidelberg_de.pdf (visited 19 October 2003), at 10 *et seq*.

[34] Consistent in this respect the approach of *Basedow,* Der kollisionsrechtliche Gehalt der Produktfreiheiten im europäischen Binnenmarkt: favor offerentis, 59 RabelsZ 1 (1995).

[35] *Cf.* Art. 1(4) E-Commerce Directive.

[36] *Cf.* namely *Mankowski,* Internet und internationales Wettbewerbsrecht, 1999 GRUR Int. 909, and now the proposal of the *Hamburg Group for Private International Law, supra* note 25, at 19 *et seq*.

of the basic freedoms to inner-community advertising on the internet. Furthermore, the secondary-law country-of-origin principle is much more effective than the ECJ's *Dassonville/Cassis* doctrine because it no longer allows the justification of restrictions of the basic freedoms by mandatory requirements, such as fair commercial practices or consumer protection, except by way of a complicated preliminary procedure in Art. 3(4)–(6) of the E-Commerce Directive, which will most likely remain of little relevance.[37] For this reason a U-turn towards the purely private-international-law solution, interpreting the country-of-origin principle as referring to the private international law of the state of origin (resulting typically in the application of the market law principle), does not appear to be the best alternative.

Likewise, the other extreme position, the proposal of the *Hamburg Group*[38] to transfer the country-of-origin principle into a proper conflict-of-laws rule of private international law as far as inter-community advertising is concerned, would at least partially contradict the original objective of the principle as it was formulated in the E-Commerce Directive, aimed at minimising restrictions of the basic freedoms originating in Member States other than the country of origin. Hence, the Commission was right not to follow this proposition in its official Rome II Proposal text. Only a middle-ground (not a compromise) solution that accepts the complex co-application of the future EC conflict-of-laws rule at the first stage, and the country-of-origin rule as a substantive law principle that expresses the basic freedoms and that may result in corrections of the result of the choice-of-law rule at the second stage (non-application of overprotective provisions of the applicable law), leads to appropriate results with respect to the completion of the Internal Market. This shall be shown by the following example, which again focuses on the question of supplementary unfair competition imitation protection for non-registered designs. Two substantive law instruments overlap in this field, the unfair competition protection, with Art. 5 of the Rome II Proposal as the conflict-of-laws rule (which has to be seen in combination with the e-commerce country-of-origin principle) and, on the other hand, the new unitary unregistered Community design protection, which can potentially apply. The latter, as for the non-harmonised sanctions, follows the general choice-of-law rules,[39] which, in the field of industrial property rights, are explicitly not subject to the country-of-origin principle. This three-level private international law situation makes the area particularly attractive for demonstrating the co-functioning of choice-of-law rules, the substantive country-of-origin principle and the development of secondary European law harmonisation.

---

[37] Although it proves the inner relation of the secondary law country-of-origin principle with the ECJ-jurisdiction concerning the basic freedoms, *cf.* for example *Ohly*, Herkunftslandprinzip und Kollisionsrecht, 2001 GRUR Int. 899, 902.

[38] *Hamburg Group for Private International Law, supra* note 25.

[39] *Cf.* the articles by *Schaper* and *Metzger* in this book.

3. Case Example: Unfair Competition Law Protection Against Imitations

In our case, company A, established in England, publishes an advertisement on the internet in which it systematically uses icons or graphic elements that have been copied from his competitor, company B, established in Germany. The website is in the English language and is accessible throughout Europe. Company B files an action for an order to cease and desist and a claim for damages in Germany. German Courts have jurisdiction according to Art. 5(3) of European Regulation No. 44/2001 on jurisdiction and the recognition and enforcements of judgments in civil and commercial matters (Jurisdiction and Judgments Regulation)[40] for the cease-and-desist order and for the damages claim, as far as damage is incurred in the German market. We will assume that supplementary unfair competition protection is applicable under German law (because of the systematic character of the imitation), while the requirements to bring a claim of passing-off under English law are not met.

Let us first solve the case under the assumption that the elements of company A's icons and graphics are not protected by IP rights, setting aside for the moment the new unregistered Community design protection. If we understand the country-of-origin principle as a choice-of-law rule, the German judge would have to compare English and German law concerning the issue and would then have to apply the more liberal English law from the very beginning, even if the defendant did not appear or raise a defence. Using the country-of-origin principle as a *substantive* European law principle governed by the aim to protect the Internal Market against restrictions on the basic freedoms would also lead to the same end-result, since the higher protection standard in Germany results in a restriction of the freedom to provide services as compared to the more liberal English law standard. However, there are some remarkable differences between the approaches, especially at the procedural stage. If the judge follows the substantive European law understanding of the country-of-origin principle, he would first have to apply the traditional unfair competition conflict-of-laws rule which would require the application of German law. Then, as a second step, if and – at least with respect to the practically relevant injunctive relief actions – only if (!) the defendant reacts and objects, will the country-of-origin rule require the application of the more liberal test under English law. The application of the stricter German law standard will be suppressed by the substantive European law country-of-origin rule.[41] English law will not even be applied in the

---

[40] Council Regulation (EC) No. 44/2001 of 22 December 2000 on jurisdiction and the recognition and enforcements of judgments in civil and commercial matters, 2001 OJ EC L 12, at 1.

[41] *Cf. Ahrens*, Das Herkunftslandprinzip in der E-Commerce-Richtlinie, 2000 CR 835; *Leistner, supra* note 26, at 55; more reserved also *Ohly, supra* note 37, at 903.

strict sense, but the German judge would only refer to it as an object for a basic-freedoms-oriented comparison, which nonetheless naturally results in a factual conflict-of-laws rule being applied in this case when the English standard is more liberal. The procedural difference to the private international law understanding is significant, because in cases in which the defendant does not react at all, the private international law understanding of the country-of-origin principle would lead to a different result. This is because, under German law, the Court would have to apply the conflict-of-laws rule *ex officio*, even when the defendant does not invoke this argument, whereas the substantive-law understanding would require the defendant to raise a defence. Paradoxically, the conflict-of-laws understanding of the country-of-origin principle would thus lead to a lack of harmonisation with respect to intra-Community private international law application, since, for example in the United Kingdom, the conflict rule, *i.e.* the non-applicability of English law, would have to be invoked by the defendant. Moreover, under German procedural law, the private international law understanding would lead to an almost systematic, and potentially unjustified, split between jurisdiction and applicable law. This is particularly true in the field of consumer protection and advertisement law, since Art. 5(3) of the Jurisdiction and Judgments Regulation typically envisages jurisdiction in the target country.[42] A private international law country-of-origin rule, on the other hand, would inevitably require the application of the origin country's substantive law, even when there is no reaction from the defendant at all, therefore typically requiring the national court to apply foreign substantive law.

---

[42] The obvious counter-argument that the E-Commerce Directive exempts consumer contract law from the application of the country-of-origin principle (*cf.* Art. 3(3), Annex, E-Commerce Directive) is not valid. Because the exemption applies only to "*contractual* obligations concerning consumer contracts", whereas actions for damages arising out of an act of unfair competition, and likewise all other forms of torts, delict and quasi-delict, remain untouched. Thus, not only with respect to the individual action of competitors, but also with respect to the partly far-reaching collective actions of consumer associations under national law, the "structural" split of jurisdiction and applicable law would typically occur. *Cf.* the recent decision of the ECJ, decision of 1 October 2002, Case C-167/2000, *Henkel*, [2002] ECR I-8111, available at www.curia.eu.int, where the Court held that "a preventive action brought by a consumer protection organisation for the purpose of preventing a trader from using of terms considered to be unfair in contracts . . . is a matter relating to tort, delict or quasi-delict within the meaning of Art. 5(3) of that convention [now the Jurisdiction and Judgments Regulation]". This can be easily transposed to the wide range of collective actions of consumers' and competitors' organisations in the field of (continental European) unfair competition law. Hence, in "internet multistate cases" the inevitable result would be that jurisdiction would be given in the target state, while a choice-of-law understanding of Art. 3 E-Commerce Directive (or even a clear-cut conflicts rule in Art. 5 Rome II convention in favour of the applicability of the country-of-origin's substantive law, as it has been proposed (*cf. supra* 2)) would, at the same time, lead to the applicability of the source state's substantive law. A structurally typical and inevitable split of jurisdiction and applicable law to such an extent cannot be efficient for the functioning of the Internal Market.

The substantive Internal-Market-oriented understanding of the country-of-origin principle, on the other hand, guarantees a procedurally consistent application of the principle throughout Europe and, moreover, ensures that the inefficient gap between jurisdiction and applicable law, which may result from the application of the country-of-origin rule, exists only when it is made unavoidable by the necessity to protect the basic freedoms of the Internal Market. The resulting duty of the defendant to at least react to the action and invoke the more liberal standard in his country seems acceptable. Therefore, while leading to the substantially same result with respect to the basic freedoms, the substantive-law concept of the country-of-origin principle seems to be the more efficient way to reach that goal. Thus, while at first sight the two-tier solution of applying the traditional choice-of-law rule at the first stage and correcting the result through application of the country-of-origin principle at the second stage may appear to be more complicated than a clear-cut choice-of-law rule, our case shows that it is the only efficient way to reduce the number of cases in which jurisdiction and applicable law diverge to the degree at which it is impossible to guarantee the functioning of the basic freedoms.[43]

The procedural law difference between the two approaches becomes an even more significant substantive law difference when we change the circumstances of the case by "twisting it around". Let us now imagine that the defendant, company A, is established in Germany, where he publishes the imitating advertisement on the internet and is subsequently sued in England by an English competitor, company B. The choice-of-law understanding, at least in its clear-cut version as it was proposed by the *Hamburg Group*[44] as an amendment to the Draft Regulation (which in this respect would even have exceeded the version of the E-Commerce Directive that establishes a comparison of the laws[45]), leads to the result that the English judge has to apply

[43] Furthermore, with respect to defendants from third countries outside the European Economic Area, the solution seems even clearer than a split conflict norm, which would otherwise be inevitable in these cases. The substantive understanding leaves the general choice-of-law rule untouched even for parties from third countries, and restricts only the correction on the second stage to defendants from the European Economic Area states. This result follows directly from the character of the basic freedoms. *See* further *Ohly, supra* note 37, at 902.

[44] *Cf.* the proposed Art. 6(2) of the *Hamburg Group for Private International Law, supra* note 25.

[45] However, the formulations of the "Internal Market", or "country-of-origin" rules by the Commission in the newly proposed instruments in the unfair competition law field, *i.e.* Art. 4 Unfair Practices Directive Proposal and Art. 3 Sales Promotion Regulation Proposal (*cf. supra* notes 12 and 13), seemed to follow a different, more conflict-of-laws-oriented approach. These newly proposed provisions explicitly state that in the unified or harmonised areas "traders shall comply only with the national provisions of the Member State in which they are established". These new formulations of the country-of-origin rule through the Commission could arguably only be read as providing for a proper private international law-style principle of mutual recognition. However, the new

German law, therefore generating another inconvenient split of jurisdiction and applicable law. Moreover, in this case the non-application of English law is not at all justified by the protection of the basic freedoms since the position under English law is even more liberal. Thus, the choice-of-law understanding leads to an unnecessary split of jurisdiction and applicable law, which, in addition, restricts the freedoms to supply services and to trade in goods. This result seems not only inefficient but almost contradictory to the development of the Internal Market. By comparison, the Internal-Market-oriented understanding of the country-of-origin principle leads to an acceptable result in this case: the conflict-of-laws rule of Art. 5 of the Rome II Proposal implies the application of English law. As the English standard is more liberal than that under German law, no correction of this result is necessary and the choice-of-law rule remains untouched. The English judge applies English law.

In summary, in areas (like e-commerce) where European law already provides for the country-of-origin principle,[46] the two-tier co-application of the choice-of-law rule in Art. 5 of the Rome II Proposal (first stage), and of the secondary law country-of-origin provisions in an interpretation oriented towards the protection of the basic freedoms (second, Internal-Market-oriented "correction" stage), as provided for in Art. 23(2) of the Rome II Proposal, leads to the best result with respect to the further development of the Internal Market. It is, moreover, coherent with the formulation of the Internal Market rule in the E-Commerce Directive, which explicitly does not establish additional rules on private international law.[47] For all of these reasons Art. 5 of the Rome II Proposal should remain as it is and the inter-

---

formulation of the country-of-origin principle in the Unfair Commercial Practices Directive Proposal of the Commission was politically not accepted by the Member States. Hence, as regards the Unfair Commercial Practices Directive Proposal, the political agreement reached in the Council (cf. Council Doc. 9667/04 of May 25 2004) explicitly cancels the private international law-style formulation in Art. 4 (1) of the Commission's Proposal. This leaves only the provision regarding restrictions on the freedom to supply services or goods (*cf.* Art. 4(2) Unfair Practices Directive Proposal) which again provides for a clear substantive law understanding of the country-of-origin principle forbidding the Member States to "restrict the free movement of goods" for reasons falling within the approximated field. Hence, the new formulation of the Unfair Commercial Practices Proposal even affirms the substantive-law understanding of the existing country-of-origin rules, as it is brought forward here. As regards the Sales Promotion Regulation Proposal (which at present seems deadlocked politically), a similar political decision in the Council can arguably be predicted. Cf. further on the Unfair Commercial Practices Proposal (in its original form) *Leistner*, in: Cambridge Yearbook of European Law Studies 2004.

[46] *Cf.*, for the new proposals of the Commission in the fields of Unfair Commercial Practices, and of Sales Promotions, *supra* note 45.

[47] *Cf.* Art. 1(4) E-Commerce Directive. For the extensive discussion on the relevance of this limitation, *cf.* the original metaphor of *Ohly*, *supra* note 37, at 900 *et seq.* ("Magritte theory", inspired by the painting "Ceci n'est pas une pipe" by René Magritte), with further references.

play with the country-of-origin rules should be interpreted in the manner proposed above.

4. The Country-of-Origin Principle as a Part of Substantive European Law and Its Proper Application

However, the *Hamburg Proposal*, a horizontal conflict-of-law concept for intra-Community advertising establishing a proper, clear-cut country-of-origin conflict-of-laws rule, would go far beyond the sector-specific secondary-law country-of-origin provisions (e-commerce, cross-border TV). This could at least be useful for the development of the Internal Market in respect of traditional advertising methods in intra-community cases.

Remarkably, the proposal of the *Hamburg Group* in this respect is explicitly based on the assumption that the harmonisation of substantive law is "particularly far advanced" in the area of "advertising law".[48] This assumption, at least at present, seems highly disputable with respect to unfair advertising. Moreover, even the envisaged Unfair Practices Directive will not essentially change this situation, because, regrettably, its scope is limited to the business-to-consumer area, while general advertising law also applies in "B2B" situations. In addition, the dividing line between advertising law (where the country-of-origin principle should apply according to the *Hamburg Proposal*) and the general law of unfair competition (where the market-effects principle would prevail) may be hard to identify and is inextricably interwoven with substantive law questions, as our example case of an advertisement using imitated elements without leading to a passing-off action in the strict sense shows.

The status quo in European unfair competition law gives rise to a more general objection. The country-of-origin principle can only work effectively when two conditions are given.[49] The first condition is, indeed, a certain minimum harmonisation framework that does not exist in the field of unfair competition in general and hardly even in the smaller field of advertising law.

Remarkably, in the area of copyright, where up to now the country-of-origin principle has not even been seriously considered in European law, the level of harmonisation is much higher. The minimum harmonisation level is required because the implementation of the secondary-law country-of-origin principle fails to incorporate an important part of the warning system that the ECJ's *Dassonville/Cassis* doctrine represents with respect to "blind

---

[48] *Cf. Hamburg Group for Private International Law, supra* note 25, at 19.

[49] *Cf.* in general, for the conditions that must be given to make the concept of regulatory competition (*competitive federalism*) work without market failure, *Barnard*, Social Dumping Revisited: Lessons from Delaware, 2000 European Law Review, 57; *Charny*, Competition among Jurisdictions in Formulating Corporate Law Rules: An American Perspective on the 'Race to the Bottom' in the European Communities, 32 Harvard International Law Journal, 422 (1991); *Kieninger*, Wettbewerb der Privatrechtsordnungen im Europäischen Binnenmarkt, 2002.

spots" of harmonisation. The way this warning system works can again be demonstrated by an example from the field of IP law. In this respect, we only have to remember that no fewer than three of the European copyright directives, the Cable and Satellite Directive,[50] the Rental and Lending Directive[51], and the Term of Protection Directive,[52] resulted more or less directly from the refusal of the ECJ to "overrule" national copyright law provisions, leading to restrictions of the free movement of goods and the freedom to provide services in the Internal Market.[53] Without going into detail, in all these cases the ECJ has stated that the differences between national copyright laws may give rise to restrictions of the basic freedoms, but that such restrictions were justified under Art. 30 EC as long as they were the result of differences that were inseparably linked to the very existence of the exclusive copyright. Thus, the cases where the ECJ did not succeed in giving precedence to the basic freedoms because of the inevitable possibility of justification on the basis of Art. 30 EC along the lines of the *Dassonville/Cassis* doctrine, *i.e.* where copyright law prevailed over the freedoms of free trade of goods and providing of services in the Internal Market, helped to find the blind spots of harmonisation, leading more or less directly to the adoption of respective Community instruments.

The secondary-law, country-of-origin principle in the E-Commerce Directive almost entirely removes this warning system, because derogations from the principle in the coordinated area can no longer be justified by public policy reasons except by way of the complicated preliminary procedure of Art. 3(4)(b) of the E-Commerce Directive, which has virtually no relevance outside the field of legislation.[54] The flexible interplay of basic freedoms and exclusive IP rights is replaced by a predominant Internal

---

[50] 1993 OJ EC No. L 248/16–21. The Cable and Satellite Directive can be associated with the ECJ ruling in ECJ, decision of 6 October 1982, Case 262/81, *Coditel SA v. Ciné Vog Films SA*, [1982] ECR 3381, where the court decided that the split licensing of film-performance rights was part of the substance of national copyright provisions, and therefore not affected by the provisions of the treaty on the free supply of services. This decision with respect to Cable and Satellite TV had weighty implications regarding the basic freedoms of the Treaty, which pressed the Commission into action.

[51] OJ EC 1992 L 346, p. 61–66, which can be seen as rooted in the ECJ, decision of 17 May 1988, *Warner Brothers v. Christiansen*, [1988] ECR 2605, which pressed the Commission into action with respect to the resulting restrictions of free trade of (rental) videotapes in the Community.

[52] OJ EC 1993 L 290 p. 9–13, which can be associated in a similar way to ECJ, decision of 24 January 1989, *EMI Electrola v. Patricia*, [1989] ECR 79, which – obviously – held that the national provisions on the term of protection of copyright and related rights prevailed (as part of the substance of national protection rights) over the basic freedoms of the Treaty.

[53] This development has been very clearly pointed out by *Cohen Jehoram*, The EC Copyright Directives, Economics and Authors' Rights, 25 IIC 821, 822 *et seq.* (1994).

[54] With the small exception of the possibility, in urgent cases, to file notification of measures after their application; Art. 3(5)–(6) E-Commerce Directive.

Market approach, which generates a less focussed harmonisation pressure in the whole coordinated area and leaves it to the Commission to discover the "neuralgic points" where further harmonisation is needed. Any "workable" competition between the national law systems of the Member States to be promoted by the country-of-origin rule therefore presupposes a certain minimum harmonisation framework and an active role for the Commission. In areas governed by country-of-origin rules the Commission will now be responsible for discovering, on its own account, future "neuralgic points" in the coordinated area that need further harmonisation.

This leads us to the second condition that ideally should be fulfilled to make this system work and that has been formulated most clearly by *Ohly*.[55] The necessary development of certain unitary Community minimum standards in the coordinated area can only be effectively promoted when the country-of-origin principle is understood as a part of substantive European law derived from the basic freedoms, which only indirectly leads to a superseding of private international law conflict rules. The decisive consequence of this understanding is that in *harmonised* areas, where European secondary law either follows the approach of minimum or factually conclusive harmonisation by means of directives, the respective national laws of the target market Member State (chosen according to Art. 5(1) of the Rome II Proposal) should be compared with the standard of European law and not the law of the country of origin, when applying the country-of-origin rule of the E-Commerce Directive or other future comparable provisions.[56] In any case, in areas unified by regulations, national law is no longer applied anyway, and the proper interpretation of the Community instrument has to be left to the ECJ by way of preliminary references according to Art. 234 EC.

Similarly, with respect to national law implementing conclusive provisions of directives, the national court could simply apply the national law provision; the subsequent question, whether the national law provision meets the harmonised European protection standard (and thus cannot lead to a restriction of the basic freedoms in the sense of the country-of-origin principle), would then again be a question that has to be referred to the ECJ in the framework of Art. 234 of the EC Treaty. With respect to minimum provisions in directives, the standard of the national law should be compared with the (minimum) standard set by the directive, the interpretation of which, if necessary, again has to be referred to the ECJ. If the national provision or case law does not exceed the minimum standard, a restriction of the freedom to trade goods or supply services cannot result from it.[57] This

[55] *Ohly, supra* note 37, at 902 *et seq*.

[56] For a further description of this approach, *see Ohly, op.cit*.

[57] *Cf. also* Art. 1(3) E-Commerce Directive: "This Directive complements Community law applicable to information society services without prejudice to the level of protection for, in particular, public health and consumer interests, as established by Community acts and national legislation implementing them in so far as this does not restrict the freedom to provide information society services."

solution would encourage the further development of European substantive law standards by promoting the essential role of the ECJ in this respect. At the same time, it would help minimise the inconvenient splitting of jurisdiction and applicable law (which as a result of this approach could only occur in non-harmonised fields of law) to the level that is absolutely necessary for the functioning of the Internal Market. Nonetheless, the objectives of the country-of-origin principle would be met, since the application of a national provision that implements either a conclusive or a minimum-harmonisation provision of a directive, and does not exceed the latter, cannot lead to a restriction of the basic freedoms, as it properly reflects the protection standard of European secondary law.[58]

However, some objections to this approach weigh heavily and have to be considered carefully. First, it seems indeed doubtful that the Court, given its organisational structure and capacity, could at present fulfil such a significantly extended role efficiently. Then again, it could be advantageous, from a long-term political perspective, to promote the jurisdiction of the Court as discussed above and hence push on its institutional development into a proper court of appeal of the European Union, a development that has already led to the installation of the Court of First Instance. Second, the approach proposed here could be objected to on the basis that at first glance it inevitably entails a comparison of national standards with European directives,[59] leading to a direct horizontal effect of the latter, which is improper according to the case law of the ECJ.[60]

However, on consideration, this is not the case when the two-tier system proposed here is applied properly. According to this interpretation, at the first stage, the national court applies the national law, which is determined by Art. 5 of the Rome II Proposal. It then applies the *national* provision, which implements the country-of-origin rule of the E-Commerce Directive into national law (*i.e.* in Germany, Sec. 4 of the Teleservices Act, or TDG). This provision, for example in Germany, provides that the national law must not be applied in the coordinated area if and insofar as its application would lead to a restriction of the freedom to supply services or goods. Only in applying this (national law) test, *i.e.* in determining if a restriction of the basic freedoms would result from the application of the national law, does a national court have to compare "its" respective (target country's) national law with secondary European law. If this test determines that a restriction of the free movement of goods or services would follow from the application of the national law, the national court does not, however, apply the provisions of a directive directly. On the contrary, the national court simply does *not* apply

[58] *Cf.* Art. 1(3) E-Commerce Directive, *supra* note 57.

[59] This highly valuable argument was first told me by *Axel Metzger* in the very fruitful discussions we had on that subject.

[60] ECJ, decision of 19 January 1982, *Ursula Becker v. Finanzamt Münster-Innenstadt*, 1982 ECR 53.

the respective (less liberal) provisions of its national law. Therefore, the issue raised by the country-of-origin principle is not so much about the choice of which law to apply, but rather about which provisions of national law *not* to apply. Hence, following the approach proposed here, a national court would only apply the national provision that implements the European country-of-origin principle and interpret it in the light of secondary European law (which, again, according to the ECJ case law, has to be taken into account anyway[61]).

5. Conclusion

From this flexible approach it follows that the country-of-origin principle is the less invasive and the more acceptable the higher the level of harmonisation is in the relevant area. This inner relation of the level of harmonisation with the country-of-origin principle is also clearly demonstrated by our example case, to return to the new uniform unregistered Community design protection. Let us assume that the icon or graphic element in our case is protected under the new unregistered Community design right.[62] This right doubtlessly provides for an acceptable standard of design protection throughout Europe. Compared with the existing Community trademark system and the protection of registered Community designs, this instrument is unique in that it requires no registration and therefore directly cumulates with national instruments of protection in this field. Therefore, the remaining field of application for German and continental European unfair competition imitation protection (for elements of an even lower level of novelty and individuality than required for the community instrument) can, without further ado, be made subject to the country-of-origin principle, since a certain average protection standard is directly available in secondary European law. The comparison with other, more liberal national laws in this field will sooner or later lead to the abolishment of German supplementary unfair competition law protection of designs, and this development should not be regretted, as European secondary law provides for a sufficient standard of protection in this field.

At the same time, the new Community instruments should be promoted as far as possible. An efficient way to do this could be the harmonisation of sanctions for the Community rights only. However, this approach has not really been followed in the Community trademark and design protection Regulations, which instead rely largely on the complementary function of national laws in this field.[63] Therefore, for the remaining choice-of-law

---

[61] ECJ, decision of 14 July 1994, *Faccini Dori v. Recreb Srl*, [1994] ECR I-3325.

[62] *Cf.* further on that issue *Kur, supra* note 4.

[63] For this reason the envisaged far-reaching harmonisation of sanctions in the framework of the Directive on measures and procedures to ensure the enforcement of intellectual property rights of 29 April 2004, OJ L 157, 16, seems the more contestable. In particular it has to be taken into account that the new instrument seems not sufficiently

questions with respect to non-harmonised sanctions (including damage claims), solutions should be found that promote as far as possible the development of the unitary Community instruments as compared to the national protection rights. Here, no correction by country-of-origin rules is needed, as the unitary European standard combined with the system of specialised national European Courts[64] guarantees the necessary legal certainty of the potential defendant with respect to substantive law. In the field of sanctions, conflict rules therefore can be determined more freely. Choice-of-law rules should be formulated that effectively allow rightholders to claim their rights and that are aligned with jurisdiction principles as far as possible.

When these comments were conceived, the then-Draft Proposal of the Commission contained no explicit provision concerning the infringement of intellectual property rights, however. Moreover, *Josef Drexl* has brought forward impressive arguments showing that the time to include such provisions into the Rome II Regulation may not yet have arrived. However, the official Rome II Proposal of the Commission now incorporates, in Art. 8, explicit provisions for intellectual property rights, which try to differentiate between national intellectual property rights and the new uniform Community industrial property rights. The question as to whether these provisions are really capable of reaching their goal is not the topic of this presentation; ongoing discussion on this issue should be followed with some interest.

V. Results

It remains to sum up the results of our analysis of the relationship between Art. 5 of the Rome II Proposal and the European secondary-law country-of-origin principle. Basically, some clear conclusions can be drawn and a somewhat provocative issue opened up.

The clear results can be summed up in the form of theses:

1. the Rome II Proposal should be adopted in their present form. The amendments made to the original Draft Proposal are justified and can be met with approval.

---

co-ordinated with the sanctions of the Community instruments, the more so with respect to the future Community Patents Regulation, which will contain separate provisions on sanctions and procedure. In this respect, and for the reasons mentioned here, it would have been more recommendable, first, to harmonise the sanctions for the Community instruments, and then in a longer-term perspective, to tackle the harmonisation of sanctions in general, which moreover should have been adjusted to the more general issue of a thinkable future approximation of general tort law. *Cf.* further on the criticism regarding the original Directive Proposal (COM (2003) 46 final, of 30 January 2003), *Cornish/Drexl/Hilty/Kur,* Procedures and Remedies for Enforcing IPRs: The European Commission's Proposed Directive, 25 (10) E.I.P.R. 447 (2003).

[64] *Cf.* Art. 80 Community Designs Regulation.

2. The European secondary-law country-of-origin principle of the E-Commerce Directive has to be interpreted in a substantive sense in line with the basic freedoms of the Internal Market. It does not state a choice-of-law rule in itself, although it may lead to a correction of the private-international-law connection of Art. 5 of the Rome II Proposal. This result remains unchanged, and should apply mutatis mutandis even with respect to possible new country-of-origin ("Internal Market") provisions in the Sales Promotion Regulation and in the Unfair Practices Directive.
3. The co-application of the choice-of-law rule in Art. 5 of the Rome II Proposal (at the first stage) and of substantive European secondary-law country-of-origin provisions in specific areas of law (at the second, Internal Market-oriented "correction" stage), as it is envisaged in Art. 23(2) of the Rome II Proposal, is the best guarantee for the further development of the Internal Market.
4. Article 5 of the Rome II Proposal should not include a general conflict-of-laws rule specifying the law of the country of origin in cases of intra-Community advertising.
5. Choice-of-law rules should deliberately be used to promote the further acceptance of unitary Community IP rights and thus to promote the completion of the Internal Market

With respect to the last point of the summary, an entirely new and, admittedly, highly provocative prospect is disclosed when we recall another observation mentioned earlier: in copyright law, which has reached a much higher level of harmonisation than advertising law, the country-of-origin principle as a substantive principle has never been considered. This is understandable with respect to the international copyright system, which traditionally grants the copyright holder a bundle of national copyrights and is, for the moment, without an alternative. However, what if in a long-term perspective a "Community Copyright Regulation" were established parallel to national copyright laws,[65] thus – as a "minimum" standard – exposing the national copyright laws to competition with one another, pressured by a possible country-of-origin rule on restrictions of the basic freedoms exceeding the uniform European rules in cross-border cases? The model of unregistered Community design protection shows that such a proposition is not entirely unimaginable, even in the area of unregistered IP rights. Of course, this is not a prospect for the foreseeable future. However, from this perspective, the future co-existence of Community and national design protection should be followed with even higher interest.

[65] This bold and rather visionary idea has been developed in several talks with *Annette Kur*, in the wider framework of the informal "Fridays' round" of the Max Planck Institute, organised by *Josef Drexl* and *Reto Hilty*.

Choice-of-Law Rules in the EU – Special Issues with Respect to Community Rights – Infringement of Community Trade Marks and Applicable Law*

EIKE SCHAPER**

I. Insufficiency of the *lex loci protectionis* Rule

Like all registered industrial property rights, the Community trade mark is limited territorially. This territoriality has consequences with respect to private international law: Community trade marks are governed by the *lex loci protectionis*.

Seen in the context of national trade mark rights, the *lex loci protectionis* rule means that the applicable law is that of the country in which the right is protected, or, more precisely, the law of the country for which protection is claimed.[1]

However, this definition of the *lex loci protectionis* rule needs to be adapted for Community rights.[2] For example, unless provided otherwise in the Community Trade Mark Regulation (CTMR), Community trade marks have equal effect or "universal character" throughout the entire Community.[3] Therefore, if protection is claimed for the European Community, it is not the law of a particular country, but the law of the

* Talk held on July 21, 2003, at Frauenchiemsee during the symposium on Jurisdiction and Choice of Law in Intellectual Property Matters – Perspectives for the Future (EU and World-Wide), organised by the Max Planck Institute for Intellectual Property, Competition and Tax Law.

See on this topic also the recent article by Knaak, Das auf die Sanktionen gem. Art. 98 der Gemeinschaftsmarkenverordnung anwendbare Recht, in: Keller & Plassmann & von Falck (ed.), Festschrift für Winfried Tilmann zum 65. Geburtstag, 2003, at 373–382, which has not been considered.

** Lawyer in Munich. The author can be reached at eike.schaper@gleisslutz.com.

[1] *Ulmer*, Die Immaterialgüterrechte im internationalen Privatrecht, 1975, No. 18 *et seq.*, No. 110, and at 108, 110: proposed Art. A(1), H; *cf.* ECJ, judgement of 22 June 1994, Case C-9/93, *IHT Internationale Heiztechnik GmbH v. Ideal Standard GmbH* [1994] ECR I-2789: "it is the law of the country where protection of a trade mark is sought which determines the conditions of that protection."

[2] *Cf. Ulmer, supra* note 1, No. 109, and at 110: proposed Art. G(3).

[3] Art. 1(2) CTMR, Council Regulation (EC) No. 40/94 of 20 December 1993 on the Community trade mark, OJ EC 1994 L 11/1–36.

European Community that applies. Accordingly, Community trade marks are governed by EC law itself. The CTMR is the *lex loci protectionis*.[4]

This application of the *lex loci protectionis* would be straightforward if the CTMR were to contain comprehensive provisions governing Community trade marks. However, since not all aspects of the Community trade mark are covered by the CTMR, a special choice-of-law issue arises. This is especially the case in relation to the sanctions available upon infringement of a Community trade mark. The CTMR specifies very few sanctions in case of Community trade mark infringement. Instead, with the important exception of injunctive relief in Art. 98(1) CTMR, Community trade mark courts must apply national law in respect of sanctions. This affects claims for damages or accounts of profits in particular. Other sanctions, such as erasure of the infringing mark, destruction of unlawfully marked products, disclosure of information concerning the origin and the channels of distribution of the product or concerning the publication of the judgement, may also be able to be granted depending on the respective national law of the Member State. Needless to say, there are considerable differences between the Member States as to the sanctions provided for and the preconditions governing their availability.

Which national law is to be applied to sanctions for infringement of Community trade marks?

The *lex loci protectionis* rule is not in itself sufficient to determine the applicable national law. The unitary character of the Community trade mark right means that the *locus protectionis* is the Community,[5] and the *lex loci protectionis* simply states that European Community law must therefore be applied with respect to these rights. The rule does not identify which national law must be applied where this is necessary.

As the *lex loci protectionis* rule is founded on the territorial limitation of industrial property rights, it can be deduced from that rule that only the national law of a Member State can be applied and not that of a third-party country. This is because Community rights are territorially limited to the European Community. It would be against the *lex loci protectionis* rule to apply the law of a third country or non-Member State. However, the *lex loci protectionis* rule does not identify one specific set of national laws; the national laws of all Member States are *lex loci protectionis*.

---

[4] *Fezer*, Markenrecht, 3rd ed. 2001, Einl.MarkenG, No. 174; *Fawcett & Torremans*, Intellectual Property and Private International Law, 1998, at 480.

[5] *Hamburg Group for Private International Law*, Comments on the European Commission's Draft Proposal for a Council Regulation on the Law Applicable to Non-Contractual Obligations, http://europa.eu.int/comm/justice_home/unit/civil/consultation/contributions/max_planck_en.pdf, at 23; also published in: 67 RabelsZ 1 (2003); *Basedow*, Europäisches Internationales Privatrecht, 1996 NJW 1921 at 1927; *Knaak*, Die Durchsetzung der Rechte aus der Gemeinschaftsmarke, 2001 GRUR 21, 27; now also *Commission of the European Communities*, Brussels, 22 July 2003, COM (2003) 427 final (in the following: Rome II Proposal); http://europa.eu.int/eur-lex/en/com/pdf/2003/ com2003_0427en01.pdf, at 21.

II. Conflict Rule in Art. 98(2) CTMR

The CTMR contains various conflict rules for determining the applicable national law. These can be found in particular in Title X, Arts. 97, 98 and 99 of the CTMR. We will not examine Art. 99, which deals with jurisdiction in respect of and the law applicable to provisional and protective measures.

Article 97(1) of the CTMR contains the general rule that the Community trade mark courts shall apply the provisions of the Community Trade Mark Regulation. This is in accordance with the *lex loci protectionis* rule. Article 97(2) and (3) of the CTMR also contain established rules: According to Art. 97(2), when a matter is not covered by the Regulation, the Community trade mark court shall apply national law, including the private international law provisions of such national law. As regards the applicable rules of procedure, Art. 97(3) of the CTMR provides that those of the *lex fori* shall be applied unless otherwise provided for in the Regulation.

Article 98(2) of the CTMR contains a special provision for determining the applicable national law with respect to sanctions for infringement. Whereas Art. 98(1) provides for injunctive relief, Art. 98(2) reads as follows:

> In all other respects [*i.e.*, in respect of sanctions other than injunctive relief] the Community trade mark court shall apply the law of the Member State to which the acts of infringement or threatened infringement were committed, including the private international law.

Article 98(2) CTMR is itself a conflict rule.[6] It contains a connecting factor (*see* 1. below), but also refers to the private international law of the Member States (*see* 2. below).

1. Connecting Factor

According to Art. 98(2) of the CTMR, the applicable law is that of the Member State to which the acts of infringement or threatened infringement were committed. The connecting factor is the place where the acts of infringement were committed, in other words: the *locus delicti comissi*.[7]

a. National Intellectual Property Rights

At first glance, Art. 98(2) seems to contain a classic conflict rule. It is often stated that the applicable law in case of infringement of intellectual property rights is the *lex loci delicti*.[8]

---

[6] *Tilmann*, Gemeinschaftsmarke und Internationales Privatrecht, 2001 GRUR Int. 673, 675.

[7] *Kreuzer*, in: Münchener Kommentar zum BGB, 3rd ed. 1998, Nach Art. 38 EGBGB Anh. II, No. 53.

[8] *Pfaff*, Das Internationale Privatrecht des Ausstattungsschutzes, in: *Schricker & Stauder* (ed.), Handbuch des Ausstattungsrechts, 1986, at 1109, 1158, No. 107; *Schack*, Urheberrechtsverletzung im internationalen Privatrecht – Aus der Sicht des Kollisionsrechts, 1985 GRUR Int. 523, 524; *Stauder*, Einheitliche Anknüpfung der

Due to their territorial limitation, national intellectual property rights can only be infringed in one state, *i.e.*, in their country of protection. For example, a German trade mark can only be infringed if the infringing act occurs in Germany. A German trade mark is not protected outside Germany and cannot be infringed by acts that occur exclusively abroad. Therefore, the *locus delicti* concerning a German trade mark can only be Germany. Consequently, it makes no difference whether the *lex loci delicti* or the *lex loci protectionis* is applied. Due to the territorial limitation of national intellectual property rights, the result is the same.[9]

For national intellectual property rights therefore, the relevant question is not *where* the infringing act took place. The right can in any case only be infringed in the country of protection. The relevant question is *whether* the right was infringed or not.

b. Locus Delicti with Respect to Community Rights

The situation is entirely different with respect to Community rights: because Community rights are by their nature unitary and therefore not subject to national territorial limitation, the *locus delicti* may be located in different Member States within the Community. According to the classic tort law conflict rule, both the place where the infringing act occurs and the place where the infringement affects the right may provide a connecting factor.[10] Therefore, in contrast to national intellectual property rights, which can only be infringed in their country of protection, a Community right can be infringed in different Member States at the same time. The reference to the "country of protection" – the Community – is therefore not sufficient to determine the applicable national law in this case.[11]

To give an example: A product is branded with a trade mark that infringes a Community trade mark. This unlawfully marked product is offered by someone in Germany to persons in several Member States. On the one hand, one may locate the infringing act in Germany since this is where the person making the offer is located. However, at the same time, the very same Community trade mark is also affected in those Member States in which the offer is received. With respect to the infringement of national trade marks, it is sufficient that either the place where the offer was made or the place where the offer was received is in the country of protection. Places outside the country of protection cannot provide the connecting factor in private international law, because an intellectual property right cannot be infringed in

---

Verletzungssanktionen im Gemeinschaftspatentübereinkommen, 1983 GRUR Int. 586, 588; *Fawcett & Torremans, supra* note 4, at 623.

[9] *Kreuzer, supra* note 7, No. 26; *Sack*, Das internationale Wettbewerbs- und Immaterialgüterrecht nach der EGBGB-Novelle, 2000 WRP 269, 271; *Schack, supra* note 8, at 524; *Stauder, supra* note 8, at 586.

[10] In German private international law those places are termed "*Handlungsort*" and "*Erfolgsort*".

[11] *Basedow, supra* note 5, at 1927.

countries where it does not enjoy protection. In contrast, a Community right may be infringed "over a distance". In our example, the place where the offer was made and the places where the offer was received are all in the "country of protection" – namely the Community – but in different Member States.

As in general private international tort law, determination of the applicable national law depends on how the connecting factor is defined. Is it to be the place where the infringing act occurs, the place where the infringement affects the right, or both? Usually, private international law states which of these places is to provide the relevant connecting factor.

2. Reference to Private International Law

Which private international law is to be applied? According to the traditional rule – which is included in Art. 97(2) CTMR – the private international law of the *forum* must be applied.

Article 98(2) of the CTMR diverges from this rule, stating that

> the Community trade mark court shall apply the law of the Member State to which the acts of infringement or threatened infringement were committed, including the private international law.

This means that it is not the private international law of the *forum* that must be applied, but the private international law of the *locus delicti*. This leads to the following paradoxical result.

If the *locus delicti* is identified by Art. 98(2) of the CTMR, then it is clear which private international law is to be applied. However, in this case there would be no need for the additional application of the national private international law because the CTMR itself already determines the applicable national law.

In contrast, if the applicable national law is not determined by Art. 98(2), then, because the *locus delicti* can be located within several Member States, it is also not clear which national private international law is to be applied.

Even if a national private international law could be identified, it is questionable whether this would solve the problem. The national private international law of the Member States usually refers to the *lex loci protectionis* with regard to intellectual property rights. As we have seen, the *lex loci protectionis* rule is not sufficient to determine the applicable national law if Community rights are infringed. Since the infringement of intellectual property rights can be classified as a tort,[12] the national private international law of tort may be applied.[13] The common rule in the Member States corresponds to the

---

[12] *Ulmer, supra* note 1, No. 14; *Pfaff, supra* note 8, at 1158, No. 107; *Fawcett & Torremans, supra* note 4, at 623.

[13] *Schulte-Beckhausen,* Die gerichtliche Durchsetzung von Ansprüchen wegen Verletzung der Gemeinschaftsmarke, 1999 WRP 300, 303 *et seq.*; *Knaak, supra* note 5, at 27 *et seq.*; *Knaak,* Grundzüge der Gemeinschaftsmarke und Unterschiede zum nationalen Markenrecht, 2001 GRUR Int. 665, 673.

connecting factor in Art. 98(2) of the CTMR, *i.e.* reference is to the *lex loci delicti*. Hence, the problems in determining the applicable national law remain if the *locus delicti* can be located in different Member States.

In addition to the common general rule, some – but not all – national laws of the Member States contain provisions that cover the case in which the tort was committed over a distance and therefore the *locus delicti* can be located in different states: according to German[14] and Italian[15] legislation, the plaintiff may choose between the law of the place where the infringing act occurs and the law of the place where the infringement affects the right. According to UK legislation the applicable law is that of the country in which the most significant element or elements of the events constituting the tort occurred.[16] This solution is similar to that in French private international law, which is based on case law. According to the French *Cour de Cassation*, if the elements of the infringement occur in different countries, the applicable law is determined by the closest connection.[17]

It is not difficult to see that there are many cases in which it is virtually impossible to determine the applicable national law. This is the case, for example, where the elements of the infringement occur in different countries and the applicable conflict rules in these countries differ from each other or do not provide a solution for torts committed over a distance.

A unified conflict rule would not only solve the problem that Art. 98(2) CTMR often does not even identify the applicable private international law, but could also address some of the problems specific to the infringement of Community rights.

III. Perspectives for a Conflict Rule *de lege ferenda*

Article 98(2) of the CTMR refers to the *lex loci delicti* (including private international law) in respect of sanctions for infringement of Community trade marks. The solution provided by Art. 89(1)(d) of the Council Regulation on Community Designs is similar.[18] Article 8(2) of the Rome II Proposal of July 22, 2003[19] provides for a special conflict rule where unitary Community industrial property rights are infringed:

---

[14] § 40 Einführungsgesetz zum Bürgerlichen Gesetzbuche (EGBGB), law of 12 May 1999.

[15] Art. 62, law of 31 May 1995, note 218, Riforma del sistema italiano di diritto internazionale privato.

[16] Sec. 11(2)(c) Private International Law (Miscellaneous Provisions) Act 1995 (c. 42).

[17] Cour de cassation 1re chambre civil, decision of 11 May 1999, *Mobil North Sea*, 1999 (126) Journal du Droit international, founded by Edouard Clunet (JDI / Clunet) 1048, 1049.

[18] Council Regulation (EC) 6/2002 of 12 December 2001 on Community designs, OJ EC 2002 L 3/1–24.

[19] *Supra* note 5. Such a provision was not contained in the preliminary draft Rome II Proposal; *cf.* http://europa.eu.int/comm/justice_home/unit/civil/consultation/index_en.htm.

In the case of a non-contractual obligation arising from an infringement of a unitary Community industrial property right, the relevant Community instrument shall apply. For any question that is not governed by that instrument, the applicable law shall be the law of the Member State in which the infringing act is committed.

This provision contains the same connecting factor as Art. 98(2) of the CTMR, but it excludes a possible *renvoi* because, in contrast to Art. 98(2) of the CTMR, it does not contain a reference to the private international law of the individual Member State (*cf.* Art. 20 Rome II Proposal). Hence, the same outcome with regard to sanctions for infringement of Community trade marks could have been achieved by simply deleting the reference to the private international law of the *locus delicti* contained in Art. 98(2) of the CTMR.[20]

The common connecting factor in these rules is the *locus delicti*. As we have seen, the connecting factor does not determine the applicable national law if the *locus delicti* can be located in different Member States. A future European conflict rule must provide a solution for such cases. Such a unified conflict rule for the infringement of Community rights should form part of the future Rome II Regulation.

1. Interpretation of the Connecting Factor by the ECJ

The connecting factor in Art. 98(2) of the CTMR and Art. 8(2) of the Rome II Proposal corresponds to the connecting factor regarding the *forum delicti* jurisdiction in Art. 93(5) of the CTMR; it is the *locus delicti*.

Concerning the *forum delicti* jurisdiction in Art. 5(3) of the Brussels Convention,[21] the ECJ ruled in the *Shevill* case that a defamation claim can be brought either before the courts in the country of publication – which have jurisdiction to award damages for all the harm caused by the defamation – or before the courts of the countries in which the publication was distributed, which only have jurisdiction in respect of the harm caused in their state.[22] The *Shevill* opinion can be applied to the *forum delicti* jurisdiction provided in the CTMR,[23] since a comparable restriction on jurisdiction is

[20] This corresponds to Art. 35(2) Protocol on the settlement of litigation concerning the infringement and validity of Community Patents (not in force), 1989 OJ EC L 401/34, 40, and was initially also proposed for Community trade marks; *cf.* Art. 76a of Council Doc. 5865/88, dated May 11, 1988 (German version printed in 1989 GRUR Int. 388, 403).

[21] Replaced, in all Member States with the exception of Denmark, by Council Regulation (EC) 44/2001 of 22 December 2000 on jurisdiction and the recognition and enforcement of judgements in civil and commercial matters, OJ EC 2001 L 12/1–23; Art. 5, No. 3 insofar unchanged.

[22] ECJ, judgment of 7 March 1995, Case C-68/93, *Shevill v. Presse Alliance S.A.* [1995] ECR I-415.

[23] *Bumiller*, Durchsetzung der Gemeinschaftsmarke in der Europäischen Union, 1997, at 17, No. B 23 *et seq.*; *Kouker*, Verteidigung und Durchsetzung der Gemeinschaftsmarke in der Europäischen Union, 2000 Mitt. 241, 245; *cf. also Scordamaglia*, Jurisdiction and

expressly provided for by Art. 94(2) of the CTMR. The infringement of unitary Community industrial property rights concerns intangible rights without territorial limitation within the Community. The situation seems similar to defamation cases, which also concern the infringement of intangible rights without territorial limitation.

The ECJ emphasises in the *Shevill* defamation case that the *forum delicti* rule is based on the existence of a particularly close connecting factor between the dispute and the courts.[24] The private international law conflict rules of the Member States are also based on this principle of the closest connection. Therefore, the distinction made by the ECJ may be transferred to the interpretation of the connecting factor in private international law. In the *Shevill* case the ECJ ruled that the courts in the country of publication have jurisdiction to award damages for all the harm caused by the defamation "since that is the place where the harmful event originated and from which the libel was issued and put into circulation",[25] whereas the courts of the countries in which the publication was distributed have only jurisdiction to rule in respect of the harm caused in their state.[26] This shows that the distinction made by the ECJ is based on the causal chain. Accordingly, in private international law, the place where the infringing act occurs is the connecting factor with regard also to all places where the infringement affects the right, provided that the infringement in those places was also caused by the infringing act. On the other hand, a place where the right is affected by the infringement is usually not the place of origin of infringing effects in other countries. Therefore, jurisdiction (Art. 94(2) CTMR) and the applicable national law under Art. 98(2) of the CTMR is usually restricted to sanctions for infringement in this country only.

This leads to the following distinction, depending on whether the place where the infringing act occurs or where it affects the right is regarded as the connecting factor.

2. Place Where the Infringing Act Occurs as Connecting Factor

The place where the infringing act occurs may be the connecting factor for all elements of the infringement.

To come back to our example: a product is branded in Germany with a trade mark that infringes a Community trade mark. This product is offered and sent from Germany to several Member States. Since Germany is the

---

Procedure in Legal Actions relating to Community Trade Marks, in: *Franzosi* (ed.), European Community Trade Mark, 1997, at 369, 387; and *von Bomhard*, Community Trade – Enforcement Issues, [25] 2 BMM bulletin 92, 93 (1999) (both concerning ECJ, judgement of 30 November 1976, Case 21/76, *Bier B.V. / Mines de potasse d'Alsace S.A*,. [1976] ECR 1735).

[24] ECJ, *supra* note 22, para. 19.

[25] ECJ, *supra* note 22, para. 24; *cf. also* para. 25.

[26] ECJ, *supra* note 22; *cf.* end of head note 1, para. 30.

place where the harmful event originated and from which the infringing products were issued and put into circulation, German law can also be applied with respect to sanctions for distribution in other Member States.

It is therefore not true to say that the connecting factor cited in Art. 98(2) CTMR necessarily leads to a territorial, mosaic-like application of national laws.[27] This is simply a consequence of national intellectual property rights, which are territorial by their very nature. Within the European Community, the Community trade mark has a unitary character and one objective of the CTMR was to overcome the territoriality of national trade mark rights.[28] Also, the reference to national private international law was included in Art. 98(2) CTMR precisely in order to avoid a territorial application of national laws and allow sanctions not regulated by the CTMR to be dealt with by just one set of national laws.[29]

If the place where the infringing act occurs is regarded as the connecting factor, just one set of national laws – the law of the Member State in which the infringing act occurs – need be applied with regard to sanctions (unless the CTMR itself applies to the sanctions). Not only does this solution respect the private international law principle of the closest connection, it also gives the owner of a Community trade mark the opportunity to effectively enforce its rights. We all agree that in the case of a Community-wide infringement it would be very difficult, if not impossible, for a Community trade mark court to apply thirteen,[30] soon to be twenty-three, different sets of national laws regarding sanctions.[31] The application of the law of the Member State in which the infringing act occurs allows the Community trade mark court to apply just one set of national laws even if the infringing act is on a Community-wide scale.

However, there are cases in which the place where the infringing act occurs cannot be located within a Member State. Because of the *lex loci protectionis* rule, a place outside the European Community cannot be the connecting factor for the infringement of a Community right. In these cases,

---

[27] For a territorial-split application of national laws as a consequence of Art. 98(2) CTMR, *see* the majority opinion in the literature: *Bumiller, supra* note 23; *Wichard*, Markenrecht zwischen Territorialität und Binnenmarkt, 2002 ZEuP 23, 51; *Gastinel & Milford*, The Legal Aspects of the Community Trade Mark, 2001, No. 416; *Knaak*, Die Rechtsdurchsetzung der Gemeinschaftsmarke und der älteren nationalen Rechte, 1997 GRUR Int. 864, 869; *von Mühlendahl & Ohlgart & von Bomhard*, Die Gemeinschaftsmarke, 1998, at 213 *et seq*.; *Scordamaglia, supra* note 23, at 408; *Tilmann, supra* note 6, at 675 *et seq*.

[28] *Cf.* the preamble of the CTMR, *supra* note 3, recital 3.

[29] *Cf. von Mühlendahl*, Von der EWG-Marke zur Gemeinschaftsmarke – Teil II, in: *Schricker & Beier* (ed.), Die Neuordnung des Markenrechts in Europa, 1997, at 81, 99.

[30] There are currently just thirteen different national trade mark laws, since the trade mark law in Belgium, Luxemburg and the Netherlands is unified.

[31] *Cf. von Gamm & Schaper*, Tagung des Max-Planck-Instituts für ausländisches und internationales Patent-, Urheber- und Wettbewerbsrecht über die Gemeinschaftsmarke – Berlin 14.–16. Mai 2001, 2001 GRUR Int. 965, 966.

the connecting factor can only be the place where the infringement affects the right.

3. Place Where the Infringement Affects the Right as Connecting Factor

The Hamburg Group for Private International Law has proposed the place where the infringement affects the right as the sole connecting factor for the infringement of Community industrial property rights.[32] Based on this proposed conflict rule, the law of the Member State where the infringement affects the right would be applicable.

One advantage of this connecting factor is that the remedies available in that particular country would be the same regardless of whether a Community trade mark has been infringed or a national trade mark. In contrast, where an infringement has an effect in several Member States and the national law of the Member State in which the infringing act occurs is applicable, this can lead to a situation where the remedies available in a particular country for breach of a Community trade mark right are less effective or offer less protection than those available for breach of a national trade mark right. A conflict rule with the place where the infringement affects the right as the connecting factor means in practice that the sanctions available in a particular country for infringements of national trade marks and Community trade marks are the same. It thus provides for equivalent treatment.

In addition, in the case of multi-state infringements, the application of the law of the Member State where the infringement affects the right may lead to the application of several sets of national laws in relation to the same infringement. In practice it is virtually impossible to apply thirteen, or soon twenty-three, different sets of national laws in order to impose sanctions for the infringement of a Community trade mark the effect of which has been felt Community-wide.

The above said, an infringement action may also be brought before the Community trade mark court, which is competent according to the *forum delicti* rule in Art. 93(5) of the CTMR because the infringement has affected a Community trade mark in the respective Member State. In this case, Art. 94(2) provides that jurisdiction is limited to acts in this Member State. Hence, the application of the law of the Member State where the infringement affects the right would not lead to difficulties in practice. On the contrary, the court would simply apply the *lex fori* in relation to the sanctions for infringement.

4. Determination of the Relevant Connecting Factor

As we have seen, there are good reasons for a conflict rule that takes both connecting factors into consideration. The application of the law of the

[32] *Hamburg Group for Private International Law*, *supra* note 5 at 21 *et seq*.

Member State in which the infringing act occurs enables just one set of national laws to be applied even in cases of multi-state infringement, whereas the application of the law of the Member State where the infringement affects the right allows for breaches of national trade marks and breaches of Community trade marks to be treated equally in the respective country. Any future conflict rule should therefore consider both connecting factors.

But how can the relevant connecting factor be determined if the *locus delicti* is located in different Member States? Basically two different solutions seem possible: One alternative would be for the court to determine the relevant connecting factor using the principle of closest connection. The other is for the plaintiff to choose the applicable national law of one Member State concerned.

The Community trade mark court could apply the law of the Member State(s) to which the closest connection exists. This solution would allow a flexible case-by-case approach, but it may make it difficult for a plaintiff to predict which national law will be applied by the court. Therefore the principle of closest connection could be concretised at the *forum delicti* by reference to the *lex fori* (excluding private international law), since the jurisdiction is limited to acts committed or threatened within the territory of the Member State in which that court is situated.[33] At the forum of general jurisdiction, the law (excluding private international law) of the Member State where the defendant is domiciled could be declared applicable, assuming that the infringing act usually occurs in his country of domicile.[34]

To allow the owner of a Community trade mark to enforce his rights effectively, one could give the plaintiff the right to choose between the law of the Member State in which the infringing act occurs and the law(s) of the Member State(s) in which the infringement affects the right. This corresponds to the solution in German and Italian private international law.[35] In this case, the conflict rule must also provide a solution for the case in which the plaintiff has not chosen the applicable law.

5. Freedom of Choice, Escape Clause

Any future conflict rule concerning the infringement of Community rights could also provide for an "escape clause", and should allow the parties to expressly choose the law of another Member State.

A choice of law by the parties is generally not admitted in relation to national intellectual property rights because it is regarded as being in conflict with the *lex loci protectionis* rule, which is founded on the territorial limitation

---

[33] Article 94(2) CTMR; almost identical: Art. 83(2) Council Regulation (EC) 6/2002 on Community designs, *supra* note 18; corresponding: Art. 101(3) Council Regulation (EC) 2100/94 of 27 July 1994 on Community plant variety rights, OJ EC 1994 L 227/1–30.

[34] *See also* the proposition by *Axel Metzger* in this publication.

[35] *See supra* notes 14 and 15.

of those rights.[36] With respect to unitary Community rights, the Community is the *locus protectionis*. Therefore, providing that the national law of one or another Member State is chosen, the *lex loci protectionis* rule does not stand in the way of a choice of law by the parties. A choice of law would also allow the parties to multi-state infringement proceedings to determine one applicable set of national laws. For this reason, the future conflict rule for unitary Community rights should allow the parties to expressly and mutually choose which national law is to apply.

For the same reason, an "escape clause" could also be included in the future conflict rule applicable to the infringement of Community rights. Like the escape clause proposed for the future Rome II Regulation,[37] this escape clause could allow a deviation from the general rule if there is a significantly closer connection to another Member State than to the Member State whose law would be applicable under the regular rules. Such a significantly closer connection might be established by, in particular, a pre-existing relationship between the parties, *e.g.*, a contract that is linked to the tort in question. In the case of a Community trade mark infringement, this may be the case if the parties have concluded a license agreement which refers to the law of a Member State.

A conflict rule concerning the infringement of Community industrial property rights should not refer to the law of the country in which both parties have their habitual residence. As Community industrial property rights may be transferred to other parties, there is no inherent close connection between the right and the domicile of the owner. The common domicile of the current proprietor and the infringing party therefore does not provide for a connection close enough to justify a deviation from the general *lex loci delicti* rule.

In no case should a future conflict rule lead to the application of a set of national laws belonging to a state other than a Member State. This is a direct consequence of the *lex loci protectionis* rule.

IV. Conclusion

The private international law issue in respect of the infringement of unitary Community industrial property rights will not be solved by the Rome II proposal. According to the proposed provision, the applicable law shall be the law of the Member State in which the infringing act is committed. This

[36] *Kreuzer, supra* note 7, at No. 15; *Beier & Schricker & Ulmer*, Stellungnahme des Max-Planck-Instituts für ausländisches und internationales Patent-, Urheber- und Wettbewerbsrecht zum Entwurf eines Gesetzes zur Ergänzung des internationalen Privatrechts (außervertragliche Schuldverhältnisse und Sachen), 1985 GRUR Int. 104, 106.

[37] Article 3(3) Rome II Proposal, *supra* note 5; *cf. also Hamburg Group for Private International Law, supra* note 5 at 39 *et seq.*

rule does not determine the applicable national law if the infringing act can be located in different Member States. The rule needs supplementing for cases of this type. One alternative would be to allow the plaintiff to determine the applicable national law (differentiating, as set out above, between the law of the Member State in which the infringing act occurs and the law of the Member State where the infringement affects the right), or to refer to the principle of closest connection. The latter could be concretised at the *forum delicti* by reference to the *lex fori*, whereas at the forum of general jurisdiction the law of the Member State where the defendant is domiciled could be declared applicable, assuming that the infringing act usually occurs at his domicile. In addition, it should be possible for the parties to mutually agree on the law of another Member State.

This private international law issue will be solved if all important questions, in particular the sanctions for infringement, are unified by Community regulations.[38] The proposed directive on measures and procedures to ensure the enforcement of intellectual property rights[39] is merely a first step in this direction, and whether one should strive for a complete unification in this regard remains open to question.

[38] *Cf.* Proposal for a Council Regulation on the Community Patent, *Commission of the European Communities*, Brussels 1 August 2000, COM (2000) 412 final.

[39] *Commission of the European Communities*, Brussels 30 January 2003, COM (2003) 46 final; now: Directive 2004/48/EC of the European Parliament and of the Council of 29 April 2004 on the enforcement of intellectual property rights, OJ EC 2004 L 157/45–86, corrigendum: OJ EC 2004 L 195/16–25.

Community IP Rights & Conflict of Laws – Community Trademark, Community Design, Community Patent – Applicable Law for Claims for Damages

AXEL METZGER*

I. Introduction

After coming home from the *Frauenchiemsee* meeting on Jurisdiction and Choice of Law in Intellectual Property Matters, the author of this paper found the Commission's proposal for a "Rome II" Regulation[1] (Rome II Proposal) on his desk. Article 8 of the proposal provides for a choice-of-law rule for infringements of intellectual property rights that has some similarities to the proposition made by the author during the meeting and that is obviously inspired by the solution advocated by the Hamburg Group for private international law, of which the author was a member.[2]

Therefore, the following remarks have to defend, on the one hand, the Commission's proposal. On the other hand, the author proposes to go a step further towards a broader application of the general conflict-of-laws rules in the field of Community IP rights. Infringements of Community IP rights with a unitary character, especially Community trademarks, Community designs and future Community patents,[3] should be governed by a combination of the *lex loci protectionis* and the general conflict-of-laws rules for torts.

To this very day, harmonisation of intellectual property law in Europe focuses on substantive law. The Commission's "Proposal for an Enforcement Directive"[4] nourishes the hope for a future harmonised law of claims for damages. Therefore, one could ask, why should we go on

---

* Dr.jur. (Munich and Paris), Max Planck Institute for Foreign Private and Private International Law, Hamburg. This text is a slightly modified version of a comment presented at the Frauenchiemsee Conference on Jurisdiction and Choice of Law in Intellectual Property Matters – Perspectives for the Future, 22–23 July 2003.

[1] Proposal of 22 July 2003 for a Regulation of the European Parliament and the Council on the law applicable to non-contractual obligations ("Rome II"), COM (2003) 427 final.

[2] *See* Art. 6a of the proposal of *Basedow, Magnus, Mankowski, Metzger et al.* ("Hamburg Group for Private International Law"), 67 RabelsZ 1, 11 (2003).

[3] The Council Regulation (EC) 2100/94 of 27 July 1994 on Community plant variety rights, OJ EC 1994 L 227, p. 1, will not be treated in the following contribution. *See* in addition ECJ, decision of 10 April 2003, Case C-305/00, 2003 EuZW, 404 – *Schulin*.

[4] Proposal for a Directive of the European Parliament and of the Council on measures and procedures to ensure the enforcement of intellectual property rights, 30 January 2003, COM (2003) 46 final.

working on conflict of laws and IP rights? Four answers must be given. Firstly, future perspectives are interesting – but they do not help us with today's questions. We have to solve the problems that have arisen from the great variety of European trademark laws regarding claims for damages.[5] Secondly, it is not clear whether the enforcement directive will be adopted, and if so, when this will be the case. Thirdly, even if the directive is adopted soon, it is not certain that the laws of the Member States will be substantially harmonised afterwards. Since the beginning of the European Community, harmonisation by directives has never succeeded in completely unifying the law of the Member States. This is particularly the case for directives with a "minimum harmonisation" purpose like the Commission's proposal for an enforcement directive.[6] Fourthly, claims for damages are linked to a lot of questions concerning general private law, such as contributory negligence, duty to pay interest and vicarious liability. These topics will not be dealt with in the future directive. Therefore, one must certainly expect that private international law will retain a significant importance for European IP rights.

This paper will treat the law applicable to infringements of Community trademarks (I) and Community designs (II), and say some words on the future Community patent (III).

II. Community Trademark

Which law is applicable to damages arising from an infringement of a Community trademark today? While Art. 98(1) of the Community Trademark Regulation[7] provides for a claim for a permanent injunction, Art. 98(2) establishes that all other claims are to be dealt with by the "law of the Member State to which the acts of infringement . . . were committed, including the private international law."

1. Infringements in Only One Member State

a) Community Trademark and Territoriality

Even if an infringement affects the Community trade mark in only one Member State, the rule of Art. 98(2) is insufficient. Article 98(2) merely provides a meta-rule for the applicable law, because it refers to the law of a Member State in its totality – including its conflict-of-laws rules. Therefore Art. 98(2) does not define which domestic law is applicable, because every *renvoi* is accepted. In German legal parlance this type of rule is called

[5] *See Bastian/Götting/Knaak/Stauder*, Der Markenverletzungsprozess in ausgewählten Ländern der europäischen Wirtschaftsgemeinschaft, Cologne 1993.

[6] *See* Art. 2(1): "Scope: Without prejudice to the means which are or may be provided for in Community or national legislation, in so far as those means may be more favourable for right holders, the measures provided for by this Directive shall apply . . .".

[7] Council Regulation (EC) No. 40/94 of 20 December 1993 on the Community trade mark OJ EC 1994 L 11/1.

Gesamtverweisung. For that reason, the conflict-of-law rules of the Member States determine the applicable domestic law.

Unfortunately, the traditional private international law of the Member States does not really help in the case of Community trade marks. In all Member States and international conventions infringements of industrial property rights are governed by the *lex loci protectionis*. This principle is also laid down in the Rome II Proposal as Art. 8(1): "The law applicable to a non-contractual obligation arising from an infringement of an intellectual property right shall be the law of the country for which protection is sought."

If, for example, a trademark is infringed by offering goods in France under a protected sign, Art. 98(2) points to French private international law. Under French private international law, a trademark infringement is governed by the law of the protecting country. In the case of a Community trademark, the whole Community is the protecting "country", with its very varying internal rules on trademark infringements. After applying the *lex loci protectionis* it is still unclear which Member State's law is applicable to claims for damages. The only clear result is that the act giving rise to liability must occur within the Community. Otherwise the Community trademark is not infringed.

Therefore the principle of territoriality needs a supplementary rule for Community IP rights with a unitary character. The Rome II Proposal advocates the application of the basic conflict-of-laws rule for non-contractual obligations, the *lex loci delicti*, in Art. 8(2).

b) Application of General Rules

A conflict-of-laws rule for claims for damages should be inspired by the general rules for non-contractual obligations. Trademark infringements have the character of torts. The basic rule for torts is the *lex loci delicti* (Art. 3(1) Rome II Proposal). The applicable law is that of the country in which the events constituting the delict occur.[8] The Rome II Proposal modifies this rule slightly for infringements of Community IP rights, in Art. 8(2):

> In the case of a non-contractual obligation arising from an infringement of a unitary Community industrial property right, the relevant Community instrument shall apply. For any question that is not governed by that instrument, the applicable law shall be the law of the Member State in which the act of infringement is committed.

This was also the solution proposed by the Hamburg Group for private international law.[9] For ordinary injuries, *e.g.* violation of personality rights,

---

[8] The wording of Art. 3(1) Rome II Proposal and the wording of Art. 3(1) of the Commission's Draft Proposal of May 2002 (*see* the Consultation on a Preliminary Draft Proposal for a Council Regulation on the law applicable to non-contractual obligations, http://www.europa.eu.int/comm/justice_home/unit/civil/consultation/index_en.htm _DP_) are nearly identical. For a detailed critique on this wording, *see Hamburg Group*, *supra* note 2, at 11.

[9] *See* Art. 6a(2) of the proposal of the *Hamburg Group*, *supra* note 2, which provides a slightly different wording.

the place of injury and the place where the act giving rise to liability has taken place may be allocated in different states. Regarding IP rights, the place of the act giving rise to liability and the place of the infringement are always identical: A Community trademark can only be affected by using it in a way that is conferred to the proprietor of a trademark. Wherever a trademark is injured, the act giving rise to liability takes place.[10] Therefore, the *lex loci delicti* unambiguously determines the applicable law as long as the infringements occur in only one Member State. Moreover, the *lex loci delicti* provides a suitable solution with regards to jurisdiction rules of the Community Trademark Regulation. Article 93(5) Community Trademark Regulation allows actions to be brought in the courts of the Member State in which the act of infringement has been committed. If this court is chosen, it is appropriate to apply the law of this Member State.

c) Freedom of Choice

One of the crucial questions in these cases is whether the parties should be granted freedom of choice. From a liberal point of view, it cannot be questioned that freedom of choice should be allowed. The question must be whether there are good reasons to forbid agreements on the applicable law. German practitioners are favourable to freedom of choice.[11] This shows that there is a practical need for such agreements.

It is true that freedom of choice in a case of trademark infringement is subject to the same reservations as in other cases.[12] Moreover, regarding the principle of territoriality, the further reservation has to be mentioned that the law of a non-Member State cannot be chosen;[13] otherwise the territoriality of the trademark could easily be circumvented.[14]

---

[10] *See Martiny*, 40 RabelsZ 218, 225 (1976). Contrary to that point: *Schulte-Beckhausen*, 1999 WRP 300, 304; *von Mühlendahl/Ohlgart*, Die Gemeinschaftsmarke, München 1998, 214.

[11] *See von Mühlendahl/Ohlgart supra* note 10, at 214; *Schulte-Beckhausen*, 1999 WRP 300, 304.

[12] *See e.g.* Art. 10(2) Rome II Proposal:

> If all the other elements of the situation at the time when the loss is sustained are located in a country other than the country whose law has been chosen, the choice of the parties shall be without prejudice to the application of rules of the law of that country which cannot be derogated from by contract.

[13] This leads to a "split" conflict-of-laws rule. For the question of split conflict-of-laws rules, *see Basedow*, 59 RabelsZ 1, 20 (1995); *Schwarz*, 101 ZVglRWiss 46, 69 (2002); *Nuyts*, 1999 Rev.crit.dr.int.pr. 245, 265. *See also* the more critical remarks of *Mankowski* in: *Basedow et al.* (ed.), Aufbruch nach Europa – 75 Jahre Max-Planck-Institut für Privatrecht, Tübingen 2001, 595, 610.

[14] This is one of the reasons why a conflict-of-laws rule for Community IP rights should provide the principle of territoriality as a general principle and the *lex loci delicti*, freedom of choice, etc. as supplementary rule. Art. 8 Rome II Proposal follows this pattern.

The Rome II Proposal does not contain a provision allowing the parties to choose the law to apply to non-contractual obligations. An appropriate amendment would be useful.

d) Displacement of the General Rule

Another important question is whether the general rule can be displaced if it appears, all things considered, that another applicable law is more appropriate.

If in the case of a trademark infringement in France both parties are domiciled in another Member State, one could ask whether the connection with this Member State is closer than the connection with the *lex loci delicti*. Article 3(2) of the Rome II Proposal answers this question in the affirmative for all types of delicts, because the handling of the case is easier under the law of the country of domicile.

The application of the law of the common domicile is also in harmony with the jurisdiction rules of Art. 93(1) of the Community Trademark Regulation. This provision states that proceedings in respect of claims for damages shall be brought in the courts of the Member State in which the defendant is domiciled. If plaintiff and defendant are domiciled in the same Member State, the proceeding should be governed by the law of this state. If both are domiciled in a non-Member State, the *lex loci delicti* governs the case.

The same principles apply to an accessory choice of law in respect of pre-existing relationships. If there is a contractual relationship between the parties that is governed by the law of a Member State, this law should also be applied to torts linked to that contract, to prevent a fragmentation of law.[15] Here, too, the Rome II Proposal is less extensive. Especially in the case of a pre-existing relationship, an additional rule in Art. 8 of the Proposal would be useful.

2. Infringements in More Than One Member State

Conflict-of-laws rules for claims for damages are rather complicated if the infringement arises in only one Member State. They are incomparably difficult for infringements arising in more than one Member State. The Rome II Proposal does not contain a special provision for these cases. The following remarks should therefore be understood as an interpretation of the *lex loci delicti* as stated in Art. 8(2) of the Rome II Proposal. The crucial question is whether it is possible in these cases to apply one single substantive law for the whole claim, or whether a bundle of different substantive laws is to be applied (the "mosaic approach"). The following remarks examine both hypotheses.

---

[15] *See von Mühlendahl/Ohlgart, supra* note 10, at 214; *Anduleit*, Die Rechtsdurchsetzung im Markenrecht, Baden-Baden 2001, 205.

a) Application of Several Laws (Mosaic Approach)

One solution for multi-state infringements could be the application of the laws of all Member States in which the acts of infringement were committed.[16]

This approach is applied by Dutch, German und English courts to infringements of European patents, but only concerning prohibitive injunctions.[17] To give an example: though it is possible to commence injunction proceedings for the Netherlands, Germany, or France in a Dutch court, the court has to apply Dutch, German and French law to adopt an injunction. For the European patent, the application of several laws is appropriate, because the European patent is an IP right without a unitary character, but a bundle of national patents. For that reason, the principles applied to European patents should not be transferred to the European trademark.

Regarding the principle of "harmony of law", the mosaic approach poses no problems. If every court applied the domestic law of every Member State, uniform solutions would be attained. Regarding jurisdiction rules of the Community Trademark Regulation, the mosaic approach also seems to be suitable. Articles 93(1) and 94(1) provide jurisdiction to the courts of the Member State in which the defendant is domiciled for damages arising in any Member State. Following the mosaic approach, the court would apply the laws of all the Member States in which the acts of infringement were committed. The same principle would be applied for the subsidiary jurisdictions of Art. 93(2) and (3). The court of the Member State in which the act of infringement had been committed (Art. 93(5)) would have jurisdiction only in respect of acts committed within the territory of the Member State in which that court is situated. The mosaic approach would allow the court to apply the law of its country.

However, the mosaic approach has strong disadvantages. The main inconvenience is the fragmentation of laws. If the court has to apply several laws, the parties will have higher legal costs. If a plaintiff has to plead in four laws he might need four lawyers to perform a serious procedure. He might also require expert opinions. Moreover, the proceeding will take more time, because it will be more complicated. In addition, legal security is threatened if several laws with which the judge is unfamiliar govern the case.

---

[16] *See Bumiller*, Durchsetzung der Gemeinschaftsmarke in der Europäischen Union, München 1997, 59 *et seq*.

[17] *See* Gerechtshof Den Haag, 3 February 1994, 1995 GRUR Int. 253 – *Follikelstimulationshormon I*; Gerechthof Den Haag, 12 December 1996, 1996 Intellectuele Eigendom en Reclamerecht 237 – *NASBA*; High Court of Justice (Chancery Division), 26 March 1997, [1997] 3 All E.R. 45 – *Coin Controls Ltd.*; Düsseldorf District Court, 1 February 1994, quoted from *Rospat*, 1997 GRUR Int. 861.

b) Application of one Substantive Law

The application of one domestic law for multi-state infringements avoids the main disadvantages of the mosaic approach. The advantage of this solution is its feasibility. If only one law is to be applied, legal costs are lower and procedures are faster. Applying only one law also means fostering legal security. Predicting the result of a court that applies one law is much easier than predicting the result of a court procedure under several laws. Nevertheless, the crucial question is which law should apply to these cases. The laws of two Member States are conceivable: either the law of the domicile of the defendant or the law of the country in which the most important infringements were committed. There are strong arguments for and against both solutions.

aa) Law of the Country of the Most Important Infringement From an economic point of view it seems appropriate to apply the law of the country in which the most important infringements were committed. The defendant has earned or wanted to earn his money mainly in this country by injuring the plaintiff's trademark. Therefore he should pay damages under the law of that Member State. This solution could be reached by a slightly modified interpretation of the *lex loci delicti*.

Regarding the jurisdiction rules of the Community trademark, however, this approach is not satisfactory. Article 94(1) gives jurisdiction for infringements occurring in "any Member State" only to the courts of the Member State in which the defendant is domiciled. The courts of the Member State in which the act of infringement is committed have jurisdiction only in respect of acts committed or threatened within the territory of the Member State in which that court is situated. If the country of the most important infringement and the country of the domicile of the defendant differ, the court has to apply the law of another Member State. In this case the advantages over the mosaic approach are nearly eliminated.

Another argument against applying the law of the country where the most important infringements were committed is that this rule does not help in difficult cases. If, for example, a trademark is used in television advertisements in several countries, it is impossible to determine the country of the most important infringement.

bb) Law of the Country of Domicile of the Defendant Another solution could be to apply the law of the country where the defendant is domiciled. Such an approach would supplement the rules of jurisdiction of Art. 93(1) of the Community Trademark Regulation in a practical manner. The courts of the Member State in which the defendant is domiciled are the only ones with jurisdiction for infringements taking place in any Member State. Proceedings before this court should end within a reasonable time and carry low legal costs. Therefore, the courts should apply the law of their own country. The proposed rule fosters legal security, because it is easy to handle and gives clear results. It moreover respects the principle of "harmony of laws" and avoids a fragmentation of laws.

However, claims for damages in the Member State in which the act of infringement has been committed should be governed by the law of that country. Otherwise the freedom of choice of forum given by Art. 93(1) and (5) would be neutralised. Moreover, for these claims the *lex loci delicti* gives clear results.

A considerable number of scholars have proposed a similar rule for multi-state injuries of personality rights. The choice-of-laws rule for these cases was energetically discussed after the *Shevill vs. Press Alliance* decision of the European Court of Justice.[18] In this decision the Court of Justice developed a concept of jurisdiction for multi-state injuries by interpreting Art. 5(3) of the Brussels Convention:[19]

> The victim of a libel by a newspaper article distributed in several Contracting States may bring an action for damages against the publisher either before the courts of the Contracting State of the place where the publisher of the defamatory publication is established, which have jurisdiction to award damages for all the harm caused by the defamation, or before the courts of each Contracting State in which the publication was distributed and where the victim claims to have suffered injury to his reputation, which have jurisdiction to rule solely in respect of the harm caused in the state of the court seised.

The court did not treat the conflict-of-laws question, but scholars concluded that the choice-of-law rule has to follow the jurisdiction rule.[20]

Nevertheless, this solution also has some disadvantages. First, the applicable law is different for legal proceedings in the country of the domicile of the defendant than in the country in which the infringements were committed. This is not the case if injuring acts are also committed in the country of the domicile of the defendant. Here, the court has to apply its law irrespective of whether a claim is brought for the whole of the damages or only part of the damages for this country.

Another inconvenience might arise in rare cases. If no injuring act is committed in the country of the defendant's domicile, the connection of an action with this country is not very close. But these cases are rather theoretical. Usually, if a person commits an act that can be qualified as a trademark infringement, it is at his domicile. As long as the infringing act is committed in this country the solution advocated here can be reached by an interpretation of the *lex loci delicti*.

---

[18] Decision of the ECJ, 7 March 1995, Case C-68/93, *Shevill v. Presse Alliance S.A.*, [1995] ECR I-415.

[19] Convention of 27 September 1968 on Jurisdiction and the Enforcement of Judgments in Civil and Commercial Matters. Now Art. 5(3) of the Council Regulation (EC) No 44/2001 of 22 December 2000 on jurisdiction and the recognition and enforcement of judgments in civil and commercial matters.

[20] *See Kropholler*, Internationales Privatrecht, 4th ed., Tübingen 2001, 515; *Kegel/Schurig*, Internationales Privatrecht, 8th ed., Munich 2000, 633; *Spindler*, 1996 ZUM 559.

When weighing up the pros and cons, it seems that applying the law of the domicile of the defendant is the better solution. But note that this rule applies only if the plaintiff chooses to commence legal proceedings in a court of the country of the defendant's domicile. If he wants to enjoy the laws of the countries where the injuring acts were committed, he can initiate actions in the courts in these countries.

c) Freedom of Choice, Displacement of the General Rule

In regard to freedom of choice and displacement of the general rule, the same principles apply as for an infringement in only one Member State. If both parties are domiciled in the same Member State, the law of this country ought to be applied. In addition, a choice of law by the parties should be allowed. If the parties are linked by a pre-existing relationship, especially a contract, the law of that relationship should govern the infringements. But note that for the application of these rules Art. 8 Rome II Proposal needs to be amended.

III. Community Design

The Community design is governed by the same principles as the Community trademark. For infringements concerning a design, Art. 89(1) of the Community Design Regulation[21] provides for a particular prohibitive order and secondary sanctions.[22] Article 89(1)(d) establishes for all other sanctions the application of the law of the Member State in which the acts of infringement are committed, including its private international law. The jurisdiction rules of the Community Design Regulation follow the same principles as the *Shevill* decision[23] and the Community Trademark Regulation.[24] Therefore, all rules developed for trademarks can be applied to design infringement cases.

IV. Community Patent

The future Community Patent Regulation seems to follow a different pattern. The draft of the Regulation[25] determines that the Community patent

---

[21] Council Regulation (EC) No 6/2002 of 12 December 2001 on Community designs, OJ EC 2002 L 3/1.

[22] These are Art. 89(1)(b) [order to seize the infringing products], and Art. 89(1)(c) [order to seize materials and implements predominantly used in order to manufacture the infringing goods].

[23] *Shevill v. Presse Alliance S.A.*, *supra* note 18.

[24] *See* Arts. 82 and 83 of the Community Design Regulation.

[25] The latest version of the Proposal for a Council regulation on the Community patent is Council Document Number 10404/30, 11 June 2003, http://register.consilium.eu.int/pdf/en/03/st10/st10404en03.pdf.

shall have a unitary and an "autonomous character". Article 2(2) stipulates that the patent shall be subject only to the provisions of the Regulation. Therefore it is not surprising that Art. 44 provides for a special claim for damages. As a consequence, the application of the law of the Member States is excluded.

It will be very interesting to see how the courts fill the numerous gaps in the Regulation. Claims for damages are linked to a lot of general questions of a legal system. Which rule will apply if more than one person is acting? What about defences like contributory negligence or *venire contra factum proprium*? Even the proposed enforcement directive will not answer all questions connected with a claim for damages. These claims need a fully functioning legal system.[26] The task would fall to the European Court of Justice to develop a whole system of private law out of the current "General Principles of Law". European scholarship has made a lot of efforts in this field.[27] The Commission's Action Plan of February 2003 on a European contract law[28] shows that further progress is to be expected – not only in the field of contract law but also regarding non-contractual obligations.[29] But the end is still far from being in sight. Fifteen or 20 years of hard work on the planned "common frame of reference" is still an optimistic point of view.

Therefore – at least in the meantime – the Community Patent Regulation should provide a choice-of-law rule for the questions not treated in the Regulation, especially regarding claims for damages. And here the provisions of the Community Trademark and Design Regulations could certainly serve as examples.

V. Conclusion

The result of this analysis can be summarised in the following rule. Paragraphs 1 and 2 are taken from the Rome II Proposal. The proposed amendment is to be found at the end of paragraph 2.

Article 8 – Infringement of intellectual property rights

1. The law applicable to a non-contractual obligation arising from an infringement of an intellectual property right shall be the law of the country for which protection is sought.

2. In the case of a non-contractual obligation arising from an infringement of a unitary Community industrial property right, the relevant Community instrument shall apply. For

---

[26] *See Tilmann*, 2003 GRUR Int. 381, 386.

[27] *See e.g.* the works of the Lando commission, published as *Lando/Beale* (ed.), Principles of European Contract Law: Parts 1 and 2, The Hague 2000, and *Lando/Clive/Prüm/Zimmermann*, Principles of European Contract Law: part 3, The Hague 2003.

[28] *See* Communication from the Commission to the European Council and the Parliament: A more coherent European Contract Law – An Action Plan, 12 February 2003, COM (2003) 68 final.

[29] *See especially* page 18, No. 67.

any question that is not governed by that instrument, the applicable law shall be the law of the Member State in which the act of infringement is committed. *The general rules on non-contractual obligations, especially freedom of choice, application of the law of the common domicile and accessory choice of law in respect of pre-existing relationships shall be applied to those infringements provided that the law of a Member State is determined. If those infringements occur in more than one Member State, the applicable law for claims for the whole of the damage is the law of the country of the domicile of the defendant provided that the law of a Member State is determined; claims restricted to the damage occurring in only one Member State shall be governed by the law of that country.*

III.

International Issues

Recent Judgments in Japan on Intellectual Property Rights, Conflict of Laws and International Jurisdiction

TOSHIYUKI KONO*

I. International Jurisdiction of Japanese Courts and Intellectual Property Rights

The number of reported cases on IPR and international jurisdiction in Japan was until recently very small. Therefore Japanese precedents on international jurisdiction over the infringement of foreign IPRs was not clear. In 1953, although the Tokyo District Court[1] had an opportunity to state its position on IPR and international jurisdiction, the court stressed the territorial character of patents and dismissed the claim, applying private international law[2] without even mentioning the jurisdiction of the Japanese court.

There was no established rule on international jurisdictions in general at that time. Even today, there is no law in Japan and no international convention on international jurisdiction of which Japan is a Member State. Thus precedent plays a very important role.

The Supreme Court clarified its stance on international jurisdiction in general in its judgment of October 16, 1981[3], for the first time. In this case, a Japanese national was killed in a plane crash in Malaysia. According to the court, the international jurisdiction of the Japanese court should be determined in accordance with *Jori*, which could be translated as "fairness" or "justice." As to its contents, the provisions on venue in the Japanese Code of Civil Procedure should be referred to.

The Supreme Court confirmed the jurisdiction in this case, since the defendant has an office in Tokyo. This judgment was criticised, because the Japanese passenger purchased his ticket in Malaysia and the office in Tokyo had nothing to do with the transportation contract.

---

* Professor of Law, Kyushu University.

[1] Judgment of Tokyo District Court, June 12, 1953, Kaminshu Vol.4, No. 6, at 847.

Facts of this case (slightly simplified by the author): In 1935, X (Japanese corporation, plaintiff) bought a Japanese patent from A, and this patent was registered in 1936. In the same year, X applied for the registration of this patent in Manchuria and it was registered in 1937. B (Japanese corporation) obtained the license of X to use its Japanese patent and it was registered in 1937. Z manufactured radios, using products from B, and exported them to Manchuria. X sued Z with the argument that Z infringed X's Manchuria patent and requested the compensation of damage.

[2] Horei, Japanese Private International Law, Art. 11(2).

[3] 35 Minshu 1224, 1226, 26 Japanese Annual of International Law 122, 123 (1983).

Since this framework was inflexible, inferior courts have developed the so-called special circumstances test, *i.e.*, in cases where special circumstances exist and the exercise of the jurisdiction of the Japanese court would hamper the fairness between parties and the provision of a speedy and fair trial, the jurisdiction of the Japanese court could be denied. The Supreme Court also adopted this test in its judgment of November 11, 1997[4]. We could say that the Japanese court has established a three-step framework to examine its jurisdiction[5], consisting of 1) Jori, 2) provisions of the Code of Civil Procedure, and 3) special circumstances.

This judgment of the Supreme Court, however, at the same time showed problems with the framework; the court rendered this judgment without specifying which provision of the Japanese Code of Civil Procedure should be referred to. In other words, the court skipped the second step. Since Jori itself has no concrete contents, in practice the Japanese courts have only one instrument as the jurisdictional rule, *i.e.*, the special circumstances test. There is no clear criterion yet to determine what kind of elements should be taken into consideration within the framework of special circumstances. In fact, the court tends to bring all kinds of elements into this framework. In addition, the number of judgments is still too small to extract certain types out of the precedent. It would lead to the results becoming unpredictable, perhaps even more unpredictable than the "doing business" jurisdiction or activity-based jurisdiction in US law.

We can draw two questions from this:

1) As long as we have no black-letter rule and have only this precedent, should this be the test to be adopted for the examination of international jurisdiction on IPR issues?

2) Or should the territorial nature of IPRs be stressed and should it override other considerations in international civil procedure? Then would it lead to the exclusive jurisdiction of the country where the IPR is registered or protected?

For the first question, one finds a few judgments that followed the Jori special circumstances approach. Two recent judgments are cited below.

The judgment of the Tokyo District Court of November 18, 2002[6], examined international jurisdiction *ex officio* based on the facts of this case: In 1999, Y, a US company, defendant, licensed B to distribute comic books and T-shirts of a manga figure, Tetsujin No. 28 (Iron man). In 2001, in California, Y sued X, a Japanese national, seeking a declaratory judgment

---

[4] 51 Minshu 4055, 4058, 41 Japanese Annual of International Law 117, 119 (1998).

[5] For a critical comment on the precedent, *see Toshiyuki Kono*, Some Considerations on International Jurisdiction and the Draft Convention on Jurisdiction and Foreign Judgments in Civil and Commercial Matters from a Japanese Perspective, in: *Chi Carmody/Yuji Iwasawa/Sylvia Rhodes* (eds.), Trilateral Perspectives on International Legal Issues: Conflict and Coherence, 2002, 157–170, at 158.

[6] Hanreijiho, No. 1812, at 139; Hanrei Taimuzu, No. 1115, at 277.

that Y had the copyright in animation films of Tetsujin No. 28. The US court dismissed the claim based on *forum non conveniens*. X filed a suit in Japan based on US copyright law for compensation of damages caused by infringement in the US and injunction against the distribution of the books and T-shirts in the US. The defendant did not appear.

The Tokyo District Court examined several jurisdictional grounds based on provisions in the Japanese Code of Civil Procedure, *i.e.*, domicile of the defendant, place of tort, and appearance. But none of these were accepted as a jurisdictional ground by the Japanese court.

The place of performance (according to the Japanese Civil Code, the place of obligee's domicile) of tortuous claim could be a jurisdictional ground. According to the Court, however, it would be too unfair for the defendant with the US domicile to appear and follow the proceedings in Japan. Thus there are special circumstances to deny the jurisdiction based on the place of performance. Hence the court denied the jurisdiction of the Japanese court.

The plaintiff argued that in the Californian suit the defendant's claims for a declaratory judgment on his copyright in Iron Man was dismissed due to *forum non conveniens*, and that this could be a reason to affirm the jurisdiction of the Japanese court. The court responded that the denial of the jurisdiction by the US court cannot be a reason for a Japanese court to exercise the jurisdiction, and the statement of the US court defining Japan as "*forum conveniens*" does not justify the jurisdiction of the Japanese court either.

In this case, the plaintiff practically tried the extra-territorial enforcement of his Japanese copyright, although all the defendant's acts were conducted outside of Japan, and it failed. The result seems reasonable.

As for the second case, the judgment of the Tokyo District Court of May 14, 2001[7], also followed the same Jori special circumstances approach. This judgment is however different from the judgments cited so far, since the plaintiff sued a Japanese company together with its US parent company and a Swedish company, which belongs to the same parent company, arguing that these companies infringed the plaintiff's Japanese patent. The Japanese defendant company is incorporated in Japan only to sell the products of the US parent company, manufactured by the Swedish company. The Court stated that the Japanese court has no jurisdiction over these companies, since the foreign companies so far carried out only promotional activities in Japan and therefore conducted no tortuous act. Moreover, no joint tortuous act was conducted by the three defendant companies. Considering the following facts that the US company is the parent company and exports the products to Japan, that the volumes of Japanese defendant company's sales in Japanese market is big (ca. 10,000 million yen a year), and that the defendant Japanese company has not only formally, but also substantially an independent legal identity, there is no reason to pierce its independent legal identity and to confirm the jurisdiction over the parent company.

---

[7] Hanreijiho, No. 1754, at 148; Hanrei Taimuzu, No. 1080, at 208.

The result of this judgment also seems appropriate. If the defendant were a paper company, this judgment might have opened a new way to such consequence that its foreign parent company as co-infringer should be subject to the jurisdiction over the Japanese defendant company. Or the foreign parent company might need to be subject to the jurisdiction of Japanese court, when its Japanese subsidiary is fully controlled by her. Then how to identify the way of "control" and to measure its degree would become important. We have to see the further development of this judgment.

As for the second question, one should pay attention to the judgment of the Japanese Supreme Court of September 26, 2002[8]. The core issues of this so-called *Card Reader* case were the laws applicable to the infringement of a US patent and to the injunction against the plaintiff's production in Japan[9]. In this case, both parties were Japanese nationals, living in Japan. Since both parties did not argue the jurisdiction of the Japanese court to decide on the US patent infringement, its jurisdiction did not arise as a major issue. However, since the jurisdiction has to be examined *ex officio* by the court, this judgment should be understood to mean that the Supreme Court confirmed the jurisdiction of the Japanese court in the infringement of a foreign IPR, or, perhaps more importantly, that it at least did not refer to the exclusivity of the jurisdiction of the US court in the infringement of US patent.

To sum up, we could perhaps say the following: Japanese courts would not take the idea of exclusive jurisdiction for IPR-related infringement and injunction cases. Also, in the field of the intellectual property law, it will further follow the precedent developed so far. We have to then remember that the Jori special circumstances test would give the court great flexibility with unpredictable consequences. In fact, shortly after the judgment of the Supreme Court that adopted the special circumstances test, under a very similar factual situation to that of the Supreme Court judgment, the Tokyo High Court rendered a judgment with a completely opposite consequence[10]. This suggests that Japan needs legislation for international jurisdiction.

The Supreme Court handed down another important judgment on international jurisdiction in 2001[11]. Although this was an international case concerned with copyright, its infringement was not the major issue: In this

---

[8] Hanreijiho, No. 1802, at 19.

[9] Facts of this case: X, plaintiff, is the holder of a US patent (no Japanese patent). Y, defendant, manufactured its products, which fall within the scope of X's US patent, and exported them to the United States. Z, incorporated in the United States as a sister company of Y, imported Y's products and sold them in the United States. X argues that Y's conduct constitutes the "active inducement of infringement of a patent" in Sec. 271(b) of the US Patent Act and also that Y shall be liable as an infringer (35 USC 271). Y shall therefore stop manufacturing and exporting, abandon the products and pay compensation for X's damages caused by Y's tortuous acts.

[10] Hanreijiho No. 1700, at 41.

[11] June 8, 2001, Minshu Vol. 55, No. 4, at 727.

case, according to defendant Y, a Thai national living in Thailand, he was exclusively licensed to use the copyright of the TV program figure "Ultra Man" outside of Japan by X, a Japanese company, the copyright holder of Ultra Man in Japan. X licensed A, a Japanese company, to make and sell Ultra Man products in Southeast Asia. Y sent warnings to A through a law firm in Hong Kong that the manufacturing of Ultra Man products would violate Y's license.

X brought a suit in Tokyo against Y for the following 5 points: (1) declaratory judgment that the license contract between X and Y is null and void, (2) declaratory judgment that X is the copyright holder of Ultra Man in Thailand, (3) declaratory judgment that Y is not licensed to use it, (4) injunction against distribution of false facts and statements, and (5) compensation.

The Tokyo District Court, at the first instance[12], stated that the international jurisdiction of the Japanese court could be exercised despite the defendant's absence from Japan. It should be determined according to the Jori special circumstances test developed by the Japanese precedent. Although the plaintiff argued that Japan should have jurisdiction as the place of the tortuous act (sending warnings) and as the location of assets (copyright), there are special circumstances to deny the jurisdiction of the Japanese court based on the facts of this case. Even if sending warnings could be considered a tort, the main part of it was conducted outside of Japan; copyright is granted by the law of each country and, in terms of the use of the work outside of Japan, Japan is not the location of the copyright.

X appealed, changing its second claim to request negative declaratory judgment that Y is not the copyright holder in Japan. The Tokyo High Court, at the second instance[13], dismissed the appeal of X. For the new claim, Japan should be considered as the location of assets (copyright in Japan) and thus its jurisdiction should be confirmed. However, no concrete dispute concerning Japanese copyright between these parties has arisen yet, so there is no procedural interest in this case.

The Supreme Court reversed the judgment of the Tokyo High Court:

X argued the following 6 points: (1) compensation of damages caused by tortuous acts, (2) negative declaratory judgments that Y was not the copyright holder in Japan, (3) declaratory judgment that the contract between X and Y was forged, (4) declaratory judgment that X was the copyright holder in Thailand, (5) negative declaratory judgment that Y was not licensed to use the work, (6) an injunction against sending letters that Y was the copyright holder outside of Japan and that doing business with X would violate Y's exclusive right.

---

[12] January 28, 1999, Hanreijiho No. 1681, at 147.

[13] March 16, 2000, Minshu Vol. 55, No. 4, at 778.

The court confirmed the jurisdiction for (1) and (2), *i.e.*,

(1) compensation of damages caused by tortuous acts, and
(2) negative declaratory judgments that Y is not the copyright holder in Japan.

The jurisdiction for the rest, (3) through (6), was then confirmed based on a joinder of the claims, since these claims are closely related.

Four issues can be raised:

[1] The first question concerns the proof of jurisdictional grounds and its extent. In this judgment, the Supreme Court clarified its stance for the first time: Tort as a jurisdictional ground should be proved "to some extent," and the proof of only objective elements of the tortuous act would suffice. When the fact that the warnings were sent to B in Japan is proven, the objective elements of the tort are fulfilled and thus jurisdiction can be affirmed.

However, sending warnings seems to be routine in legal practice. When a Japanese company receives such warnings from its foreign business partner, the foreign partner should be subject to the jurisdiction of Japanese court. This may easily lead to exorbitant jurisdiction.

[2] According to the court, Japanese copyright should be considered as being located in Japan. Jurisdiction based on the location of assets could be therefore affirmed. Since Y argues in the litigation filed by X in Thailand that the copyright in Thailand is shared by X and Y, Y has legal interest in negative declaratory judgments.

The court confirmed the jurisdiction for negative declaratory judgments on Japanese copyright, although who holds the Japanese copyright was not the issue between the parties in this case. To justify its conclusion, the court cited the Thai litigation between the same parties. On this basis, a party could create the jurisdiction of Japanese court whenever a suit is filed overseas at a certain stage.

[3] For the rest of the claims, the court said that when there is a close relationship between them, jurisdiction based on the joinder of claims could be exercised. Claims (3) through (6) in this case are closely related, so that the Tokyo High Court should have exercised its jurisdiction over these claims as well.

This is very generous. Some questions could be raised. For example, are claims (2) (negative declaratory judgment for Japanese copyright) and (4) (positive declaratory judgment for Thai copyright) so closely related that they should be dealt with together? Or would (4) (Thai copyright) be related to (1) (tortuous acts), although the act at issue was sending warnings to Japan, not the infringement of an IPR?

[4] According to the court, there is no special circumstance to deny the jurisdiction in this case: it focuses on the Thai litigation. The subject matter of jurisdiction in this case and that of the Thai case is different. Although one issue in the Thai litigation is who exclusively holds the right to use the work in Thailand, and this issue is common to the Japanese case, to subject the defendant to the jurisdiction of a Japanese court is not in opposition to the principle of fairness between parties and a fair and speedy trial.

The application of the special circumstance test here is not elaborately done. The main concern of the court in the framework of this test was *lis pendens* only. On the other hand, the court missed other elements to be considered in the framework of this test, such as the difference in economic power of the parties. This judgment again highlighted the problems involved with the special circumstances test.

II. Choice-of-Law Issues and IPRs in Japan

The above-cited judgment of the Supreme Court in the *Card Reader* case should be further examined in the context of private international law. The Tokyo High Court as the second instance adopted the opinion, which has been the prevailing scholarly opinion, that due to the territoriality principle of IPRs, there is no room to discuss the choice-of-law issues. It is *a priori* excluded.

The Supreme Court took a different approach; it recognised that IPRs have a territorial nature because IPRs are closely related to the industrial policies of each country. However, the territorial nature of IPRs does not necessarily exclude the choice of law in the field of intellectual property.

The court then classified infringement and injunction differently: infringement as a tort, and injunction as effect of patent. As for the effect of patent, according to the court, Japanese private international law (*Horei*) does not have a provision, so that the applicable law, *i.e.*, the law with the closest connection to the concerned legal relationship, should be determined by Jori. The law of the country where the patent is registered should be the applicable law. It is, in this case, US law. According to the US Patent Act, Secs. 271(b) and 284, not only the infringer in the US, but also the person who induced the infringement overseas is liable. However, Japanese patent law does not know such extraterritorial applicability, so the policy of the US patent law is too foreign and collides with the fundamental value of Japanese law. Therefore the application of US patent law would violate Japanese public policy (Art. 33 Horei).

As for the infringement, Art. 11 of Horei applies and the law of the place of occurrence of tort is applicable. It is the place where tortuous effect occurred, *i.e.*, the United States. According to Art. 11(2), however, Japanese law has to be cumulatively applied. The question is whether, according to

Japanese law, the inducing acts conducted abroad constitute a tort or not. Since Japanese law does not have any provision or convention setting the territoriality principle aside, such inducement would not be unlawful. Therefore the requirements of tort could not be fulfilled. Hence the plaintiff's claims were dismissed.

The Supreme Court made it clear that the court took the choice-of-law approach, not the territoriality-principle approach. One could raise the following questions: Should infringement and injunction be treated separately; would the territoriality principle constitute public policy in Japan; and is the law of the country where a patent is registered the appropriate applicable law? Whatever the answer to these questions should be, the most important thing is that abandoning the old theory based on the territoriality principle opens the discussion of these issues.

As for the concrete law to apply to the claim for tort and compensation, a foreign "right" can be a legal basis of tortuous liability in Japanese tort law. Therefore one question is whether a foreign "patent" could be the foreign "right" to be protected by Japanese tort law. If this is affirmed, then the second question is whether the defendant's acts constitute "joint tort" under Japanese law (Art. 719 Japanese Civil Code). The majority opinion of this judgment denied the first question, while the dissenting opinion of Justice Fujii affirmed both questions and urged that the case be remanded to the second instance. His opinion seems appropriate.

Two recent cases show some important choice-of-law issues: P, an American national, who became the holder of the registered copyright of the "Kewpie" figure in 1913, obtained copyright also in Japan based on the US–Japan Copyright Treaty. After her death in 1944, her copyright in Japan is valid until 2005 based on a law made as a special measure after World War II. X, a Japanese national, purchased the copyright in Japan from P's heir, T, in 1998. X filed two separate suits against Japanese companies; the one is Y, a Japanese mayonnaise manufacturer, which uses the figure for its trademark and other purposes[14], the other Z, a Japanese bank, which used this figure for its advertisements[15].

[1] In both cases, the issue of the validity of the transaction between X and T and its applicable law was raised. According to the Tokyo High Court[16], the causal relationship for the transfer of rights (ex. contract) should be distinguished from the transfer of the property right or of similar rights such as copyright. The law applicable to the causal relationship is to be determined by the parties' agreement (Art. 7(1) Horei). When it is lacking, the judge should try to find a concluding agreement. In this case, one should

---

[14] Tokyo District Court, November 17, 1999, Hanreijiho No. 1704, at 134; Hanrei Taimuzu No. 1019, at 255.

[15] Tokyo District Court, November 17, 1999, Hanreijiho No. 1704, at 147; Hanrei Taimuzu No. 1019, at 269.

[16] May 30, 2001, Hanreijiho No. 1797, at 131; Hanrei Taimuzu No. 1106, at 235.

assume that the parties agreed to choose Japanese law, since the object of the transaction is the right with exclusive effect in Japan and one party is a Japanese national. On the other hand, the transfer of a property right or of similar rights should be governed by *lex rei sitae*; in the case of copyright, it should be the law that determines the contents and effects of the right, *i.e.*, Japanese law.

[2] In the second case against the bank, the bank Z argued that the copyright of this figure belonged not to P, but to the company that published P's illustrations of Kewpie in its magazine in 1909. The copyright issues between an employer and its employees should be governed by the law applicable to the labour contract. It would be US law in this case. However the labour-contractual relationship between P and the publishing company cannot be confirmed in this case. In addition, the illustrations were published in the name of P, not of the publishing company. Therefore Z's argument cannot be accepted.

It should be pointed out that this judgment is based on the theory under German influence, *das Abstraktionsprinzip*, which separates transactions into two parts, the causal (contractual) relationship of transfer and the transfer of rights itself. This has been the prevailing opinion on the international property law in Japan, but it has been criticised and one should doubt whether this idea would be widely accepted. Since the parties appealed to the Supreme Court, we have to further observe the development of discussion on this issue.

III. The Most Recent Judgment – Does It Suggest the Direction of Japanese Precedent?

The most recent judgment, rendered in October 2003[17], draws attention because it is the first judgment on a foreign IPR since the judgment of the Supreme Court in the 2002 *Card Reader* case, and because it contains issues on both international jurisdiction and private international law. This case again concerns a US patent, and both plaintiff and defendant are Japanese corporations. The plaintiff is a manufacturer who sells, in both Japanese and American markets, products using coral powder. The defendant is the US patentee of an invention for production of coral powder. The defendant sent warnings to the plaintiff's American client that the plaintiff's products infringe his US patent. The plaintiff sought:

(1) a negative declaratory judgment that the plaintiff's products do not fall within the scope of the defendant's US patent, so that no injunction order against both the plaintiff and his US client should be granted, and

(2) compensation and an injunction order against the defendant that he should stop sending warnings to the plaintiff and the plaintiff's client: since the defendant's warnings contain false information, sending them violates the Law for the Prevention of Unfair Competition in Japan.

---

[17] Tokyo District Court, October 16, 2003, unpublished.

The issues included in these contentions are as follows: [1] international jurisdiction of Japanese Court over the negative declaratory judgment (contention (1)); [2] procedural interest of plaintiff in the negative declaratory judgment and injunction (contentions (1) and (2)); [3] sales of plaintiff's products and violation of US patent law; [4] defendant's sending warnings and Law for Prevention of Unfair Competition.

1. International Jurisdiction of Japanese Court

The Tokyo District Court followed the Jori special circumstance approach; the defendant in this case has its principal place of business in Japan, which in principle justifies the exercise of jurisdiction of a Japanese court over any kind of claim against the defendant (Art. 4(4) Japanese Code of Civil Procedure).

According to the court, the territoriality principle in patent law cannot be a ground to deny the international jurisdiction, since this jurisdiction concerns a matter related to private law.

In litigation, where an injunction based on a patent is sought, the issue of patent validity is often raised as an objection by the defendant. It is generally accepted that the country of patent registration has exclusive jurisdiction over the claim on the validity of patent. However, if this objection based on the validity of the patent is accepted by the court, such judgment on the validity of the patent binds only the parties. Therefore, even if it may give the defendant an opportunity to assert its interpretation of the validity of patent, it does not prevent the court from exercising jurisdiction to decide on injunction.

The same logic should apply to litigation, as in this case, where a negative declaratory judgment against injunction based on a patent is sought. Also, it is not difficult for the defendant in this case to appear in court, since he has his principal place of business in Japan. Hence there is no special circumstance to deny the above affirmed jurisdiction.

2. Procedural Interest

A negative declaratory judgment of this court against injunction on the *plaintiff* in this case should be recognised by the state of Nevada, where the plaintiff's client has his principal place of business. Once the negative declaratory judgment is rendered, the plaintiff could prevent injunctions in Japan as well. Thus the plaintiff has a procedural interest in such a negative declaratory judgment.

On the other hand, there is no ground to render a negative declaratory judgment against injunction on the *plaintiff's client*. This is because the core issue of this case is whether the plaintiff's products fall within the scope of the defendant's patent. The judgment on this does not create any legal relationship between the defendant and the plaintiff's client.

3. Violation of US Patent Law

Here, to determine the applicable law, the Tokyo District Court apparently followed the judgment of the Supreme Court in the *Card Reader* case: injunction based on patent should be classified as "effect of patent." Since there is no provision on "effect of patent" in Horei, Japanese private international law, it should be determined by Jori. The law of the country of patent registration has the closest relationship to the patent and it should thus be applicable. Since (1) a patent is granted as a right through application and registration in each country, (2) according to the territoriality principle adopted in many countries, the effect of patent is determined by each country and recognised only by such country, and (3) therefore, as long as the effect of patent is recognised only in such country, the country where the protection of patent is sought is the country of patent registration, hence US patent law is applicable to such an injunction.

Applying US patent law to this case, the court concluded that the plaintiff's products do not fall within the scope of the defendant's patent. Thus selling these products does not constitute a violation of US patent law, and thus no injunction should be ordered. Therefore there is a ground to render a negative declaratory judgment in this case.

4. Violation of Law for Prevention of Unfair Competition

Injunction and compensation are sought based on the fact of sending false information. The court affirmed the jurisdiction of a Japanese court on the same ground as that for the above-mentioned negative declaratory judgment. Injunction sought by the plaintiff is addressed to the defendant's acts that hamper the plaintiff's business. His claim for compensation is a tortuous claim. Therefore the law applicable to such injunction and claim should be determined by Art. 11 of Horei, which governs tort. Japanese law should be applicable in this case, since the defendant sent his warnings by way of e-mails and letters from Japan, and thus Japan was the place of tort. Hence the Law for the Prevention of Unfair Competition is applicable. The court then concluded that Law for the Prevention of Unfair Competition had been violated.

This judgment contains many issues to be analysed. At this stage, one could say at least that it suggests the directions the developing Japanese precedent will take: (1) Jurisdiction should be determined following the Jori special circumstance approach despite its unpredictability; and (2) for the determination of the law applicable to patents, the judgment of the Supreme Court in the *Card Reader* case will be followed.

Choice of Law in the Digital Environment – Problems and Possible Solutions

ANSGAR OHLY*

I. Introduction

In the global world created by the internet, national boundaries lose their significance. International intellectual property law, which is firmly rooted in the notion of territoriality, therefore faces new challenges.

The principle of territoriality provides that the scope of intellectual property rights is limited to the territory for which they have been granted. Parallel rights relating to identical intangible objects may exist in various countries, but they are independent of one another. According to the view prevailing in most jurisdictions, a choice-of-law rule can be deduced from this principle: Intellectual property disputes are governed by the lex loci protectionis, or, in the words of Article 110(1) of the Swiss Act on Private International Law: "Intellectual property rights are subject to the law of the state for whose territory protection is sought". It can be argued that this rather straightforward rule has comforted intellectual property lawyers and has prevented many of them from venturing deeper into the world of private international law. In recent years, however, conflicts and infringements of intellectual property rights on the internet make a fresh analysis of the traditional approach to the choice of law in intellectual property disputes inevitable. Academics in several countries have become attentive to this issue.

Apart from some impressive academic work that has been published in the last few years,[1] three initiatives are worth mentioning. In 1998, the WIPO Standing Committee on the Law of Trademarks, Industrial Designs and Geographical Indications started elaborating principles concerning the use of

---

* Dr.jur. (Munich), LL.M. (Cantab.); Professor of Civil Law and Intellectual Property Law at the University of Bayreuth.

[1] *See* in particular: *Bettinger/Thum*, Territoriales Markenrecht im Global Village, 1999 GRUR Int. 659 = 31 IIC 285 (2000); *Dinwoodie*, Private International Aspects of the Protection of Trademarks, WIPO Forum on Private International Law and Intellectual Property, Geneva 2001, available online at http://www.wipo.int/pil-forum/en/documents/pdf/pil_01_4.pdf; *Fawcett/Torremanns*, Intellectual Property and Private International Law, 1998; *Schack*, Internationale Urheber-, Marken- und Wettbewerbsrechtsverletzungen im Internet, 2000 MMR 59 *et seq.*, 135 *et seq.*; *Thum*, Internationalprivatrechtliche Aspekte der Verwertung urheberrechtlich geschützter Werke im Internet, 2001 GRUR Int. 9; *van Eechoud*, Choice of Law in Copyright and Related Rights: Alternatives to the Lex Protectionis, 2003.

marks and other distinctive signs on the internet. After several rounds of discussions, the Joint Recommendation Concerning Provisions on the Protection of Marks, and Other Industrial Property Rights in Signs, on the internet (hereinafter: WIPO Recommendation)[2] was adopted at a joint session of the Paris Union and the WIPO General Assembly in 2001. This recommendation seeks to restrict the legally relevant use of signs on the internet in a particular country to acts having a commercial effect within that country. Additionally, the introduction of a "notice and avoidance of conflict" procedure and a principle of proportionality between the commercial effect of the use of a mark within the jurisdiction and the subsequent court sanctions are recommended. At the outset of the second project stood the efforts of the Hague Conference for Private International Law, aimed at the elaboration of an international convention on jurisdiction and enforcement.[3] While initially issues concerning intellectual property rights were to be included in the convention, they were later dropped from the agenda, except for matters resulting from B2B contracts. However, since an international agreement on jurisdictional matters would be as desirable in the area of intellectual property law as in other areas of commercial law,[4] *Rochelle Dreyfuss* and *Jane Ginsburg* presented a private draft,[5] which was later adopted as a project by the American Law Institute (ALI). Meanwhile, the Institute has charged a working group with the task of formulating principles governing jurisdiction, choice of law, and judgments in transnational disputes. While the *Dreyfuss/Ginsburg* draft was still restricted to matters of jurisdiction, the first preliminary ALI draft principles, which were tabled in January 2003 (hereafter: ALI draft principles) also address choice-of-law issues.[6] Thirdly, the Max Planck Institute for Intellectual Property has initiated a

---

[2] Published in 2001 WRP 833, available online at http://www.wipo.int/sct/en/documents/session_6/pdf/sct6_7p.pdf,*see also* the commentary, http://www.wipo.int/docu-ments/session_6/pdf/sct6_notesrev.pdf. On the Recommendation *see Bettinger*, Die WIPO-Vorschläge zum Schutz von Marken und anderen Zeichenrechten im Internet, 2001 WRP 789; *Kur*, Die WIPO-Empfehlungen zur Benutzung von Marken im Internet, 2001 GRUR Int. 961; *see also infra*, III 2, and the analysis of the principles by *Christian Wichard* in this volume.

[3] On this project *see Dreyfuss*, An Alert to the Intellectual Property Bar: The Hague Judgments Convention, 2001 U.Ill.L.Rev. 421; *Dreyfuss/Ginsburg*, Principles Governing Jurisdiction, Choice of Law, and Judgments in Transnational Disputes, 2003 CRi 33; *Kur*, International Hague Convention on Jurisdiction an Foreign Judgments: A Way Forward for IP? 2001 E.I.P.R. 175; *Wagner*, Die Bemühungen der Haager Konferenz für Internationales Privatrecht um ein Übereinkommen über die gerichtliche Zuständigkeit und ausländische Entscheidungen in Zivil- und Handelssachen, 2001 IPRax 533 *et seq.*

[4] *See Dreyfuss/Ginsburg*, *supra* note 3, at 34; *Kur*, Principles Governing Jurisdiction, Choice of Law and Judgments in Transnational Disputes: A European Perspective, 2003 CRi 65.

[5] Published in 77 Chicago-Kent L.Rev. 1065 (2002).

[6] While this draft has not been published yet, *Dreyfuss* and *Ginsburg* give an outline of its contents in their article cited in note 3, *supra*; *see also* the comment by *Kur*, *supra* note 4.

working group on questions of jurisdiction and choice of law in intellectual property matters. While the group has already presented draft provisions on jurisdiction,[7] the elaboration of choice-of-law rules has been reserved for the second stage of the project.[8]

Not only the principles of international intellectual property law, however, are put to a test in the new global online world. Also, the fundamental assumption of private international law according to which the one legal system with the closest connection to the dispute can always be identified may need to be reconsidered. While the idea of a global "cyberlaw" may remain an illusion, private international law has to take account of the fact that the application of well-established choice-of-law rules to information available on the internet may result in the applicability of a multitude of legal systems. Problems similar to multi-state infringements of intellectual property rights on the internet exist in other areas of private law,[9] most notably in the law of unfair competition[10] and in the law of defamation.[11] Private international law, which has traditionally aimed at the determination of the applicable law, may also have to consider new instruments.

My task is twofold. I have been asked to identify problems and possible solutions. It is evident that the analysis of the problems (II) will be the much easier enterprise. While some possible solutions, both conventional and unconventional, will be canvassed (III), many questions will only be asked rather then answered. The discussion is only beginning.

II. Problems

1. Territoriality Versus Globalisation

The *problem* is evident. It is the clash between the territorially parcelled world of intellectual property and the global universe of the internet.

Since the beginnings of modern intellectual property law, the principle of territoriality has been the bedrock of international cooperation in this area. As early as the 19th century the principle was embodied in both great international conventions (Arts. 4bis, 6 Paris Convention, Art. 5 Berne Convention). According to traditional wisdom, territoriality is the natural

---

[7] *See* the information on the Max Planck Institute's website: www.ip.mpg.de.

[8] *See*, however, the discussion proposal by *Kur*, *supra*, note 4, at 72.

[9] For an overview of the various issues, *see Leible* (ed.), Die Bedeutung des Internationalen Privatrechts im Zeitalter der neuen Medien, 2003.

[10] *See Dethloff*, Europäisierung des Wettbewerbsrechts, 2001, at 48 *et seq.*; *Höder*, Die kollisionsrechtliche Behandlung unteilbarer Multistate-Verstöße, 2002; *Kieninger*, Die Lokalisierung von Wettbewerbsverstößen im Internet – Ist das Marktortprinzip zukunftsfähig?, in: Leible (ed.), *supra*, note 9, at 121 *et seq.*; *Mankowski*, Internet und internationales Wettbewerbsrecht, 1999 GRUR Int. 909.

[11] *See Helle*, Persönlichkeitsrechtsverletzungen im Internet, 2002 JZ 593; *v. Hinden*, Persönlichkeitsrechtsverletzungen im Internet, 1999.

consequence of the fact that the grant of intellectual property rights is a sovereign act of state. In recent years, however, the principle of territoriality has come under attack from two sides. On the one hand, copyright lawyers challenge its traditional justification and point out that copyright in a work does not depend on an act of state but rather comes into existence as a mere consequence of the creation of the work. Copyright, it is argued, should therefore not be conceived of as territorial but as universal.[12] Secondly, private international lawyers object to an idea that seems to be firmly rooted in 19th-century national state doctrine. In particularly forceful words, *Kurt Siehr*[13] has recently voiced the following criticism:

> Not infrequently this territorial orientation leads to results which, even if perfectly explainable by IP principles, make an impartial observer shake his head. (. . .) It remains to be hoped that within this system some relaxations will come to be accepted in order to avoid ludicrous and grotesque results. Every area of law can only benefit from a little grain of international justice, a touch of common sense and a bit of courage to allow exceptions to the rules.

Later in this paper it will indeed be argued that the principle of territoriality may need to be relaxed in certain respects. However, at this stage it should already be pointed out that the criticism is much more forceful with respect to unregistered rights, particularly copyright and neighbouring rights, than with regard to registered industrial property rights. The grant of a patent or the registration of a trade mark is still an act of state or of a *supra*national body, respectively.

2. Case Example: The "Maritime" Case

Indeed, particularly in the digital environment, the idea of a territorially fragmented world may seem outdated. Since there are no *reliable* technical means of restricting the accessibility of an internet website to a particular country,[14] the internet defies national boundaries. The *Maritime* case recently decided by the Oberlandesgericht (Court of Appeal) Hamburg[15] may serve as an example.

"Maritime" is the name of a small hotel in the city of Copenhagen. The hotel's website, which is accessible at the URL "www.hotel-maritime.dk", not only contains information in Danish, but also in English and German. Reservations can be made online. The owners of the hotel also own the

---

[12] For German law *see Schack*, Urheber- und Urhebervertragsrecht, 2nd ed., 2001, para. 806 *et seq.*, 900 *et seq.*; *v. Welser* in: *Wandtke/Bullinger* (eds.), Praxiskommentar zum Urheberrecht, 2002, para. 11 vor §§ 120 ff.; for US law *see Itar-Tass Russian News Agency v. Russian Kurier, Inc.*, 153 F.3d 82 at 90 = 1999 GRUR Int. 639 (case-note *Schack*); *Goldstein*, International Copyright, 2001, at 102 *et seq.*

[13] *Siehr*, Internationales Privatrecht, 2001, at 303.

[14] *See Bettinger/Thum*, *supra* note 1, at 660; *Höder*, *supra* note 10, at 19 *et seq.*; *Ubber*, in: *Ubber* (ed.), Markenrecht im Internet, 2002, at 206.

[15] OLG Hamburg 2002 MMR 822 – *hotel-maritime.dk*.

Danish trade mark "maritime", registered *inter alia* for accommodation services. In Germany, however, a well-known hotel chain bears an almost identical name; only the letter "e" at the end of the word is missing. Based on its German trade mark right in the word "Maritim", the owners of this chain sued for infringement before the Landgericht Hamburg (District Court).[16] According to the principle of territoriality, both marks are territorially restricted and independent of one another. Offline they coexist peacefully, but online they conflict. A national court called upon in an infringement suit could certainly ignore the international nature of the conflict, hold that because of the mere accessibility of the website the trade mark is used within the country and give judgment for the claimant accordingly.[17] Such an outcome, however, would amount to a Pyrrhic victory for the claimant, since its own internet presence could also be enjoined by a court in the defendant's home country. On a strict application of the principle of territoriality, both parties could thus preclude each other's internet activities completely.

There is no easy answer to this problem.[18] Some possible solutions will be canvassed later. At this point, the case should only highlight the fact that there are two quite distinct issues involved. On the one hand there is a *conflict of laws*. Two legal systems – Danish and German law – may be applicable to this dispute. The rules of private international law are called upon to decide which of the two legal systems should apply. In this respect, the case does not differ fundamentally from other cases concerning the choice of law. In particular, there are evident parallels to disputes about tangible property. It is possible to distinguish between questions regarding the existence and the initial ownership of the right, issues of infringement and questions concerning the transfer of title and licensing.

However, in the *Maritime* case these issues are not the most pertinent ones. Substantive trade mark law in the European Union has been harmonised by the Trade Marks Directive of 1988. Thus, the relevant provisions of Danish and German law do not differ much. In particular, according to both legal systems, a registered trade mark is infringed where a similar sign is used for identical services.[19] The main issue in the *Maritime* case is not the conflict of

---

[16] The judgment of the LG Hamburg at first instance is published in 2002 GRUR Int. 163.

[17] Such an approach has indeed been adopted by courts in some jurisdictions, *see* for Germany: KG Berlin, 1997 CR 685 – *concert-concept*; LG München I, 2000 CR 464 – *intershopping.com*, confirmed by OLG München, 2000 MMR 277; for France: Tribunal de Grande Instance de Nanterre, *SG 2/Brokat Informationssysteme GmbH*, referred to by *Bettinger/Thum*, *supra* note 1, at 661; for the USA: *Inset Systems, Inc. v. Instruction Set, Inc.*, 937 F.Supp. 161 (165) (D.Conn. 1996).

[18] Certainly the solution offered by one of my assistants – the court should ask which country had the prouder seafaring tradition – will have to be rejected: Too big is the risk that a Hamburg and a Copenhagen court might not agree on this point.

[19] *See* § 4(1) No. 2 of the Danish Trade Marks Act and § 14(2) No. 2 of its German counterpart.

laws but the *conflict of rights*.[20] Two territorially restricted rights conflict in a global medium. The task is to balance the interests of two right owners when one intangible object may legitimately be used in one territory while infringing an intellectual property right in another territory. The solution to this problem will not be found in private international law. Rather, the same dispute can arise in a purely domestic context, as German experience shows. After the German unification the territorial scope of the laws of the Federal Republic of Germany was extended to the former German Democratic Republic.[21] Nevertheless, the conflicts between rights formerly registered for different owners in both German states remained.[22] Legislation had to make specific provisions governing this conflict.[23] But even apart from this very special situation the need for conflict-of-rights rules may arise. Similar trade marks can be registered by different persons for different goods or services. However, a particular internet domain name can only be allocated to one person. Thus the conflict between several legitimate users of a sign may have to be resolved by specific conflict rules such as those enunciated by the German Federal Supreme Court in the recent domain name cases *shell.de*[24] and *vossius.de*.[25]

The difference between the *conflict of rights* and the *conflict of laws* is sometimes overlooked because under the traditional approach they are resolved in a similar manner: according to the principle of territoriality, the scope of intellectual property rights is restricted to one territory, and these rights are subject to the law applicable within that territory. However, this coincidence is not a necessary one. First, one can imagine choice-of-law rules under which the scope of various territorially restricted rights is determined by the law of one single country. The introduction of a country-of-origin principle into European trade mark law, for example, could leave the territoriality of trade mark rights intact while determining all conflicts under one set of national provisions. Secondly, there could be one monolithic universal right, the scope of which is determined differently in different countries. This is the scenario envisaged by the proponents of the principle of universality in copyright law. One of the purposes of this paper is to show that the traditional approach should not cloud the view: both questions should be distinguished clearly.

20 *See Bettinger/Thum*, *supra* note 1, at 669 *et seq.*; *Dinwoodie*, *supra* note 1, para. 62; *Kur*, Territorialität versus Globalität – Kennzeichenkonflikte im Internet, 2000 WRP 935 at 937; *Ohly*, Kennzeichenkonflikte im Internet, in: Leible (ed.), *supra* note 9, at 135 at 145.

21 Art. 8 Einigungsvertrag (Treaty of Unification, 1990).

22 *See*, for example, the *Altenburg playing cards* case, 1995 GRUR 754.

23 *See* the conflict rules in §§ 26 *et seq.* Erstreckungsgesetz (Act of Extension, 1992).

24 BGHZ 149, 191 = 2003 IIC 315.

25 BGH, 2002 GRUR 706.

III. Possible Solutions

1. First Issue: Determination of Initial Ownership

At first glance there seem to be evident parallels between the choice-of-law rules concerning property in tangible objects on the one hand and intellectual property on the other. Both property rights create a relation between an object and a person. Thus it is necessary to identify the initial owner. When a new object is created – be it corporeal or incorporeal – there can be doubts as to whether the actual creator or rather the employer or investor should be regarded as the initial owner. In this respect, determining which legal system to apply in order to determine initial ownership is a classic *conflict of laws* issue. As for property in tangibles, the most widespread rule provides that the *lex rei sitae*, the law of the country where the object is situated, should be applied.[26] In intellectual property law things are more complex, as an intangible object cannot be localised in a particular country. Thus there is an alternative between the application of the *lex loci protectionis*, which results in a determination of first ownership on a country-by-country basis, and the application of criteria such as the domicile of the creator or the place of first publication, which allow a universal determination. This issue is most pertinent in copyright law, where a heated discussion between the advocates of both approaches has been going on for decades.

However, there is also a related, yet distinct *conflict of rights* issue. Unlike tangible property, information can be used by different persons concurrently.[27] Thus rights in one intangible object can be allocated to different persons in different jurisdictions, and these rights can coexist. This coexistence is most evident in trade mark law: since trade marks often consist of common words such as "Maritime", it is likely that different and unrelated persons will register similar marks in different countries. In this situation the existence of different owners is not the result of a choice of law, as the legal rules on the allocation of trade mark rights on the basis of priority can probably claim universal acceptance. Even within one jurisdiction several rights in distinctive signs may coexist. While registered marks are usually granted for the entire territory of a state, the concept of a locally restricted goodwill is well established in the law of unregistered marks.[28]

---

[26] For German law, *see* Art. 43 EGBGB (Introductory Act to the Civil Code); for English law, *see Collins* (ed.), Dicey and Morris on the Conflict of Laws, 13th ed., 2000, rules 111 and 116 (paras. 22R-001 and 24R-001).

[27] On the economic implications of this aspect, *see Ullrich*, Grenzen des Rechtsschutzes: Technologieschutz zwischen Wettbewerbs- und Industriepolitik in: *Schricker/Dreier/Kur* (eds.), Geistiges Eigentum im Dienst der Innovation, 2001, p. 83 at 91.

[28] For German trade mark law, *see* BGHZ 21, 182 at 196 – *Ihr Funkberater*; *Ingerl/Rohnke*, Markengesetz, 2nd ed., 2003, § 4, para. 22; for the English law of passing-off, *see Brestian v. Try* [1958] R.P.C. 161 (C.A.); *Chelsea Man v. Chelsea Girl* [1987] R.P.C. 189 at 201 (C.A.); for US law *see* the "TEA ROSE" case, *Hanover Star Milling Co. v.*

Under the traditional approach, however, it is not necessary to distinguish between the two issues. The principle of territoriality limits the scope of both registered and unregistered rights to the country for which they have been granted and the initial ownership is determined according to the *lex loci protectionis*. As far as registered rights are concerned, the burden of multi-state applications is eased by mechanisms such as the PCT application in patent law, or the international registration under the Madrid Agreement or the Protocol to the Madrid Agreement in trade mark law. However, these mechanisms are still based on the principle of territoriality. The same is true for *supra*national rights such as the Community rights[29] (Community trade mark, Community design, possibly the Community patent in the future) or the Benelux trade mark and design rights. Internally they abolish territoriality to a great extent, but externally their scope remains restricted to a certain *supra*national territory.

In the digital environment, however, universal ownership of intellectual property rights would make life much easier, since conflicts between coexisting rights in a global medium would vanish. The ALI draft principles in their first version (January 2003) made a bold attempt at achieving universality by stating simply that initial title to an intellectual property right other than an unregistered trade mark should be governed by the law of the country of origin.[30] The "country of origin" was defined as the country in or from which the work has first been made available to the public, or, if this country lacks a significant relationship to the creation of the work, the country of the creator's residence.[31] As for unregistered trade marks, the draft offered two alternatives. According to one alternative, initial title should be governed by the law of the country where the mark was first used, whereas the other alternative favoured the principle of territoriality by applying the law of each country where the mark was first used.[32] It was evident from the terminology of the proposal that it was drafted with copyright and neighbouring rights in mind. Indeed, in copyright law the universal determination of ownership seems possible. The arguments for and against this approach shall not be repeated here, since they are discussed by *Dorothee Thum* and *Mireille van Eechoud* elsewhere in this volume.

However, it is not clear from the draft whether the proposed principle is also meant to extend to registered rights.[33] At this point it should be remem-

---

Metcalf, 240 U.S. 403, 60 L.Ed. 713, 36 S.Ct. 357 (1916); McCarthy on Trademarks and Unfair Competition, 2002, § 26:2.

[29] On choice-of-law issues of community rights, *see* the contributions by *Eike Schaper* and *Axel Metzger* in this volume.

[30] ALI draft principles (January 2003), Art. 25.1; the approach was changed in the 2nd version of the draft, published in January 2004.

[31] ALI draft principles (January 2003), Art. 23.3.

[32] ALI draft principles (January 2003), Art. 25.3.

[33] Since registered rights are granted by an administrative body, the application to register rights might be excluded by Art. 17.1, which limits the scope of the following

bered that registered rights are granted by an act of state. Their territorial limitation is the inevitable consequence of the existence of different national patent and trade mark offices. Under a "country-of-origin principle" the grant of a patent or the registration of a mark (or, possibly, even the "first publication" of an invention or mark) in one country would bar applications in all other countries. Such a system would not only be inconsistent with the principles of independence of national industrial property rights and of union priority set forth in the Paris Convention,[34] it would also unduly restrict competition. Leaving aside the Convention rules on priority for a moment, the registration of a right in one country has no impact on the competition in other states under the present system. If initial ownership were determined under a country-of-origin principle, however, the first use or the first application would automatically result in a world-wide monopoly.

The same argument applies to unregistered trade marks and designs, where the universal determination of initial ownership would be possible in theory.[35] In practice, however, such an approach would not only hamper competition, it would also be undesirable to apply different choice-of-law rules to parallel registered and unregistered rights. International universality would have to be paid for with inconsistencies in national law, since both forms of protection overlap. First, quite frequently the use of a mark or a design gives rise to an unregistered right before its owner applies for registration.[36] Secondly, in some jurisdictions it is common for a claimant in trade mark infringement proceedings to rely on both his registered mark and his unregistered right in the same sign.[37]

The universal determination of first ownership according to a country-of-origin principle is therefore not an option for intellectual property law as a whole. Its introduction is only workable with respect to copyright and neighbouring rights. Thus, even a principle of universality in international copyright law would cause additional problems since it would result in different choice-of-law rules for copyright on the one hand and industrial property rights on the other hand. Since intellectual property rights have an

---

principles to substantive law while excluding administrative law. However, it would hardly seem convincing to exclude the substantive requirements for patent or trade mark protection, including the rules determining initial ownership, from the area of substantive law.

[34] Articles 4A(1), 4bis(1), 6(3) of the Paris Convention.

[35] *See Schack, supra* note 1, at 62.

[36] *See*, for example, Art. 7 (2) of the Council Regulation (EC) No. 6/2002 of 12 December 2001 on Community designs, OJ EC L 3 of 5 January 2002, at 1, which explicitly allows for a design to be registered within 12 months after it has first been made available to the public by the designer or related persons.

[37] In English law, a claimant will frequently add a claim in passing-off "as a second string" to actions for trade mark infringement, *see Kitchin etc.* (eds.), Kerly's Law of Trade Marks and Trade Names, 13th ed., 2001, para. 14–34; *Howe/Abrahams* in: *Lord Mackay of Clashfern* (ed.), Halsbury's Laws of England, Vol. 48 – Trade Marks, 2000, para. 406.

increasing tendency to overlap,[38] as the example of copyright and patent protection for computer software shows,[39] it can be doubted whether this distinction is desirable.

There is, however, one mechanism in trade mark law that is indeed based on a universal approach. ICANN's Uniform Domain Name Dispute Resolution Policy (UDRP) determines the ownership of a domain name which includes a generic top-level-domain on a world-wide level.[40] If a person has registered a domain name in bad faith without having a right or legitimate interest with respect to the name, the panel can order the cancellation or transfer of the domain name. However, for several reasons the UDRP is far from being the nucleus of a future universal "cyber-IP law". First, ICANN is a quasi-administrative body governing the allocation of certain domain names. Outside this rather restricted field, there is no comparable organisation that could claim jurisdiction over international intellectual property disputes. Secondly, the adjudicative power of the panels established under the UDRP is limited to disputes in which only one party has a right or legitimate interest in the name whereas the other party has registered the name in bad faith. Thus the UDRP has its merits in evident cases of domain-grabbing, but it does not provide any guidance in disputes between two legitimate users of conflicting national marks. Thirdly, the UDRP does not

---

[38] *See Dinwoodie*, Trademark And Copyright: Complements Or Competitors, in: *Ginsburg/Besek* (eds.), Adjuncts and Alternatives to Copyright, Proceedings of the ALAI Congress 2001, at 498 *et seq.*; *Kur*, Does/should trademark law prohibit conduct to which copyright exceptions apply?, in *Ginsburg/Besek* (*loc. cit.*), at 594 *et seq.*

[39] An overlap between copyright and patent protection for computer software is common in US law, where no specific restrictions on the patenting of computer software exist, *see State Street Bank & Trust Co. v. Signature Financial Group Inc.*, 149 F.3d 1368, 47 U.S.P.Q.2d 1596 = 1999 GRUR Int. 633 – *Finanzdienstleistungs-Anordnung* (case note *Nack*); *Cohen/Lemley*, Patent Scope and Innovation in the Software industry, 89 Cal.L.Rev. 1 at 7 *et seq.* (2001); *Nack*, Die patentierbare Erfindung unter den sich wandelnden Bedingungen von Wissenschaft und Technologie, 2002, at 101 *et seq.* In the European Community, computer programs qualify for copyright protection, *see* the Council Directive of 14 May 1991 on the legal protection of computer programs (91/250/EEC); OJ EC L 122 of 17 May 1991, at 42. On patent protection, *see* the Commission's proposal for a directive on computer-implemented inventions of 20 February 2002, COM (2002) 92 final, available online at http://www.europa.eu.int/comm/internal_market/en/indprop/comp/com02-92en.pdf.

[40] Available online at http://www.icann.org/dndr/udrp/policy.htm; on the UDRP, *see Bettinger*, ICANN's Uniform Domain Name Dispute Resolution Policy, 2000 CR 234 *et seq.*; *Bousonville* in: *Ubber* (ed.), *supra* note 14, at 229; *Gibson*, Digital Dispute Resolution, 2001 CRi 33 *et seq.*; *Lührig*, Online-Schiedsgerichte für Domainstreitigkeiten, in: *Hohl/Leible/Sosnitza* (eds.), Domains, Frames und Links, 2002, at 71 *et seq.*; on first experiences with the UDRP system, *see Kur*, Abschlußbericht zur UDRP-Studie des Max-Planck-Instituts für Geistiges Eigentum, Wettbewerbs- und Steuerrecht in Zusammenarbeit mit den Universitäten Karlsruhe und Stockholm, available online at www.zar.uni-karlsruhe.de/admin/get_data.php?resID=95.

preclude recourse to national courts.[41] Panel decisions are thus not final: whoever loses the dispute before the panel still has the possibility of firing a second shot.[42]

Hence, although it may seem disappointing, international intellectual property law will have to live with territorially restricted rights that have the potential to conflict in a global medium. A universal determination of ownership only seems feasible for copyright and neighbouring rights. In industrial property law, however, a universal approach is not sustainable as long as national patent and trade mark offices exist.

2. Second Issue: Infringement

While it is impossible to avoid territoriality as far as ownership is concerned, the harshness of the principle of territoriality can be relaxed to some extent when it comes to questions of infringement. Again, *conflict of laws* and *conflict of rights* issues should be distinguished.

The *conflict of laws* question is: Is it possible to apply one set of national rules to infringements occurring on the internet or does the mere accessibility of a website in a country render the law of that country applicable? Similar questions arise in several areas of tort law, particularly in unfair competition law. According to Art. 5(1) of the Commission's proposal for a "Rome II" Regulation[43] and according to the approach traditionally prevailing in most Member States,[44] disputes concerning unfair competition are subject to the law of the market place. Whenever the market is global, this approach results in the applicability of several national legal systems. Since, however, even within the European Union the levels and methods of protection against unfair competition (despite the Commission's best efforts[45]) still differ widely,[46] the "market place principle" is an obstacle for commercial communication on the internet. In practice, a person trading on the internet will have to look for advice about many different national legal systems, and eventually he will have to conform to the strictest national rules. In order to cope with this problem, the Commission and the Council adopted the

---

[41] Para. 4(k) UDRP.

[42] Para 4(k) UDRP; *see also* the case of *Sallen v. Corinthians Licenciamentos LTDA*, 273 F.3d 14 (C.A. 1, Mass. 2001).

[43] Proposal for a Regulation of the European Parliament and the Council on the law applicable to non-contractual obligations ("ROME II") of 22 July 2003, COM (2003) 427 final; *see also* the analysis of this proposal by *Josef Drexl* and *Matthias Leistner* in this volume.

[44] *See* the comments on Art. 5 in the explanatory memorandum, *loc cit.*, at 16.

[45] *See* the Commission's Proposal for a Directive of the European Parliament and of the Council concerning unfair business-to-consumer practices in the Internal Market and amending Directives 84/450/EEC, 97/7/EC and 98/27/EC (the Unfair Commercial Practices Directive) of 25 May 2004, Doc. 9667/04, on the acquis communautaire in the field on unfair competition law, *see Schricker/Henning Bodewig*, [2002] E.I.P.R. 271.

[46] *See Schricker/Henning-Bodewig*, *supra* note 45, at 274 *et seq.*

country-of-origin principle, which provides that commercial communication on the internet must not be prohibited in the receiving state if it is legal under the law of the country of origin.[47] Although the E-Commerce Directive does not acknowledge it,[48] the country-of-origin principle is, at least to some extent, a choice-of-law rule.[49]

Similar choice-of-law problems exist in intellectual property law. Whoever uses the internet for commercial purposes not only has to be aware of potentially conflicting intellectual property rights in other countries. Even when he has found out about all potentially conflicting rights, he must still take into account that the scope of rights may differ. The "Arsenal story" is a good example. Arsenal Football Club is the owner of several registered trade marks in the word "Arsenal" and in the club emblem. A London trader had offered unauthorised Arsenal fan articles for sale that showed the club emblem. However, the trader had tried to avoid any confusion by putting up a sign in his shop explaining that all the articles sold by him were "unofficial". In the English High Court, Laddie J. held that the sale of the articles did not amount to a "trade mark use" and that there was no likelihood of confusion and referred the case to the European Court of Justice for a preliminary ruling.[50] The ECJ decided both issues in favour of the claimant,[51] as probably most courts in continental jurisdictions would have. The case highlights the problem that even within the European Union, where the law of registered trade marks was harmonised in 1988, national opinions about the scope of intellectual property rights may differ. Under the traditional approach, the scope of each national right is determined by the *lex loci protectionis*. As in unfair competition law, this principle may cause obstacles to e-commerce. For a trader who intends to sell fan articles for various European Champions League teams it will be rather easy to ascertain which names and emblems are protected by trade mark rights in which countries. However, it will be much more difficult to find out whether the sale of fan articles amounts to "trade mark use" according to the national trade mark laws of all European countries. True, within the European Union most issues will be decided by the

---

47 Article 3(2) of the E-Commerce Directive, Directive 2000/31/EC of the European Parliament and of the Council of 8 June 2000 on certain legal aspects of information society services, in particular electronic commerce, in the Internal Market; OJ EC L 178 of 17 July 2000, at 1 *et seq*.

48 Article 1(4) of the Directive provides: "This Directive does not establish additional rules on private international law nor does it deal with the jurisdiction of Courts".

49 The question is disputed; *see Kieninger, supra* note 10; *Mankowski, supra* note 10 and Herkunftslandprinzip und deutsches Umsetzungsgesetz zur e-commerce-Richtlinie, 2002 IPrax 257 *et seq*.; *Ohly*, Herkunftslandprinzip und Kollisionsrecht, 2001 GRUR Int. 899 at 900 *et seq*.; *Spindler*, Herkunftslandprinzip und Kollisionsrecht – Binnenmarktintegration ohne Harmonisierung?, 66 RabelsZ 633 at 648 *et seq*.

50 *Arsenal Football Club plc v. Reed*, (2001) R.P.C. 46.

51 ECJ, decision of 12 November 2002, Case C-206/01, *Arsenal Football Club v. Reed*, [2002] ECR I-10273.

European Court of Justice sooner or later. After the Arsenal decision of the Court of Justice[52] the trader in our example will have to obtain licences from the various football clubs. Nevertheless, the example begs the question of whether it might be possible to determine the scope of all intellectual property rights under one single set of national rules. Similar issues may arise in patent law, given that computer-implemented business methods are patentable in some jurisdictions.[53] It may be easier to obtain information about the existence of relevant patents than about the rules applicable to the interpretation of claims in various jurisdictions.

The European E-Commerce Directive explicitly excludes intellectual property law from its ambit.[54] Nevertheless, one could argue in favour of a country-of-origin principle in European intellectual property law that, while acknowledging the existence of independent rights in various states, determined the scope of these rights according to the law of the country of origin. This approach would ensure that every trader would be free to rely on the various exceptions provided by the intellectual property statutes as interpreted in his home jurisdiction. Many of the arguments that have been advanced in favour of or against the country-of-origin principle in unfair competition law[55] have force here too. On the one hand, it would make life easier for traders using the internet; on the other hand, a strong intellectual property protection in one country could be undermined by traders conducting business on the internet from "intellectual property havens". One can also object that the traditional "*lex loci protectionis*" rule ensures the application of the same national law to issues concerning the requirements for registration on the one hand and infringement on the other. Since a generous registration practice is often counter-balanced by a narrow scope of "weak" rights, whereas a restrictive registration practice often results in strong protection, there is much to be said for a parallel choice-of-law rule for questions of registration and for issues of infringement. Finally, particularly in trade mark law, questions of infringement often depend on the circumstances of the domestic market, especially on language and customer habits. Certainly, here as well as in unfair competition law,[56] a country-of-origin principle would require some degree of harmonisation first. However, within the European Union, where the level of harmonisation in intellectual property law is much higher than in unfair competition law, the

---

[52] *See also* the subsequent decisions by the English High Court and the Court of Appeal, (2003) R.P.C. 9 *et seq*. (Ch.D.), 39 (C.A.) *et seq*.

[53] *See supra*, note 39.

[54] *See* the appendix to the Directive.

[55] On this discussion *see supra* note 49 and *Bodewig*, Elektronischer Geschäftsverkehr und unlauterer Wettbewerb, 2000 GRUR 475 at 482; *Kur*, Das Herkunftslandprinzip in der E-Commerce-Richtlinie: Chancen und Risiken in: *Ahrens*, etc. (ed.), Festschrift für Willi Erdmann zum 65. Geburtstag, at 629 *et seq*.

[56] For the arguments for and against a global country-of-origin principle in unfair competition law *see Kieninger*, *supra* note 10, at 132 *et seq*.

idea of a country-of-origin principle might deserve discussion despite the objections raised above.

Another attempt at a universal determination of the law governing infringement issues is made by the ALI working group. The ALI draft principles allow exceptions to the *lex loci protectionis* rule in two situations. First, when, in cases of multi-state infringement, ascertaining the law of the countries of infringement is unduly burdensome, the court should apply "international substantive norms" such as set forth in the TRIPS Agreement or in other international conventions.[57] Secondly, the court may apply the law of the country with which the claim as a whole has the greatest connection if it appears that the connection to other countries is only very loose.[58] Both principles concern the *choice of law*, as they allow the application of the laws of country X to the infringement of an intellectual property right that came into existence under the laws of country Y. However, while both principles are well worth discussing, some objections can be raised. As for international conventions, they are not directly applicable in most jurisdictions. Also, these conventions only reflect a minimum international standard,[59] not a thorough and detailed balance between the right level of protection and the proper scope of exceptions. What is more, the provisions of TRIPS and the other international conventions are framed in very general terms. A judge, in applying these provisions to a particular dispute, will thus probably tend to look at his own familiar legal system for more guidance. Thus, the resort to convention law may eventually result in the application of the *lex fori*. A similar argument can be advanced against the "closest connection" approach: particularly judges in big countries with important electronic markets may be tempted to assume that the dispute has the closest connection to their own country. Again, the departure from the *lex loci protectionis* might not be a step forward towards more international harmony in the adjudication of international disputes, but a step back towards the application of the *lex fori*.

However, in the majority of cases, it is not the *conflict of laws* but the *conflict of rights* that causes the problems. The "Maritime" case is a case in point: German and Danish law by and large determine the scope of trade marks according the same rules. The crucial question in the case was not whether Danish or German law should govern the dispute, but whether the mere use of a sign on the internet by itself amounted to an infringing use of a conflicting national trade mark.

---

[57] ALI draft principles (January 2003), Art. 24.2; for changes introduced in the 2nd version (January 2004) *see* the following note.

[58] ALI draft principles (January 2003), Art. 24.3. The approach was slightly changed in the second version (January 2004), Sec. 302. According to that provision, courts shall take the following factors into account for choosing the law to be applied in exceptional cases: (a) the law of the country with the closest connection to the dispute, and (b) the degree to which the desirability of such regulation is generally accepted as evidenced by TRIPS and successive international laws.

[59] *See Kur, supra* note 4, at 72.

As seen above, a strict application of the principle of territoriality would be unsatisfactory, since it would give precedence to the intellectual property right protected within the jurisdiction while neglecting the legitimate interests of the owner of the foreign right. Thus, for these conflicts every national legal system is faced with the task of developing rules of coexistence and proportionality. Orientation is offered by the WIPO Joint Recommendation, which envisages a restricted concept of "trade mark use", a procedure for notice and avoidance of conflict, and a principle according to which the scope of national judgments should be proportionate to the use of the sign within the jurisdiction. Since *Christian Wichard* will introduce and analyse this recommendation in depth, I do not need to go into any detail here. Suffice it to say that these principles provide valuable guidelines.

The restriction of the concept of "infringing use" to a use that has commercial effect within the jurisdiction has already been applied by courts in various countries.[60] It is also the argumentational basis for the Hamburg Court of Appeal's judgment for the defendant in the "Maritime" case.[61] The Oberlandesgericht held that the internet advertisement for the Copenhagen hotel did not have a significant commercial effect on the German market. The court did not attach any weight to the fact that the website contained information in English and German, since both languages were used in international commerce and thus did not constitute a link to particular countries. The court also pointed out that the services offered by the hotel could by its nature only be rendered in Denmark. However, this approach is limited in an important aspect: it only helps where the use of a sign has no significant commercial effect within the jurisdiction. In cases concerning offers for the sale of goods made online, the commercial effect on the market in many jurisdictions will be the rule rather than the exception.

Another important feature of the Recommendation is the principle of proportionality. Increasingly, courts are aware of the extraterritorial implications of their judgments in internet disputes. Rather than making global injunctions, the courts should look for possibilities to allow for a coexistence of various national rights. Practical possibilities such as disclaimers or portals are outlined in the WIPO recommendations. It should also be pointed out that an injunction not to deliver goods or offer services to customers within the jurisdiction will often be more adequate than a global injunction prohibiting any use of a sign, work or invention on the internet. As Annette *Kur* has pointed out in her recently published proposal,[62] the principle of

---

[60] *See*, for example, *1-800-Flowers Inc. v. Phonenames Ltd.*, [2000] F.S.R. 697 (English High Court), [2002] F.S.R. 191 (Court of Appeal); *Bensusan Restaurant Corp. v. King*, 937 F.Supp. 295 (US District Court, S.D.N.Y. 1996), 126 F.3d 25 (Court of Appeals, 2nd cir., 1997); TGI Paris, 28 March 2003, *Nestlé v. Mars*, available online at http://www.foruminternet.org/telechargement/documents/tgi-par20030328.pdf.

[61] *Supra*, note 15.

[62] *Kur, supra* note 4, at 72.

proportionality has the potential of becoming an internationally accepted guideline for judges, not only in trade mark disputes but in all transnational intellectual property disputes. However, it should be remembered that a principle of proportionality along the lines envisaged in the WIPO Recommendation would not be a choice-of-law rule but rather a procedural rule that restricts the ambit of national jurisdiction rather than determining the applicable law. In particular, it specifies the general rule familiar to most legal systems that an injunction should not be broader than is necessary for the protection of the claimant's rights.

IV. Conclusion

There is no easy way of avoiding the tension between the territoriality of intellectual property rights and the globality of the internet. While a universal approach may be conceivable in copyright law, the territorial restriction of industrial property rights will remain as long as the idea of a world patent and trade mark office is utopian. At least in industrial property law, initial ownership therefore will have to be determined according to the *lex loci protectionis*.

As for the infringement of intellectual property rights on the internet, however, the rigour of the principle of territoriality can be relaxed in some respects. The use of a mark, an invention or a work on the internet should only be regarded as infringing a national right if this use has a commercial effect within the jurisdiction. Also, the courts should be aware that unrestricted injunctions in transnational disputes are likely to have an extra-territorial effect. Sanctions should therefore be proportionate to the commercial effect that the act complained of has within the jurisdiction. While these principles do not concern the choice of law but the scope of national rights, there may also be a case for allowing certain exceptions to the *lex loci protectionis* rule in private international law.

The Joint Recommendation Concerning Protection of Marks, and Other Industrial Property Rights in Signs, on the Internet

JOHANNES CHRISTIAN WICHARD*

I. Trademarks on the Internet: Territorial Rights in a Global Medium

Private international law and trademark law have a long history of avoiding each other. Trademark law has been – and still is – firmly rooted in territoriality, reinforced by the principles of national treatment and the independence of national trademark rights (Arts. 2.1, 6.2 and 6.3 of the Paris Convention for the Protection of Industrial Property). Trademarks are protected wherever the legal requirements for protection are satisfied. In all other countries, the trademark right has no legal existence. In private international law terms, the *lex loci protectionis* principle has remained largely unchallenged. Choice of law has therefore hardly been an issue in trademark law.

As with intellectual property rights in general, the territorial foundation of trademark rights is at least partially explained by their use as an instrument of economic and cultural policy by states, and the corresponding desire of states to preserve the ability of striking their own balance between exclusive rights and public access to intangible assets. Trademark law is part of the legal framework that regulates behaviour in a territorially defined market. Core concepts of trademark law rely on territorial connecting factors. Most notably, the use of a trademark is only relevant under a country's trademark law (as a condition for obtaining or maintaining trademark protection, or for finding trademark infringement) if such use has taken place in that country, i.e. the country of protection.

Since markets never completely coincided with territorial borders, trademark law had to deal, almost from the outset, with the international aspects of trademark use. This was, however, hardly done in the framework of private international law. Trademark law, like intellectual property law in general, instead relied, since the late 19th century, on international conventions, which, like the Paris Convention and the TRIPS Agreement, harmonised national laws and introduced general principles, or which, like the Madrid Agreement and the Madrid Protocol, facilitated trademark registration in

---

* The author is Deputy Director and Head of the Legal Development Section of the WIPO Arbitration and Mediation Center. The views expressed in this article are those of the author.

several countries. While these international norms and principles alleviate the potentially detrimental effect of territoriality on international commerce, they leave the territorial basis of trademark law unchallenged.

With the advent of the internet the territorial basis of trademark law has come under strain. The markets in which trademarks are being used are potentially as global as the internet. Such use is difficult to fit into the traditional territorial concepts of trademark law, which has resulted in considerable legal uncertainty. The following cases might illustrate some of these issues.

SG2 v. Brokat ("payline").[1] A German company (Brokat), the owner of the German trademark "payline" for internet payment systems, used this trademark on its web site (brokat.de). The payment system could not be sold to French customers since it did not comply with French regulations on cryptography. A French competitor (SG2), the owner of an identical trademark registered in France for the same services, sued Brokat in a French court for infringement of its French trademark. The French court held for the plaintiff. The court based its jurisdiction on the fact that the word "payline" appeared on a web site that was accessible to internet users in France. The mere use of that sign on the internet was regarded as an infringement, in France, of the French trademark. The court therefore enjoined the defendant from using the trademark "payline" on its internet web site.

Playboy v. Chuckleberry.[2] An Italian publisher of adult journals operated a web site under the domain name "www.playmen.it". The owner of the US trademark "Playboy" initiated trademark infringement litigation in the USA. The court found for the plaintiff because the web site was visible in the USA, and because the Italian publisher had actively solicited electronic subscribers in the USA. The court, however, allowed the Italian defendant to continue operating its web site, provided it did not permit access to users from the USA. The court stated that "[to] hold otherwise would be tantamount to a declaration that this Court, and every other court throughout the world, may assert jurisdiction over all information providers on the global World Wide Web."

Among the questions raised by these and other cases are the following:

(i) What should be done in cases where the same or a similar trademark has different owners in different states? Can each of them use its mark on the internet, or will such use be considered as infringing the other's trademark so that, effectively, no one would be able to use it? If this were the case, then rights that coexist offline in different territories enter into conflict on the internet.

(ii) Is it fair when courts pass injunctions prohibiting every use of a sign on the internet? The effect of such injunctions is as global as the internet, while the scope of the infringed trademark right is territorially limited.

---

[1] *SG2 v. Brokat Informationssysteme GmbH*, Tribunal de grande instance Nanterre, October 13, 1997, www.legalis.net/jnet/decisions/marques/ord_tgi_nanterre_131097.htm.

[2] *Playboy Enterprises Inc. v. Chuckleberry Publishing, Inc.*, 939 F. Supp 1032, 1039-40, 39 USPQ 2d 1746 (SDNY 1996).

A more general question is whether such issues can be addressed on the basis of the existing territorial trademark laws, or whether they call for a separate cyber-trademark law regulating this potentially global marketplace.

The World Intellectual Property Organisation (WIPO) has addressed these issues since 1998 in the framework of the Standing Committee on the Law of Trademarks, Industrial Designs and Geographical Indications (SCT). Based on the results of a comprehensive study,[3] supplemented by information gathered with the help of a questionnaire,[4] and directed by an issues paper,[5] WIPO prepared several drafts for provisions concerning the protection of marks and other distinctive signs on the internet.[6] On the basis of this preparatory work, the Assembly of the Paris Union for the Protection of Industrial Property and the General Assembly of WIPO adopted the WIPO Joint Recommendation Concerning the Protection of Marks, and Other Industrial Property Rights in Signs on the internet (the "Joint Recommendation") in September 2001.[7]

II. Approach and Scope

The approach of the Joint Recommendation is best characterised by three negatives:

(i) It does not establish a self-contained trademark law for the internet;
(ii) It does not address choice-of-law issues;[8]
(iii) It does not attempt to re-territorialise the internet by imposing unreasonably burdensome obligations on those who use signs on the internet.

[3] WIPO document SCT/2/9, http://www.wipo.int/sct/en/documents/session_2/doc/sct2_9p.doc.

[4] WIPO document SCT/3/2, http://www.wipo.int/sct/en/documents/session_3/doc/sct3_2.doc.

[5] WIPO document SCT/3/4, http://www.wipo.int/sct/en/documents/session_3/doc/sct3_4.doc.

[6] WIPO document SCT/4/4, http://www.wipo.int/sct/en/documents/session_4/doc/sct4_4.doc; WIPO document SCT/5/2, http://www.wipo.int/sct/en/documents/session_5/doc/sct5_2.doc; WIPO document SCT/6/2, http://www.wipo.int/sct/en/documents/session_6/doc/sct6_2.doc.

[7] WIPO Publication No. 845, http://www.wipo.int/about-ip/en/index.html?wipo_content_frame=/about-ip/en/development_iplaw/index.htm; *see also Bettinger*, Die WIPO-Vorschläge zum Schutz von Marken und anderen Zeichenrechten im Internet, 2001 WRP 789–796; *Buri*, WIPO/PVÜ: Gemeinsame Empfehlung zum Schutz gewerblicher Kennzeichen im Internet, 2001 sic! 848–852; *Kur*, Die WIPO-Empfehlungen zur Benutzung von Marken im Internet, 2001 GRUR 961–965; *Wichard*, Übersicht über aktuelle Aktivitäten der Weltorganisation für geistiges Eigentum (WIPO) im Markenrecht, 2001 MarkenR 201 and 2002 MarkenR 13.

[8] *See* note 0.04: "The question of determining the applicable law is not addressed by the present provisions, but left to the private international laws of individual Member States. Once the applicable national or regional law has been determined, it should be applied, directly or by analogy, wherever this is possible."

In line with the tradition of international norm-setting in trademark law, the Joint Recommendation addresses international dimensions of trademark use within the framework of national trademark laws. It accepts both the territorial character of existing trademark laws as well as the global nature of the internet as given factors, but aims to reduce the tension between both factors by making national and regional trademark laws "internet-compatible".

The Joint Recommendation covers all registered and unregistered "industrial property rights" in distinctive signs (Art. 1(ii)). This includes all rights in signs that are exclusive, are protected in a commercial context, and are of a "territorial" nature, in particular trademarks, trade names or geographical indications. While the Joint Recommendation does not itself contain a comprehensive list of such rights the definition of "industrial property" in Art. 2(2) of the Paris Convention would, however, provide a minimum. Rights that are protected in a purely non-commercial context, such as personal names, are not explicitly covered. Member States are, however, free to apply the provisions to such rights as well.

III. Linking the Use of Signs on the Internet to Individual Territories

As stated earlier, trademark use is one of the core concepts of trademark law because it determines whether certain activities are legally relevant under a national or regional trademark law. As such, trademark use is fundamentally territorial since it must be linked to a particular territory in order to gain legal relevance. Use of a sign can only establish, maintain or infringe a trademark in a particular country if the sign has been used in that country. This link may be hard to establish where a sign has been used on the internet

For the Joint Recommendation, this link consists in the "commercial effect" of internet use. Only use that has a "commercial effect" in a particular territory shall be treated as having occurred in that territory (Art. 2). Mere visibility on a computer screen alone does not suffice. Article 3 provides a detailed, but non-exhaustive, list of factors that can be relevant for determining commercial effect, such as the interactivity of the web site in question, registration under a country code Top-Level Domain (ccTLD – such as ".de" for Germany), etc. Actual delivery of goods or services is an important factor but not necessarily required. Preparatory activities can suffice, where a web site, for example by virtue of the language used, the currency in which prices are expressed, or the contact addresses indicated, is (also) directed at the public in a particular territory. The use of "disclaimers", *i.e.* statements not to serve customers in a particular territory, can be relevant, but does not provide complete protection when a commercial effect can be established on the basis of other factors, most notably, actual delivery to customers based in the country concerned.

The Joint Recommendation applies the general principle expressed in Art. 2 to instances where trademark use is of legal relevance. Where it is relevant for obtaining or maintaining trademark rights under a national or regional trademark law, use on the internet shall be taken into consideration where such use has a commercial effect in the territory concerned (Art. 5). Similarly, such use can be regarded as infringing a right protected in the territory concerned (Art. 6), while use without a commercial effect is legally irrelevant.[9] By thus clearly defining the territorial reach of national or regional trademark laws, Art. 6 serves to avoid conflicts between rights from different jurisdictions on the internet.

IV. Resolving Conflicts Between Territorial Rights

Because the scope of trademark rights is territorially limited, different owners can hold rights in identical or similar signs in different countries. As in the "payline" case, this can create problems when such signs are used on the internet. Because of the necessarily global nature of the internet, such use might be considered as infringing a right under the law of a state in which the right of the user is not recognised. The "commercial effect" principle alone cannot avoid all conflicts. The question is whether any user of a sign on the internet should be required to undertake a comprehensive worldwide search for conflicting registered and unregistered rights in order to avoid a commercial effect in any country where such a right might exist. In many instances this may be impossible or at least not commercially viable. The resulting risk of liability would place a heavy burden on commercial internet users, particularly on small and medium-sized enterprises.

To address such conflicts, the provisions introduce a "notice and avoidance of conflict" procedure (Part V, Arts. 9 to 15). Under certain conditions, the use of a sign on the internet is exempt from liability up to the point when the user is notified of a conflicting right (Art. 9). To facilitate such a notification, the user must provide contact details. The exemption applies to users who own a right in the sign they are using, provided the right has not been acquired in bad faith (as defined in Art. 4), for example with a view to take unfair advantage of the reputation of a third party's right. The exemption also applies in instances in which the use is legitimate under the law of a country to which the user has a close connection, for example because it is the user's personal name or because the term is considered generic or descriptive, provided that such use has not been made in bad faith.

Once a user has been notified of a conflicting right, he or she has to take certain measures for avoiding the conflict. Otherwise the user can be held

[9] A similar approach has been adopted by the Landgericht (district court) Hamburg in its decision of 3 August 2001 (416 O 294/00), 2002 GRUR Int. 163. According to this decision, a German trademark right can only be infringed by the use of a sign on the internet if such use has a special connection ("besonderer Inlandsbezug") with Germany. This is determined in light of all relevant circumstances of the individual case, including the competing interests.

liable for any infringement resulting from such use. The measures for avoiding liability are described in general terms in Art. 10. The user must send a reply explaining why his or her use is legitimate, and must use "reasonable" means to avoid a commercial effect in the country where the conflicting right is protected. In order to prevent abuse of the notification system, a notification is only relevant if it is sufficiently specific and enables the user to assess the seriousness of the claim raised (Art. 11).

In order to provide right holders and other legitimate users with a sufficient degree of legal certainty as to how to avoid liability, Art. 12 obliges Member States to accept a qualified disclaimer as a sufficient measure under Art. 10. The user must declare that the user has no relationship with the owner of the conflicting right, and that he or she does not intend to deliver goods or services to customers located in the state where the conflicting right is protected. The disclaimer is only effective if the user acts on this stated intent by asking customers where they are located, and refusing delivery to those who have indicated that they are based in the country disclaimed. Since users can only be expected to take "reasonable" measures, *i.e.* measures that do not place an unreasonable burden on their commercial activity, they would not be required to verify the statements made by customers. Where the transaction involves the physical delivery of goods, customers will necessarily make correct statements. Where, however, the whole transaction takes place over the internet (*e.g.* delivery of software, music, information) a verification may be close to impossible. In such cases, a certain degree of unintended commercial effect cannot be avoided.

Through the notice and avoidance of conflict procedure, the Joint Recommendation restricts the scope of trademark rights in certain, limited, situations, in order to manage conflicts that cannot be avoided on the basis of the "commercial effect" principle. At the same time the procedure avoids the mutual blocking effect of conflicting rights, and provides some degree of legal certainty as to how users in good faith can avoid liability in potentially remote jurisdictions without unreasonably burdening commercial activities on the internet.

V. Territorial Remedies in a Global Medium

The tension between territorial rights and a global medium is also evident in the area of remedies. As stated earlier, an injunction to cease every use of a sign on the internet would have a potentially global effect and would go far beyond the territory in which the conflicting right is protected. A decision as to remedies should therefore take account of the territorial limitation of such rights. Remedies should be limited, as far as possible, to the territory in which the right is recognised, and they should only be available if the allegedly infringing use of the sign can be deemed to have taken place in that territory.

These issues are addressed in Part VI (Arts. 13 to 15) of the Joint Recommendation, which introduces a general principle of proportionality is established. Pursuant to Art. 13(1), remedies should be proportionate to the commercial effect in the Member State where the conflicting right is protected. Thus, the "commercial effect" serves as a yardstick for determining a proportionate remedy. Injunctions should generally be limited to what is necessary to prevent or remove the commercial effect in the Member State (or Member States) in which the infringed right is protected, and damages should cover only use that has a commercial effect in the country concerned. Article 14 requires courts to consider limitations – rather than prohibitions – of use, which are designed to avoid a commercial effect in the country concerned, and to avoid any confusion with the owner of that right. Such limitations could include, for example, "qualified disclaimers" (as set out in Art. 12), gateway web pages and the like. The Joint Recommendation recognises that "global injunctions" may be unavoidable in certain cases, for example if the user has targeted a well-known mark in bad faith (as in the case of "cybersquatting"). Pursuant to Art. 15, however, such global injunctions shall not be granted against good-faith users who hold a right in the sign or who are otherwise permitted to use the sign.

VI. Status and Effect of the Joint Recommendation

The Joint Recommendation was adopted as part of WIPO's policy to accelerate the development of international harmonised common principles through "soft law" instruments.[10] It is the third Joint Recommendation in the area of trademark law adopted by the Assemblies of the Paris Union and by the WIPO General Assembly.[11] While it does not have the same legal effect as an international treaty, it has strong persuasive authority as an expression of an international consensus in this particular area of the law.

In substance, the Joint Recommendation is an example for the tendency of international trademark law to address international aspects of trademark use on the basis of harmonised principles of substantive law, thereby avoiding issues of private international law. As explained above, this is (at least partly) due to the principle of territoriality, which limits the relevance of acts that take place outside of the country of protection. The analysis adopted in

---

[10] On function and status of soft law instruments in public international law *see* *Hilgenberg*, A Fresh Look at Soft Law, 10/3 European Journal of International Law 499–516 (1999); *Thürer*, "Soft Law" – eine neue Form von Völkerrecht? 1985 Zeitschrift für Schweizerisches Recht 429–453; *Wengler*, "Nichtrechtliche" Staatenverträge in der Sicht des Völkerrechts und des Verfassungsrechts, 1995 JZ 21–26.

[11] The two earlier instruments are the Joint Recommendation Concerning Provisions on the Protection of Well-Known Marks of 1999, WIPO Publication 833, and the Joint Recommendation Concerning Trademark Licenses adopted in 2000, WIPO Publication 835.

the Joint Recommendation is, however, comparable to an analysis under private international law. Both seek to link a certain fact pattern, in the case of the Joint Recommendation: the use of a sign on the internet, to a certain territory. Unlike private international law, however, the Joint Recommendation does not attempt to determine the applicable (substantive) law, but to situate the fact pattern within the framework of a given substantive law: "use", a substantive legal requirement, is only relevant in a particular country if it has a "commercial effect" in that country. The factors listed in Art. 3 to assist in this determination may however be helpful, beyond the scope of the Joint Recommendation, wherever a certain activity on the internet needs to be linked to a certain territory, for example, in the context of determining jurisdiction for internet-related disputes.

Who Decides on the Colours of Films on the Internet? Drafting of Choice-of-Law Rules for the Determination of Initial Ownership of Film Works vis-à-vis Global Acts of Exploitation on the Internet

DOROTHEE THUM*

I. Introduction: Different Attitudes in National Copyright Laws Towards the Attribution of First Ownership in a Work

1. The Fundamental Difference Between Droit d'Auteur Systems and Copyright Systems

The question of who shall be considered as the author of a creative work is one of the fundamental questions of each copyright system. This question has been answered quite differently in different societies. On the one hand, there are societies that have opted for a *droit d'auteur* system, where the first owner of copyright is always the *natural person* who has actually created the work. Countries with a long tradition of author protection in this respect are for example France and Germany.[1] This tradition of author protection is founded on the respective constitutions and is reflected in the Declaration of Human Rights, which says, in its Art. 27(2): *"Chacun a droit à la protection des intérêts moraux et matériels découlant de toute production scientifique, littéraire ou artistique dont il est l'auteur"*.[2]

Thus, *droit d'auteur* systems vest authorship and initial ownership in the copyright to a work only in natural persons who have made creative contributions to the work.

---

* E-mail: d.thum@dts-law.com. This contribution to the Max Planck Symposium on Jurisdiction and Choice of Law in Intellectual Property Matters at Frauenchiemsee, July 2003, originates from and further develops the round table contribution of the author to the 2002 ALAI study days in Neuchâtel: Thum, Time for compromise in international private law for copyright?, in: Brügger (ed.), Copyright-Internet World, 2003, at 48–65.

[1] *Cf.* Art. L 111-1 CA (France):

> Nature du droit d'auteur Art. L. 111-1. – *L'auteur d'une oeuvre de l'esprit jouit sur cette oeuvre, du seul fait de sa création, d'un droit de propriété incorporelle exclusif et opposable à tous. Ce droit comporte des attributs d'ordre patrimonial, . . . l'existence ou la conclusion d'un contrat de louage d'ouvrage ou de service par l'auteur d'une oeuvre de l'esprit n'emporte aucune dèrogation à la jouissance du droit reconnu par l'alinéa Ier.*; similarly, Sec. 7 CA (Germany): "*Urheber ist der Schöpfer des Werkes*"; also Art. 6 CA (Italy).

[2] Art. 27(2) Declaration of Human Rights of 1948.

On the other hand, there are societies that have opted for a *copyright system* with a *work-made-for-hire doctrine*. This doctrine allows for legally vesting all rights to a creative work not in the author himself or herself, but in an employer or producer, who may even be a legal entity. Such copyright systems exist, for example, in the United States, Great Britain and The Netherlands.[3] All three countries know regulations according to which – in the case of works being created under commission or employment contracts – the whole copyright in these works covering exploitation rights as well as *moral rights*, is owned by the producer or employer *ab initio*. The main reason given for these work-made-for-hire regulations is that the employer or producer shall be able to exercise all exploitation rights unhindered by any restrictions, whether based on moral rights or economic rights of the actual creators of the works. Only with such an unlimited position of rights it is said, the producer would be able to achieve an amortisation of his investment.

It should be stated though that also in copyright systems initial ownership in copyright is generally conferred to the person who actually created the work, the work-made-for-hire doctrine being only an exception to the general rule with a limited scope of application compared to the total number of works being created.

2. Particularly Wide Variety of Answers to the Question of Initial Ownership in the Area of Cinematographic Works

As if this fundamental difference between copyright systems and *droit d'auteur systems* did not complicate matters enough, questions of initial ownership become even more complicated in the area of cinematographic works, to which the following analysis will be confined.

---

[3] *Cf.* Sec. 201 b U.S.C. (1976) CA (USA):

§ 201. Ownership of copyright (a) Initial Ownership. Copyright in a work protected under this title vests initially in the author or authors of the work. . . . (b) Works Made for Hire. In the case of a work made for hire, the employer or other person for whom the work was prepared is considered the author for purposes of this title, and, unless the parties have expressly agreed otherwise in a written instrument signed by them, owns all rights comprised in the copyright;

similarly, Sec. 9(2a) CDPA (1988) CA (GB):

Authorship and ownership of copyright. 9.–(1) In this Part "author", in relation to a work, means the person who creates it. (2) That person shall be taken to be – (a) in the case of a sound recording or film, the person by whom the arrangements necessary for the making of the recording or film are undertaken; . . . 11.–(1) The author of a work is the first owner of any copyright in it, subject to the following provisions. (2) Where a literary, dramatic, musical or artistic work is made by an employee in the course of his employment, his employer is the first owner of any copyright in the work subject to any agreement to the contrary;

similarly, Arts. 6, 7, 8 CA (The Netherlands).

Here, in the area of film works, a wide variety of answers exists to the question of who, among the group of persons contributing to a film, can possibly be considered as "author" or "co-author" of the film. It might be the producer only, the principal director only, producer and principal director as co-authors, the principal director and specifically listed authors of underlying works of literature (like script, scenario, dialogue, adaptation) and of the film music as co-authors and, as a final example, co-authorship of all persons who have made creative contributions to the film, including, besides the principal director, for example also the director of photography, the editor and the sound designer.[4] This list could still be continued.

To sum up: the question of initial ownership, while being one of the most fundamental questions of each national copyright regime, turns out to be, at the same time and especially in the area of film works, regulated in the most diverse manner one can think of.

II. Does the Multitude of Solutions in National Copyright Laws Correspond to Significant Differences and Difficulties in Legal Practice?

Being alerted by this observation and the ongoing intense disputes about initial ownership issues at the same time, the question arises of whether and in what respect this multitude of individual national regulations for the determination of initial ownership in film works leads to great differences in practical results. This question will be looked at separately for the following specific areas of substantive copyright law: the area of limitations and exceptions (1), the area of exploitation rights (2), and the area of moral rights as well as other author-protective regulations of copyright (3).

1. Limitations and Exceptions

If we start with the limitations and exceptions to copyright and ask whether the question of who the initial owner of copyright in a specific work is has any significant effect on the limitations and exceptions to copyright, the answer obviously has to be "no"; as for the question of whether I am allowed

---

[4] Producer only: USA (formerly also Great Britain, The Netherlands and Ireland, before the rental directive 92/100/EC); principal director only: Greece (but authors contributing to the production of the film generally enjoy specific rights in their own creative contributions if they can be exploited independently of the film); producer and principal director as co-authors: Luxemburg, Great Britain (before 1992 it had been the producer only, transformation of the rental directive into national law required additional copyright protection for the principal director), Ireland; principal director and specifically listed authors of underlying works of literature and film music as co-authors: Spain, Italy, Portugal; co-authorship of all persons having made a creative contribution to the film: France, Belgium, Germany, Austria, the Netherlands, Denmark, Finland, Sweden; *cf.* the Report from the Commission, *infra* note 7.

to make a private (digital) copy, whether and to what extent I may quote from a work, whether I am allowed to store a copy of the work in an archive, etc., it does not matter whether the copyright in the work that is copied, quoted, or stored, etc., is owned by the employer, the producer or its actual creator(s), may there be one, two, three or even hundreds of right owners.[5]

The reason for this independence of limitations and exceptions of the answers to authorship and ownership in a copyright work is that limitations and exceptions only affect the "external" relationship between the copyright owner(s) and the public as *users* of the work, whereas the question of initial ownership only affects the "internal" relationship between the possible right owners (producer, principal director, etc.).

2. Exploitation Rights

Does the multitude of individual national answers to the question of initial ownership lead to great differences in the practical results with respect to exploitation rights? Aside from the very specific question of the transfer of exploitation rights for forms of exploitation unknown at the time of the conclusion of a contract, we have to state that in legal practice the attributions of the authorship status to different "authors" by the national copyright laws have in the past caused neither severe difficulties for the exploitation of film works by their producers nor for the efficient prosecution of the unauthorised use of film works in general. One basic reason for this is that *droit d'auteur* regimes also allow for an efficient exploitation by providing *special rules for the transfer of exploitation rights* from the original author to the producer or employer. And remaining difficulties for the exploitation of works that result from the fact that there may be, besides the producer, one or more or even different authors in different countries as original owners of exploitation rights, or from the fact that these transfer rules differ as concerns the method as well as the coverage of the transfer of rights, are – in daily practice – overcome by contractual arrangements between the producer or employer and the potential "authors".[6] These contractual arrangements, together with the statutory rules on the transfer of rights in film works and underlying works, provide the necessary framework for a problem-free cross-border exploitation of film works on a worldwide scale, as all rights needed for such an exploitation can be concentrated in the hands of the producers.

[5] Certainly, the question of ownership becomes relevant for questions of procedural law, like the "power to sue", as, for example, could be seen in *Itar Tass*, for example (*see* the text accompanying *infra* note 22). And also with respect to the duration of copyright, the question whether a specific person is to be seen as (co)author of a work can be of quite some relevance, if the duration of copyright in a film work is determined by the death of the longest living co-author. In the end the duration of copyright protection might differ by 30, 40 or even 50 years.

[6] *Cf.* Report from the Commission, *infra* note 7.

Thus, the amortisation of an investment in a film production can be secured in *all* systems, whether the film is produced under the legal regime of a work-made-for-hire country or under the legal regime of a *droit d'auteur* country. We might quote in this regard a report from the European Commission of December 2002 on the question of authorship of cinematographic or audiovisual works in the European Community,[7] which concludes, after thorough study of the factual evidence:

> Contrary to the fears expressed before the adoption of the Directive 92/100/EEC,[8] there is no evidence that vesting original authorship in the principal director of a film would have caused difficulties in the exploitation or distribution of films, or in the effective tackling of piracy and other unauthorised use of such works. Although it was argued at the time of the adoption of the directive that this provision might lead to increased complexity in dealing with rights, in practice, relevant exploitation rights are transferred to the producer by operation of law or by contractual arrangements. Within the margins of contractual freedom, relations between the producer on one hand and other right holders on the other are determined by agreements concerning the film production. Also potential difficulties resulting from disparities in Member States' legislation are levelled by contractual arrangements.[9]

3. Moral Rights and Other Author-Protective Regulations of Copyright

The situation becomes quite different when we enter the area of moral rights, of inalienable, author-protective statutory limitations of transfer of rights and of inalienable remuneration rights. First of all it is obvious that such restrictions to the unlimited exploitation rights of the producer or employer only exist in *droit d'auteur* systems without a work-made-for-hire doctrine, as, in order to enjoy "author protection " at all in the form of moral rights, limitations on the transfer of rights, remuneration rights, etc., the creator of a work needs to be legally vested with "authorship".

If one considers that, at the same time, these author-protective statutory regulations – among them especially the granting of moral rights – belong to the essence of any *droit d'auteur* system, then it is obvious that *droit d'auteur*

---

[7] *Cf.* Report from the Commission on the question of authorship of cinematographic or audiovisual works in the Community (COM (2002) 691 final of December 6, 2002), which is based substantially on a study carried out by external consultants and the Commission's own findings. The background of this report is as follows: on the occasion of the adoption of the common position on Directive 92/100/EEC on rental right and lending right, *whose Article 2(2) obliged the Member States to recognise the principal director of a film as its author (or one of its authors)*, the Commission made a political commitment to produce a report on the notion of authorship of cinematographic or audiovisual works, as three Member States which did not provide for author's rights for film directors were fundamentally opposed to this provision and suspected it would cause difficulties for the exploitation of films in their territories.

[8] Directive 92/100/EEC, OJ EC L 346, p.61.

[9] *Cf.* Report from the Commission, *supra* note 7, at 3 (Executive Summary) and at 12 (Conclusion).

countries face a serious and fundamental value conflict if being asked to deny the actual creators of works not only all exploitation rights but also all moral rights to their works, including for example even the right to prohibit exploitation of their works in a distorted form.

But exactly this is the intended legal effect of a work-made-for-hire doctrine: if the initial ownership is vested in the producer or employer while the actual creator of the work is left with "nothing", there is no possibility for the actual creator to object to or to participate in any exploitation of the film work at all. The reason for this is that someone who is in legal terms not regarded as the "author" of a work does not enjoy any moral rights in "his" or "her" work at all because legally it is not "his" work or "her" work, and at the same time that person cannot be protected by any statutory limitations of transfer of rights, because he or she does not "own" any rights and, additionally, does not participate in any remuneration rights at all.[10]

Thus, all restrictions regarding the unlimited attribution or transfer of unrestricted exploitation rights to the producer of a work, with which *droit d'auteur* countries show respect for those persons who contributed with their creativity to the making of a film, become null and void, if – by definition of law – these persons are denied the status of being (one of) the "authors" of the film.

On the other hand, copyright systems do not face a comparable value conflict, when being asked to accept the initial ownership of the actual creators of film works. The reason for this is, firstly, that copyright systems are also built on the general principle that generally it is the actual creator of a work who should be rewarded with the "copyright" in his or her work, whereas the work-made-for-hire doctrine represents only a limited and very specific *exception* to this general principle. As copyright systems share this general principle with *droit d'auteur* systems, vesting "authorship" in the actual creators of films does not contrast with or violate any *fundamental* principle of the copyright law. And secondly, if one takes into account that the reason behind the specific exemption of "works made for hire" from the commonly shared fundamental rule is the safeguarding of the amortisation of the producers' investment in a film production, while, as we have seen above, this amortisation can also be secured without a work-made-for-hire doctrine, it is evident that copyright systems would *not* face a major value conflict, were they asked to vest – besides the producers – also the actual creators of cinematographic works with initial ownership.[11]

---

[10] *Cf. Dietz*, Die USA und das "droit moral": Idiosynkrasie oder Annäherung?, 1989 GRUR Int. 627.

[11] It should be emphasised that we are talking about the system as such at this point and not about the interests of particular interest groups. Certainly, lobbying groups will *never* be value-indifferent at this point, but special interest groups, as for example the interest group "film producers", are obviously only *part* of the system. And it should have become obvious that the argument used by the producers in this debate according to which only vesting initial ownership with the producers leads to a secure amortisation of investments

In other words, here we are confronted with a major, but only a *one-directional* value conflict: while copyright systems are fairly value-indifferent with respect to initial ownership in a work, *droit d'auteur systems* are not, as for them, with the question of initial ownership, the question of moral rights and, thus, a very high value, is at stake, as could be seen in the *Huston* case, where the French courts called in the "ordre public" in order to establish John Huston with French *droit moral.*[12]

Thus, with respect to the question of applicable law to initial ownership issues in copyright we encounter the difficulty that, whereas private international law is based on the assumption that national laws are interchangeable, copyright systems and *droit d'auteur systems* are *not* interchangeable when it comes to issues of author-protective limitations to unlimited producer's rights and, in particular, to the sensitive, fundamental and highly political issue of moral rights.

4. Conclusion

The analysis of the relevance of first-ownership issues carried out separately for three main aspects of copyright protection, *i.e.*, limitations and exceptions (1), exploitation rights (2) and inalienable author-protective regulations, in particular moral rights (3), has lead to the observation that (1) questions of "initial ownership" apparently do not concern the interests of the public as users of copyrighted works and, thus, questions of limitations and exceptions, but the interests at stake rather relate to the "internal" relationship between the different potential right owners (like producers and employers on the one side and the actual creators on the other side) instead,[13] and that (2) questions of "initial ownership" also do not really affect the efficient exploitation or prosecution of unauthorised use of film works, as film producers can obtain the necessary exploitation rights via either special rules for the transfer of rights or contractual arrangements. But in the area of

---

in film productions cannot be upheld after thorough investigation of the legal and factual situation, as the results of the Report of the Commission (*supra* note 7) have shown. The remaining question is why the actual creator should be deprived of *all* rights in the work he or she has created. Certainly, the investment has to be secured, as otherwise no one would invest in the production of such a work. But the interests at stake have to be balanced, and simply denying the actual creator all rights to the work is obviously no "balancing".

[12] *Cf.* Cour de Cassation, 28 May 1991, Cass.Civ. 1re, JCP II 21731 with comment by *Françon*, also published in German translation in 1992 GRUR Int. 304 – *John Huston II.*

[13] It is this limitation to the internal sphere of the right owners and irrelevance of the external relation to the public as users, that with questions of initial ownership it is possible to enter the "choice-of-law process", which Professor *Fentiman* has invoked (*cf.* his contribution at 129). This is because all the policy concerns connected with the external sphere which lead to the application of the territorial country-of-protection rule are blended out when it comes to questions of initial ownership. Thus, with respect to first ownership issues we are actually allowed to "make a choice".

moral rights and other inalienable author-protective regulations in national copyright laws (3), the question of initial ownership turned out to be of utmost importance from the perspective of author-protective national copyright laws, as the whole effectiveness of such author-protective regulations depends on vesting the actual creators with initial ownership of the works created by them.

Thus, the *question of initial ownership* turned out to be nothing else (and nothing less) than the question of "*inalienable author-protective regulations in copyright*" and among them, in the first place, the question of moral rights.

But at the same time, it is in this area, and mainly in the area of moral rights, that the substantive rules of national copyright laws show significant differences and, thus, "*true conflicts*" arise in international private law when it comes to the decision to apply one national copyright law or another to the question of initial ownership. In addition, we have seen that, firstly, this "choice of law" is not only a formal decision of choosing one or the other "rule of law" – but, for *droit d'auteur* countries, fundamental values are at stake that do belong to the national cultural identity of these countries, and secondly, we have also seen that this value conflict is not bi-directional, but only one-directional, as only for *droit d'auteur* countries are these fundamental values at stake.

Thus, we will have to undertake the difficult task of drafting a compromise choice-of-law rule in an area where a basic assumption for drafting rules of international private law, the *exchangeability* of substantive rules of law, is – at least for *droit d'auteur* systems, and thus half of the world – missing. Obviously, some creativity as well as openness for new types of solutions will be needed for such an undertaking.

But before turning towards the task of drafting a new choice-of-law rule for issues of initial ownership with respect to the specific questions of global acts of use on the internet, we will carry out a short survey of the recent approaches that countries have taken in their national conflicts laws in order to determine the initial ownership in a copyright work in cases of classical forms of multinational exploitation in the analogue or off-line world, and then check afterwards which consequences these approaches lead to when being transposed to global acts of exploitation on the internet.

III. The Different Approaches in National Conflicts Laws to Determining the Law Applicable to Initial Ownership in Copyright

1. Country-of-Protection Rule

First, there are countries that determine the initial ownership in a work according to the domestic copyright law of each country "for which", *i.e.*, for whose territory copyright protection is claimed (country-of-protection rule).[14] This approach obviously leads to the consequence that the question of who is the first owner of copyright in a specific film work will, according to the great variety of individual regulations for the initial ownership in a film work in national copyright laws, be answered in nearly as many different ways as there are countries in which the exploitation of the film takes place. To use the familiar metaphor: the ownership in a work will change each time "*the work crosses a border*". This effect of the country-of-protection rule when applied to first-ownership issues attracted the condemnation of copyright scholars, who argued that the question of authorship for one and the same work must "necessarily" be (or at least should be) answered uniformly all over the world, as otherwise the efficient international exploitation of film works would be disturbed by legal chaos.[15]

But taking a closer look, we have to note that this invocation of legal chaos does not really correspond to reality in daily legal practice. As we have seen above, irrespective of the multitude of different national regulations with respect to first ownership of copyright in film works, the film producer also in *droit d'auteur* countries is enabled to concentrate all rights required for an efficient worldwide exploitation in his hands via contractual arrangements and by the aid of a framework of statutory rules of transfer of rights. Thus, even with application of the country-of-protection rule to questions of first ownership, the efficient international exploitation of film works is secured. as no "true conflicts" between the applicable laws arise, since the rules of law may differ but not the results of their application. This has also been the conclusion of the above-cited Report of the European Commission on the question of authorship of cinematographic or audiovisual works in the Community.[16] The only and very specific area where the differences between national copyright laws with respect to the attribution of initial ownership being allowed by the country-of-protection rule make themselves felt is the area of fundamental and inalienable author-protective regulations of *droit d'auteur* countries, especially the area of moral rights.

But, as these author-protective regulations are part of the fundamental essence of *droit d'auteur* systems, the territorially based country-of-protection rule seems to be indeed the natural and just choice-of-law rule (also) for the question of initial ownership, as it allows *droit d'auteur* countries to safeguard their fundamental values against work-made-for-hire doctrines by conferring

[14] Germany, decisions of the BGH: 1998 GRUR Int. 427 – *Spielbankaffaire*, with further references; 1992 GRUR 697 – *ALF*, with further references. As this country-of-protection rule is also the general approach for all countries insofar as questions of existence and scope of protection are concerned, countries following this general approach also for questions of initial ownership determine all copyright questions uniformly according to the same choice-of-law rule.

[15] *Schack*, Internationale Urheber-, Marken- und Wettbewerbsrechtsverletzungen im Internet – Internationales Privatrecht, 2000 MMR 59, 63 *et seq*. with further references; *Schack*, comment on *Itar Tass*, 1999 GRUR Int. 645, 647.

[16] *See supra* II. 2.

to the "authors" of film works, *i.e.* the actual creators of the film works, on their territory inalienable author-protective rights provided for by domestic copyright law, among them moral rights, in the first place. If it is the general opinion in copyright law that, in questions where fundamental constitutional and social aspects are involved, every country is allowed to set its own rules for its own territory,[17] which means, in terms of conflicts law, application of the territorial country-of-protection rule, it has to be accepted that *droit d'auteur* countries also apply this rule to issues of (authorship and) first ownership insofar as *inalienable author-protective regulations* are concerned. Other countries with "author-less" areas of copyright have to acknowledge that these author-protective regulations belong to the constitutional aspects of copyright in *droit d'auteur* countries and, thus, have to be placed on the same level as, for example, the questions of fair use, freedom of speech or the "*constitutional right to copy unoriginal material*" in the United States.[18]

And it should be noted, without going into depth with regard to problems of interpretation of international treaties, that prominent copyright scholars are of the opinion that the Berne Convention even obliges other countries to respect the territorial approach of the country-of-protection rule for initial ownership taken by *droit d'auteur* countries by ruling in Art. 14bis (2)(a) BC[19] that "*ownership of copyright in a cinematographic work shall be a matter for legislation in the country where protection is claimed*".[20] But although

---

[17] *Cf. Patry, infra* note 18; *Van Eechoud*, Choice of Law in Copyright and Related Rights, Alternatives to the Lex Protectionis, 2003, at 178, 226, 229; *Katzenberger*, in *Schricker* (ed.), Urheberrecht Kommentar, 1999, vor §§ 120 ff. note 163 *et seq.*

[18] *Cf. Feist Publications, Inc. v. Rural Telephone Serv.*, 499 U.S. 340, 345 (1990) and *Patry*, Choice of Law and International Copyright, 2000, American Journal of Comparative Law, Vol. XLVIII, No. 3, at 383–470, 387: "The Court has also written that the flip side of the originality requirement is a constitutional right to copy unoriginal material", (at 349) "This constitutional right is, the Court noted, 'the essence of copyright'. . . . In the choice of law context, this means there can be no choice of law on the question of originality: U.S. law must apply."

[19] Article 14bis Berne Convention:

> (1) Without prejudice to the copyright in any work which may have been adapted or reproduced, a cinematographic work shall be protected as an original work. The owner of copyright in a cinematographic work shall enjoy the same rights as the author of an original work, including the rights referred to in the preceding Article.
> (2) (a) Ownership of copyright in a cinematographic work shall be a matter for legislation in the country where protection is claimed.

[20] *See Ricketson*, The Berne Convention for the protection of literary and artistic works 1886–1986, 1987, at 582:

> Ownership of copyright in a cinematographic work: Paragraph 2(a) confirms the previously accepted position that the ownership of copyright in a cinematographic work is a matter for legislation in the country of the Union where protection is claimed. . . . Thus, if protection for a French film is claimed in the UK it is British law which applies, and conversely it is French law which will govern a claim for protection of a British film in France.

we also favour the interpretation of Art. 14bis (2)(a) BC as stating that the ownership of the copyright of an imported film is to be determined by the law of the country of importation – which means that Art. 14bis (2)(a) BC contains a direct reference to the substantive rules of copyright law and thus stipulates the "country-of-protection" rule for the question of initial ownership in film works – we omit this old controversy about the interpretation of Art. 14bis (2)(a) Berne Convention and, while for the purpose of our further analysis accepting that this interpretation of Art. 14bis (2)(a) BC is not unanimously shared among the Member States of the Berne Union, turn from theory to legal practice instead, where some countries have solved things differently.

2. "Country-of-Origin" Rule

Some countries apply, or at least it is said that they apply (see the discussion below), a *country-of-origin rule* for the determination of initial ownership to a copyright work. According to this rule it is the law of the "country of origin" of a work that determines who is the "author" and "initial owner" of the copyright in the work. As this *country-of-origin rule* – at least in principle – leads to application of one and the same national law with respect to initial ownership in a work, wherever the work is being used or exploited, it is sometimes also referred to as the "principle of universality". This is because, if the initial ownership is determined for one work according to only one single national copyright law no matter where the work is used or exploited, *i.e.* the law of the "country of origin" is acknowledged as the relevant law for the determination of ownership in all other countries of the world, the ownership does not "change" when the work "crosses" a border.

It is obviously necessary to define *which* country shall actually play the role of being "country of origin" for a specific work. The most common approach in this respect has been to define "country of origin" as a connecting factor for questions of international private law analogous to Art. 5(4)(a) BC as the country *of first publication of the work* – if the work has been published (*lex primae publicationis*) – and, if it has not been published, the country of which its author is a national (*lex auctoris*, Art. 5(4)(c) BC) or, in the specific case of unpublished cinematographic works, as the country where the film producer has his headquarters or habitual residence (*lex producentis*, Art. 5(4)(c)(i) BC).[21] Two countries that supposedly apply a country-of-origin rule to questions of first ownership are France and the United States.

If we start with the legal situation in the United States, the US Court of Appeals in 1998 issued a widely received decision regarding the *Itar Tass* case in which, according to some scholars, it affirmed the application of a

[21] This also seems to be the approach of the ALI proposal, which, in Art. 25(1), stipulates as the general rule the application of the law of the country of origin to questions of first ownership.

"country-of-origin rule" for first-ownership issues.[22] The issue in the *Itar Tass* case was the unlawful publication by the weekly magazine "Russian Kurier" in New York of numerous newspaper articles that had first been published in Russia. As there were several plaintiffs, in particular the Russian news agency *Itar Tass*, several Russian newspaper publishers and the Journalist Union of Russia, the court had to decide, who among the several plaintiffs was the one who owned the copyright and, thus, had the power to sue Russian Kurier for copyright infringement. With respect to the question of international private law according to which national copyright law the initial ownership should be determined, the Court of Appeals ruled that in the present case with Russia being the country with the "most significant relationship to the works", Russian law should determine about the (initial) ownership.[23]

While at first sight this decision seems to apply a "country-of-origin principle", a closer look at the reasoning given by the Court of Appeals reveals that the court was far from applying any such principle. Instead, what the court did was to apply a multi-factor analysis as prescribed by the Second Restatement of American conflicts law, and tried to find the law "*with the most significant relationship to the work*" in the specific case, by "*weighing*" the "*connecting factors*".[24] The court decided that in this case, where all possible connecting factors with exception of the place of the infringing publication, pointed towards Russian law, this multitude of factors "outweighed" under the circumstances of the present case the single connecting factor "place of infringement in the United States" pointing to US law.[25] However; no one knows how the court would have decided if, having been faced with a different fact pattern, for example, if articles from US journalists written in English and translated into Russian for the purpose of first publication in Russia had first been published in Russia by the subsidiary of a US newspaper agency residing in Moscow. The court might have been inclined to apply US copyright law to decide the question of initial ownership in such a case, as a multitude of connecting factors would have pointed towards US copy-

[22] *Itar Tass Russian News Agency v. Russian Kurier, Inc.*, US Court of Appeals, August 27, 1998, 153 F.3d 82 (2d Cir. 1998), also published in German in 1999 GRUR Int. 639 with comment by *Schack*.

[23] *Cf. Itar Tass, supra* note 22.

[24] Restatement of the Law Second, Conflict of Laws 2d (St. Paul, Minn., 1971), American Law Institute (ed.). The Restatement replaces abstract general choice-of-law rules by policy considerations in form of open principles of preference; *cf.* in German literature *von Bar & Mankowski*, Internationales Privatrecht, Bd. I, 2003, at 544 with further references.

[25] Among the connecting factors which the Court had to consider were, besides the place of infringement, the nationality, domicile and place of habitual residence of the authors or co-authors of the articles, the nationality, domicile or habitual residence of the alleged right owners, the one or more places of creation of the articles, the language of the original publications as well as the one or more places of first publication.

right law, and thus not have applied Russian law as the law of the "country of first publication" and, thus, "country of origin". In other words, the choice-of-law process in the form of "weighing of connecting factors" as contained in the Second Restatement is an open process with fairly unpredictable results and will never be comparable to a choice-of-law rule like the "country-of-origin rule" in some other countries.

Therefore, it cannot be said that in the United States a country-of-origin rule is applied to questions of initial ownership, as in US law such connecting factors as "country-of-origin" etc. do not rise to the level of presumptions but are only weighted considerations.[26] Even after the *Itar Tass* ruling, US courts do not apply "rules" of international private law and especially not a "country-of-origin rule" for the determination of initial ownership.

If we now turn to the legal situation in France, the second prominent country which is generally said to apply a "country-of-origin" rule to initial ownership issues of copyright works, it has first to be stated that the role the "country of origin" (as country of first publication) of a work plays in French conflicts law for copyright cases is a very complex and highly debated one which has its roots in the law of foreigners.[27] We will not go into depth of this discussion and for the purpose of our present analysis only highlight the following aspects of the legal situation in France. French courts generally refer to the law of the country of first publication if the question of who is the initial owner of a copyright work becomes relevant for aspects of exploitation rights, but – every time the question of initial ownership becomes relevant for aspects of moral rights – French courts apply *French* law and *not* the possibly conflicting country-of-origin law.[28] Certainly, as they achieve this by either declaring the French *droit moral* as "*loi d'application impérative*" against the US work-made-for-hire doctrines in foreign law, which deprives the principal director of all moral rights,[29] or by invoking the "*ordre public international*" (via reference to the Declaration of Human Rights of 1948) against a contractual waiver of all moral rights in a ghost-writer contract validly concluded under US foreign copyright law,[30] this approach

[26] *Cf. Patry, supra* note 18:

> Given the wide variety of possible fact patterns and the number of possible connecting factors, it is easy to appreciate why the *Itar Tass* court wisely avoided reaching issues beyond those of its own facts. But what should future courts do when faced with one of these more complex fact patterns? One ill-advised approach is to focus mechanically on one factor, such as the place of first publication, as some lower courts have already done in a mistaken interpretation of *Itar Tass*.

[27] *Cf. Bergé*, La protection internationale et communautaire du *droit d'auteur* – Essai d'une analyse conflictuelle, 1996, at 178.

[28] *Cf.* Cour de Cassation in *John Huston II, supra* note 12 and *Anne Bragrance c. Olivier Orban et Michel de Grèce*, Cour d'Appel de Paris (1re ch.), 1 February 1989, 142 RIDA 301 (1989) with comment by *Sirinelli*.

[29] Cour de Cassation in John Huston, *supra* note 12.

[30] Cour d'Appel in *Anne Bragrance, supra* note 28.

can be criticised from a purely methodological point of view.[31] But if we recall the above findings that in the area of "inalienable author-protective regulations of national copyright laws" the basic assumption for the choice-of-law process in form of exchangeability of rules of substantive law is missing, these attempts of French courts to assert the "author-protective" French *droit moral* against "author-less" copyright regimes via the concepts of "*loi d'application impérative*" or "*ordre public international*" only prove that the underlying choice-of-law rule "country of origin" lacks justification in the area of inalienable author-protective regulations in national copyright laws.

To summarise, it cannot be said that French courts apply a "country-of-origin" rule for all questions of initial ownership to copyright. In fact, when it comes to questions of author-protection via moral rights, they do *not* apply the law of the country of origin to first-ownership issues.

3. Conclusion

The above very brief analysis of the choice-of-law approaches that countries are currently taking with respect to the determination of the law applicable to first ownership in copyright works has shown that this area of copyright conflicts law is far from being regulated in a uniform, satisfying and broadly accepted manner.

As regards first-ownership issues in *substantive* copyright law, the United States probably found the best copyright law for its society, and France found the best copyright law for its society and – in the analogue world—there is no need to change this by forcing either the United States to switch to a French-style *droit d'auteur* system or France to switch to a US-style copyright system. Therefore, as each system works well on its territory, the territorially based country-of-protection rule seems to be indeed the natural and just choice-of-law rule for all questions of copyright in the analogue world and, therefore, also for the question of initial ownership in the analogue world. The reason for this is that for all questions regarding the constitutional aspects of copyright every country should be allowed to set the rules on its own territory, and the question of authorship is – at least for *droit d'auteur countries* – on the same constitutional level as are, in other countries (for example the United States), the questions of fair use, freedom of speech or the "constitutional right to copy unoriginal material", which all lead to the application of domestic copyright law to domestic copyright cases.

In addition, quite a number of arguments can be raised against the country-of-origin concept. First of all, the place of the first publication could only ensure legal certainty if it were easy to determine and were certain to be determined *uniformly* in all countries. This is not the case, though, as on the one hand, national copyright laws have different opinions about the *require-*

[31] *Ginsburg & Sirinelli*, Authors and Exploiters in International Private Law: the French Supreme Court and the Huston Film Controversy, 15 Colum.-VLA J.L. & Arts 135 (1991).

ments for "publication": do 500, 100 or 10 printed copies suffice to affirm "publication" in a legal sense? And what about *simultaneous publication* in several countries? Which country should be chosen as country of origin? And should "simultaneous" publication mean publication on the same day, or should the regulation of the Berne Convention prevail according to which publication within thirty days is regarded as simultaneous publication? And can a "country of origin" be determined at all if a work is first published on the internet? Thus, the country-of-origin concept as "*lex primae publicationis*" does not in fact achieve the legal certainty it pretends to achieve.[32]

But the main argument against any country-of-origin concept remains that application of such a rule would lead to a one-sided abandonment of fundamental values, as *droit d'auteur* countries would be obliged not to apply their concepts of moral rights and author protection in cases where the work has been created under a commission or employment contracts in a work-made-for-hire country *even if* exploitations on their own territory and works of their own nationals are concerned.

Thus, the country-of-origin concept is not able to solve the dilemma that the work-made-for-hire doctrine poses to *droit d'auteur* countries. Therefore, "classical" forms of exploitation should continue to be treated according to the law of each individual country for which copyright protection is sought, including first-ownership issues, which are in fact questions of moral rights and author-protective statutory limitations on the transfer of rights. This means that in the analogue world there is no need to apply a choice-of-law rule other than that of the country-of-protection rule to issues of first ownership as well and this analysis could be summarised by a quotation of Art. 14bis (2)(a) BC: "*Ownership of copyright in a cinematographic work shall be a matter for legislation in the country where protection is claimed.*"

Nevertheless, things become quite different in the area of global acts of exploitation on the internet.

IV. Need for Compromise Regarding Global Acts of Exploitation

In order to clarify the following line of thought, let us turn to the well-known example of colourisation of black and white movies. Because this example is so well known, it might be appropriate in order to "colourise" the discussion in the abstract field of international private law with respect to

[32] *Cf.* report of *Lucas*, Private international law aspects of the protection of works and of the subject matter of related rights transmitted over digital networks, 1998 (Doc. No. GCPIL/1/01), WIPO Group of Consultants on the Private International Law Aspects of the Protection of Works and Objects of Related Rights transmitted Through Global Digital Networks, Geneva, December 16 to 18, 1998; *Thum*, Internationalprivatrechtliche Aspekte der Verwertung urheberrechtlich geschützter Werke im Internet, 2001 GRUR Int. 9 *et seq.*

first-ownership issues on the internet. Everybody knows from the case of "Asphalt Jungle" that the colourisation of a film whose director has deliberately chosen the black-and-white format as the artistic language of his film constitutes a violation of his moral rights according to French (and other *droit d'auteur* countries) copyright law and can thus be objected to by him. On the other hand, if the film has been produced under a work-made-for-hire regime, the director of the film does not enjoy any rights to "his" or "her" film at all, whether moral or exploitation rights, and would thus not at all be able to object to the exploitation of the film in a colourised version on the internet. While in the analogue world different answers to first-ownership issues according to different rules of substantive and/or conflicts law in each country can be tolerated, as acts of exploitation can be split territorially, the question of the applicable law, *i.e.* which country's domestic copyright law shall determine the legitimacy of global acts of exploitation, becomes of utmost importance on the internet. This is due to the specific nature of global acts of exploitation as they can be either allowed or not allowed in all countries at the same time: *i.e.* either the director can object to the distribution of "his" film in a colourised version on the internet or he can't. There is no middle course.[33]

Thus, in the end, as long as national copyright laws differ (and we probably will not be too unrealistic if we assume that differences in national copyright laws with respect to initial ownership will continue to exist for decades to come) and only one single national copyright law can be the decisive one, courts cannot avoid deciding between application of the law of country A or that of countries B, C, D, etc.

Obviously, if ever we want – for the benefit of authors, producers and users – to establish a reasonable, workable international copyright regime for the internet, at least the question, *which* national copyright law should be decisive in a global copyright case needs to be answered in the same way by courts all over the world, no matter which country's courts will eventually have to decide the case. Otherwise, if we allow national diversity to continue not only for questions of substantive copyright law itself but also for questions of international private law, we end up with contradictory rules of substantive copyright laws concurrently claiming applicability to global acts of exploitation – a situation which, evidently, can only be termed legal chaos.

Therefore, in the following, we will first have a look at how the approaches "country-of-protection" rule (1) and "country-of-origin" rule (2) would solve the problem of conflicting substantive initial ownership rules if being applied to global acts of exploitation on the internet. And afterwards

---

[33] In the context of the present analysis the term "global exploitation" will be used for truly global forms of exploitation, and not for forms of exploitation with a possibility of "territorially shaping" these acts of exploitation via password systems or billing mechanisms.

we will, led by the idea that the notion of "compromise" prohibits unilaterally giving preference to one of the existing solutions in substantive copyright laws by neglecting the interests of other countries in having their law applied to global copyright cases, try to draw the outlines of a possible compromise solution (3).

1. Consequences of a "Country-of-Protection Rule" for First-Ownership Questions of Global Acts of Exploitation

As we have seen, application of a country-of-protection rule means to apply successively the laws of all countries, for whose territory copyright protection is claimed. As global acts of exploitation affect all countries of the world at the same time, the country-of-protection rule, if being applied to global acts of exploitation, leads to parallel and simultaneous application of all national copyright laws to each act of global exploitation.

What would "simultaneous application" mean in practice? If all national copyright laws were to be applied simultaneously to one and the same global act of exploitation, obviously any person who qualifies as "author" by any national copyright law would enjoy all the rights reserved to him by this copyright law. In other words, any person regarded as "author" by any of the world's copyright laws could exercise all his or her rights against the global act of exploitation of the work on the internet, and consequently the maximum number of "authors" would enjoy the maximum amount of author protection.

If we turn to our example of the distribution of colourised black and white movies via the internet, a country-of-protection rule[34] would allow all film directors to invoke the French *droit moral* against any global act of exploitation and thus stop the global use and distribution of colourised versions of their films on the internet, no matter whether the contract with the film producer had been concluded under the regime of a work-made-for-hire country, and no matter whether they were French nationals or not. Even if the film were a US film production with all potential "authors" being US nationals, the "authors" from the United States could rely on French moral rights in order to prohibit the global exploitation of a colourised version of "their" film on the internet. Thus, with the application of a *country-of-protection rule* to first-ownership issues on the internet, a work-made-for-hire doctrine would be rendered ineffective.

[34] In the context of the internet the "country-of-protection" rule is sometimes also referred to as "country of reception" rule. Although in theory the concept of the country of protection is different from the concept of the country of reception as also the country of emission is a country of protection, there will be no practical difference for truly global acts of exploitation as it will also be possible to receive the work in the country of emission with the result that the country of emission will at the same time also be a country of reception.

Simultaneous application of all national copyright laws to global acts of exploitation via a *country-of-protection rule* on the internet would thus not only be quite tedious but would also one-sidedly favour the interests of *droit d'auteur countries* in having their idea of author-protection prevail over the interests of *copyright countries* with less or even non-existing author protection.

2. Consequences of a "Country-of-Origin Rule" for First Ownership Questions of Global Acts of Exploitation

As we have seen above, application of a country-of-origin concept would, at least in principle, result in the question of who is the initial owner of the copyright in a film work being answered for each individual work uniformly all over the world, as only one single national copyright law would be decisive. But, as we have also seen above, it would be necessary to determine which country shall be regarded as the country of origin for a specific work.

While the concept of the *lex primae publicationis* (country of first publication as country of origin) already lacks justification and practicability in the analogue world, it appears to be almost impossible to determine a country of first publication, if works are first being published on the internet.[35] Thus, "country of origin" would have to be defined in a different way for global acts of exploitation on the internet. One possibly would be to take the law of the country where the film producer has his headquarters or habitual residence as relevant law for the determination of initial ownership on the internet,[36] along with the definition of "country of origin" in Arts. 4(b) and 5(4)(c)(i) of the Berne Convention.[37] From the perspective of "work-made-

[35] *Cf.* reports of *Lucas, supra* note 32, and *Ginsburg*, Private international law aspects of the protection of works and objects of related rights transmitted through digital networks, 1998 (Doc. No. GCPIC/2), WIPO Group of Consultants on the Private International Law Aspects of the Protection of Works and Objects of Related Rights Transmitted Through Global Digital Networks, Geneva, December 16 to 18, 1998; *Thum, supra* note 32 at 9 et seq.

[36] *Cf. also Van Eechoud, supra* note 18, at 227: the law of the habitual residence (for natural persons) or the law of the principal place of business (for legal persons) of those who actually create the work should govern the determination of initial ownership, while in case of works made by employees, accessory allocation of the initial ownership issue to the employment contract prevails, with the proviso that the actual creators cannot be robbed of the protection that is afforded to them under the law of the place where they normally work.

[37] Article 4 Berne Convention (Criteria of Eligibility for Protection of Cinematographic Works):

> The protection of this Convention shall apply . . . to: (a) authors of cinematographic works the maker of which has his headquarters or habitual residence in one of the countries of the Union; (b) authors of works of architecture erected in a country of the Union or of other artistic works incorporated in a building or other structure located in a country of the Union.; Art. 5 Berne Convention (. . . Country of origin) . . . (4) The country of origin shall be considered to be: (a) in the case of works

for-hire countries" this would certainly be the "perfect solution" for the determination of initial ownership for global acts of exploitation: Application of this rule would allow them to "export" their concept of (missing) authorship on a worldwide scale. And they would not mind application of the same country-of-origin rule to cases where the film producer has his headquarters or habitual residence in a *droit d'auteur* country, as the concept that the actual creators of works are vested with the initial ownership to the copyright in their works is not only familiar to copyright systems, too, but also implemented in wide areas of their national copyright laws. And as long as only film productions from such *droit d'auteur* countries would be concerned, copyright countries would not perceive any foreign legal effect on their territory at all, because as long as the scope of application of the country-of-origin rule would be confined to questions of initial ownership, whereas the *scope of rights* would still be determined according to the country-of-protection rule, copyright countries would not be obliged to assert to "authors" from *droit d'auteur* countries more rights than the "producers" would be granted in their own system.

But the situation is quite different for *droit d'auteur* countries. Application of the country-of-origin rule would force these countries – contrary to their fundamental values – to accept even blatant violations of moral rights and even if works are being domestically exploited as they can be viewed or downloaded by the public in their own countries via the internet. In addition, *droit d'auteur* countries would even have to deny moral rights protection to their own nationals in such cases of domestic exploitation of their works. For example, French courts would have to deny French directors protection by French moral rights – even if the films can be downloaded by the public in France – if their films have been produced by US production companies. As a result, France would have to accept these global violations of moral rights, even if French directors were concerned. Via any country-of-origin rule the "author-less" work-made-for-hire doctrine would thus be exported on a worldwide scale.

3. Conclusion

None of the traditional approaches provides an acceptable solution as to which law should be applicable to questions of initial ownership of global

---

first published in a country of the Union, that country; in the case of works published simultaneously in several countries of the Union which grant different terms of protection, the country whose legislation grants the shortest term of protection; (b) in the case of works published simultaneously in a country outside the Union and in a country of the Union, the latter country; (c) in the case of unpublished works or of works first published in a country outside the Union, without simultaneous publication in a country of the Union, the country of the Union of which the author is a national, provided that: (i) when these are cinematographic works the maker of which has his headquarters or his habitual residence in a country of the Union, the country of origin shall be that country.

acts of exploitation: the "country-of-protection" rule would one-sidedly favour the most author-protective copyright regimes and render the work-made-for-hire concept of copyright systems ineffective, while the "country-of-origin" rule would one-sidedly favour the spread of author-less regulations of copyright systems like the work-made-for-hire doctrine at the expense of author-protective regulations of *droit d'auteur* systems. Therefore, none of the traditional approaches provides an acceptable solution to the dilemma of applicable law vis-à-vis initial ownership questions of global acts of exploitation of film works. What could a compromise possibly look like?

V. Draft Compromise Rule on First-Ownership Issues in Global Acts of Exploitation

1. General Considerations

Legal certainty implies predictability of the results of the application of legal rules and, thus, legal certainty also implies legal simplicity. Therefore, if we want to achieve legal certainty with respect to questions of initial ownership of works on the internet, the possible number of applicable laws to a global act of exploitation has to be confined to a few, or—ideally—to only one. Therefore, from a mere technical point of view, the territorial concept of the country-of-protection rule with its multitude of potentially applicable national copyright laws rules itself out as a possible basis for a new model rule in a global environment. From a mere technical point of view the "country-of-origin" approach seems to be more appropriate for forming the underlying concept of a new model rule instead, as it leads to application of one law only.

But as we have seen from our analysis, from a global viewpoint the country-of-origin rule one-sidedly favours the spread of "author-less" copyright systems at the expense of "author-protective" copyright systems. If we nevertheless take the country-of-origin rule as the underlying concept of our new model rule, we have to ensure the balance between "author-less" and "author-protective" legal systems by re-enlarging the scope of applicability of the "author-protective" *droit d'auteur* systems within the model rule.

As we have also seen, the greatest problems for the acceptance of the country-of-origin rule by *droit d'auteur* countries are caused by the fact that such a rule would even prohibit *droit d'auteur* countries from protecting their own nationals against violations of their moral rights in the case of global acts of exploitation on the internet despite their fundamental values. Therefore, from a value perspective, an exemption from the general rule for these cases has to be provided for. This would also correspond to the primary objective of international copyright, as set forth in the preamble of the Berne Convention, which is "*to protect, in as effective and uniform a manner as possible, the rights of authors in their literary and artistic works*".[38] According to *Ginsburg*, this fundamental goal of the Berne Convention suggests that, where the

[38] Berne Convention, preamble cl. 1 (emphasis added).

Berne Convention does not supply a choice-of-law rule, but leaves the determination of applicable law to the member countries, those countries' determinations should be guided by the principle of *favor auctoris*: when in doubt, follow the conflicts analysis that will yield an author-favourable outcome, *i.e.* uniformity in choice-of-law approaches to copyright ownership should not lead to less effective protection of the rights of authors.[39]

Thus, a balanced compromise could consist of allowing the law of the country of which the "author" is a national prevailing over the law of the "country of origin" even if the cinematographic work has been produced under the regime of a work-made-for-hire country. Such a rule could possibly be given the following wording:

> Applicable law to initial ownership of cinematographic works in cases of global acts of exploitation
>
> (1) With respect to global acts of exploitation the initial ownership of copyright in a cinematographic work shall be determined by the law of the country where the producer has his headquarters or habitual residence.
> (2) However, if natural persons who have made contributions to a cinematographic work are, in the legislation of the country of which they are a national, included among the initial owners of copyright, such persons reserve vis-à-vis global acts of exploitation all moral, exploitation and remuneration rights they are vested with by this legislation.

2. Consequences of the Application of the Proposed Rule in Legal Practice

a) General Consequences

What would application of this rule mean in practice? On the one hand, US film producers would enjoy the benefits of the US work-made-for-hire doctrine on a worldwide scale for those works, whose creative contributions stem from US nationals or from nationals of a similar work-made-for-hire system. On the other hand, French directors would enjoy the French *droit moral* also on a world-wide scale, wherever the producer of the cinematographic work has his headquarters or habitual residence at the time of producing the film.

In the end US courts would have to assert French moral rights against US and other producers, if French directors are involved. And French courts would have to assert the work-made-for-hire doctrine against US and other directors and deny French *droits moraux* if the director (or any other "author") of the film is not a French national.[40] Evidently, this is a new perspective.

---

[39] *Cf. also Ginsburg*'s considerations with respect to the *favor auctoris* principle contained in the Berne Convention, text accompanying *supra* note 39.

[40] In the case that the director is a national of another country that provides for moral rights or other inalienable author-protective regulations in its national copyright law, these regulations have to be applied. If such author-protective regulations are missing, there will be no author protection.

The advantage of such a compromise would not only be that the much complained about territorial splitting of ownership issues would be overcome but that, at the same time, a simple and easy-to-apply rule would come into being which shows respect for the different solutions of assignment of authorship in national copyright laws.[41]

b) Application of the Proposed Rule to the Huston Case on the internet

Let us now apply the above developed compromise solution to the famous *Huston* case: "Asphalt Jungle" was produced by the US production company Metro Goldwyn Mayer that had (and still has) its principal place of business in the United States. Thus, according to the general principle, US law and, consequently, the US work-made-for-hire doctrine would apply, vesting MGM with the overall copyright in the film, leaving no rights whatsoever to the director John Huston. In a second step we would have to check whether the "personal law" of John Huston vests him with inalienable moral or economic rights. This is quite an easy task: John Huston, being a US national, can not rely on an author-protective copyright law, but instead the work-made-for-hire doctrine of his own, "personal" national copyright law would deprive him of any moral or economic rights in the movies he directed. Therefore, exploitation of "his" movie "Asphalt Jungle" in colourised form would be allowed on the internet, and French courts could not prevent access to the colourised version for internet users in France.

If this new standard rule were not only applied to internet cases but to "off-line" cases as well, Huston would have lost his case in France. But, François Truffaut for example, would have won a similar case, even if the exploitation of his film had taken place on US territory and US courts would have had to decide about a violation of his "*droit moral*".

VI. Conclusion: Transatlantic Reflections on the Notion of "Compromise"

Anticipating the reactions on both sides of the Atlantic, we imagine the following scenario. US copyright scholars will say that it is reasonable to apply the law of the country where the film producer has his principal place of business but that it is "impossible" to have foreign directors exercise their foreign moral and exploitation rights on US territory against US film producers. On the other hand, French copyright scholars will say that it is reasonable to apply the law of the country of which the director ("author") is a national but that it is "impossible" to have foreign production companies exercise their exploitation rights on French territory unrestrictedly with respect to the moral rights of the director.

---

[41] Certainly some follow-up questions would have to be solved, for example the question of how to consolidate this approach with the principle of national treatment. But this contribution is not the place to elaborate on these topics further; these follow-up questions can be solved.

Nevertheless, if we want to overcome the strictly territorial approach to international private law in copyright – and we have to with respect to global acts of exploitation on the internet – we do have to make some degree of compromise, which ultimately leads to foreign law being applied to copyright questions raised in cases having effect on one's own territory. No one denies that this is quite a difficult and unsatisfying task. But if we remember that the saying *"A compromise will only be fair, if all participants are equally dissatisfied."* is equally attributed to *Aristide Briand*, the well-known French politician,[42] and to *Henry Kissinger*, the well-known American politician[43] – who probably both knew exactly what they were talking about – we at least have a common transatlantic understanding of *how to define the "fairness"* of a compromise. And as we cannot entirely avoid dissatisfaction in principle, we have to place the emphasis on "*equally*". This is what the proposed choice-of-law rule tries to do.

---

[42] *Aristide Briand* (1862–1932), French politician, between 1908 and 1932 in diverse functions as Minister of Justice, Minister President, Minister of Foreign Affairs. Received the Nobel Peace Prize in 1926.

[43] *Henry Kissinger* (*1923), US politician, Minister of Foreign Affairs under president Nixon and president Ford, consultant to president Eisenhower, president Kennedy and president Johnson. Received the Nobel Peace Prize in 1973.

Alternatives to the *lex protectionis* as the Choice-of-Law Rule for Initial Ownership of Copyright

MIREILLE VAN EECHOUD*

I. Introduction

Conventional wisdom has it that the law of the country for whose territory protection is claimed governs copyright issues – whether it concerns existence, scope, duration, ownership, transfer or infringement. This predominance of the *lex protectionis*, or law of the protecting country (*Schutzland*), has never gone completely unchallenged. It seems that every decade's end inspires a revival in the debate on proper choice-of-law rules for intellectual property.

In the late 1970s, Ulmer's proposals to the European Commission on private international law rules for intellectual property sparked a lively debate. As we know, it took place primarily among German scholars, particularly those associated with the Max Planck Institutes in Munich (intellectual property law) and Hamburg (private international law). The debate cantered on territorialist versus universalist outlooks, which corresponded by and large to a preference for the *lex protectionis* and the *lex originis* (law of the country of origin of an author/work) respectively.

In the late 1980s, the (in)famous French *Huston* case served as catalyst. At the heart of the ensuing discussion were the position of moral rights in the choice-of-law process and the question of whether a single governing law, rather than the *lex protectionis,* should govern initial ownership.

As the 1990s drew to a close, the rapid expansion of communications via the internet became responsible for the surge in meetings and publications devoted to "IPRs" and "PIL". The ALAI picked up the subject at its 1996 Amsterdam and 2002 Neuchatel study days. The WIPO organised its first special meeting on IPRs and PIL in 1998, and has kept the topic on its agenda since. From both sides of the Atlantic, (draft) principles on applicable law, jurisdiction and recognition of foreign IP-rulings have been put forward.[1] These are to fill the gap that may be left by the proposed Hague

* Senior researcher at the Institute for Information Law, University of Amsterdam (The Netherlands).

[1] For the *Ginsburg/Dreyfuss* project (US), and *Sterling's* proposal, *see inter alia Ginsburg*, Draft Principles on Jurisdiction and Recognition of Judgments, and *Sterling*, Draft International Copyright Protection Agreement and Associated Protocols, in ALAI Study Days 2002, Copyright Internet World 2003.

Convention on Jurisdiction and Recognition of Judgments in Civil and Commercial Matters, since that treaty may not be concluded for a while. More important, even if it will see the light of day, there it will most likely not extend to intellectual property disputes even though the original idea was that it should.[2] Most relevant for the subject of this contribution is the controversy surrounding the draft WIPO Audiovisual Performances Treaty. Negotiations recently grinded to a halt as (choice-of-law) provisions on ownership and transfer could not be agreed upon.

II. Which Law to Apply?

1. The Initial Ownership Controversy

What, then, is the problem with determining who is the initial owner of copyright, or related rights for that matter? The debate currently focuses on how to address the need for legal certainty while giving due respect to the diversity in allocation regimes. From the perspective of legal certainty, the *lex protectionis* is a problem because it remands the question of who initially owns a work to the laws of all the countries where the work is protected. Thus, the legal uncertainty does not spring from the fact that it is unpredictable which law applies, but from the fact that a multitude of laws apply simultaneously. Using a conflict rule that identifies a single governing law would simplify matters greatly. The consequence would of course be that countries must accept that foreign law can govern ownership issues with respect to works exploited within their territory.

Although more than 20 years old, the Huston case offers a good illustration of how strong the aversion to apply another country's ownership rules can be. The Huston heirs disagreed with the colourisation of Huston's film "Asphalt Jungle". Before the French courts Huston's heirs successfully claimed moral rights, even though the film in question was made by an American director in America, in the course of his duties as an employee of an American film company which under American copyright law owned the initial copyright on the basis of the work-for-hire clause in the US Copyright Act. In addition, the employment contract – which was governed by American law – contained provisions ensuring that any (residual) rights Huston may have had were assigned to the film producer. At the time, American copyright law did not include moral rights (Berne Convention or European style).

The French Supreme Court in this decision seems to have qualified moral rights including the rules on who are its beneficiaries, as a matter of public policy, or possibly as priority rules. Both doctrines override the normal

---

[2] *See* www.hcch.net for the latest developments on the proposed Hague Jurisdiction Convention; *see also Andrea Schulz*'s contribution in this volume.

conflict rules.[3] In my view, the Supreme Court's ruling seems to imply that under French law initial ownership is not governed by *lex protectionis* per se. If that were the case, the Court could have applied French copyright law without having to resort to escape devices such as the public policy exception, since Huston's heirs claimed that their (moral) rights were infringed by a (planned) broadcast of the colourised film in France.[4]

Much of the commotion surrounding the *Huston* ruling can be traced to the (perceived) weaker position of creative contributors in law systems based on the so-called "copyright approach" compared to the position of such creators in civil law countries adhering to the "*droit d'auteur* approach". This issue is also a major stumbling block in the negotiations on the proposed WIPO treaty on the protection of audiovisual performances. It seems that particularly countries that think of their law as especially creator-friendly are hostile to the idea of their courts having to apply foreign rules on initial ownership in cross-border cases.

Objection can be taken to the view of those who attach great interest in the differences between copyright and *droit d'auteur* systems because these types of laws have converged considerably in the past decades and continue to do so.[5] Even if copyright laws were very different, the *lex protectionis* still is not the obvious choice if one favours a truly pro-author conflict rule (author in the sense of actual creator). The multiplicity of laws that govern ownership questions not only creates legal uncertainty for the actual creator as to his

---

[3] Cass. 28 May 1991, *Huston v. TV5*, 149 RIDA 197–199 (1991). When the action was brought the Berne Convention was not in force for the U.S. Critical comments among others: *Bertrand*, Affaire John Huston, la Cour de Cassation opte pour "la loi de la jungle", Cahiers du droit d'auteur 1–10 (1991), *De Boer*, Filmauteursrecht en Internationaal Privaatrecht, 1 AMI 3–7 (1993); *Farchy & Rochelandet*, Protection of Authors and Dissemination of Works in the Digital Universe. The Case of the French Film Industry, 39 Communications & Strategies 37 (2000); *Ginsburg & Sirinelli*, Authors and Exploitations in International Private Law: the French Supreme Court and the Huston Film Colorisation Controversy, 435 Colum.J.L. & Arts 135–159 (1991). *Françon* argued – justly in my view – against the use of the *ordre public* exception in this case, in his comment on the earlier appellate court's decision of 6 July 1989, 143 RIDA 329 (1990). *Locher*, Das Internationale Privat- und Zivilprozessrecht der Immaterialgüterrechte aus urheberrechtlicher Sicht, 1993, at 42–44, is of the opinion that the *Cour de Cassation* did not apply the public policy exception, but considered the moral rights provisions of the French Copyright act as priority rules. That characterisation is in accordance with Dutch private international law, where public policy exception can be invoked against the application of foreign law if that would yield a result that goes against fundamental Dutch legal values. Priority rules are those provisions that because of the preponderant public interest they protect are applied regardless of the (otherwise) applicable foreign law.

[4] Possibly the court recognised the contractual arrangement whereby Huston waived his rights as having effect in France, thus needing public policy rules to uphold the director's moral rights.

[5] An early spotter of this trend was *Dietz*, Transformation of author's rights, change of paradigm, 138 RIDA 23–76 (1988). For an extensive analysis *see Strowel*, Droit d'auteur et copyright. Divergences et convergences, 1993.

or her position. Applying the *lex protectionis* means applying the law of the country where exploitation of the work takes place. That law does not necessarily give the creator the best protection available vis-à-vis other potential rightsowners such as a producer, employer or investor.

There is a case to be made for the development of creator-oriented conflict rules for initial ownership issues, particularly if they also serve legal certainty by identifying a single governing law. In the coming paragraphs I will expand on how such rules may be construed using the main allocation principles of modern European private international law theory.

2. Four Principles Underlying Conflict Rules

In modern choice of law four principles[6] may be distinguished on which conflict rules are based. More precisely, the choice of connecting factor used reflects either

a) the principle of the closest connection in a factual-geographic sense,
b) the principle of party autonomy,
c) the principle of functional allocation, or
d) the favour principle.

Conflict rules come in many shapes and forms. They may be simple rules containing one connecting factor, or rules with a number of alternative ("either/or") or cumulative ("and") or tiered ("if not then . . .") connecting factors. Not only the number and nature of connecting factors may vary, but also the degree of openness. On one end of the scale are the classic rules with clear predictable criteria, usually indicating a place (where something happened, where someone resides). A good example is the rule in Art. 6(2)a of the 1980 Rome Convention on the law applicable to contractual obligations: it prescribes the place where the employee habitually carries out his duties as the connecting factor for the law governing the employment contract. On the other end, a conflict rule may have an open norm, *e.g.* where it prescribes application of the law of the country "most closely connected" to the case at hand. Article 4(1) of the 1980 Rome Convention contains such a norm. Coupled with the presumption in Art. 4(2) that the closest connection exists with the country with which the party effecting the performance that is characteristic of a contract is most closely connected, Art. 4 becomes a semi-open conflict rule.

a) Principle of the closest connection

The classic approach to selecting the applicable law in an international case is to determine with which legal system the issue at hand has the closest con-

[6] As private international law is still in large part national law, there is not really a unified European doctrine. The principles I describe can, however, be discerned in various laws of European countries and in EC instruments and conventions concluded under the ambit of the Hague Conference on private international law.

nection from a factual-geographical point of view. Traditionally this is achieved by designing a conflict rule with a single clear connecting factor, whose application in a typical case yields the law most closely connected.

As was said above, the widely held view is that the country for which protection is sought (*Schutzland*) is the appropriate connecting factor for copyright issues. This view is usually not based on a traditional choice-of-law analysis,[7] which is aimed at determining the law most closely connected. Rather, support for the *lex protectionis* stems 1) from the conventional wisdom that intellectual property is territorial and 2) from the duty that states have taken upon themselves to grant foreign works or foreign authors the same rights as nationals. It would surpass the topic of this contribution to discuss the choice-of-law implications of territoriality[8] and national treatment in detail. Suffice it to say here that the national treatment principle as laid down *inter alia* in Art. 5 of the Berne Convention of 1886 is on closer inspection not a conflict rule. Also, what we mean exactly when we say that intellectual property is territorial is often unclear, and consequently, so are the ramifications of the territorial view for the applicable law.[9]

b) Principle of Party Autonomy

The freedom of parties to choose the applicable law has a long history. Initially limited to contracts, freedom of choice has spread to other types of legal issues, thus reflecting the increased freedom of disposition in substantive law. Party autonomy features not only in the 1980 Rome Convention (Art. 3), but also in the Hague Convention on the law applicable to succession (Art. 5) and in the EC's proposed "Rome II" Regulation on the applicable law for torts of 2003[10] (Art. 10).

As will be elaborated below, I can envisage a minor role for the principle of party autonomy in initial ownership issues, notably where it concerns collective works made by authors from different countries.

c) Principle of Functional Allocation

The principle of *functional allocation*, which underlies quite a number of modern choice-of-law rules, reflects the social policy interests of states. The socialisation of private law has been an important factor in the advent of functional allocation. As the term suggests, a choice-of-law rule based on this

---

[7] *Troller*, Das internationale Privat- und Zivilprozeßrecht im gewerblichen Rechtsschutz und Urheberrecht, 1952, is an early exception.

[8] On different notions of territoriality, *see Dinwoodie* in ALAI Study Days 2002, Copyright Internet World 2003; *see also Fentiman* elsewhere in this volume.

[9] For an analysis of the concept of territoriality and the choice-of-law calibre of the Berne Convention and other intellectual property treaties, *see Van Eechoud*, Choice of Law in Copyright and Related Rights, Alternatives to the Lex Protectionis, 2003.

[10] Proposal for a Regulation on the law applicable to non-contractual obligations, COM (2003) 427 final.

principle takes account of the function of the particular field of law to which it relates.[11]

Cases of functional allocation typically involve areas of substantive law whose objective it is to protect weaker parties (children, consumers, employees). There functional allocation is used to guarantee that the "weaker" party is protected according to the laws of the country where the economic or social activities of the party are typically concerned. Thus, the European rule for the law applicable to employment contracts is that of the country where the employee habitually carries out his duties (Art. 6(2) sub a Rome Convention 1980).[12]

Functional allocation as a principle with a protective function could also be made the leading principle for issues of initial ownership. Using a creator-oriented connecting factor corresponds well with the objective of copyright and related rights law where rights allocation is concerned, namely to reward and stimulate authors – notably the actual creators of works. I will elaborate this view below.

One can imagine functional allocation not just in this narrow sense, but in the broader sense. The aim would not be to specifically protect a weaker party. Rather the function protected may be a more general policy interest, such as the public's interest in a public domain of information and knowledge.

If the perceived territoriality of intellectual property laws is a problematic basis for the *lex protectionis*, particularly in the digitally networked world, one could justify the *lex protectionis* on the basis of such a broad functional allocation principle. It can be maintained that the *lex protectionis* is the proper choice-of-law rule for existence, scope and duration of copyright given the instrumental rationale of copyright and related rights law. Intellectual property laws each strike a balance between what is and what is not (yet) in the public domain, in an attempt to do justice both to the individual creators and to the interest of the community in an optimal climate for the production and dissemination of information goods and services.

Were the applicable law to be based on, for instance, the place where a work originated, or any other law that does not coincide with the place of use, the coherence of the local intellectual property system would be in danger of being shattered. The transborder use of information products and services has become so all-pervasive (think of music, films, but also software, news services, etc.) that with respect to local use, foreign copyright and

[11] *Compare* §6 at 2c of the American Law Institute's Restatement of the Law on the Conflict of Laws (Second), which provides that where there is no statutory conflict rule, one of the factors in the selection process to be considered is "the basic policies underlying the particular field of law".

[12] The Convention also contains conflict rules for employment contracts in situations in which the employee does not habitually work in one country; these are based on factual allocation.

related rights norms would be applied not now and then, but systematically and in a large number of cases. To maintain the balance that has been struck locally, one needs to allow the *lex protectionis* to reign. The question of which intellectual property rights exist, for how long and what their scope is, should therefore be governed by the law of the place of use.

The same does not hold true for the issue of (initial) ownership. The public interest in rights with respect to the creation and use of information lies primarily in *what* is protected, not in who owns these rights.

As regards functional allocation in the narrow sense, it should be borne in mind that even though functional allocation reflects the protective function of an area of law, the outcome is by no means the "best" from the weaker party's point of view. If an employee works in a country with relatively low levels of worker protection, it is not functional allocation that gives him an opportunity to benefit from higher standards, but the freedom of disposition he and his employer have to choose a more advantageous law. The favour principle also may provide the best of both worlds for the weaker party.

d) Favour Principle

More so than is the case with functional allocation, conflict rules whose underlying principle is the favour principle are geared towards achieving a preconceived material outcome.[13] The two main groups are 1) rules that favour the validation of legal acts, and 2) rules that give one of the parties to a relationship preferential treatment.

Rules in the first group have a long history. They contain alternative connecting factors ("or" constructions) to ensure that certain juridical acts are considered valid. The *favor negotii* is possibly the oldest of these and is designed to validate legal acts as to form (*e.g.* Art. 9 Rome Convention 1980). The *favor testamenti* does the same for wills (Art. 1 Hague Convention on Testamentary Dispositions 1961).

The most far-reaching application of the favour principle is in a second group of conflict rules that are designed to benefit one particular party. Examples of rules that favour weaker parties are the Rome Convention's provisions on consumer contracts (Art. 5(2)) and on employment contracts (Art. 6(1)). They provide that if a choice for the applicable law has been made, this cannot rob the consumer or employee of the protection of mandatory provisions of the law of the habitual residence (consumer), or the law that is objectively applicable to the employment contract (usually the law of the place where the employee works), respectively.[14] The consumer and

---

[13] *De Boer*, Bescherming en begunstiging op het terrein van de international onrechtmatige daad, in De Boer *et al.*, Vijftig jaar lex loci delicti. Van Dubbinks proefschrift tot een Wet conflictenrecht onrechtmatige daad, 1998, at 290–296; *Strikwerda*, Inleiding tot het Nederlandse internationaal privaatrecht 2000, at 39.

[14] One could also view this type of rule as reflecting functional allocation, not the favour principle. *See Strikwerda* 2000, *supra* note 13, at 168–169.

employee are thus given the best of both worlds, as they can invoke the law more favourable to them.

Where it concerns initial ownership, the favour principle could play a role in work-for-hire situations. As I propose below – along with many other writers – in case of works made by employees, the initial ownership question should be subjected to the law that governs the employment contract. Under the Rome Convention of 1980 the employer and employee can choose the law that governs their contract. To protect the author-employee from a disadvantageous law chosen in effect by the employer, the favour principle can be used as a correction mechanism (see below).

3. The Creator's Law: Functional Allocation as a General Rule

As a rule, copyright is vested in the actual creator of a work. Domestic laws do, however, tend to deal differently with the allocation of rights in the case of works made for hire and works created by two or more co-contributors (*e.g.* films). If one were to let the *lex protectionis* govern issues of initial ownership, the result would be legal uncertainty as to who qualifies as initial right owner. As was said above, the question of ownership of one and the same work would be subjected to as many laws as there are legal systems protecting the work in question. Apparently inspired by the wish to avoid this legal uncertainty, a number of French and US courts tend to use some form of the *lex originis* for initial ownership questions.[15] Dutch courts sail a less clear course, but currently the *lex protectionis* does not seem to enjoy the same unchallenged position that it still has in for instance German case law.[16] Among scholars also, the use of the *lex originis* or other single governing law is increasingly advocated.[17]

---

[15] *ITAR Tass v. Russian Kurier* 153 F3d 82 (2nd Cir 27 August 1998); Cass. 29 April 1970, *Lancio v. Editirice Fotoromanzi Internazionali*, [1971] Rev.crit.dr.int.priv.; CA Versailles 17 December 1993, *Sarl F2S v. Pravda*, 162 RIDA 448 (1994); CA Paris 6 July 1989, *Turner v. Huston*, 143 RIDA 329 (1990); CA Paris 1 February 1989, *Bragance v. Orban*, 142 RIDA 302 (1990); District Court and Court of Appeals in *Saab Scania v. Diesel Technic*, cited in Cass. 7 April 1998, (1999) Rev.crit.dr.int.priv. 1, 76.

[16] The predominance of the lex protectionis for all copyright issues under German law has been confirmed by a number of BGH decisions: *Lara's Tochter*, 1999 GRUR 984; *Spielbank*, 1998 MMR 35, and *Alf*, 1992 GRUR 697. In the Netherlands some district courts do seem to apply the law of the country of origin (of a work or of its author) to the issue of initial ownership, but typically a clear choice-of-law analysis is lacking. Possibly this is due to the fact that copyright cases in the Netherlands are often litigated in "kort geding" proceedings (a type of summary proceedings). *See Van Eechoud, supra* note 9, at 110, 123–4.

[17] *See*, for instance, *Ginsburg*, The Private International Law of Copyright, 273 Receuil des Cours, 1998, at 356–357; *Goldstein*, International Copyright. Principles, Law and Practice, 2001, at 103 *et seq.*; *Schack*, Internationale Urheber-, Marken- und Wettbewerbsrechtverletzungen im Internet – Internationales Privatrecht, 2000 MMR 64; *Torremans*, The law applicable to copyright: Which rights are created and who owns them?, 188 RIDA 75 (2001). Contra: *Lucas*, Private International Law Aspects of the Protection of Works and of the Subject Matter of Related Rights Transmitted over Digital Networks, 1998 WIPO doc. GCPIL/1/01 at pt. 45 *et seq.*; *Sterling, supra* note 1, at 153–4.

In my opinion, a move away from the *lex protectionis* towards a single governing law is a development to be welcomed, as it could increase legal certainty and thereby facilitate the cross-border exploitation of works. However, there is another, better reason not to use the *lex protectionis* as the conflict rule for initial ownership. It lies in the central position the author has historically enjoyed in copyright law.

At the centre of the first modern copyright laws of the 19th century was the author – *i.e.*, the creative natural person – rather than publishers or printers, who formerly enjoyed printing privileges. Consequently, it is traditionally the author as the natural person who creates a work in whom copyright is vested, rather than the person or company that invests or is otherwise involved in the production of works. This allocation of rights is to date the predominant norm in most copyright acts and has found its way into performer's rights as well. It reflects the "justice" rationale of copyright, both in terms of the respect that is due to the bond between creator and his or her work, and in terms of the Lockean notion of just reward for labour spent.

In the past decades, the expansion of intellectual property rights has seen an increasing group of beneficiaries that are often corporate entities. In the course of time, record producers, broadcasting organisations, film producers, database producers and software manufacturers – all of whom are typically legal rather than natural persons – have come to benefit from exclusive rights in the information products or services that they produce. The rationale for the protection of these producers is primarily a utilitarian one, *i.e.*, the allocation of exclusive rights serves as an incentive for production. Traditionally the "copyright systems" have been based more (but not exclusively) on utilitarian rationale, whereas the "*droit d'auteur* systems" were based more (but also not exclusively) on the justice rationale.

One would expect that the increased importance of the utilitarian rationale in both copyright and *droit d'auteur* systems has led to an increase in the direct allocation of exclusive rights to those who invest, produce or are otherwise instrumental in the creation of information goods. However, in cases where creative input is also required, direct allocation to producers has remained the exception. Instead, the traditional rule that the person who actually does the creative work is invested with ownership remains dominant.[18]

As a result, producers acquire intellectual property directly through allocation by law only to a limited extent. More often, they acquire rights indirectly, by way of transfer of rights from the actual creators or performers.

---

[18] *E.g.*, where it concerns software and databases as original – *i.e.*, copyrighted – works, the allocation of exploitation rights to the employer rather than to the employee was prescribed by the EC's Software Directive 91/250/EEC of 1991 (OJ EC L122, p. 41). The more recent Database Directive 96/9/EC (OJ EC L77, p. 20) does not, however, grant rights in copyrighted databases directly to employers, but to employees (although Member States remain free to provide that initial ownership rests with the employer, or that employees are presumed to have transferred their rights to the employer).

Given the protective function of the law of copyright and related rights towards the actual creator or performer, who are regarded as the weaker parties compared to other parties involved in the production and dissemination of works (producers, publishers, etc.), in my view, functional allocation should be the guiding principle for initial ownership. That means the use of connecting factors linked to the actual creator or performer, notably the habitual residence at the time the work was created or first performed.[19]

a) Identification of the Creator

The connecting factor proposed above for initial ownership of copyright does not refer to the *author*. The term "author" is not a factual definition, but a legal one. Even though the term often coincides with, or denotes the actual creator,[20] legal definitions of who the "author" of a work is or can be, do substantially differ. In some countries – like Germany – the author must of necessity be a natural person; in others – like the Netherlands – it can be a legal person. With regard to films, under some laws the film producers rather than the creative contributors, are regarded as authors or co-authors and therefore initial (co-)right owners.

If one were to let initial ownership be governed by the author's law, one would first have to determine which law's definition of author should be used. The normal solution to this type of problem is to decide who qualifies as the (co-)author under the *lex fori*. Obviously it is of no use if ownership questions arise outside litigation. Short of situations where litigants are allowed to choose their (future) court, the lex fori rule does not contribute to legal certainty either. Alternatively, the term "author" could be given an autonomous "supranational" interpretation. However, copyright treaties are not a satisfactory source for such a country-independent definition, since they do not contain a clear definition of "author" either.[21]

By referring to the *actual creator of a work* – which is a more factual definition – the interpretation problem is reduced. More importantly, where the actual creator and another party (producer, investor, or any other entity that could under some laws qualify as the author) each claim initial ownership, this wording allows for the law of the actual creator to decide the issue. This solution – functional allocation by reference to the actual creator – is in accordance with the objective of most copyright laws, which primarily seek to protect and reward actual creators.

[19] If the author changes his or her habitual residence during the creation, the last habitual residence, *i.e.*, the one at the time of completion of the work, rather than the one at the beginning or in between, seems the more appropriate connecting factor. Alternatively, one could use the country where most of the creative work took place as connecting factor.

[20] *Drexl* states that the Berne Convention is based on the idea of the author as a natural creative person (Europarecht und Urheberkollisionsrecht, in: *Ganea et al.*, Urheberrecht Gestern-Heute-Morgen, 2001).

[21] *See Van Eechoud*, *supra* note 9, chapter 3.

As long as the question is who owns the initial rights in a copyrighted work,[22] there will always be a natural person who actually did the creative work involved – however low the required standard of originality may be – and under the conflict rule I propose, it would be the law of that person's habitual residence that decides who owns the copyright.

In case two or more natural persons both claim to be the initial owner to the exclusion of the other, while they do not share the same habitual residence, application of the law of shared nationality is an option.[23] If that does not yield one applicable law either, the *lex fori* will have to be applied as a last resort.[24]

The general rule proposed above does not work in cases of co-operation between creators from different countries. An alternative solution must be found for such collective works. Also, the relationship between employer and employee with regard to ownership of rights in works created in the course of an employee's duties deserves special attention. These issues will be dealt with next.

b) Collective Works

The creator's law is no answer to the choice-of-law problem in cases of multi-authorship, or for performances with more than one performer, unless of course all creators or performers involved share the same habitual residence.[25] To arrive at the identification of one single law, we must therefore look for another solution.

It seems logical to make a choice between the various creators' laws involved. Who the co-creators are is a matter of fact, not law, so it should not

---

[22] Some copyright laws also grant rights in non-original creations (*e.g.*, protection of non-original writings in the Netherlands, or of non-original photography in Scandinavian countries), in which case the habitual residence of the actual maker could be used as the connecting factor.

[23] One could also give the parties the opportunity to choose between the laws of either of their habitual residences or the *lex fori* so as to settle their position. Chances are of course that they will not agree on such a choice. Connecting factors related to the work, such as the place of creation or the place of first publication, could serve as alternatives but may be difficult to determine, especially in the digital environment.

[24] This is the solution used for divorce in the Dutch *Wet Conflictenrecht Echtscheiding* (Act on the law applicable to divorce), *Stb.* 1981, 66. In default of a choice by the spouses and in default of common nationality or habitual residence, the *lex fori* is the applicable law.

[25] Alternatively, common nationality could be used as connecting factor if there is no common habitual residence. However, there should be a meaningful connection between the creator and the country of which he or she is a national. Such a connection could be lacking if for instance a writer has long been in exile, or moved from his or her native country as a child. In practice, the relevance of nationality as connecting factor will be limited, as it is not that likely that co-contributors who do not share a habitual residence do share the same nationality.

be too difficult to determine which persons and therefore which laws are to be considered.[26]

aa) Choice by the Co-Creators The choice between laws can be made objectively, but also subjectively, by giving the co-creators the opportunity to decide jointly which law governs the allocation of rights in the work they helped to create. The justification for leaving the choice to the co-creators is that the idea behind the use of a creator-oriented connecting factor for issues of initial ownership is to protect their interests to begin with. One may assume that by choosing the applicable law themselves, the co-creators can take care of their interests at least as well as the legislator can by providing an objective conflict rule. From that perspective, it can be argued that they should also be allowed to opt for a "neutral" law, rather than for the law of one of their habitual residences or principal places of business.

Not unimportant either is that party autonomy provides legal certainty and predictability for the co-contributors. Such a choice would not affect the rights of third parties, but only determine the respective positions of the co-creators involved.

bb) Applicable Law in Default of a Choice by Co-Contributors It is, of course, quite conceivable that the co-contributors will not agree on the applicable law. In default of a choice, the question of initial ownership may best be answered by using a semi-open conflict rule, bearing in mind the protective function of copyright law towards actual creators.[27] Such a rule would prescribe that the law of the country with the *closest connection* to the case should govern the ownership question and list connecting factors that may be considered in search of that closest connection.

These factors could, for instance, be based on the relative creative input of the co-contributors, or more neutrally, on majority characteristics. In the first case, the fact that someone is a primary creative contributor or the initiator of the work suggests that his or her habitual residence should be given more weight than that of contributors with less (creative) input. In the latter case, if a (considerable) majority of the contributors share the same habitual residence, this can be viewed as indicative of a close connection. If the parties have made a more or less equal contribution, or if there is no majority habitual residence, the (principal) place of creation may serve as an alternative.

One drawback of using a semi-open conflict rule as described above is that it leaves a measure of legal uncertainty. It does not provide for much predictability as to the applicable law. If one considers the alternatives, however, these do not appear to be ideal either.

---

[26] As we have argued above that the actual creators (in cases of copyright) should be the point of departure, these are also the parties to consider in cases of collective works, rather than the corporate entities that may under some laws have a claim to initial ownership, for instance because they commissioned a work.

[27] A conflict rule based on functional allocation in the narrow sense would not work here, since it is aimed at determining the creator's law. The problem that needs addressing here is what to do when there are various creators' laws involved.

The classic territorial or *lex protectionis* approach, for instance, entails at least as much uncertainty. With respect to the same work, a co-contributor may be regarded as initial co-owner in one country, but not in the next. This causes limping legal relationships among co-contributors. It also means that a chain of title cannot be traced back to one single law, but can end in as many applicable laws as there are countries that recognise an intellectual property right in a work. For the transfer of intellectual property later on in the exploitation chain, this yields uncertainty as to the validity of title.

Instead of a semi-open conflict rule, one could also opt for a hard-and-fast rule, for instance, that the law applicable to initial ownership in collective works is that of the country in which the work was created, or first published. The problem with such connecting factors – apart from the fact that the places they point to may be difficult to determine – is that they do not necessarily lead to the identification of a law with a significant relationship to the case. All in all, a semi-open conflict rule that leads to identification of a single governing law has my preference over a hard-and-fast rule.

c) Works Created by Employees

The creation of information products and services continues to gain in economic importance. As the much heralded Information Society takes shape, intellectual creations are increasingly made by employees in the course of their duties. Few domestic laws have a general work-for-hire clause that attributes copyright to the employer – such as Art. 7 of the Dutch Copyright Act and Sec. 11(2) of the UK Copyright, Designs and Patents Act – or to employer and commissioner alike, such as Sections 101 and 201(b) of the USCA.[28]

Less far-reaching than the outright allocation of rights are the legal presumptions that the employer has an (exclusive) licence to exploit the work or performance created by employees. The Dutch Neighbouring Rights Act (*Wet Naburige Rechten 1993)*, for instance, contains an extensive clause on the rights of employers, who are entitled to exercise the performer's economic rights if parties have an agreement to that effect, or if it follows from the nature of the employment contract, from convention or standards of equity and fairness (Art. 3 Neighbouring Rights Act).[29]

Laws that do not contain a general work-for-hire clause or presumption with regard to the employer's rights may contain specific provisions for certain categories of works such as film or software. Such provisions often lay down a (often rebuttable) presumption that the employer or producer owns the economic rights.

---

[28] *E.g.*, under German law copyright is inalienable, but the courts have accepted that the employer is presumed to have been licensed the rights necessary for business purposes, unless there is an express agreement to the contrary. *See Seignette,* Challenges to the creator doctrine, 1994, at 34.

[29] Art. 38(1) Austrian Copyright Act provides that for films, the exploitation rights rest with the producer; Art. 79 German Copyright Act provides that the employer owns the exploitation rights in performances made in the context of an employment or service contract.

In EU legislation, granting initial ownership to the employee is the preferred method of rights allocation.[30] Even the introduction of legal presumptions of transfer enabling the employer to exploit the intellectual property in the work of employees is controversial. The 1991 Software Directive is an exception as it provides in Art. 2(3) that "Where a computer program is created by an employee in the execution of his duties or following the instructions given by his employer, the employer exclusively shall be entitled to exercise all economic rights in the program so created, unless otherwise provided by contract."[31]

A few years later it was not possible to reach such an agreement in favour of the employer again concerning copyright in databases.[32] The 1996 Database Directive does however (in Recital 29) make clear that "nothing in this Directive prevents Member States from stipulating in their legislation that . . . the employer exclusively shall be entitled to exercise all economic rights in the database . . ."[33] According to Article 4(1) the creator of a database is the natural person or persons who makes the database, or, if the law of a Member State so allows, the legal person that the law of the Member State designates as right owner.

At the European level then, there is no real trend towards granting initial ownership of intellectual property rights to the employer rather than to the employee.[34] It could be argued that the creator's law as proposed above should therefore also be used for situations where protected subject-matter is created by employees. After all, the employees, and not the corporate entity that employs them, deliver the creative performance. The law of the habitual residence of the employee/creator then governs the question of (initial) rights allocation between employer and employee.

---

[30] *See Spoor & Verkade*, Auteursrecht 1993 at No. 27 for a discussion of legal theories behind the employer (and legal persons in general) as authors/creators. *Id. Seignette, supra* note 28, 1994, and *Nimmer & Nimmer*, Nimmer on Copyright, 2001, at § 1.06). On the relationship between intellectual property law and labour law, especially where it concerns financial interests, *see Quaedvlieg*, Denker im Dienstverhältnis. Kernfragen des Arbeitnehmer Immaterialgüterrechts, 2002 GRUR Int. 11, 901–914.

[31] Implemented in *e.g.*, Art. 59 Danish Copyright Act, Art. L113–9 French Intellectual Property Code, Art. 40a Austrian Copyright Act, Art. 69b German Copyright act, Art. 14(3) Portuguese Copyright Act.

[32] The *sui generis* right in databases (Sec. III Database Directive) is vested directly in the database producer, which will often be a corporate entity.

[33] In the Netherlands, the normal copyright rules concerning ownership apply to databases protected under copyright, *i.e.*, the employer is regarded as author of a database that is created by employees in the course of their duties (Art. 7 Aw). For databases protected under the *sui generis* regime, the producer, *i.e.*, the (legal) person who bears the risk of investment, owns the exclusive rights (Art. 1(1)b Dw).

[34] *Guibault & Hugenholtz*, Study on the conditions applicable to contracts relating to intellectual property in the European Union, 2002, at 25–26, conclude that there "seems to be a growing tendency at the European level to recognise, either statutorily or judicially, the existence of the presumption of ownership in favour of the employee . . ." (study for the EC, available at www.ivir.nl).

However, the employee's duties – including the creation of information that is potentially the subject-matter of intellectual property – are embedded in the broader labour relationship of employer and employee. It can therefore be maintained that the question of who owns any exclusive rights in the work may as well be subjected to the law that governs this labour relationship, *i.e.*, the law that governs the employment contract.[35] For employment contracts the 1980 Rome Convention provides – apart from a choice by parties – for functional allocation, *i.e.*, the law that governs the employment contract is the law of the country where the employee habitually works.

aa) Accessory Allocation to the Employment Contract Accessory allocation to the employment contract means that initial ownership of works created by employees is subjected to functional allocation, not by reference to the creator as such, but by reference to the creator in his or her capacity as employee. In practice, the country of habitual residence of the employee will, of course, also be the place of work, as is the case with, for instance, the many Indian software developers who work in Silicon Valley firms.[36] From that perspective, both connecting factors point towards the same law.

The situation will be different if there is no habitual place of work. For such "mobile" employees,[37] the 1980 Rome Convention provides in Art. 6(2b) that the employment contract is governed by

[35] In favour of accessory allocation, among others: *Birk,* Arbeitnehmer und Arbeitnehmerähnliche Person im Urheberrecht bei Auslandbeziehungen, in: *Forkel & Kraft,* Beiträge zum Schutz der Persönlichkeit und ihrer schöpferischen Leistungen, 1985, at 6; *De Boer,* Aanknoping in het internationaal auteursrecht, 5414 WPNR (1977), at 692; *Brem,* 'Das Immaterialgüterrecht im zukünfitigen IPR Gesetz, in: Beiträgen zum neuen IPR des Sachen-, Schuld-, und Gesellschaftsrechts, 1987, at 65; *Fawcett & Torremans,* Intellectual Property and Private International Law, 1998, at 515; *Katzenberger,* Urheberrechtsverträge in internationalen Privatrecht und Konventionsrecht, in: Urhebervertragsrecht, 1995, at 252; *Mankowski,* Besondere Formen von Wettbewerbsverstößen, 1999 GRUR Int. 522; *Ulmer,* Intellectual Property Rights and the Conflict of Laws, 1978, at 38 *et seq.*, 99–100. Contra, if there is no real consensus between employer and employee as to the applicable law: *Quaedvlieg,* Een multiple personality syndrom in het IPR: de identificatie van de auteursrechthebbende, in Kortmann *et al.*, Oprecht: bundel opstellen, aangeboden aan prof. mr. A.V.M. Struycken ter gelegenheid van zijn zilveren ambtsjubileum aan de Katholieke Universiteit Nijmegen 1997, at 263.

[36] *The Economist* (21 April 2001) actually described Indian engineers and scientists as the back-bone of Silicon Valley's workforce.

[37] Incidental work carried out elsewhere does not make an employee mobile in the sense of Art. 6(2b) Rome Convention. Exactly when there is no longer a place of habitual work is unclear. In the *Weber* case, the ECJ ruled that if an employee works in various places, the place where the employee habitually works is the place where the employee fulfils the most important part of his duties towards the employer (ECJ 27 February 2002, case C–37/00, [2002] ECR I-2013). As this ruling pertained to the habitual place of work for issues of jurisdiction under the Brussels Convention, one should be cautious as regards its extension to applicable law issues.

> the law of the country in which the place of business through which [the employee] was engaged is situated; unless it appears from the circumstances as a whole that the contract is more closely connected with another country, in which case the contract shall be governed by the law of that country.

Applied to our area this Article means, for instance, that set designers or other contributors to a film that work on films in various countries, can invoke the provisions on initial ownership of the law of the country where the company that employs them has its principal place of business, unless, all circumstances considered, the law of another country is more closely connected.

bb) Favour-Restricted Choice by Parties The primary reason to subject the initial ownership question to the law of the employment contract is that the creative activities of the author are embedded in labour relations. Another reason is that (written) employment contracts, or any collective labour agreements[38] to which the contract refers, often contain provisions on intellectual property. If the material validity of the intellectual property clauses and their interpretation are subjected to the law of the contract, but the initial ownership question is governed by another law, it may become difficult to assess which prerogatives with regard to intellectual property lie with the employer or employee.[39]

The drawback of treating initial ownership as an issue accessory to an employment contract is that in contract law there is a large measure of freedom of disposition to choose the applicable law. Since the terms of an employment contract are usually stipulated by the employer, a choice for an employer-friendly intellectual property law is easily made. However, the favour principle could always be used to restrict the freedom of disposition. In that case, a choice of the applicable law by the parties cannot have as an effect that the employee-creator loses the protection of the mandatory provisions of the copyright or related rights law of the country where he or she habitually works.

Article 6(1) of the 1980 Rome Convention contains such a "favour restriction" for employment contracts. As it stands, this Article probably applies at best only to provisions in intellectual property law that pertain specifically to employer-employee relations. Such provisions can be said to belong to the realm of labour law addressed by Art. 6.[40]

---

[38] On collective labour agreements and intellectual property, *see Birk*, *supra* note 35.

[39] *Locher*, *supra* note 4, at 49 *et seq*., notes that provisions on ownership and transfer in national copyright acts tend to protect the author, but that subjecting them to the *lex protectionis* leads to a fragmentation that easily becomes detrimental to the creator's interest. He suggests that the division of rights between employer and employee, commissioner and commissionee, be governed by the employment or commission contract, including the question of which rights are transferable.

[40] From *Giuliano & Lagarde*'s report on the Rome Convention it is not clear exactly which mandatory rules are covered by Paragraph 2 of Art. 6. It seems one may interpret the provision broadly, as it applies not only to the law of labour contracts, but also for instance to standards of safety and hygiene (*see Giuliano & Lagarde* 1980, comment on Art. 6(2)).

The question is whether the intellectual property law's general provisions on initial ownership can also be invoked by the employee under the Rome Convention. If not, the effect of the favour principle correction is largely annulled, because those laws that contain special provisions on works made for hire or presumptions of ownership with respect to rights in works created by employees, usually do so to the advantage of the employer. Laws without any special provision will be based on the idea that the employee is the initial owner. Another reason to allow employees to invoke the totality of provisions on initial ownership and employer–employee relations in substantive intellectual property law lies in the fact that these general and specific provisions are related.

In sum, it is the protective function of copyright law towards actual creators combined with the fact that the creative work of employees is embedded in their labour relationship with the employer, that warrants accessory allocation of the initial ownership issue to the law that governs the employment contract.

The Rome Convention's functional allocation principle (Art. 6(2)) as used to objectively determine the applicable law to employment contracts should in my view extend to the provisions of intellectual property law that determine the respective position of employee and employer where ownership is concerned. The same goes for the favour principle (Art. 6(1)), which serves as a restriction to the freedom of employer and employee to determine the applicable law to the benefit of the employee.

III. In Conclusion

In this contribution, though concise, I have attempted to view the issue of the applicable law for issues of initial ownership in copyrighted works in the light of the four main allocation principles that are used in European private international law. These are closest connection, party autonomy, functional allocation and the favour principle.

It has been argued that even if, for the issues of existence, scope and duration of copyright, the *lex protectionis* – based on the functional allocation principle in a broad sense – is the appropriate conflict rule, the same does not follow for the question of initial ownership (or transfer, for that matter).

All four allocation principles have in my view a role to play where initial ownership of copyright is concerned. I would suggest that functional allocation in the narrow sense should be the leading principle, as this best corresponds with the predominant objective of ownership rules in copyright, namely to reward and stimulate the actual creators of a work. The creator's law, meaning the law of the country where the actual creator has his or her habitual residence, should then be the principal candidate to determine who owns copyright.

In the case of works or performances made by employees, accessory allocation of the initial ownership issue to the employment contract is to be preferred, with the proviso that the actual creators cannot be robbed of the protection that is afforded them under the law of the place where they normally work.

In the case of collective works, either common habitual residence or a choice by the co-contributors, should determine initial ownership. In default of a party choice and lacking a common habitual residence, a semi-open conflict rule must be used to determine the country most closely connected. Possible factors to be considered are:

- the common habitual residence or principal place of business of the large majority of the co-contributors;
- the habitual residence or principal place of business of the initiators or primary contributors; and
- the (principal) place of creation of the work.

The chance that in practice the *lex protectionis* will be replaced by a single governing law where initial ownership is concerned remains slim as long as the conventional wisdom persists that copyright is territorial, and with it the view that the lex protectionis is the only plausible conflict rule. The tendency in doctrine and in the courts of some countries – albeit careful – to develop alternatives to the *lex protectionis* can in my view only be reinforced if we are prepared to closely examine what we mean exactly when we label copyright as "territorial" and reconsider whether it should of necessity imply the reign of the *lex protectionis*.

Annex

I. General Directions

Most of the topics treated in this volume are concerned with legal fields and projects that are very much in flux. The material compiled in the Annex is therefore not conclusive in the sense that it represents the final outcome of endeavours presently conducted on the regional and international level. In part, the texts printed in the following are no longer of actual relevance, like the 1999 Draft Hague Jurisdiction Convention (infra, III). Nevertheless, its publication was considered as useful, as it did form the general framework for the elaboration of the MPI proposal (infra, II). For the actual state of the Hague project, including the latest draft of the Draft Hague Contracts Convention (May 2004), it is highly recommended to consult the Hague Conference's website, at www.hcch.net.

A special problem was posed to the editors of this book by the fact that the Draft ALI principles in their present version (January 2004) are not publicly available. Although it might have been possible to obtain the kind permission of the American Law Institute to print the black letter text in the Annex, this was not considered useful, as the versions presently available will be changed again in the course of the project, which may go on for several years. For information about the Dreyfuss/Ginsburg proposal that has formed the incentive for the ALI project, and still constitutes the basis for the jurisdiction chapter, it is recommended to consult previous internet publications that can be found at http://www.wipo.int/pil-forum/en/documents/pdf/pil_01_7.pdf (version presented at the WIPO forum on private international law and intellectual property, 2001) and http://www.kentlaw.edu/depts/IPp/intl-courts/docs/treaty10_10.pdf.

II. The MPI Proposal

Special Provision on I.P.: Text of Proposed Art. 12a[1]

Art. 12a – Jurisdiction in Intellectual Property Matters

Paragraph 1

(1) In proceedings in which the relief sought is a judgment on the grant, registration, validity, abandonment, or revocation of a patent, a mark, an industrial design or any other industrial property right required to be registered or protected on the basis of registration, the courts of the Contracting State where the right has been registered or is deemed to have been registered under the terms of an international convention shall have exclusive jurisdiction, unless the judgment would only become effective inter partes.

(2) Notwithstanding paragraph 4, 1st sentence, the courts in the Contracting State where the right has been registered or is deemed to have been registered under the Aterms of an international convention shall have exclusive jurisdiction if the judgment would entail a prohibition of further use of the right in that Contracting State, even though the issue of invalidity has not been raised expressly in the proceedings.

[(3) In proceedings in which the relief sought is a judgment on the validity of any other intellectual property right, the courts in the Contracting State where the judgment would have effect erga omnes shall have exclusive jurisdiction.

(4) Even if, in proceedings in which the relief sought is a judgment on the validity of an intellectual property right, exclusive jurisdiction pursuant to sentences 1 to 3 does not apply, the courts in the Contracting State in regard of whose territory the judgment shall become effective inter partes shall have jurisdiction.]

Paragraph 2

(1) Paragraph 1 shall not apply where the matter arises as an incidental question in proceedings before a court not having exclusive jurisdiction. [However, the incidental ruling in that matter shall have no binding effect in subsequent proceedings, even if they are between the same parties].

(2) A matter arises as an incidental question if the court is not requested to give a judgment on that matter, even if a ruling on it is necessary in arriving at a decision.

---

[1] Unless otherwise indicated, and pending further deliberations in the working group, it is submitted that other relevant provisions correspond to the 1999 DHJC text (printed *infra*, III a). *In order to avoid misunderstandings, it is emphasized that relying on the 1999 DHJC text as a general framework for the present draft is merely a matter of working convenience and does not express the view of the MPI working group that the 1999 DHJC still is, will be, or should remain, unchanged in the future.*

Paragraph 3

(1) Absent an agreement valid under Art. 4,[2] the courts in the Contracting State where an intellectual property right

a) has been registered or is deemed to have been registered under the terms of an international convention;

b) has otherwise acquired protection, e.g. by use in commerce, or by acquisition of the degree of public recognition required by national law and/or an international convention, or through an act conferring protection under copyright law

shall have jurisdiction in proceedings which have as their object the infringement, including declaration of non-infringement, of that right.

(2) No other court shall have jurisdiction except for the courts in the Contracting State where the defendant is habitually resident[3] pursuant to Article 3.

(3) Art. 10[4] does not apply with respect to proceedings concerning infringement or declaration of non-infringement of intellectual property rights.

Paragraph 4

(1) Subject to Paragraph 1, 2nd sentence, courts in the Contracting State where the defendant is habitually resident pursuant to Article 3 have jurisdiction with respect to all infringement claims raised against that defendant.

(2) If jurisdiction in infringement proceedings is solely founded on the fact that the right has been registered, is deemed to have been registered or has otherwise acquired protection in the Contracting State, the courts in that Contracting State have jurisdiction only with respect to infringements occurring in that territory, unless regulated otherwise in paragraph 5.

Paragraph 5

If the infringement claim concerns behaviour related to the Internet or similar ubiquitous media, courts in other Contracting States than the Contracting State where the defendant is habitually resident pursuant to Article 3 shall have jurisdiction with respect to infringements occurring in other territories, if

a) an essential part of the activities which are claimed to have caused the infringement has been carried out by the defendant in the Forum State, and

b) the activities which are claimed to have caused the infringement are not aimed at the market in the Contracting State where the defendant is habitually resident, and have no substantial commercial effect there.

---

[2] Art. 4 of the 1999 DHJC text deals with contractual agreements on jurisdiction. These are now regulated in the draft Hague Convention on Jurisdiction clauses; *see* the contributions by Andrea *Schulz* and Alexander *Peukert*.

[3] The Brussels Convention uses the term "domicile", whereas the DHJC prefers using "habitual residence" to denote the defendant's forum.

[4] Art. 10 of the 1999 DHJC text deals with torts or delicts.

Paragraph 6

(1) For the application of paragraph 4, 2nd sentence, an infringement is held to occur in a Contracting State where the right exists, provided that
a) the activity or omittance by which the right is claimed to be infringed has commercial effect or, if commercial effect is lacking, a substantial impact in that Contracting State, or
b) the activity by which the right is claimed to be infringed is intentionally directed towards that Contracting State.
(2) Courts shall deny jurisdiction if the defendant has taken reasonable steps to avoid creating a commercial effect in, or directing activity to, that Contracting State.

Paragraph 7

If, in proceedings involving the existence, validity and/or infringement of an intellectual property right in the territory of another Contracting State than the Forum State, the question of initial ownership of that right constitutes a decisive issue in the proceedings, and the legal doctrines applying in the Contracting State where the deciding court is situated and in the Contracting State where the right is claimed to exist and/or to have been infringed diverge with respect to the law governing the issue of initial ownership, the deciding court shall, upon motion of the defendant, stay the proceedings with respect to the existence and/or infringement of the right in the other Contracting State, unless the plaintiff provides relevant evidence proving, to the satisfaction of the deciding court, that the defendant will not be subject to legal proceedings concerning the same subject-matter initiated by, or on behalf of, another person who, according to the legal doctrine applying in the other Contracting State, may have a valid claim to ownership of the right concerned.

Comments

1. Heading and Numbering of the Provision

Proposed Art. 12a is modelled on the provisions set out in Art. 12 paragraphs 4 et seq. of the 1999 prel. DHJC. In the DHJC, the heading of Art. 12 is "exclusive jurisdiction", and the provisos contained therein exclude any possibility of a choice of courts by the parties. In contrast, proposed Article 12a lists in its third paragraph three alternative grounds for jurisdiction in infringement proceedings. As it might create confusion to insert such a rule under the old heading, and also in view of the fact that the rules proposed in the following are rather lengthy and complex, this proposal has preferred to create a new article specifically dealing with intellectual property matters under a separate heading.

It is important to note in this context that the rules set out in the proposed article should not be subject to a *forum non conveniens* rule, i.e. a court whose competence can be established on the basis of that provision cannot deny jurisdiction on the ground that another court is more competent to hear the case.[5]

2. *Paragraph 1 – Exclusive Jurisdiction in (In)Validity Cases*

Text:

> (1) In proceedings in which the relief sought is a judgment on the grant, registration, validity, abandonment, or revocation of a patent, a mark, an industrial design or any other industrial property right required to be registered or protected on the basis of registration, the courts of the Contracting State where the right has been registered or is deemed to have been registered under the terms of an international convention shall have exclusive jurisdiction, unless the judgment would only become effective inter partes.
> (2) Notwithstanding paragraph 4, 1st sentence, the courts in the Contracting State where the right has been registered or is deemed to have been registered under the terms of an international convention shall have exclusive jurisdiction if the judgment would entail a prohibition of further use of the right in that Contracting State, even though the issue of invalidity has not been raised expressly in the proceedings.
> [(3) In proceedings in which the relief sought is a judgment on the validity of any other intellectual property right, the courts in the Contracting State where the judgment would have effect erga omnes shall have exclusive jurisdiction.
> (4) Even if, in proceedings in which the relief sought is a judgment on the validity of an intellectual property right, exclusive jurisdiction pursuant to sentences 1 to 3 does not apply, the courts in the Contracting State in regard of whose territory the judgment shall become effective inter partes shall have jurisdiction.]

2.1 General considerations

It is a general and widely uncontested rule[6] that courts in the state where industrial property rights have been registered or are deemed to be registered on the basis of an international convention (state of registration) have exclusive jurisdiction in proceedings where the relief sought is the declaration of (in)validity or the cancellation etc. of the right. This is a matter of national sovereignty: The Act of State which is manifested in the registration must be respected abroad, and cannot be declared invalid by the courts of other countries.

While this much is clear, there is no consensus on the question of how much respect must be paid to the sovereign power vested in the courts in the state of registration. The following antagonistic positions can be assumed in regard of this issue. A cautious approach would reserve exclusive jurisdiction

---

[5] That is, based on the working assumption that the new article is included in the DHJC text, it should be listed in the catalogue contained in Article 22.1.

[6] A different approach is however chosen in the ALI Principles, Preliminary Draft No. 2 (2004), where it is stipulated under § 223 (2) (b) that "if the declaration is sought with respect to the validity of registrations in more than one State, the courts of the State in which the defendant has its principal place of business shall have jurisdiction to the exclusion of courts of third countries"

to the courts in the state of registration whenever the question of (in)validity arises in the proceedings, even as an incidental matter. On the other hand, it can be argued that the unique position to be reserved for the courts in the registration state would only be jeopardized if and in so far as the judgment handed down by a foreign court would concern the legal effects of the right in their entirety, i.e., the legal validity of the right *erga omnes*.

The first, cautious position corresponds to the approach endorsed by a large part of the IP community. It may also be in compliance with a correct interpretation of Art. 22.4 of the Brussels Regulation.[7] By contrast, the second, more liberal and flexible solution to date appears to be supported by a minority only. In essence, this position puts more emphasis on party autonomy than on those aspects of public policy which may weigh in favour of an extensive application of the exclusivity principle.

After thorough deliberations, the MPI working group has chosen to follow the second, liberal approach. Having made that fundamental decision, it further determined that the approach should be implemented in a consistent fashion. This means that exclusive jurisdiction should only, and always, be prescribed for proceedings in which relief is sought whose legal effects would affect the right in its very existence. The consequences ensuing therefrom are set out in more detail in the following. At this point, they shall only be summarized briefly:

- The rule that exclusive jurisdiction applies to proceedings in which the relief sought is a judgment on the grant, registration, validity etc. of a registered industrial property right is only maintained if and insofar as the judgment would have effect *erga omnes* (paragraph 1, 1st sentence, last half-sentence).
- Exclusive jurisdiction of the courts in the registration state shall also apply if in consequence of the judgment, it will no longer be possible to make use of the right in that state (paragraph 1, 2nd sentence).
- If and to the extent that proceedings having as their object the (in)validity of an unregistered IP right would have effect *erga omnes*, the courts in the state where that effect would accrue shall have exclusive jurisdiction (paragraph 1, 3rd sentence).
- Even if exclusive jurisdiction does not apply pursuant to sentences 1 to 3, the courts in the country of registration/protection would still be competent to adjudicate claims seeking a declaration of (in)validity of an intellectual right *inter partes*, if and to the extent the judgment shall become effective for the territory of that state (paragraph 1, 4th sentence).

[7] The issue is pending before the ECJ (case C-4/03-1), upon reference for a preliminary decision by the Düsseldorf Court of Appeals, 2003 GRUR Int. 1030.

2.2 Registered Industrial Property Rights (Paragraph 1, 1st sentence)

As was pointed out before, Paragraph 1, 1st sentence embeds the generally accepted principle that proceedings in which the relief claimed has a direct impact on the existence of the right which has been granted by an Act of State must be conducted before the courts in the country where that Act has been executed or is deemed to have been executed. However, in consequence of the concept underlying this draft, this rule shall only apply if the judgment has effect *erga omnes*, typically by ordering cancellation of the registration, or by ordering its transfer to another person.

It can be assumed that in most cases falling under the scope of paragraph 1, the relief claimed will indeed be such that it does take effect *erga omnes*. However, this is not necessarily so. It is at least not generally excluded that a declaration of invalidity of a trademark, industrial design or patent is confined in its effects to the relationship between the parties, and does not entail (consent of the holder to) cancellation or similar consequences effecting the validity of the right vis-á-vis third parties. It may even be possible that in certain situations, national law does not offer the option to claim for cancellation etc. of a right that is deemed to be registered in that state, leaving no other choice than to revert to a declaration of invalidity *inter partes*.[8] In these cases, the proceedings would, according to paragraph 1, 1st sentence, last half-sentence, not be subject to exclusive jurisdiction of the courts in the country of registration.[9]

The approach endorsed in paragraph 1 1st sentence differs from the system that presently applies under the Brussels Regulation. Art. 22.4 (previously: Art. 16.4 Brussels Convention), the general rule establishing exclusive jurisdiction for (in)validity proceedings, applies to all proceedings in which such relief is claimed, irrespective of the legal effects entailed by the judgment. Likewise, the present proposal deviates from the wording of provisions that have been debated so far in the framework of the Hague Conference. However, as was pointed out above (sub 2.1, at the end), these differences result from the decision to endorse, and implement in a consistent fashion, the principle that only decisions affecting the legal existence of the right in its

---

[8] This situation could arise e.g. in Germany, when a claim is raised for declaration of invalidity of an industrial design right which has acquired legal effect in Germany on the basis of an international deposit according to the Hague Agreement Concerning the International Deposit of Industrial Designs. The German Design Act does not provide for a possibility to claim cancellation or similar measures with respect to such rights, meaning that the claim for declaration of invalidity to be raised against the right owner will become valid between the parties only. For an example of such a case, *see* the decision by the Munich Court of Appeals, 15 May 2003 (29 U 1977/03), with comments by *Kur*, IPRax 2004, 331.

[9] However, pursuant to the 4th sentence, the courts in that state would still be competent to exercise jurisdiction, i.e. the plaintiff has a choice to initiate proceedings either there or before the courts in the country of defendant's domicile.

entirety should be reserved to the courts in the country where the right has been granted by an Act of State.

2.3 The Case of Relative Invalidity (Paragraph 1, 2nd sentence)

The second sentence in paragraph 1 is a novel feature which is not contained in any of the previous DHJC texts or alternative proposals. It is intended to take care of possible problems resulting from the concept of relative invalidity, which is of particular importance in trademark law. This is illustrated by the following case: X and Y have taken out trademark registrations in country A, where they also make use of their marks. Y, the owner of the younger mark, is domiciled in country B. Pursuant to the proposal set out in paragraph 4 below, X might initiate infringement proceedings in country B. If Y's mark is found to be infringing, an injunction may be issued against her by a court in country B. Furthermore, it would follow from the fact that X owns a senior mark that Y's mark can be declared invalid on relative grounds. However, the declaration of invalidity of Y's mark may not be claimed in the proceedings, and it may not even have been mentioned by the parties. Nevertheless, although the registration remains unaffected as such, the mark is "dead" for all practical purposes; Y may never use it in country A again. This effect would clash with the respect to be paid to the foreign Act of State in no lesser degree than an order for cancellation of the right.

Admittedly, the practical relevance of the problem seems to be minimal. It hardly ever occurs in practice that infringement of a senior right by a younger registered right is claimed without joining a claim for cancellation to the infringement claim – something that would bring the matter immediately under the exclusivity rule set out in the first sentence. This estimation is confirmed by the fact that the situation has obviously never occurred before under the regime of the Brussels and the Lugano Conventions. It should therefore be a matter for discussion whether the issue needs any specific regulation at all, or whether it can safely be ignored.

Pending further deliberations, the present draft has chosen to regulate the issue in an affirmative manner, extending the rule of exclusive jurisdiction in validity matters to those cases where a total prohibition of further use of a registered right would ensue from an injunction based on an infringement claim.

2.4 Unregistered Intellectual Property Rights (Paragraph 1, 3rd sentence)

As was pointed out in the contribution contained in the first part of this volume,[10] it has been a fundamental objective of the present proposal to avoid discrimination between different fields of intellectual property law to the best possible degree. On the basis of this approach, the question must be considered whether the exclusivity rule generally held to apply with respect to proceedings concerning the validity or cancellation etc. of registered

[10] A. *Kur*, at II.1.

industrial property rights should also pertain to other intellectual property rights, including copyright.

At first glance, it might seem odd to pose the question at all. For practical reasons, such a rule would probably be of very little relevance anyway for copyright and neighbouring rights. The typical relief sought in proceedings relating to those rights is not a declaration of (in)validity, but a claim for injunction or damages with respect to infringement. Validity issues usually only arise as incidental matters, which are addressed in paragraph 2 of proposed Article 12a.

Nevertheless, raising an isolated claim for declaration of (in)validity is not something which would be excluded *per se*. For instance, the Community Design Regulation expressly allows for such claims with respect to unregistered Community designs (UCDs). And although this may occur very rarely in practice, the issue might also be of relevance in copyright, for instance if a claim is raised for declaration that the term of copyright protection has lapsed with respect to a certain work.[11]

When assessing the issue of exclusive jurisdiction with respect to these cases, the following must be taken into account. First, the situation differs from the type of invalidity proceedings addressed in the first sentence, as neither the UCD nor copyright comes into existence through an Act of State manifested by an entry in a public register. Second, a declaration of (in)validity of an unregistered intellectual property right will typically have legal effect between the parties only, meaning that it corresponds to the situation where, according to this proposal, even proceedings concerning registered industrial property rights shall not be subject to the rule of exclusive jurisdiction.

On the other hand, it cannot be excluded that under certain circumstances and in certain jurisdictions, proceedings in which the relief claimed is the declaration of (in)validity of an unregistered intellectual property right will have effect *erga omnes*. If and to the extent that this effect would be attainable in legal proceedings, it seems to be the most sensible solution that the power to declare the right (in)valid should be vested exclusively in the courts or other competent authorities in the territory where the right, in consequence of the decision, shall cease (or be confirmed) to exist with effect vis-á-vis everyone. In other words, if the finding with respect to protectability or lapse of protection etc. becomes binding in the sense that future decisions have to accept it without the deciding court being entitled to any further evaluation of the subject matter, the exclusive competence to exercise juris-

[11] In a previous version of Art. 12a, the exclusivity rule with respect to unregistered IP rights was also extended to ownership of rights. This was meant to form a parallel to the rules applying to registered rights, where claims challenging the ownership of a registered right (e.g. interference proceedings in patent cases) would also fall under the exclusivity rule, because, and to the extent that, they directly affect the registration. In that respect, however, the situation is different with unregistered rights, as is elaborated in more detail in the contribution by Alexander *Peukert*, Part One of this volume.

diction should rest with the courts in the state with respect to which this effect shall accrue.

However, it appears doubtful that proceedings concerned with the (in)validity of an unregistered IP right will ever have the effect described above. This is a matter of national procedural rules, concerning the scope and effects of *res iudicata*, which cannot be ascertained here. With a view to these uncertainties, and in order to indicate that the rule contained in the third sentence of paragraph 1 may be of theoretical value only, it has been placed in square brackets.

2.5 Judicial competence in cases not falling under the exclusivity rule (Paragraph 1 4th sentence)

The last sentence in paragraph one, also placed in square brackets, deals with the situation that the exclusivity rule set out in sentences 1 to 3 does not apply to proceedings in which the remedy claimed is the (in)validity of an intellectual property right, in particular because the judgment will only become effective between the parties. In these situations as well, it appears appropriate to grant jurisdiction to the courts in the country in respect of whose territory the judgment will become legally effective, as they regularly have the closest connection to the case, given the fact that the assessment will regularly be made on the basis of the law applying in that country. While this appears natural, it was decided that it should be set out expressly in the provision for the sake of clarification, and in order to avoid the impression that in such cases, the plaintiff must always revert to the courts having general jurisdiction.

3. Paragraph 2 – (In)Validity Matters as Incidental Questions

Text:

> (1) Paragraph 1 shall not apply where the matter arises as an incidental question in proceedings before a court not having exclusive jurisdiction. [However, the incidental ruling in that matter shall have no binding effect in subsequent proceedings, even if they are between the same parties].

3.1 Effects of Invalidity Inter Partes

Paragraph 2 deals with (in)validity matters arising as incidental questions in the framework of proceedings where another court than the court having exclusive jurisdiction pursuant to paragraph 1 is competent to decide the case. The proviso is closely linked with paragraph 3, where the principle is set out that the courts at the defendant's forum are also competent to decide in infringement proceedings. The wording was adopted from the provision inserted into the text of Art. 12, paragraph 5 DHJC during the negotiations at the 2001 Diplomatic Conference. It is submitted that this clause will ease concerns voiced in previous discussions that the concept of invalidity *inter partes* is not universally known or accepted, entailing the risk that absent an express rule about *res iudicata*, it would not be possible to prevent *erga omnes* effects of judgments involving an assessment of the invalidity of an IP right, even if the matter arises as an incidental question.

Nevertheless, the fact remains that on the basis of the proposed clause in connection with paragraph 3, a foreign court would be enabled to render a judgment which, in spite of being effective only between the parties, has

(i) direct consequences on the market in the country of registration that might clash with aspects of public policy and national sovereignty, and
(ii) would regularly be fatal for the right anyhow, as it would no longer be respected by third parties.

These arguments have been considered to some extent in the contribution contained in Part One of this volume.[12] The attitude taken towards them in the MPI working group can be summarized as follows:

Concerning (i): The question whether it is tolerable that a verdict handed down by a foreign court has an impact on the national market, is ultimately a matter of the weight attributed to party autonomy. If it is accepted that a right-holder does not enforce the right at all, or settles a conflict by private agreement, or, on the basis of an agreement with the alleged infringer, submits the case to binding arbitration, it is difficult to see why it should be irreconcilable with public policy if the same party submits the conflicts to a foreign court, with the verdict, like an arbitration award, becoming effective only between the parties.

Concerning (ii): It is true that a finding on invalidity between the parties may regularly prove to be disastrous for the right owner, because in spite of the restrictions with respect to the legal effects of the judgment, the right would no longer be respected by anyone in practice. However, this concern is particularly valid for the situation arising in the same jurisdiction, i.e. where different courts (or even the same courts) located in the same territory deal with conflicts between the right holder and subsequent infringers. It is less convincing in the situation when the right holder enforces his right in other jurisdictions. The latter is however the typical situation to which paragraph 3 applies: The *inter partes* effect will (only) accrue if the right holder initiates infringement proceedings before courts in another country than the country of registration – i.e. regularly in the country of the alleged infringer's habitual residence. If the same right is infringed by another person, nothing prevents the right-holder from taking the matter, this time, to the supposedly more competent courts in the country of registration. If that court should come to the result that the right is valid and infringed, the judgment can be enforced without difficulties under the proposed rules.

---

[12] A. Kur, at II.5.

3.2 General Inter Partes Effect or Restriction of Legal Effects to the Concrete Proceedings?

In addition to the issue of restricting the legal effects of judgments to the parties in a given lawsuit, it has to be decided whether the *res iudicata* effect shall relate to subsequent proceedings conducted between the same parties, or whether it shall be confined to the current proceedings only. After the problem had been debated at some length in the framework of the Hague Conference, it was decided that incidental findings on (in)validity – if acceptable at all – should be ascribed the most restrictive legal effect possible, i.e. they should leave subsequent proceedings unaffected, even if these are conducted between the same parties. No final decision has been made on this point in the MPI working group. Paragraph 2, 2nd sentence, which adopts the narrow approach tentatively adopted at the 2001 Hague Diplomatic Conference,[13] was therefore put in square brackets.

In this context, however, it must be pointed out that in any case, the additional restriction of the *res iudicata* effect reflected in paragraph 2, 2nd sentence would only apply in the situation regulated in paragraph 2, i.e. if the issue of (in)validity has arisen as an incidental question. The situation is different in the cases encompassed by paragraph 1, in proceedings where the relief sought in the proceedings is a declaration of (in)validity of the right. As was explained above, the principle of exclusive jurisdiction does *not* apply in those cases if the judgment becomes effective between the parties only. However, in such a case, contrary to the situation dealt with in paragraph 2, the effect *does* extend to subsequent proceedings between the same parties. This difference is justified by the fact that in proceedings falling under paragraph 1, the (in)validity of the IP right constitutes the core subject matter of the lawsuit, and not just an incidental aspect.

3.3 Alternative Solutions Recommended for Further Discussion

While the position assumed by the MPI working group is firmly grounded, it has to be acknowledged that its approach is not shared by a substantial part of the intellectual property community. In particular with respect to patent rights, it appears highly doubtful whether it will be possible in the foreseeable future to win acceptance for a Convention rule granting jurisdiction for (in)validity rulings with effect *inter partes* to a court that is not competent in general to decide on registration or validity pursuant to Paragraph 1.

On the other hand, extending exclusive jurisdiction in IP matters to all infringement proceedings potentially involving (in)validity issues would constitute a serious drawback, resulting in severe impediments for the efficient enforcement of IP rights in case of multiterritorial infringement. Instead of taking a full step back from the position endorsed here, the

---

[13] For an explanation of the reasons and more details, *see* the contribution by Andrea *Schulz*, Part One of this volume.

following intermediate solutions could be considered and discussed as a compromise.

—*Alternative 1*: As a general rule, infringement proceedings involving the assessment of the validity of an IP right must be conducted before the courts in the country of grant or registration. However, an exemption is made for cases concerning the infringement, in more than one territory, of an IP right or IP rights relating to the same subject matter, if a close relationship exists between the infringing acts and the person or persons against whom the claims are directed (exemption for consolidation).
—*Alternative 2*: In proceedings involving the validity of a (registered) right, other courts than the courts in the Contracting State of grant or registration may only decide the case on the assumption that the right is valid. If they consider the right invalid, they must stay the proceedings until a decision on that point has been made by the competent authority/ies in the country of grant or registration (*exemption on assumption of validity*).
—*Alternative 3*: Whenever the validity of a (registered) right becomes an issue in infringement proceedings before a court that is not situated in the Contracting State of grant or registration, the court is obliged (upon motion of the parties) to consult with the competent authorities in the Contracting State of grant or registration about the legal situation in that state. For this purpose, each Member State would have to name one instance – a specialised court or an authority – that is competent to give advice in these matters (*consultation principle*).

3.4 *Definition of "Incidental Matter"*

Finally, it remains to be considered how the concept of "incidental matter" should be defined. The wording agreed upon during the 2001 Diplomatic Conference confines the notion to subject matter which is considered in the proceedings, without the court being requested to give a judgment on that matter. It follows that if the matter is raised by way of counterclaim, it would be excluded from the concept.

It seems important to note in this context that in some countries and in some areas of I.P. law, it may not be possible to raise the issue of invalidity in infringement proceedings other than by filing a counterclaim. This applies for instance to Community Design law.[14] Consequently, even if both parties, including the defendant, would prefer to have the case decided by another court than the court in the country of registration, the Convention would not allow it as soon as the issue of invalidity is brought up (necessarily by way of counterclaim) in the proceedings.

This situation calls for further deliberation. From the approach underlying the MPI proposal, it would appear more consistent to allow counterclaims for invalidity to be raised at the forum of the infringement claim, even if it does not have exclusive jurisdiction, provided that the decision will only

[14] *See* Art. 85 para 1, 2nd sentence of the Community Design Regulation No. 6/2002.

become valid between the parties. As this point has not been finally discussed in the working group, however, the proposed text still follows the wording proposed in the framework of the Hague Conference.

4. *Paragraph 3 – Courts Having Jurisdiction in Infringement Proceedings*

Text:

> (1) Absent an agreement valid under Art. 4,[15] the courts in the Contracting State where an intellectual property right
> a) has been registered or is deemed to have been registered under the terms of an international convention
> b) has otherwise acquired protection, e.g. by use in commerce, or by acquisition of the degree of public recognition required by national law and/or an international convention, or through an act conferring protection under copyright law shall have jurisdiction in proceedings which have as their object the infringement, including declaration of non-infringement, of that right. (2) No other court shall have jurisdiction except for the courts in the Contracting State where the defendant is habitually resident[16] pursuant to Article 3. [(3) Art. 10[17] shall not apply with respect to proceedings concerning infringement or declaration of non-infringement of intellectual property rights.]

4.1 *Structure of the Provision*

Paragraph 3 enumerates in a conclusive manner the courts to which competence is granted to decide in IP infringement proceedings. These are – listed in order of their importance – (1) the courts in the country where the right is registered, is deemed to have been registered or has otherwise acquired protection, (2) the courts in the country where the defendant is domiciled, and (3) if an agreement exists between the parties, the courts of the Contracting State that have been indicated in the agreement as having jurisdiction in disputes arising in connection with a particular legal relationship (see further on this point the contribution by Alexander *Peukert*). Again, it is deemed undesirable and unnecessary to discriminate between different types of IP rights in this respect.

4.2 *Competence of Courts in the Country of Registration/Protection*

It follows from the listing contained in paragraph 3, 1st sentence that nothing in the proposal will detract from the prominent role presently assumed by the courts in the country of registration/protection in IP infringement proceedings. There can be no doubt at all that for many reasons, those courts provide the most competent and appropriate fora in the overwhelming majority of IP infringement cases. One particularly important aspect weighing in favour of those courts is the fact that they, and in principle only they, will regularly be

---

[15] *I.e.*, Art. 4 of the DHJC.

[16] *See* supra note 3.

[17] *I.e.*, Art. 10 of the DHJC.

in a position to apply domestic law when assessing the infringement.[18] This follows from the generally accepted rule that the law applying in IP infringement cases is the *lex loci protectionis*, i.e. the law of the country where protection is claimed. Because, as a consequence of the territoriality principle, IP rights can only claim protection in a country where the right exists[19] – having come into existence by virtue of registration or otherwise –, the country of protection in the meaning of the PIL rule mentioned above is usually the same as the country of registration or protection in the meaning of the rule on which jurisdiction is founded in infringement cases. It is mainly this congruence normally existing between competent forum and applicable law, which guarantees that the paramount importance of the rule granting competence in infringement proceedings to the courts in the country of registration or protection will remain largely unaffected even in presence of the possibility to choose another forum, which is set out in the second sentence.

The same considerations as for IP infringement proceedings also apply with respect to claims seeking a declaration of non-infringement. An explicit regulation of this aspect is lacking in the DHJC as well as the in the text of the Brussels Convention on which it was modelled.[20] In a decision of the Swedish Supreme Court concerning the application of the corresponding provision in the Lugano Convention,[21] this has been interpreted as meaning that claims for declaration of non-infringement may only be raised at the defendant's forum, i.e. (possibly) in a state other than that where the alleged infringement is taking place.[22] The same result had been endorsed in a decision by the Tribunale di Bologna in a case where an alleged infringer had applied for declaration of non-infringement of a European patent which had been granted in Belgium, Germany, France, the UK Italy, and the Netherlands.[23] Apart from the fact that the latter decision was a reaction to

[18] This rule must however be qualified with respect to the issue of initial ownership in copyright.

[19] Like all aspects of the territoriality principle, even this basic rule is not uncontested. However, it still constitutes a sufficiently sound working assumption.

[20] The issue is however addressed expressly in Art. 93 CTMR, pursuant to which – in contrast to the present draft – the competence of the courts based on the *delicti commissi* rule does not extend to claims for declaration of non-infringement.

[21] The Lugano Convention was concluded between the former EFTA states as a parallel agreement to the Brussels Convention. It is still valid today with respect to Switzerland, Norway, Iceland and Poland in their mutual relations and their relations with the European Communities and its Member States.

[22] Swedish Supreme Court, Case Ö 2095–99, 14 June 2000, 32 IIC 231 [2001]. Unfortunately, as the case regarded the application of the Lugano Convention, which does not fall under the jurisdiction of the ECJ, it was not possible to refer the issue to Luxembourg for a preliminary ruling.

[23] Decision of 16 September 1998, German version published in 2000 GRUR Int.1020, with (critical) comment by *Stauder*.

the so-called torpedo problem,[24] the reasoning may be in accordance with the structure and underlying objectives of the Brussels and Lugano Conventions (and the Brussels regulation) in a case where the weaker party in a dispute, e.g. a consumer having suffered damage from a defective product manufactured abroad, is the defendant in proceedings for declaration of non-infringement by the product's manufacturer, the rule makes little sense in IP proceedings, where the aspect typically prevails that the courts in the country where the infringement is alleged to have taken place or to be threatening have the closest connection to the dispute.[25]

In order to avoid misunderstandings and ambiguities in this respect, the present proposal expressly includes actions for declaration of non-infringement in the notion of infringement proceedings in the meaning of paragraph 3. In this context, it needs to be pointed out that claims for declaration of non-infringement will not entail a barring effect under the *lis pendens* rule in relation to subsequent proceedings by which substantive remedies are claimed with respect to the same subject matter (4.3.2 (iv)).

Finally, another aspect to be considered in the framework of paragraph three, first sentence, is whether the rule making reference solely to the country of registration/protection must be supplemented by a proviso stating that the infringement claimed in the proceedings must take place in the same territory. Absent such a rule, it might be feared that courts in country X are deemed competent to decide a claim for copyright infringement occurring in country Y, simply because Y might in principle also qualify as a country where the right is protected. Whereas it is true that paragraph three, first sentence might in principle be construed in that way, the detrimental effects of such interpretations would be kept to a minimum not least because it is set out expressly in paragraph four, first sentence that the jurisdiction of courts whose competence is solely founded on the registration/protection rule is confined in principle to infringements occurring in that territory. In view of this mechanism, it appears superfluous to introduce further requirements.

4.3 Alternative Fora in Infringement Cases

4.3.1 Contractual Jurisdiction Clauses

The question to what extent it should be possible for the parties to agree on a forum that is competent to settle any dispute which has arisen or may arise in connection with a particular legal relationship, as is generally provided for in Art. 4 of the DHJC, seems to be of limited relevance for proceedings dealing with infringement and/or validity, which are dealt with in Art. 12a. On

---

[24] *See* the comment by *Stauder* (previous footnote). The problem is solved in a different manner in the framework of the DHJC (also endorsed here) than in the Brussels system, *see infra* 4.3.2 (iv).

[25] *See L. Lundstedt*, Jurisdiction and the Principle of Territoriality in Intellectual Property Law: Has the Pendulum Swung Too Far in the Other Direction? 32 IIC 124 [2001], at 140.

the other hand, although they mostly arise out of non-contractual relationship, such conflicts may also emerge in other situations, e.g. in the framework of license agreements. From the concept of the present proposal, it was deemed consistent to accept the validity of jurisdiction clauses contained in such agreements, though with the exception that the court designated by the parties is not entitled to decide upon validity matters with *erga omnes* effect. A more detailed motivation as well as deliberations concerning other aspects connected with contractual jurisdiction clauses is set out in the contribution by Alexander *Peukert.*

4.3.2 Competence of Courts at Defendant's Forum

The central question with respect to IP litigation in the framework of the DHJC has been whether it should be possible to raise infringement claims before the courts having general jurisdiction, i.e. the courts at defendant's forum. As is pointed out in the contribution by Annette *Kur* in the first part of this volume, and as indicated sub 3 above, the MPI proposal in that respect does not follow the majority opinion endorsed by the patent and trademark community in the discussions concerning Art. 14 of the 1999 DHJC, but instead allows infringement proceedings to be raised (*inter alia*) before the courts at the defendant's forum. As a consequence of the structure underlying the MPI proposal, those courts are, as a matter of principle, the only courts competent to adjudicate multi-state or even global infringements in their entirety. Apart from courts whose competence is founded on contractual agreements between the parties, and notwithstanding the exceptions to be treated below, i.e. the multiple- defendants rule (see the contribution by Marcus *Norrgård*) and infringements occurring in cyberspace, no other courts are competent to hand down decisions in IP matters having cross-border effects.

The reasons for this attitude have been elaborated in several publications[26] and are also briefly treated in the contribution in part one as well as in the comments dealing with paragraphs 1 and 2. It suffices therefore to make reference to the most important arguments on which the MPI proposal is based.

(i) It should be kept in mind that the possibility to claim infringement[27] of IP rights registered or otherwise protected abroad before the courts at defendant's forum, and to consolidate multi-state infringement proceedings there, is nothing but an additional option. Nothing in the draft will

---

[26] *See* in particular A. *Kur*, International Hague Convention on Jurisdiction and Foreign Judgments: A Way Forward for IP? 24 E.I.P.R. 175–183 (2002).

[27] The same applies, *mutatis mutandis*, to claims for declaration of non-infringement; *see* 4.2 above. This means that such claims can be initiated (a) before the courts in the rightholders home country or (b) in the country or countries where the allegedly infringed right exists. However, with respect to claims for non-infringement it is important to note that the court seized by the right-holder with claims for substantive remedies will always prevail, even if another court was seized first (*see* below).

take away or interfere with a plaintiff's freedom to initiate infringement proceedings in the place where the right is registered and allegedly infringed. It is contended that it would be unwise to preclude the additional option now and for the future, provided that the interests of the parties are taken into account to the best possible degree, and that misuse can be prevented.

(ii) As regards the plaintiff, his interests are only adversely affected in the case that his choice of forum turns out to be unwise, be it because the courts at the defendants' forum cannot be trusted to make the right decision, or because procedural rules are applied that are unfamiliar to, or even tend to disfavour, a foreign plaintiff. This hardly amounts to a sufficient reason to discard the possibility of making choices altogether.

(iii) Whereas there is no reason to worry about the position of the plaintiff, the defendant is exposed to a considerably higher risk, as he will have to answer the claim in the forum chosen by the former. It follows that it is of primary importance that the defendant's interests are protected as much as possible against serious detriment, which is mainly achieved by restricting the possible choice of fora, and by allowing only rather limited exceptions to the general rule according to which consolidation of multistate infringement proceedings can only take place before the courts at defendant's forum.

(iv) Fears of abusive "torpedo" litigation, which is frequently held to be an inevitable consequence of granting any choice of forum in IP infringement cases, are unfounded under the system endorsed in the present draft, which does not attribute a blocking effect to proceedings for declaration of non-infringement which have been commenced before the right-holder raises a claim for substantive remedies relating to the same cause of action.

4.3.3 *Difficulties Facing the Courts*

It may seem odd at first glance to consider the idea that courts might also figure among the "parties" whose interests should be taken into account when discussing the availability of alternative fora in IP infringement proceedings. Nevertheless, one sometimes gets the impression that the arguments used to promote exclusive jurisdiction are to some extent rooted in the fear that granting an additional choice of fora might confront national courts with a task they are unable to deal with, and that they must be protected against the assignment of such an overly ponderous burden.

Indeed it should not be ignored that having to assess claims relating to the infringement of foreign IP rights constitutes a major challenge for the deciding judge, who must be ready to set aside the principles of domestic law he is accustomed to, and place himself in the unfamiliar shoes of someone having been brought up in a different legal system. This is certainly not an easy task, from both an intellectual and a psychological point of view. On the other hand, it has been done for many years in other legal fields, where it is more easily accepted that pursuant to the rules of private international law, judges may have to consider foreign law in their decision-making. And, with all due respect for the complex character of IP law, it is hardly convincing to say that courts may master the intricacies of foreign family or contract law, but that they are helpless when it comes to copyright, patent or trademark law. Of course, obtaining the relevant knowledge will regularly require expert help, and this may lead to consequences that are undesirable in principle, like prolongation of the proceedings and extra costs. However, this is an aspect for the parties – in particular the plaintiff–, rather the court, to worry about (*see supra*).

Although the difficulties regularly arising in decisions involving the application of foreign law thus appear manageable in principle, the problems may be considerably aggravated in situations when courts are faced with the task of adjudicating infringements occurring simultaneously in a multitude of countries, or even on a world-wide scale. As a matter of principle, the deciding judge has to take into account the law and facts in all the countries to which the ruling shall extend. This may already be problematic in an area where IP laws are largely harmonised, like the EU; it is even more demanding in view of countries which do not even have this common background, and it is hardly feasible at all when it comes to decisions having a potentially global impact. If in the latter situation one were compelled to abide by the principle that the legal situation in each country affected by the judgment has to be evaluated in the decision, the legal assessment of such claims would indeed amount to a "mission impossible" for the deciding judge.

The issue addressed in the previous paragraph is one of the many challenges facing international IP law in the age of cyberspace. On the one hand, it is indisputable that it must be possible to claim a total, i.e. actually world-wide ban on dissemination of infringing content, including its being posted on the Internet, and that the hurdles for such a claim to be granted must not be set at a level that is, for all practical purposes, insurmountable On the other hand, granting a claim with world-wide impact without taking into account the legal situation in the countries affected by the decision clashes to some extent with established principles of private international law, and it may also be considered as disrespecting the constitutional confinements of judicial power.

It will primarily be a matter for harmonisation of substantive law as well as for private international law proper (specifically, the rules dealing with choice of law) to devise adequate solutions for this dilemma. However, the present lack of generally accepted schemes for the assessment of IP conflicts with global impact does not furnish a sufficient reason for not allowing consolidation of proceedings. In order to cope with the problems posed by global communication, it is necessary to adopt a combined, dynamic and simultaneous approach, trying to devise compatible solutions on all the levels involved, i.e. substantive law, private international law, and also in matters of jurisdiction.

4.4 *Exclusion of Applicability of General Rules*

In the third sentence of paragraph 3 the application of Art. 10 DHJC, the provision on torts and delicts, is generally excluded with respect to proceedings concerning infringement or declaration of non-infringement of intellectual property rights. This can be viewed as a logical consequence of the structure underlying paragraph 3, with competence being granted exclusively to the courts mentioned in the first and second sentences.

Supplementing the general rule on torts and delicts to be found in a Convention of the DHJC type with a specific provision that has exclusive application in cases of intellectual property infringement allows for a better differentiation with respect to the terminology used as well as the structure of the provision. Concentrating on intellectual property rights makes it possible to replace general notions of tort law like "act" and "omittance" with the more specific term "infringement".[28] Furthermore, while rules concerning torts and delicts usually undertake a fundamental distinction between the place where an act or omittance actually occurs and the place where its results are felt, this distinction is of no, or at least only of secondary,[29] importance for intellectual property law, the essential, primary question always being whether the right exists in the territory in question. For example, even if the distribution of a product in country B definitely infringes the patent held by X in that country, there is no point in raising a claim for infringement on the basis of the *forum delicti commissi* rule before the courts in country A where the product is manufactured, unless X's right is also valid there.

Apart from the consequences with respect to terminology and structure, the promulgation of separate rules for IP infringement proceedings is also of importance because it allows some deviation from the provisions set out in Art. 10 DHJC in certain aspects. One of these was already addressed in the context of the first sentence in paragraph 3; it concerns the possibility to raise a claim for declaration of non-infringement at the *forum delicti commissi*. It is unclear whether this possibility also exists – or whether it should rather be excluded – with respect to tort claims in general, where the positions and the relative strength of the parties involved may not be as evenly balanced as in IP law. Another concern regards consolidation of claims at the victim's – i.e. the rightholder's – forum. Here as well, the considerations on which to base a solution in IP infringement cases differ substantially from tort cases in general, leading to the result that the MPI proposal definitely excludes the

---

[28] On the other hand, this creates the need to define the notion of "infringement", which is done in paragraph 6.

[29] In the present proposal, the distinction is only of certain relevance in the context of paragraph 5, the provision regulating the territorial reach of jurisdiction with respect to e-commerce.

infringed person's habitual residence as a relevant point of attachment for extraterritorial jurisdiction.[30]

5. Paragraph 4 – Reach of Jurisdiction I: General Principle

Text:

> (1) Subject to Paragraph 1, 2nd sentence, courts in the Contracting State where the defendant is habitually resident pursuant to Article 3 have jurisdiction with respect to all infringement claims raised against that defendant. (2) If jurisdiction in infringement proceedings is solely founded on the fact that the right has been registered, is deemed to have been registered or has otherwise acquired protection in the Contracting State, the courts in that Contracting State have jurisdiction only with respect to infringements occurring in that territory, unless regulated otherwise in paragraph 5.

Paragraph 4, 1st sentence contains a restatement of the principle that jurisdiction is not confined to infringements occurring in the forum state if the courts have general jurisdiction, i.e. when the defendant is habitually resident in that state. Although this result is self-evident in view of the structure of the Convention, it is of paramount importance for the understanding of the system underlying Art. 12a that it deserves to be pointed out explicitly.

By contrast to courts having general jurisdiction, a court whose competence is founded solely on the aspect that the right is registered or protected in the forum state is only granted power to exercise jurisdiction with regard to the infringement occurring in the territory of the Contracting State where the deciding court is situated.

This rule appears to comply with the interpretation given by the ECJ to Art. 5.3 in the Brussels Convention (now: Brussels Regulation). As is explained in the contribution in Part One of this volume,[31] the MPI draft does not set that rule aside in order to grant more extended jurisdiction to the courts in the country where the party whose rights have been infringed is habitually resident, as this would amount, for all practical purposes, to granting a favourable position to the holder of IP rights acting as a plaintiff, which cannot be justified by considerations of equity and fairness.[32]

---

[30] A. *Kur*, Part One of this volume, II.4 and *infra*.

[31] A. *Kur*, II.4.

[32] As was revealed during the Frauenchiemsee conference by Andrea *Schulz*, it was already decided during the 2001 Diplomatic conference to delete the last half-sentence in Art. 10.4 DHJC, which, in its original form, privileged the courts in the country where the injured party has its domicile. However, in her words, "during the turbulences of the Diplomatic Conference in June 2001, it was simply forgotten to submit the proposal".

6. *Paragraph 5 – Reach of Jurisdiction II: E-Commerce*

Text:

> If the infringement claim concerns behaviour related to the Internet or similar ubiquitous media, courts in other Contracting States than the Contracting State where the defendant is habitually resident pursuant to Article 3 shall have jurisdiction with respect to infringements occurring in other territories, if
> a) an essential part of the activities which are claimed to have caused the infringement has been carried out by the defendant in the Forum State, and
> b) the activities which are claimed to have caused the infringement are not aimed at the market in the Contracting State where the defendant is habitually resident, and have no substantial commercial effect there.

Paragraph 5 provides for alternative fora with competence to exercise multistate jurisdiction with respect to infringements resulting from unauthorised use of content posted on the Internet. As explained in the contribution in Part One,[33] an exemption from the rule granting general jurisdiction only to the courts in the country of the defendant's habitual residence is needed for infringements occurring in cyberspace, taking into account the fact that persons carrying out their business on the Internet may easily move their seat and even the centre of their activities to countries offering relatively safe havens for IP infringements. It was also explained that the exemption should remain confined to the situation when it is actually needed, i.e. it should not apply to infringements of the traditional kind, which are still the rule e.g. in patent cases.

Paragraph 5 contains two requirements. First, an essential part of the activities which are claimed to have caused the infringement has been carried out by the defendant in the Forum State, and second, the activities which are claimed to have caused the infringement are not aimed at the market in the Contracting State where the defendant is habitually resident, and have no substantial commercial effect there. The background for these requirements has been explained in the contribution in Part One,[34] where it was emphasized in particular that although the second, negative criterion may be controversial and certainly needs further discussion, it was deliberately chosen in order to mark the importance attributed to the protection of defendant's interests in the context of the MPI proposal.

As regards the first, positive requirement, the following remarks may be added to what has been stated before. From a civil law perspective, it is a conspicuous disadvantage of that proviso that it does not offer the degree of clarity which is generally deemed desirable for provisions determining jurisdiction. However, it must be admitted that in the fuzzy world of cyberspace, it is difficult to impossible anyhow to devise solutions that are as clear and straightforward as they used to be in an analogue environment. While it is

---

[33] A. *Kur*, II.3.
[34] A. *Kur*, II.3.

therefore inevitable that concessions must be made to the specific character of the new medium, we should nevertheless attempt to achieve the broadest consensus possible on the meaning of relatively vague and open requirements such as an "essential part" of allegedly infringing activities having to be carried out in the forum state. Pending further discussions, it is proposed here that the requirement should be considered as met if either

(i) the activities causing infringements in the forum state as well as in other states have been carried out in the forum state, and/or if
(ii) activities carried out in the same or another member state have resulted in a substantial number of infringements, or have caused substantial economic harm, in the forum state.

Whether this or another definition should be included in the final text of the provision is also a matter for discussion. In any case, it should be clear that the threshold for an "essential part" of the infringing (multiterritorial) activities to be taking place in a member state is more elevated than the standard set in Art. 6 for the finding of (simple) infringement in order to determine the *locus delicti commissi*.

7. *Paragraph 6 – Place of Infringement*

Text:

(1) For the application of paragraph 4, 2nd sentence, an infringement is held to occur in a Contracting State where the right exists, provided that
the activity or omittance by which the right is claimed to be infringed has commercial effect or, if commercial effect is lacking, a substantial impact in that Contracting State, or
the activity by which the right is claimed to be infringed is intentionally directed towards that Contracting State.
(2) Courts shall deny jurisdiction if the defendant has taken reasonable steps to avoid creating a commercial effect in, or directing activity to, that Contracting State.

7.1 *The Basic Rule*

Pursuant to paragraph 3, 3rd sentence, the MPI proposal has excluded the applicability of the general jurisdiction rule for torts and delicts. It is therefore not possible to rely, for the determination of the *locus delicti commissi*, on traditional notions established in private international law, like the place of the act and the place of result. Instead, the only issue of relevance is whether the activities forming the cause of action have resulted in, or are threatening to result in, an infringement.[35]

As a matter of principle, that assessment is guided and governed by the substantive IP law applying in the forum state (or other states where the

[35] Or, in the case of a claim for declaration of non-infringement, whether the activities undertaken by the plaintiff have *not* resulted, and are not threatening to result, in an infringement.

infringement is claimed to occur). Without, at this stage, entering into a full evaluation of the merits, the court seized will regularly pose the question whether it is plausible that the activities claimed to have been carried out by the defendant have resulted in a violation of national provisions protecting national rights. In this way, national substantive law has at least an indirect impact on jurisdiction issues. From the point of view of national policy, it appears important that the logical sequence reflected therein is not reversed, i.e. that it remains for national substantive law to influence and delimit the notions governing jurisdiction rather than letting decisions ultimately belonging into the sphere of substantive law be pre-empted by determinations regarding competence of courts.[36]

From that point of departure, it would appear advisable for an international jurisdiction convention not to deal with the notion of infringement at all, but to leave the issue to be decided by national substantive law. However, that approach hardly appears feasible, for reasons that, again, mainly concern infringements occurring in cyberspace. First, in that novel area, national law is still in a stage of development, so it is hardly possible to rely on secure and easily retrievable sources in order to decide whether acts carried out on the Internet will be considered as resulting in an infringement occurring in a particular state. Second, and more importantly, there is a strong desire in the IP community to arrive at a set of internationally accepted rules delimiting the fora competent to adjudicate infringements occurring in cyberspace to a foreseeable number, instead of leaving the issue to national law.

Taking into consideration the provisos included in the 1999 DHJC plus supplements added during the 2001 Diplomatic Conference as well as the texts endorsed by *Dreyfuss* and *Ginsburg*, the MPI proposal adopts as a general rule that, as a minimum requirement for an infringement taking place in a particular territory, the conflicting content must have "commercial effect" there, or, absent a demonstrable commercial effect, the measure must be targeted at the territory in question. This approach has already found international consensus in the WIPO Joint Recommendation Concerning Provisions on the Protection of Marks, and Other Industrial Property Rights in Signs, on the Internet (treated in the contributions by Christian *Wichard* and Ansgar *Ohly* in Part One of this volume).

Whereas the Recommendation does not deal with jurisdiction proper, but rather with issues of substantive law, the underlying concept also makes sense with respect to the former. Furthermore, there is no pertinent reason why the approach should not work for patent law and industrial design law as well. In copyright law, however, the situation does not lend itself to an equally straightforward solution, as in contrast to industrial property, copyright infringement may also occur outside the commercial sphere, for instance if the moral rights of an author are severely encroached upon,

---

[36] The same applies, *mutatis mutandis*, to the determination of the applicable law in multinational conflicts.

without any commercial activities being carried out or directed to the relevant territory. In order to ensure that jurisdiction can be established even with a view to infringements of a non-commercial character, it is therefore stipulated in the proposal that a different kind of "substantial impact" in a particular territory will be sufficient to establish jurisdiction under the *forum delicti commissi* rule.

In addition to the rule set out in the first sentence of paragraph 6, the proposal embraces the principle that jurisdiction should be denied if the alleged infringer has taken reasonable measures to avoid creating a commercial effect or directing activities to the member state in question. This principle is reflected in the modifications made in the DHJC text as a result of discussions at the 2001 Diplomatic Conference, and it is also contained in the Dreyfuss/Ginsburg draft. Whether its inclusion in a convention on jurisdiction and enforcement would be a wise step might however be questioned, because its assessment would typically involve a complex and detailed evaluation of the defendant's conduct, which would appear to be a matter for a decision on the merits rather than for the, after all, somewhat summary assessment to be made at a stage when the court asserts jurisdiction. Nevertheless, for practical reasons it is recommended that the rule should be taken into further consideration.

8. *Paragraph 7 – Problems Concerning Initial Copyright Ownership*

Text:

> If, in proceedings involving the existence, validity and/or infringement of an intellectual property right in the territory of another Contracting State than the Forum State,
>
> the question of initial ownership of that right constitutes a decisive issue in the proceedings, and
>
> the legal doctrines applying in the Contracting State where the deciding court is situated and in the Contracting State where the right is claimed to exist and/or to have been infringed diverge with respect to the law governing the issue of initial ownership,
>
> the deciding court shall, upon motion of the defendant, stay the proceedings with respect to the existence and/or infringement of the right in the other Contracting State, unless the plaintiff provides relevant evidence proving, to the satisfaction of the deciding court, that the defendant will not be subject to legal proceedings concerning the same subject-matter initiated by, or on behalf of, another person who, according to the legal doctrine applying in the other Contracting State, may have a valid claim to ownership of the right concerned.

Paragraph 7 is a tentative approach towards solving problems resulting from diversity of national doctrines applying with respect to initial ownership (and assignability) of IP rights. It seems that this problem is acute mainly or even exclusively in copyright. However, absent any adverse effects ensuing for other fields of IP law, the proposed solution does not have to remain confined to that area.

The situation addressed in the proposed paragraph is basically the following. The copyright in a work which has been created in the framework of a contractual relationship between author and producer is infringed in country A, where the "work made for hire" doctrine applies, whereas the defendant is located in country B, where according to the established doctrine, copyright rests with the author. If an infringement suit is initiated by the author in country B, the courts in that country, on the basis of domestic law, may oblige the infringer to pay damages to the copyright owner, i.e. to the author. On the other hand, the defendant might be held liable for the same infringement *vis-à-vis* the producer in a lawsuit filed before the courts in the country where the infringement occurs, as the producer pursuant to the law applying in that country is in a position to claim a copyright of her own. On the basis of the present DHJC text, there is no possibility for the defendant to plead *res iudicata* in such a case.[37]

The picture may be further complicated when one takes into account that there are also different opinions on the question of whether the country-of-origin doctrine applies in the assessment of initial copyright ownership. At first glance, it might seem that the courts in a country where that particular doctrine applies would be able to avoid the problems depicted above. For instance, if in the case just mentioned the infringement courts applied the country-of-origin principle with respect to the issue of initial ownership, the producer would not be in a position to claim a valid right. On the other hand, applying the country-of-origin principle with respect to initial copyright ownership is no guarantee that the problems will disappear, as is demonstrated by the following example: Plaintiff A, a journalist, sues defendant B in state X, B's country of domicile, for copyright infringement taking place in country Z. The work was created in country Y. The courts in X apply the country-of-origin rule when assessing initial copyright ownership. If the rules applying in Y do not recognise the doctrine of works made for hire, A is considered to be the owner of the right which is infringed, and obtains full compensation for losses. On the other hand, A's employer, C, may still sue B for the same infringement in country Z, where the unlawful act has taken place, and C will win if regarded, according to the doctrines applying there, as the true copyright holder.

Before commenting on the rule we propose to insert in the present text in order to deal with these intricacies, it must be pointed out that only very seldom will these matters be of practical relevance. The discrepancies ensuing from the different doctrines applied with respect to initial ownership will hardly ever have repercussions on the position of third parties. This is a consequence, among other things, of the fact that the transfer of rights from the author to the producer, even in countries following a strict author's rights

[37] The constellation depicted above may raise issues of ordre public. This aspect is not pursued any further here.

approach, is regulated by contract, or, in absence of explicit contractual agreements, is effected by virtue of legal presumptions.

Nevertheless, it might be worthwhile to try to anchor in the present text a solution for those (few) cases for which the diversity of copyright doctrines might be of relevance. One possibility might be to promulgate rules on *res iudicata* that are more comprehensive than what is set out in paragraph 3. Another alternative, which was given preference in the present proposal, is to introduce an obligation for the deciding courts in these situations to stay the proceedings until it has been proven to their satisfaction – e.g. by provision of a declaration by (the) other potential copyright holder(s), or, more simply, by procuring the documents by virtue of which copyright was transferred to the plaintiff/producer – that the defendant will not be subject to renewed legal prosecution with respect to the same infringing act.

III. Hague Conference Project

(For more, and more actual, information, please consult the Hague Conference's website at www.hcch.net)

a) Draft Hague Jurisdiction Convention, 1999

Chapter I – Scope of the Convention

Article 1 Substantive scope

1. The Convention applies to civil and commercial matters. It shall not extend in particular to revenue, customs or administrative matters.
2. The Convention does not apply to –
a) the status and legal capacity of natural persons;
b) maintenance obligations;
c) matrimonial property regimes and other rights and obligations arising out of marriage or similar relationships;
d) wills and succession;
e) insolvency, composition or analogous proceedings;
f) social security;
g) arbitration and proceedings related thereto;
h) admiralty or maritime matters.
3. A dispute is not excluded from the scope of the Convention by the mere fact that a government, a governmental agency or any other person acting for the State is a party thereto.
4. Nothing in this Convention affects the privileges and immunities of sovereign States or of entities of sovereign States, or of international organisations.

Article 2 Territorial scope

1. The provisions of Chapter II shall apply in the courts of a Contracting State unless all the parties are habitually resident in that State. However, even if all the parties are habitually resident in that State –
a) Article 4 shall apply if they have agreed that a court or courts of another Contracting State have jurisdiction to determine the dispute;
b) Article 12, regarding exclusive jurisdiction, shall apply;
c) Articles 21 and 22 shall apply where the court is required to determine whether to decline jurisdiction or suspend its proceedings on the grounds that the dispute ought to be determined in the courts of another Contracting State.
2. The provisions of Chapter III apply to the recognition and enforcement in a Contracting State of a judgment rendered in another Contracting State.

Chapter II – Jurisdiction

Article 3 Defendant's forum

1. Subject to the provisions of the Convention, a defendant may be sued in the courts of the State where that defendant is habitually resident.
2. For the purposes of the Convention, an entity or person other than a natural person shall be considered to be habitually resident in the State –
a) where it has its statutory seat,
b) under whose law it was incorporated or formed,
c) where it has its central administration, or
d) where it has its principal place of business.

Article 4 Choice of court

1. If the parties have agreed that a court or courts of a Contracting State shall have jurisdiction to settle any dispute which has arisen or may arise in connection with a particular legal relationship, that court or those courts shall have jurisdiction, and that jurisdiction shall be exclusive unless the parties have agreed otherwise. Where an agreement having exclusive effect designates a court or courts of a non-Contracting State, courts in Contracting States shall decline jurisdiction or suspend proceedings unless the court or courts chosen have themselves declined jurisdiction.
2. An agreement within the meaning of paragraph 1 shall be valid as to form, if it was entered into or confirmed –
a) in writing;
b) by any other means of communication which renders information accessible so as to be usable for subsequent reference;
c) in accordance with a usage which is regularly observed by the parties;
d) in accordance with a usage of which the parties were or ought to have been aware and which is regularly observed by parties to contracts of the same nature in the particular trade or commerce concerned.
3. Agreements conferring jurisdiction and similar clauses in trust instruments shall be without effect if they conflict with the provisions of Article 7, 8 or 12.

...

Article 9 Branches [and regular commercial activity]

A plaintiff may bring an action in the courts of a State in which a branch, agency or any other establishment of the defendant is situated, [or where the defendant has carried on regular commercial activity by other means,] provided that the dispute relates directly to the activity of that branch, agency or establishment [or to that regular commercial activity].

Article 10 Torts or delicts

1. A plaintiff may bring an action in tort or delict in the courts of the State –
a) in which the act or omittance that caused injury occurred, or

b) in which the injury arose, unless the defendant establishes that the person claimed to be responsible could not reasonably have foreseen that the act or omittance could result in an injury of the same nature in that State.
2. Paragraph 1 *b)* shall not apply to injury caused by anti-trust violations, in particular price-fixing or monopolisation, or conspiracy to inflict economic loss.
3. A plaintiff may also bring an action in accordance with paragraph 1 when the act or omittance, or the injury may occur.
4. If an action is brought in the courts of a State only on the basis that the injury arose or may occur there, those courts shall have jurisdiction only in respect of the injury that occurred or may occur in that State, unless the injured person has his or her habitual residence in that State.
...

Article 12 Exclusive jurisdiction

1. In proceedings which have as their object rights *in rem* in immovable property or tenancies of immovable property, the courts of the Contracting State in which the property is situated have exclusive jurisdiction, unless in proceedings which have as their object tenancies of immovable property, the tenant is habitually resident in a different State.
2. In proceedings which have as their object the validity, nullity, or dissolution of a legal person, or the validity or nullity of the decisions of its organs, the courts of a Contracting State whose law governs the legal person have exclusive jurisdiction.
3. In proceedings which have as their object the validity or nullity of entries in public registers, the courts of the Contracting State in which the register is kept have exclusive jurisdiction.
4. In proceedings which have as their object the registration, validity, [or] nullity[, or revocation or infringement,] of patents, trade marks, designs or other similar rights required to be deposited or registered, the courts of the Contracting State in which the deposit or registration has been applied for, has taken place or, under the terms of an international convention, is deemed to have taken place, have exclusive jurisdiction. This shall not apply to copyright or any neighbouring rights, even though registration or deposit of such rights is possible.
[5. In relation to proceedings which have as their object the infringement of patents, the preceding paragraph does not exclude the jurisdiction of any other court under the Convention or under the national law of a Contracting State.]
[6. The previous paragraphs shall not apply when the matters referred to therein arise as incidental questions.]

Article 13 Provisional and protective measures

1. A court having jurisdiction under Articles 3 to 12 to determine the merits of the case has jurisdiction to order any provisional or protective measures.

2. The courts of a State in which property is located have jurisdiction to order any provisional or protective measures in respect of that property.
3. A court of a Contracting State not having jurisdiction under paragraphs 1 or 2 may order provisional or protective measures, provided that –
a) their enforcement is limited to the territory of that State, and
b) their purpose is to protect on an interim basis a claim on the merits which is pending or to be brought by the requesting party.

Article 14 Multiple defendants

1. A plaintiff bringing an action against a defendant in a court of the State in which that defendant is habitually resident may also proceed in that court against other defendants not habitually resident in that State if –
a) the claims against the defendant habitually resident in that State and the other defendants are so closely connected that they should be adjudicated together to avoid a serious risk of inconsistent judgments, and
b) as to each defendant not habitually resident in that State, there is a substantial connection between that State and the dispute involving that defendant.
2. Paragraph 1 shall not apply to a codefendant invoking an exclusive choice of court clause agreed with the plaintiff and conforming with Article 4.

Article 15 Counter-claims

A court which has jurisdiction to determine a claim under the provisions of the Convention shall also have jurisdiction to determine a counter-claim arising out of the transaction or occurrence on which the original claim is based.

. . .

Article 18 Prohibited grounds of jurisdiction

1. Where the defendant is habitually resident in a Contracting State, the application of a rule of jurisdiction provided for under the national law of a Contracting State is prohibited if there is no substantial connection between that State and the dispute.
2. In particular, jurisdiction shall not be exercised by the courts of a Contracting State on the basis solely of one or more of the following –
a) the presence or the seizure in that State of property belonging to the defendant, except where the dispute is directly related to that property;
b) the nationality of the plaintiff;
c) the nationality of the defendant;
d) the domicile, habitual or temporary residence, or presence of the plaintiff in that State;
e) the carrying on of commercial or other activities by the defendant in that State, except where the dispute is directly related to those activities;
f) the service of a writ upon the defendant in that State;
g) the unilateral designation of the forum by the plaintiff;
h) proceedings in that State for declaration of enforceability or registration or

for the enforcement of a judgment, except where the dispute is directly related to such proceedings;
i) the temporary residence or presence of the defendant in that State;
j) the signing in that State of the contract from which the dispute arises.
3. Nothing in this Article shall prevent a court in a Contracting State from exercising jurisdiction under national law in an action [seeking relief] [claiming damages] in respect of conduct which constitutes –

[Variant One:

[*a)* genocide, a crime against humanity or a war crime[, as defined in the Statute of the International Criminal Court]; or]
[*b)* a serious crime against a natural person under international law; or]
[*c)* a grave violation against a natural person of non-derogable fundamental rights established under international law, such as torture, slavery, forced labour and disappeared persons].
[Sub-paragraphs [*b)* and] *c)* above apply only if the party seeking relief is exposed to a risk of a denial of justice because proceedings in another State are not possible or cannot reasonably be required.]

Variant Two:

a serious crime under international law, provided that this State has established its criminal jurisdiction over that crime in accordance with an international treaty to which it is a party and that the claim is for civil compensatory damages for death or serious bodily injury arising from that crime.]

Article 19 Authority of the court seised

Where the defendant does not enter an appearance, the court shall verify whether Article 18 prohibits it from exercising jurisdiction if –
a) national law so requires; or
b) the plaintiff so requests; or
[*c)* the defendant so requests, even after judgment is entered in accordance with procedures established under national law; or]
[*d)* the document which instituted the proceedings or an equivalent document was served on the defendant in another Contracting State.]
or
[*d)* it appears from the documents filed by the plaintiff that the defendant's address is in another Contracting State.]

Article 20

1. The court shall stay the proceedings so long as it is not established that the document which instituted the proceedings or an equivalent document, including the essential elements of the claim, was notified to the defendant in sufficient time and in such a way as to enable him to arrange for his defence, or that all necessary steps have been taken to that effect.

[2. Paragraph 1 shall not affect the use of international instruments concerning the service abroad of judicial and extrajudicial documents in civil or commercial matters, in accordance with the law of the forum.]
[3. Paragraph 1 shall not apply, in case of urgency, to any provisional or protective measures.]

Article 21 *Lis pendens*

1. When the same parties are engaged in proceedings in courts of different Contracting States and when such proceedings are based on the same causes of action, irrespective of the relief sought, the court second seised shall suspend the proceedings if the court first seised has jurisdiction and is expected to render a judgment capable of being recognised under the Convention in the State of the court second seised, unless the latter has exclusive jurisdiction under Article 4 or 12.
2. The court second seised shall decline jurisdiction as soon as it is presented with a judgment rendered by the court first seised that complies with the requirements for recognition or enforcement under the Convention.
3. Upon application of a party, the court second seised may proceed with the case if the plaintiff in the court first seised has failed to take the necessary steps to bring the proceedings to a decision on the merits or if that court has not rendered such a decision within a reasonable time.
4. The provisions of the preceding paragraphs apply to the court second seised even in a case where the jurisdiction of that court is based on the national law of that State in accordance with Article 17.
5. For the purpose of this Article, a court shall be deemed to be seised –
a) when the document instituting the proceedings or an equivalent document is lodged with the court, or
b) if such document has to be served before being lodged with the court, when it is received by the authority responsible for service or served on the defendant.
[As appropriate, universal time is applicable.]
6. If in the action before the court first seised the plaintiff seeks a determination that it has no obligation to the defendant, and if an action seeking substantive relief is brought in the court second seised –
a) the provisions of paragraphs 1 to 5 above shall not apply to the court second seised, and
b) the court first seised shall suspend the proceedings at the request of a party if the court second seised is expected to render a decision capable of being recognised under the Convention.
7. This Article shall not apply if the court first seised, on application by a party, determines that the court second seised is clearly more appropriate to resolve the dispute, under the conditions specified in Article 22.

Article 22 Exceptional circumstances for declining jurisdiction

1. In exceptional circumstances, when the jurisdiction of the court seised is not founded on an exclusive choice of court agreement valid under Article 4, or on Article 7, 8 or 12, the court may, on application by a party, suspend its proceedings if in that case it is clearly inappropriate for that court to exercise jurisdiction and if a court of another State has jurisdiction and is clearly more appropriate to resolve the dispute. Such application must be made no later than at the time of the first defence on the merits.
2. The court shall take into account, in particular –
a) any inconvenience to the parties in view of their habitual residence;
b) the nature and location of the evidence, including documents and witnesses, and the procedures for obtaining such evidence;
c) applicable limitation or prescription periods;
d) the possibility of obtaining recognition and enforcement of any decision on the merits.
3. In deciding whether to suspend the proceedings, a court shall not discriminate on the basis of the nationality or habitual residence of the parties.
4. If the court decides to suspend its proceedings under paragraph 1, it may order the defendant to provide security sufficient to satisfy any decision of the other court on the merits. However, it shall make such an order if the other court has jurisdiction only under Article 17, unless the defendant establishes that sufficient assets exist in the State of that other court or in another State where the court's decision could be enforced.
5. When the court has suspended its proceedings under paragraph 1,
a) it shall decline to exercise jurisdiction if the court of the other State exercises jurisdiction, or if the plaintiff does not bring the proceedings in that State within the time specified by the court, or
b) it shall proceed with the case if the court of the other State decides not to exercise jurisdiction.

Chapter III – Recognition and Enforcement

Article 23 Definition of "judgment"

For the purposes of this Chapter, "judgment" means –
a) any decision given by a court, whatever it may be called, including a decree or order, as well as the determination of costs or expenses by an officer of the court, provided that it relates to a decision which may be recognised or enforced under the Convention;
b) decisions ordering provisional or protective measures in accordance with Article 13, paragraph 1.

Article 24 Judgments excluded from Chapter III

This Chapter shall not apply to judgments based on a ground of jurisdiction provided for by national law in accordance with Article 17.

Article 25 Judgments to be recognised or enforced

1. A judgment based on a ground of jurisdiction provided for in Articles 3 to 13, or which is consistent with any such ground, shall be recognised or enforced under this Chapter.
2. In order to be recognised, a judgment referred to in paragraph 1 must have the effect of res judicata in the State of origin.
3. In order to be enforceable, a judgment referred to in paragraph 1 must be enforceable in the State of origin.
4. However, recognition or enforcement may be postponed if the judgment is the subject of review in the State of origin or if the time limit for seeking a review has not expired.

Article 26 Judgments not to be recognised or enforced

A judgment based on a ground of jurisdiction which conflicts with Articles 4, 5, 7, 8 or 12, or whose application is prohibited by virtue of Article 18, shall not be recognised or enforced.

Article 27 Verification of jurisdiction

1. The court addressed shall verify the jurisdiction of the court of origin.
2. In verifying the jurisdiction of the court of origin, the court addressed shall be bound by the findings of fact on which the court of origin based its jurisdiction, unless the judgment was given by default.
3. Recognition or enforcement of a judgment may not be refused on the ground that the court addressed considers that the court of origin should have declined jurisdiction in accordance with Article 22.

Article 28 Grounds for refusal of recognition or enforcement

1. Recognition or enforcement of a judgment may be refused if—
a) proceedings between the same parties and having the same subject matter are pending before a court of the State addressed, if first seised in accordance with Article 21;
b) the judgment is inconsistent with a judgment rendered, either in the State addressed or in another State, provided that in the latter case the judgment is capable of being recognised or enforced in the State addressed;
c) the judgment results from proceedings incompatible with fundamental principles of procedure of the State addressed, including the right of each party to be heard by an impartial and independent court;
d) the document which instituted the proceedings or an equivalent document, including the essential elements of the claim, was not notified to the defendant in sufficient time and in such a way as to enable him to arrange for his defence;
e) the judgment was obtained by fraud in connection with a matter of procedure;
f) recognition or enforcement would be manifestly incompatible with the public policy of the State addressed.
2. Without prejudice to such review as is necessary for the purpose of

application of the provisions of this Chapter, there shall be no review of the merits of the judgment rendered by the court of origin.

Article 29 Documents to be produced

1. The party seeking recognition or applying for enforcement shall produce –
a) a complete and certified copy of the judgment;
b) if the judgment was rendered by default, the original or a certified copy of a document establishing that the document which instituted the proceedings or an equivalent document was notified to the defaulting party;
c) all documents required to establish that the judgment is *res judicata* in the State of origin or, as the case may be, is enforceable in that State;
d) if the court addressed so requires, a translation of the documents referred to above, made by a person qualified to do so.
2. No legalisation or similar formality may be required.
3. If the terms of the judgment do not permit the court addressed to verify whether the conditions of this Chapter have been complied with, that court may require the production of any other necessary documents.

Article 30 Procedure

The procedure for recognition, declaration of enforceability or registration for enforcement, and the enforcement of the judgment, are governed by the law of the State addressed so far as the Convention does not provide otherwise. The court addressed shall act expeditiously.

Article 31 Costs of proceedings

No security, bond or deposit, however described, to guarantee the payment of costs or expenses shall be required by reason only that the applicant is a national of, or has its habitual residence in, another Contracting State.

Article 32 Legal aid

Natural persons habitually resident in a Contracting State shall be entitled, in proceedings for recognition or enforcement, to legal aid under the same conditions as apply to persons habitually resident in the requested State.

Article 33 Damages

1. In so far as a judgment awards non-compensatory, including exemplary or punitive, damages, it shall be recognised at least to the extent that similar or comparable damages could have been awarded in the State addressed.
2. *a)* Where the debtor, after proceedings in which the creditor has the opportunity to be heard, satisfies the court addressed that in the circumstances, including those existing in the State of origin, grossly excessive damages have been awarded, recognition may be limited to a lesser amount.
b) In no event shall the court addressed recognise the judgment in an amount less than that which could have been awarded in the State addressed in the same circumstances, including those existing in the State of origin.
3. In applying paragraph 1 or 2, the court addressed shall take into account

whether and to what extent the damages awarded by the court of origin serve to cover costs and expenses relating to the proceedings.

Article 34 Severability

If the judgment contains elements which are severable, one or more of them may be separately recognised, declared enforceable, registered for enforcement, or enforced.

...

b) Relevant Articles of the Summary of the Outcome of the Discussion in Commission I of the First Part of the Diplomatic Conference 6-20 June 2001

Interim Text

Article 2 Territorial scope

1. The provisions of Chapter II shall apply in the courts of a Contracting State unless all the parties are habitually resident in that State. However, even if all the parties are habitually resident in that State –
   a) Article 4 shall apply if they have agreed that a court or courts of another Contracting State have jurisdiction to determine the dispute [provided that dispute is of an international character];
   b) Article 12, regarding exclusive jurisdiction, shall apply;
   c) Articles 21 and 22 shall apply where the court is required to determine whether to decline jurisdiction or suspend its proceedings on the grounds that the dispute ought to be determined in the courts of another Contracting State.
2. The provisions of Chapter III apply to the recognition and enforcement in a Contracting State of a judgment rendered in another Contracting State.

Article 12 Exclusive Jurisdiction

[1. In proceedings that have as their object rights in rem in immovable property or tenancies of immovable property, the courts of the Contracting State in which the property is situated have exclusive jurisdiction, unless in proceedings that have as their object tenancies of immovable property [concluded for a maximum period of six months], the tenant is habitually resident in a different State.]

[2. In proceedings that have as their object the validity, nullity, or dissolution of a legal person, or the validity or nullity of the decisions of its organs, the courts of a Contracting State whose law governs the legal person have exclusive jurisdiction.]

3. In proceedings concerning the validity of entries in public registers other than those dealing with intellectual property rights, the courts of the Contracting State in which the register is kept shall have exclusive jurisdiction.

Intellectual property

[Alternative A

4. In proceedings in which the relief sought is a judgment on the grant, registration, validity, abandonment, revocation or infringement of a patent or a mark, the courts of the Contracting State of grant or registration shall have exclusive jurisdiction.
5. In proceedings in which the relief sought is a judgment on the validity, abandonment, or infringement of an unregistered mark [or design], the courts of the Contracting State in which rights in the mark [or design] arose shall have exclusive jurisdiction.]

[Alternative B

5A. In relation to proceedings that have as their object the infringement of patents, trademarks, designs or other similar rights, the courts of the Contracting State referred to in the preceding paragraph [or in the provisions of Articles [3 to 16]] have jurisdiction.]

Alternatives A and B

[6. Paragraphs 4 and 5 shall not apply where one of the above matters arises as an incidental question in proceedings before a court not having exclusive jurisdiction under those paragraphs. However, the ruling in that matter shall have no binding effect in subsequent proceedings, even if they are between the same parties. A matter arises as an incidental question if the court is not requested to give a judgment on that matter, even if a ruling on it is necessary in arriving at a decision.]

7. [In this Article, other registered industrial property rights [(but not copyright or neighbouring rights, even when registration or deposit is possible)] shall be treated in the same way as patents and marks]

[8. For the purpose of this Article, 'court' shall include a Patent Office or similar agency.]

Article 21 Lis pendens

1. When the same parties are engaged in proceedings in courts of different Contracting States and when such proceedings are based on the same causes of action, irrespective of the relief sought, the court second seized shall suspend the proceedings if the court first seized has jurisdiction under Articles [white list] [or under a rule of national law which is consistent with these articles] and is expected to render a judgment capable of being recognised under the Convention in the State of the court second seized, unless the latter has exclusive jurisdiction under Article 4 [, 11] or 12.
2. The court second seized shall decline jurisdiction as soon as it is presented with a judgment rendered by the court first seized that complies with the requirements for recognition or enforcement under the Convention.
3. Upon application of a party, the court second seized may proceed with the case if the plaintiff in the court first seized has failed to take the

necessary steps to bring the proceedings to a decision on the merits or if that court has not rendered such a decision within a reasonable time.

4. The provisions of the preceding paragraphs apply to the court second seized even in a case where the jurisdiction of that court is based on the national law of that State in accordance with Article 17.
5. For the purpose of this Article, a court shall be deemed to be seized –
   a) when the document instituting the proceedings or an equivalent document is lodged with the court; or
   b) if such document has to be served before being lodged with the court, when it is received by the authority responsible for service or served on the defendant.

[As appropriate, universal time is applicable.]

6. If in the action before the court first seized the plaintiff seeks a determination that it has no obligation to the defendant, and if an action seeking substantive relief is brought in the court second seized –
   a) the provisions of paragraphs 1 to 5 above shall not apply to the court second seized; and
   b) the court first seized shall suspend the proceedings at the request of a party if the court second seized is expected to render a decision capable of being recognised under the Convention.
7. This Article shall not apply if the court first seized, on application by a party, determines that the court second seized is clearly more appropriate to resolve the dispute, under the conditions specified in Article 22.

Article 22 Exceptional circumstances for declining jurisdiction

1. In exceptional circumstances, when the jurisdiction of the court seized is not founded on an exclusive choice of court agreement valid under Article 4, or on Article 7, 8 or 12, the court may, on application by a party, suspend its proceedings if in that case it is clearly inappropriate for that court to exercise jurisdiction and if a court of another State has jurisdiction and is clearly more appropriate to resolve the dispute. Such application must be made no later than at the time of the first defence on the merits.
2. The court shall take into account, in particular –
   a) any inconvenience to the parties in view of their habitual residence;
   b) the nature and location of the evidence, including documents and witnesses, and the procedures for obtaining such evidence;
   c) applicable limitation or prescription periods;
   d) the possibility of obtaining recognition and enforcement of any decision on the merits.
3. In deciding whether to suspend the proceedings, a court shall not discriminate on the basis of the nationality or habitual residence of the parties.
4. If the court decides to suspend its proceedings under paragraph 1, it may order the defendant to provide security sufficient to satisfy any decision

of the other court on the merits. However, it shall make such an order if the other court has jurisdiction only under Article 17, or if it is in a non-Contracting State, unless the defendant establishes that [the plaintiff's ability to enforce the judgment will not be materially prejudiced if such an order is not made] [sufficient assets exist in the State of that other court or in another State where the court's decision could be enforced].

5. When the court has suspended its proceedings under paragraph 1,
   a) it shall decline to exercise jurisdiction if the court of the other State exercises jurisdiction, or if the plaintiff does not bring the proceedings in that State within the time specified by the court; or
   b) it shall proceed with the case if the court of the other State decides not to exercise jurisdiction.
6. This Article shall not apply where the court has jurisdiction only under Article 17 [which is not consistent with Articles [white list]]. In such a case, national law shall govern the question of declining jurisdiction.

[7. The court seized and having jurisdiction under Articles 3 to 15 shall not apply the doctrine of forum non conveniens or any similar rule for declining jurisdiction.]

IV. WIPO Joint Recommendation Concerning Provisions on the Protection of Marks, and Other Industrial Property Rights in Signs, on the Internet

PART I – GENERAL

Article 1 – Abbreviated Expressions

For the purposes of these Provisions, unless expressly stated otherwise:

(i) "Member State" means a State member of the Paris Union for the Protection of Industrial Property, of the World Intellectual Property Organization, or of both;
(ii) "Right" means an industrial property right in a sign under the applicable law, whether registered or unregistered;
(iii) "Act of unfair competition" means any act of competition contrary to honest business practices in industrial or commercial matters as defined in Article 10*bis* of the Paris Convention for the Protection of Industrial Property, signed in Paris on March 20, 1883, as revised and amended;
(iv) "Competent authority" means an administrative, judicial or quasi-judicial authority of a Member State which is competent for determining whether a right has been acquired, maintained or infringed, for determining remedies, or for determining whether an act of competition constitutes an act of unfair competition, as the case may be;
(v) "Remedies" means the remedies which a competent authority of a Member State can impose under the applicable law, as a result of an action for the infringement of a right or an act of unfair competition;
(vi) "Internet" refers to an interactive medium for communication which contains information that is simultaneously and immediately accessible irrespective of territorial location to members of the public from a place and at a time individually chosen by them;
(vii) except where the context indicates otherwise, words in the singular include the plural, and *vice versa*, and masculine personal pronouns include the feminine.

PART II – USE OF A SIGN ON THE INTERNET

Article 2 – Use of a Sign on the Internet in a Member State

Use of a sign on the Internet shall constitute use in a Member State for the purposes of these provisions, only if the use has a commercial effect in that Member State as described in Article 3.

Article 3 – Factors for Determining Commercial Effect in a Member State

(1) [*Factors*] In determining whether use of a sign on the Internet has a commercial effect in a Member State, the competent authority shall take into

account all relevant circumstances. Circumstances that may be relevant include, but are not limited to:

(a) circumstances indicating that the user of the sign is doing, or has undertaken significant plans to do, business in the Member State in relation to goods or services which are identical or similar to those for which the sign is used on the Internet.

(b) the level and character of commercial activity of the user in relation to the Member State, including:

(i) whether the user is actually serving customers located in the Member State or has entered into other commercially motivated relationships with persons located in the Member State;

(ii) whether the user has stated, in conjunction with the use of the sign on the Internet, that he does not intend to deliver the goods or services offered to customers located in the Member State and whether he adheres to his stated intent;

(iii) whether the user offers post-sales activities in the Member State, such as warranty or service;

(iv) whether the user undertakes further commercial activities in the Member State which are related to the use of the sign on the Internet but which are not carried out over the Internet.

(c) the connection of an offer of goods or services on the Internet with the Member State, including:

(i) whether the goods or services offered can be lawfully delivered in the Member State;

(ii) whether the prices are indicated in the official currency of the Member State.

(d) the connection of the manner of use of the sign on the Internet with the Member State, including:

(i) whether the sign is used in conjunction with means of interactive contact which are accessible to Internet users in the Member State;

(ii) whether the user has indicated, in conjunction with the use of the sign, an address, telephone number or other means of contact in the Member State;

(iii) whether the sign is used in connection with a domain name which is registered under the ISO Standard country code 3166 Top Level Domain referring to the Member State;

(iv) whether the text used in conjunction with the use of the sign is in a language predominantly used in the Member State;

(v) whether the sign is used in conjunction with an Internet location which has actually been visited by Internet users located in the Member State.

(e) the relation of the use of the sign on the Internet with a right in that sign in the Member State, including:

(i) whether the use is supported by that right;
(ii) whether, where the right belongs to another, the use would take unfair advantage of, or unjustifiably impair, the distinctive character or the reputation of the sign that is the subject of that right.

(2) [*Relevance of Factors*] The above factors, which are guidelines to assist the competent authority to determine whether the use of a sign has produced a commercial effect in a Member State, are not pre-conditions for reaching that determination. Rather, the determination in each case will depend upon the particular circumstances of that case. In some cases all of the factors may be relevant. In other cases some of the factors may be relevant. In still other cases none of the factors may be relevant, and the decision may be based on additional factors that are not listed in paragraph (1), above. Such additional factors may be relevant, alone, or in combination with one or more of the factors listed in paragraph (1), above.

Article 4 – Bad Faith

(1) [*Bad Faith*] For the purposes of applying these provisions, any relevant circumstance shall be considered in determining whether a sign was used in bad faith, or whether a right was acquired in bad faith.
(2) [*Factors*] In particular, the competent authority shall take into consideration, *inter alia*:
(i) whether the person who used the sign or acquired the right in the sign had knowledge of a right in an identical or similar sign belonging to another, or could not have reasonably been unaware of that right, at the time when the person first used the sign, acquired the right or filed an application for acquisition of the right, whichever is earlier, and
(ii) whether the use of the sign would take unfair advantage of, or unjustifiably impair, the distinctive character or the reputation of the sign that is the subject of the other right.

PART III – ACQUISITION AND MAINTENANCE OF RIGHTS IN SIGNS

Article 5 – Use of a Sign on the Internet and Acquisition and Maintenance of Rights

Use of a sign on the Internet in a Member State, including forms of use that are made possible by technological advances, shall in every case be taken into consideration for determining whether the requirements under the applicable law of the Member State for acquiring or maintaining a right in the sign have been met.

PART IV – INFRINGEMENT AND LIABILITY

Article 6 – Use of a Sign on the Internet, Infringement of Rights and Acts of Unfair CompetitionUse of a sign on the Internet, including forms of use that are made possible by technological advances, shall be taken into consideration for determining whether a right under the applicable law of a Member State has been infringed, or whether the use amounts to an act of unfair competition under the law of that Member State, only if that use constitutes use of the sign on the Internet in that Member State.

Article 7 – Liability for Infringement and Acts of Unfair Competition Under the Applicable Law

Except where otherwise provided for in these provisions, there shall be liability in a Member State under the applicable law when a right is infringed, or an act of unfair competition is committed, through use of a sign on the Internet in that Member State.

Article 8 – Exceptions and Limitations Under the Applicable Law

A Member State shall apply the exceptions to liability, and the limitations to the scope of rights, existing under the applicable law when applying these provisions to the use of a sign on the Internet in that Member State.

PART V – NOTICE AND AVOIDANCE OF CONflICT

Article 9 – Use Prior to Notification of Infringement

If the use of a sign on the Internet in a Member State is alleged to infringe a right in that Member State, the user of that sign shall not be held liable for such infringement prior to receiving a notification of infringement, if:

(i) the user owns a right in the sign in another Member State or uses the sign with the consent of the owner of such a right, or is permitted to use the sign, in the manner in which it is being used on the Internet, under the law of another Member State to which the user has a close connection;
(ii) any acquisition of a right in the sign, and any use of the sign, has not been in bad faith; and
(iii) the user has provided, in conjunction with the use of the sign on the Internet, information reasonably sufficient to contact him by mail, e-mail or telefacsimile.

Article 10 – Use After Notification of Infringement

If the user referred to in Article 9 has received a notification that his use infringes another right, he shall not be held liable if he

(i) indicates to the person sending the notification that he owns a right in the sign in another Member State, or uses the sign with the consent of the owner of such a right, or that he is permitted to use the sign, in the manner in which it is being used on the Internet, under the law of another Member State to which he has a close connection;
(ii) gives relevant details of that right or permitted use; and

(iii) expeditiously takes reasonable measures which are effective to avoid a commercial effect in the Member State referred to in the notification, or to avoid infringement of the right referred to in the notification.

Article 11 – Notification Under Articles 9 and 10

The notification under Articles 9 and 10 shall be effective if it is sent by the owner of a right or his representative, by mail, e-mail or telefacsimile, and indicates, in the language, or in one of the languages, used in conjunction with the use of the sign on the Internet, the following:

(i) the right which is alleged to be infringed;
(ii) the identity of the owner of that right and information reasonably sufficient to contact him or his representative by mail, e-mail or telefacsimile;
(iii) the Member State in which that right is protected;
(iv) relevant details of such protection allowing the user to assess the existence, nature and scope of that right; and
(v) the use that is claimed to infringe that right.

Article 12 – Disclaimer as a Measure Under Article 10

Member States shall accept, *inter alia*, a disclaimer, by a user referred to in Article 9, as a reasonable and effective measure under Article 10, if:

(i) the disclaimer includes a clear and unambiguous statement in conjunction with the use of the sign, to the effect that the user has no relationship with the owner of the right which is alleged to be infringed, and does not intend to deliver the goods or services offered to customers located in a particular Member State where the right is protected;
(ii) the disclaimer is written in the language or in the languages used in conjunction with the use of the sign on the Internet;
(iii) the user inquires, before the delivery of the goods or services, whether customers are located in the Member State referred to in item (i); and
(iv) the user in fact refuses delivery to customers who have indicated that they are located in that Member State.

PART VI – REMEDIES

Article 13 – Remedy Proportionate to Commercial Effect

(1) The remedies provided for the infringement of rights or for acts of unfair competition in a Member State, through use of a sign on the Internet in that Member State, shall be proportionate to the commercial effect of the use in that Member State.
(2) The competent authority shall balance the interests, rights and circumstances involved.
(3) The user of the sign shall, upon request, be given the opportunity to propose an effective remedy for consideration by the competent authority, prior to a decision on the merits of the case.

Article 14 – Limitations of Use of a Sign on the Internet

(1) In determining remedies, the competent authority shall take into account limitations of use by imposing reasonable measures designed:

(i) to avoid a commercial effect in the Member State, or
(ii) to avoid infringement of the right or to avoid the act of unfair competition.

(2) The measures referred to in paragraph (1) may include, *inter alia*:

(a) a clear and unambiguous statement in conjunction with the use of the sign on the Internet, to the effect that the user has no relationship with the owner of the infringed right or the person affected by the act of unfair competition, written in the language or in the languages used in conjunction with the use of the sign on the Internet, and any other language indicated by the competent authority;
(b) a clear and unambiguous statement in conjunction with the use of the sign on the Internet to the effect that the user does not intend to deliver the goods or services offered to customers located in a particular Member State, written in the language or in the languages used in conjunction with the use of the sign on the Internet, and any other language indicated by the competent authority;
(c) an obligation to inquire, before the delivery of the goods or services, whether customers are located in that Member State, and to refuse delivery to customers who have indicated that they are located in that Member State;
(d) gateway web pages.

Article 15 – Limitation on Prohibition to Use a Sign on the Internet

(1) Where the use of a sign on the Internet in a Member State infringes a right, or amounts to an act of unfair competition, under the laws of that Member State, the competent authority of the Member State should avoid, wherever possible, imposing a remedy that would have the effect of prohibiting any future use of the sign on the Internet.
(2) The competent authority shall not, in any case, impose a remedy that would prohibit future use of the sign on the Internet, where

(i) the user owns a right in the sign in another Member State, uses the sign with the consent of the owner of such a right, or is permitted to use the sign, in the manner in which it is being used on the Internet, under the law of another Member State to which the user has a close connection; and
(ii) any acquisition of a right in the sign, and any use of the sign, has not been in bad faith.

V. The Proposed Rome II Regulation

Proposal for a Regulation of the European Parliament and the Council on the law applicable to non-contractual obligations ("ROME II")
/* COM/2003/0427 final – COD 2003/0168 */

Chapter I – Scope

Article 1 – Material scope

1. This Regulation shall apply, in situations involving a conflict of laws, to non-contractual obligations in civil and commercial matters. It shall not apply to revenue, customs or administrative matters.
2. The following are excluded from the scope of this Regulation:

a) non-contractual obligations arising out of family relationships and relationships deemed to be equivalent, including maintenance obligations;
b) non-contractual obligations arising out of matrimonial property regimes and successions;
c) obligations arising under bills of exchange, cheques and promissory notes and other negotiable instruments to the extent that the obligations under such other negotiable instruments arise out of their negotiable character;
d) the personal legal liability of officers and members as such for the debts of a company or firm or other body corporate or incorporate, and the personal legal liability of persons responsible for carrying out the statutory audits of accounting documents;
e) non-contractual obligations among the settlers, trustees and beneficiaries of a trust;
f) non-contractual obligations arising out of nuclear damage.

3. For the purposes of this Regulation, "Member State" means any Member State other than [the United Kingdom, Ireland or] Denmark.

Article 2 – Universal application

Any law specified by this Regulation shall be applied whether or not it is the law of a Member State.

Chapter II – Uniform rules

Section 1 Rules applicable to non-contractual obligations arising out of a tort or delict

Article 3 – General rule

1. The law applicable to a non-contractual obligation shall be the law of the country in which the damage arises or is likely to arise, irrespective of the country in which the event giving rise to the damage occurred and irrespective of the country or countries in which the indirect consequences of that event arise.

2. However, where the person claimed to be liable and the person sustaining damage both have their habitual residence in the same country when the damage occurs, the non-contractual obligation shall be governed by the law of that country.
3. Notwithstanding paragraphs 1 and 2, where it is clear from all the circumstances of the case that the non-contractual obligation is manifestly more closely connected with another country, the law of that other country shall apply. A manifestly closer connection with another country may be based in particular on a pre-existing relationship between the parties, such as a contract that is closely connected with the non-contractual obligation in question.

Article 4 – Product liability

Without prejudice to Article 3(2) and (3), the law applicable to a non-contractual obligation arising out of damage or a risk of damage caused by a defective product shall be that of the country in which the person sustaining the damage is habitually resident, unless the person claimed to be liable can show that the product was marketed in that country without his consent, in which case the applicable law shall be that of the country in which the person claimed to be liable is habitually resident.

Article 5 – Unfair competition

1. The law applicable to a non-contractual obligation arising out of an act of unfair competition shall be the law of the country where competitive relations or the collective interests of consumers are or are likely to be directly and substantially affected.
2. Where an act of unfair competition affects exclusively the interests of a specific competitor, Article 3(2) and (3) shall apply.

Article 6 – Violations of privacy and rights relating to the personality

1. The law applicable to a non-contractual obligation arising out of a violation of privacy or rights relating to the personality shall be the law of the forum where the application of the law designated by Article 3 would be contrary to the fundamental principles of the forum as regards freedom of expression and information.
2. The law applicable to the right of reply or equivalent measures shall be the law of the country in which the broadcaster or publisher has its habitual residence.

Article 7 – Violation of the environment

The law applicable to a non-contractual obligation arising out of a violation of the environment shall be the law determined by the application of Article 3(1), unless the person sustaining damage prefers to base his claim on the law of the country in which the event giving rise to the damage occurred.

Article 8 – Infringement of intellectual property rights

1. The law applicable to a non-contractual obligation arising from an infringement of a intellectual property right shall be the law of the country for which protection is sought.
2. In the case of a non-contractual obligation arising from an infringement of a unitary Community industrial property right, the relevant Community instrument shall apply. For any question that is not governed by that instrument, the applicable law shall be the law of the Member State in which the act of infringement is committed.
Section 2 Rules applicable to non-contractual obligations arising out of an act other than a tort or delict

Article 9 – Determination of the applicable law

1. If a non-contractual obligation arising out of an act other than a tort or delict concerns a relationship previously existing between the parties, such as a contract closely connected with the non-contractual obligation, it shall be governed by the law that governs that relationship.
2. Without prejudice to paragraph 1, where the parties have their habitual residence in the same country when the event giving rise to the damage occurs, the law applicable to the non-contractual obligation shall be the law of that country.
3. Without prejudice to paragraphs 1 and 2, a non-contractual obligation arising out of unjust enrichment shall be governed by the law of the country in which the enrichment takes place.
4. Without prejudice to paragraphs 1 and 2, the law applicable to a non-contractual obligation arising out of actions performed without due authority in connection with the affairs of another person shall be the law of the country in which the beneficiary has his habitual residence at the time of the unauthorised action. However, where a non-contractual obligation arising out of actions performed without due authority in connection with the affairs of another person relates to the physical protection of a person or of specific tangible property, the law applicable shall be the law of the country in which the beneficiary or property was situated at the time of the unauthorised action.
5. Notwithstanding paragraphs 1, 2, 3 and 4, where it is clear from all the circumstances of the case that the non-contractual obligation is manifestly more closely connected with another country, the law of that other country shall apply.
6. Nowithstanding the present Article, all non-contractual obligations in the field of intellectual property shall be governed by Article 8.

Section 3 Common rules applicable to non-contractual obligations arising out of a tort or delict and out of an act other than a tort or delict

Article 10 – Freedom of choice

1. The parties may agree, by an agreement entered into after their dispute arose, to submit non-contractual obligations other than the obligations to

which Article 8 applies to the law of their choice. The choice must be expressed or demonstrated with reasonable certainty by the circumstances of the case. It may not affect the rights of third parties.
2. If all the other elements of the situation at the time when the loss is sustained are located in a country other than the country whose law has been chosen, the choice of the parties shall be without prejudice to the application of rules of the law of that country which cannot be derogated from by contract.
3. The parties' choice of the applicable law shall not debar the application of provisions of Community law where the other elements of the situation were located in one of the Member States of the European Community at the time when the loss was sustained.

Article 11 – Scope of the law applicable to non-contractual obligations

The law applicable to non-contractual obligations under Articles 3 to 10 of this Regulation shall govern in particular:

a) the conditions and extent of liability, including the determination of persons who are liable for acts performed by them;
b) the grounds for exemption from liability, any limitation of liability and any division of liability;
c) the existence and kinds of injury or damage for which compensation may be due;
d) within the limits of its powers, the measures which a court has power to take under its procedural law to prevent or terminate injury or damage or to ensure the provision of compensation;
e) the assessment of the damage in so far as prescribed by law;
f) the question whether a right to compensation may be assigned or inherited;
g) persons entitled to compensation for damage sustained personally;
h) liability for the acts of another person;
i) the manners in which an obligation may be extinguished and rules of prescription and limitation, including rules relating to the commencement of a period of prescription or limitation and the interruption and suspension of the period.

Article 12 – Overriding mandatory rules

1. Where the law of a specific third country is applicable by virtue of this Regulation, effect may be given to the mandatory rules of another country with which the situation is closely connected, if and in so far as, under the law of the latter country, those rules must be applied whatever the law applicable to the non-contractual obligation. In considering whether to give effect to these mandatory rules, regard shall be had to their nature and purpose and to the consequences of their application or non-application.
2. Nothing in this Regulation shall restrict the application of the rules of the law of the forum in a situation where they are mandatory irrespective of the law otherwise applicable to the non-contractual obligation.

Article 13 – Rules of safety and conduct
Whatever may be the applicable law, in determining liability account shall be taken of the rules of safety and conduct which were in force at the place and time of the event giving rise to the damage.
Article 14 – Direct action against the insurer of the person liable
The right of persons who have suffered damage to take direct action against the insurer of the person claimed to be liable shall be governed by the law applicable to the non-contractual obligation unless the person who has suffered damage prefers to base his claims on the law applicable to the insurance contract.

Article 15 – Subrogation and multiple liability

1. Where a person ("the creditor") has a non-contractual claim upon another ("the debtor"), and a third person has a duty to satisfy the creditor, or has in fact satisfied the creditor in discharge of that duty, the law which governs the third person's duty to satisfy the creditor shall determine whether the third person is entitled to exercise against the debtor the rights which the creditor had against the debtor under the law governing their relationship in whole or in part.
2. The same rule shall apply where several persons are subject to the same claim and one of them has satisfied the creditor.
Article 16 – Formal validity
A unilateral act intended to have legal effect and relating to a non-contractual obligation is formally valid if it satisfies the formal requirements of the law which governs the non-contractual obligation in question or the law of the country in which this act is done.

Article 17 – Burden of proof

1. The law governing a non-contractual obligation under this Regulation applies to the extent that, in matters of non-contractual obligations, it contains rules which raise presumptions of law or determine the burden of proof.
2. Acts intended to have legal effect may be proved by any mode of proof recognised by the law of the forum or by any of the laws referred to in Article 16 under which that act is formally valid, provided that such mode of proof can be administered by the forum.

Chapter III – Other provisions

Article 18 – Assimilation to the territory of a State

For the purposes of this Regulation, the following shall be treated as being the territory of a State:
a) installations and other facilities for the exploration and exploitation of natural resources in, on or below the part of the seabed situated outside the State' s territorial waters if the State, under international law, enjoys sovereign rights to explore and exploit natural resources there;

b) a ship on the high seas which is registered in the State or bears lettres de mer or a comparable document issued by it or on its behalf, or which, not being registered or bearing lettres de mer or a comparable document, is owned by a national of the State;
c) an aircraft in the airspace, which is registered in or on behalf of the State or entered in its register of nationality, or which, not being registered or entered in the register of nationality, is owned by a national of the State.

Article 19 – Assimilation to habitual residence

1. For companies or firms and other bodies or incorporate or unincorporate, the principal establishment shall be considered to be the habitual residence. However, where the event giving rise to the damage occurs or the damage arises in the course of operation of a subsidiary, a branch or any other establishment, the establishment shall take the place of the habitual residence.
2. Where the event giving rise to the damage occurs or the damage arises in the course of the business activity of a natural person, that natural person's establishment shall take the place of the habitual residence.
3. For the purpose of Article 6 (2), the place where the broadcaster is established within the meaning of the directive 89/552/EEC, as amended by the directive 97/36/EC, shall take the place of the habitual residence.

Article 20 – Exclusion of renvoi

The application of the law of any country specified by this Regulation means the application of the rules of law in force in that country other than its rules of private international law.

Article 21 – States with more than one legal system

1. Where a State comprises several territorial units, each of which has its own rules of law in respect of non-contractual obligations, each territorial unit shall be considered as a country for the purposes of identifying the law applicable under this Regulation.
2. A State within which different territorial units have their own rules of law in respect of non-contractual obligations shall not be bound to apply this Regulation to conflicts solely between the laws of such units.

Article 22 – Public policy of the forum

The application of a rule of the law of any country specified by this Regulation may be refused only if such application is manifestly incompatible with the public policy ("ordre public") of the forum.

Article 23 – Relationship with other provisions of Community law

1. This Regulation shall not prejudice the application of provisions contained in the Treaties establishing the European Communities or in acts of the institutions of the European Communities which:

– in relation to particular matters, lay down choice-of-law rules relating to non-contractual obligations; or

– lay down rules which apply irrespective of the national law governing the non-contractual obligation in question by virtue of this Regulation; or
– prevent application of a provision or provisions of the law of the forum or of the law designated by this Regulation.
2. This regulation shall not prejudice the application of Community instruments which, in relation to particular matters and in areas coordinated by such instruments, subject the supply of services or goods to the laws of the Member State where the service-provider is established and, in the area coordinated, allow restrictions on freedom to provide services or goods originating in another Member State only in limited circumstances.

Article 24 – Non-compensatory damages

The application of a provision of the law designated by this Regulation which has the effect of causing non-compensatory damages, such as exemplary or punitive damages, to be awarded shall be contrary to Community public policy.

Article 25 – Relationship with existing international conventions

This Regulation shall not prejudice the application of international conventions to which the Member States are parties when this Regulation is adopted and which, in relation to particular matters, lay down conflict-of-law rules relating to non-contractual obligations.

Chapter IV – Final provisions

Article 26 – List of conventions referred to in Article 25

1. The Member States shall notify the Commission, no later than 30 June 2004, of the list of conventions referred to in Article 25. After that date, the Member States shall notify the Commission of all denunciations of such conventions.
2. The Commission shall publish the list of conventions referred to in paragraph 1 in the Official Journal of the European Union within six months of receiving the full list.

Article 27 – Entry into force and application in time

This Regulation shall enter into force on 1 January 2005. It shall apply to non-contractual obligations arising out of acts occurring after its entry into force. This Regulation shall be binding in its entirety and directly applicable in all Member States in accordance with the Treaty establishing the European Community.
Done at Brussels, [...].
For the European Parliament For the Council
The President

VI. The Proposed Community Patent Judiciary

Proposal for a Council Decision establishing the Community Patent Court and concerning appeals before the Court of First Instance
/* COM/2003/0828 final – CNS 2003/0324 */
THE COUNCIL OF THE EUROPEAN UNION,
Having regard to the Treaty establishing the European Community, and in particular Articles 225a, 245 thereof,
Having regard to the proposal from the Commission [1],
[1] OJ C
Having regard to the opinion of the European Parliament [2],
[2] OJ C
Having regard to the opinion of the Court of Justice [3],
[3] OJ C
Having regard to the opinion of the European Economic and Social Committee [4],
[4] OJ C
Whereas:
(1) The European Council held in Lisbon in March 2000 called for the necessary steps to increase the competitiveness of the Union in a modern, knowledge-based economy underlining the importance of effective Community-wide patent protection.
(2) The system of patent protection has been characterised by patents granted either by a national patent office in a Member State or by the European Patent Office with effect in a Member State and by enforcement of those patents before the national courts of the Member State concerned.
(3) Innovative European industry relies on effective Community-wide legal protection for its inventions. The creation of a Community patent system comprising a unitary Community patent title and the possibility of enforcing such a right before a Community jurisdiction to be established at the latest by 2010 after a transitional period in which national courts retain competence will provide the missing elements completing the system of patent protection in the Union.
(4) Council Regulation (EC) No .../2003 [5] creates a Community patent title. Holders of such a title will enjoy Community wide protection of an invention according to the uniform standards of the regulation.
[5] OJ L
(5) By Decision 2003/.../EC [6], the Council confers jurisdiction on the Court of Justice in certain disputes relating to the Community patent, recommending those provisions to the Member States for adoption in accordance with their respective constitutional requirements.
[6] OJ L
(6) The second paragraph of Article 220 of the Treaty provides that judicial

panels may be attached to the Court of First Instance under the conditions laid down in Article 225a thereof, in order to exercise, in certain specific areas, the judicial competence laid down in the Treaty.
(7) The jurisdiction conferred on the Court of Justice under Article 229a of the Treaty in disputes relating to the Community patent should be exercised at first instance by a judicial panel established on the basis of Article 225a of the Treaty, to be called "Community Patent Court".
(8) Article 225(2) of the Treaty provides that the Court of First Instance has jurisdiction to hear and determine actions and proceedings brought against decisions of the judicial panels set up under Article 225a of the EC Treaty. For this purpose a specialised patent appeal chamber should be created within the Court of First Instance to hear appeals against decisions of the Community Patent Court. Decisions made by the Court of First Instance on appeal against decisions of the Community Patent Court are according to Article 225(2) of the Treaty, exceptionally, subject to review by the Court of Justice where there is a serious risk to the unity or consistency of Community law.
(9) In order to take account of the special nature of private-party Community patent litigation and to ensure a uniform procedure at both instances, amendments to the procedural rules contained in the Protocol on the Statute of the Court of Justice are necessary, both for the procedure at first instance before the Community Patent Court and on appeal before the Court of First Instance.
(10) A centralised and specialised Community court system, holding exclusive jurisdiction for Community patent disputes and composed of a first-instance Community Patent Court and an appeal chamber within the Court of First Instance, should ensure expertise and decisions of the highest quality. It should guarantee efficient patent proceedings for the whole Community, the establishment of a common body of case-law and the uniform application of Community patent law,
HAS DECIDED AS FOLLOWS:

Chapter I

Community Patent Court

Article 1
Establishment
A judicial panel, to be called "Community Patent Court ", shall be attached to the Court of First Instance of the European Communities.
Its seat shall be at the Court of First Instance.

Article 2
Application of Treaty provisions
Save as hereinafter provided for in this Chapter, Articles 241, 243, 244 and 256 of the Treaty shall apply to the Community Patent Court.

Article 3

Statute provisions for judicial panels
The following Title VI is added to the Protocol on the Statute of the Court of Justice:

"Title VI

Judicial Panels

Article 65
The provisions relating to the jurisdiction, the composition, and the organisation of judicial panels established under Article 225a of the Treaty, and the procedure before them, shall be as laid down in the annexes to this Statute."

Article 4

Annex to the Protocol on the Statute of the Court of Justice
The following Annex [II] is added to the Protocol on the Statute of the Court of Justice"

Annex [II]

Community Patent Court

Article 1
The Community Patent Court shall have, at first instance, exclusive jurisdiction in disputes relating to the application of Council Regulation (EC) No.../... [of... on the Community patent] and Council Regulation (EC) No .../... [of... on the Community supplementary protection certificate] to the extent that jurisdiction is conferred on the Court of Justice pursuant to Article 229a of the EC Treaty.

Article 2

The Community Patent Court shall consist of seven Judges, who shall be appointed for a period of six years. The membership shall be partially renewed every three years, replacing four and three members alternately. Retiring members shall be eligible for reappointment.

The Judges shall be chosen from candidates presented by the Member States having an established high level of legal expertise in patent law. They shall be appointed by the Council on the basis of their expertise after consultation of a committee to be set up in accordance with Article 3.

Article 3

An advisory committee to be set up for this purpose shall, prior to the appointment decision of the Council, give an opinion on the adequacy of the profile of candidates with a view to the function of a Judge at the Community Patent Court. It may attach to its opinion a list of candidates possessing the most appropriate high level of legal experience. Such a list shall comprise a number of candidates twice the number of Judges to be appointed by the Council.

The advisory committee shall be composed of seven members chosen from among former members of the Court of Justice, the Court of First Instance, the Community Patent Court or lawyers of recognised competence. The appointment of members of the advisory committee and its operating rules shall be decided by the Council, acting by a qualified majority, on a proposal from the President of the Court of Justice.

Article 4

The Judges shall elect the President of the Community Patent Court from among their number for a term of three years. He may be re-elected.

Article 5

Articles 2 to 7, Articles 13, 14 and 15, the first, second and fifth paragraphs of Article 17, and Article 18 of the Statute shall apply to the Community Patent Court and its members.

The oath referred to in Article 2 of the Statute shall be taken before the Court of Justice and the decisions referred to in Articles 3, 4 and 6 of the Statute shall be adopted by that Court after hearing the Court of First Instance and the Community Patent Court.

Article 6

governing his service. The fourth paragraph of Article 3 of the Statute and Articles 10, 11 and 14 thereof shall apply to the Registrar of the Community Patent Court mutatis mutandis.

Article 7

Technical experts shall assist the Judges throughout the handling of the case as Assistant Rapporteurs. The fourth paragraph of Article 3 and Article 13 of the Statute shall apply.

Assistant Rapporteurs must have a high level of expertise in the relevant technical field. They shall be appointed for a period of six years on a proposal from the Court of Justice. Retiring Assistant Rapporteurs shall be eligible for reappointment.

Assistant Rapporteurs are required, under the conditions laid down in the Rules of Procedure, to participate in the preparation, the hearing and the deliberation of cases. They shall have the right to put questions to the parties. They shall not have a right to vote.

Article 8

In certain cases governed by the Rules of Procedure, the Community Patent Court may sit in an enlarged configuration, or be constituted by a single Judge. They shall contain provisions concerning the quorum.

The President of the Community Patent Court shall preside over one of the chambers of three Judges. In addition, he shall preside where the

Community Patent Court sits in an enlarged configuration. The President of the remaining chambers shall be elected by the Judges from among their number for a term of three years. They may be re-elected.

The composition of the chambers and the assignment of cases to them shall be governed by the Rules of Procedure.

Article 9

The President of the Court of Justice or, where appropriate, the President of the Court of First Instance shall, acting by common accord with the President of the Community Patent Court, determine the conditions under which officials and other servants attached to the Court of Justice shall render their services to the Community Patent Court to enable it to function. Certain officials or other servants shall be responsible to the Registrar of the Community Patent Court under the authority of the President of the Community Patent Court.

Article 10

The procedure before the Community Patent Court shall be governed by Title III of the Statute with the exception of the second paragraph of Article 21, Articles 22 and 23, the first and third paragraphs of Article 40, Article 42 and Article 43 thereof. It shall be subject to Articles 11 to 25 of this Annex. Such further and more detailed provisions as may be necessary shall be laid down in its Rules of Procedure. The Rules of Procedure may derogate from Article 40 of the Statute in order to take account of the specific features of litigation in the field of Community patents.

Article 11

The lawyer referred to in Article 19 of the Statute may be assisted by a European Patent Attorney whose name appears on the list maintained by the European Patent Office for the purpose of legal representation before it and who is a national of a Member State or of another State which is a party to the Agreement on the European Economic Area.

The European Patent Attorney shall be allowed to speak at hearings under the conditions laid down in the Rules of Procedure.

The fifth and sixth paragraphs of Article 19 of the Statute shall apply mutatis mutandis.

Article 12

By way of derogation from the fourth, fifth and sixth paragraphs of Article 20 of the Statute the following rules shall apply:

The oral procedure shall consist of the presentation of the main features of the case by the Judge acting as Rapporteur, the hearing by the Community Patent Court of the parties, and the examination of evidence.

The Community Patent Court may, in accordance with the Rules of Procedure and after having heard the parties, dispense with the oral procedure.

The Rules of Procedure may provide that all or part of the procedure may be conducted in electronic form, and the conditions for so doing.

Article 13

By way of derogation from the first sentence of the first paragraph of Article 24 of the Statute the following rule shall apply:

Where a party has presented reasonably accessible evidence sufficient to support its claims, and has, in substantiating those claims, cited evidence which is to be found under the control of the opposing party, the Community Patent Court may order that such evidence be produced by the opposing party, subject to the protection of confidential information.

Article 14

The competence of the Community Patent Court to prescribe any necessary interim measures shall not be conditional upon main proceedings having already been instituted before it.

Where there is a demonstrable risk that evidence may be destroyed even before the commencement of proceedings on the merits of the case, the Community Patent Court may, in the event of an actual or imminent infringement of a Community patent, authorise in any place either the detailed description, with or without the taking of samples, or the physical seizure of the infringing goods, and, in appropriate cases, the documents relating thereto.

Where interim or evidence-protection measures have been revoked the Community Patent Court shall order the applicant, at the request of the defendant, to provide the defendant adequate compensation for any injury caused by these measures.

Article 15

Article 39 of the Statute relating to special orders in a summary procedure shall also apply to evidence-protection measures. The Rules of Procedure shall determine who is competent to make the orders.

Article 16

Without prejudice to Article 41 of the Statute, a judgment by default may be given against the party that, after having been duly summoned, fails to appear at the oral hearing.

Article 17

By way of derogation from the first paragraph of Article 44 of the Statute, the following rule shall apply:

An application for revision of a judgment may exceptionally be made to the Community Patent Court on discovery of a fact which is of such a nature as to be a decisive factor, and which, when the judgment was given, was unknown to the party claiming the revision, and only on the grounds of a fundamental procedural defect or of an act which was held, by a final court decision, to constitute a criminal offence.

Article 18

The parties may, at any time in the course of proceedings, conclude their case by way of settlement confirmed by a decision of the Community Patent Court. The settlement cannot affect the validity of a Community patent.

Article 19

The first and second paragraphs of Article 54 of the Statute shall apply mutatis mutandis to the Community Patent Court.

Article 20

Where the Court of Justice is seised of a case in which the same issue of interpretation is raised, or where the Court First Instance is seised of a case in which the validity of the same Community patent is called in question, the Community Patent Court may, after hearing the parties, stay proceedings before it until such time as the Court of Justice or the Court of First Instance shall have delivered judgment.

Where an opposition against the grant of a European patent designating the Community is filed with the European Patent Office, the Community Patent Court, seised of an invalidity action, may, after hearing the parties, stay proceedings until such time as a final decision is issued on the opposition.

Article 21

Article 55 of the Statute shall apply subject to the condition that Member States and institutions of the Communities which have neither intervened nor been a party to the case shall only receive the final decision of the Community Patent Court.

Article 22

Final decisions of the Community Patent Court shall be enforceable if they are no longer subject to appeal. Appeal shall have suspensory effect. However, the Community Patent Court may declare its decisions enforceable while, if necessary, subjecting enforcement to the provision of security. The order for its enforcement is appended to the decision by the Community Patent Court. Decisions shall be enforceable against Member States.

The Community Patent Court may order that non-compliance with its decisions or orders constituting an obligation to act or to abstain from an act shall be sanctioned by a penalty payment. The penalty payment may consist in a single or a recurrent fine. The individual fine must be proportionate and may not exceed EUR 50 000.

Article 23

Appropriate court fees will be charged for proceedings before the Community Patent Court.

A schedule of fees shall be adopted by the Council, acting by a qualified majority on a proposal from the Commission and after consulting the

European Parliament and the Court of Justice or at the request of the Court of Justice and after consulting the European Parliament and the Commission.

Court fees shall be paid in advance. Any party which has not paid the prescribed court fees may be excluded from further participation in the proceedings.

Article 24

The Community Patent Court may hold hearings in Member States other than that in which its seat is located.

Article 25

The Community Patent Court shall conduct proceedings in the official EU language of the Member State where the defendant is domiciled, or in one of them to be chosen by the defendant, where in a Member State there are two or more official EU languages. Where the defendant is not domiciled in a Member State, the Community Patent Court will conduct the proceedings in the official EU language in which the Community Patent was granted.

At the request of the parties, and with the consent of the Community Patent Court, any official EU language can be chosen as language of proceedings.

The Community Patent Court may, in accordance with the Rules of Procedure, hear parties in person, witnesses and experts in a language other than the language of proceedings. In that case the Registrar shall cause everything said during the oral procedure to be translated into the language of proceedings and, at the request of any party, into the language used by that party in accordance with the Rules of Procedure.

The Community Patent Court may, in accordance with the Rules of Procedure, allow the submission of accompanying documents drawn up in a language other than the language of proceedings. It may at any time order that party to produce a translation of such documents into the language of proceedings.

Article 26

An appeal against a final decision of the Community Patent Court may be brought before the Court of First Instance within two months of the notification of the decision appealed against.

An appeal against a decision of the Community Patent Court made pursuant to Article 243 of the Treaty or the fourth paragraph of Article 256 thereof or pursuant to the second paragraph of Article 14 of this Annex may be brought before the Court of First Instance within two months of its notification. However, if the order has been made without a prior hearing of the party adversely affected, that party may, within two months of the notification, lodge an objection with the Community Patent Court, whose decision shall be subject to an appeal to the Court of First Instance.

An appeal against a decision of the Community Patent Court dismissing an application to intervene may be brought before the Court of First Instance within two weeks of its notification.

The Rules of Procedure may determine the situations and conditions under which an appeal may be brought against decisions of a procedural nature taken by the Community Patent Court in the course of proceedings.

An appeal as provided for in paragraphs 1 to 4 may be brought by any party which has been unsuccessful, in whole or in part, in its submissions. The appeals referred to in paragraphs 2 and 3 shall be heard and determined under the procedure referred to in Article 39 of the Statute.

Article 27

The appeal may be based on points of law and matters of fact.

An appeal on points of law shall lie on the grounds of lack of competence of the Community Patent Court, a breach of procedure before it which adversely affects the interests of the appellant, or an infringement of Community law by the Community Patent Court.

An appeal on matters of fact shall lie on the grounds of a re-evaluation of the facts and evidence submitted to the Community Patent Court. New facts and new evidence may only be introduced if their submission by the party concerned could not reasonably have been expected during proceedings at first instance.

No appeal shall lie regarding only the amount of the costs or the party ordered to pay them.

Article 28

If the appeal is well founded, the Court of First Instance shall quash the decision of the Community Patent Court and give final judgment. The Court of First Instance may in exceptional circumstances and in accordance with the Rules of Procedure refer the case back to the Community Patent Court for judgment.

Where a case is referred back to the Community Patent Court, it shall be bound by the decision of the Court of First Instance on points of law.

Article 29

The Rules of Procedure of the Community Patent Court shall contain any provision necessary for applying and, where required, supplementing this Annex."

Chapter II

Appeal proceedings before the Court of First Instance

Article 5

Number of Judges of the Court of First Instance
Article 48 of the Protocol on the Statute of the Court of Justice is replaced by the following:
"Article 48
The Court of First Instance shall consist of 18 Judges."

Article 6

Community Patent appeal proceedings
The following Article is inserted into the Protocol on the Statute of the Court of Justice:

"Article 61a

A specialised patent chamber of the Court of First Instance with three Judges shall hear appeals against decisions of the Community Patent Court.

Without prejudice to the fifth paragraph of Article 17 and Article 50, the Judges of the patent appeal chamber shall be chosen from candidates having an established high level of legal expertise in patent law and appointed on the basis of their expertise.

Article 7 and Articles 10 to 23 of Annex [II] to the Statute shall apply to the appeal procedure before the patent chamber of the Court of First Instance mutatis mutandis. Member States and institutions of the European Community shall have the right to intervene in accordance with the first paragraph of Article 40.

The appeal proceedings shall be conducted in the language of proceedings in which the case was conducted before the Community Patent Court. The second, third and fourth paragraphs of Article 25 of Annex [II] to the Statute apply."

Chapter III

Final provisions

Article 7

Transitional provisions
The first President of the Community Patent Court shall be appointed for a term of three years in the same manner as its members. However, the Council may decide that the procedure laid down in Article 4 of Annex [II] to the Protocol on the Statute of the Court of Justice shall apply.
Immediately after all members of the Community Patent Court have taken oath, the President of the Council shall proceed to choose by lot the Judges whose terms of office are to expire at the end of the first three years.

Article 8

Entry into force
Following its publication in the Official Journal of the European Union, this Decision shall enter into force on the day following notification by the last Member State of its acceptance of the provisions of Council Decision 2003/.../EC taken pursuant to Article 229a of the EC Treaty conferring jurisdiction on the Court of Justice relating to the Community Patent.

Article 1 of Annex [II] to the Protocol on the Statute of the Court of Justice shall become applicable on the date on which Council Decision

2003/.../EC conferring jurisdiction on the Court of Justice relating to the Community patent enters into force.

Done at Brussels, [...]

For the Council

The President

[...]

Printed in the United Kingdom
by Lightning Source UK Ltd.
103821UKS00001B/103-108

9 781841 135397